Culturally Responsive Mathematics Education

At a time of rapid demographic change and amidst the many educational challenges facing the US, this critical new collection presents mathematics education from a culturally responsive perspective. It tackles the most crucial issues of teaching mathematics to an ethnically diverse school population, including the political dimension of mathematics education within the context of governmental efforts to improve achievement in school mathematics. *Culturally Responsive Mathematics Education* moves beyond a point of view that is internal to mathematics education as a discipline, and instead offers a broad perspective of mathematics as a significant, liberating intellectual force in our society. The editors of this volume bring together contributions from many of the leading teachers, teacher educators, researchers, scholars, and activists who have been working to reorient mathematics education in ways that reflect mathematics education as accomplished, first and foremost, through human interactions.

Dr. Brian Greer is an independent scholar and Adjunct Professor in the Graduate School of Education at Portland State University.

Dr. Swapna Mukhopadhyay is an Associate Professor in the Graduate School of Education at Portland State University.

Dr. Arthur B. Powell is an Associate Professor of Mathematics Education in the Department of Urban Education and Associate Director of the Robert B. Davis Institute for Learning at Rutgers University.

Dr. Sharon Nelson-Barber is a sociolinguist and directs the Center for the Study of Culture and Language in Education Research at WestEd.

STUDIES IN MATHEMATICAL THINKING AND LEARNING

Alan H. Schoenfeld, Series Editor

Artzt/Armour-Thomas/Curcio *Becoming a Reflective Mathematics Teacher: A Guide for Observation and Self-Assessment, Second Edition*

Baroody/Dowker (Eds.) *The Development of Arithmetic Concepts and Skills: Constructing Adaptive Expertise*

Boaler *Experiencing School Mathematics: Traditional and Reform Approaches to Teaching and Their Impact on Student Learning*

Carpenter/Fennema/Romberg (Eds.) *Rational Numbers: An Integration of Research*

Chazan/Callis/Lehman (Eds.) *Embracing Reason: Egalitarian Ideals and the Teaching of High School Mathematics*

Cobb/Bauersfeld (Eds.) *The Emergence of Mathematical Meaning: Interaction in Classroom Cultures*

Cohen *Teachers' Professional Development and the Elementary Mathematics Classroom: Bringing Understandings to Light*

Clements/Sarama/DiBiase (Eds.) *Engaging Young Children in Mathematics: Standards for Early Childhood Mathematics Education*

English (Ed.) *Mathematical and Analogical Reasoning of Young Learners*

English (Ed.) *Mathematical Reasoning: Analogies, Metaphors, and Images*

Fennema/Nelson (Eds.) *Mathematics Teachers in Transition*

Fennema/Romberg (Eds.) *Mathematics Classrooms That Promote Understanding*

Fernandez/Yoshida *Lesson Study: A Japanese Approach to Improving Mathematics Teaching and Learning*

Greer/Mukhopadhyay/Powell/Nelson-Barber (Eds.) *Culturally Responsive Mathematics Education*

Kaput/Carraher/Blanton (Eds.) *Algebra in the Early Grades*

Lajoie *Reflections on Statistics: Learning, Teaching, and Assessment in Grades K-12*

Lehrer/Chazan (Eds.) *Designing Learning Environments for Developing Understanding of Geometry and Space*

Ma *Knowing and Teaching Elementary Mathematics: Teachers' Understanding of Fundamental Mathematics in China and the United States*

Martin *Mathematics Success and Failure Among African-American Youth: The Roles of Sociohistorical Context, Community Forces, School Influence, and Individual Agency*

Reed *Word Problems: Research and Curriculum Reform*

Romberg/Fennema/Carpenter (Eds.) *Integrating Research on the Graphical Representation of Functions*

Romberg/Carpenter/Dremock (Eds.) *Understanding Mathematics and Science Matters*

Romberg/Shafer *The Impact of Reform Instruction on Student Mathematics Achievement: An Example of a Summative Evaluation of a Standards-Based Curriculum*

Sarama/Clements *Early Childhood Mathematics Education Research: Learning Trajectories for Young Children*

Schliemann/Carraher/Brizuela (Eds.) *Bringing Out the Algebraic Character of Arithmetic: From Children's Ideas to Classroom Practice*

Schoenfeld (Ed.) *Mathematical Thinking and Problem Solving*

Senk/Thompson (Eds.) *Standards-Based School Mathematics Curricula: What Are They? What Do Students Learn?*

Solomon *Mathematical Literacy: Developing Identities of Inclusion*

Sophian *The Origins of Mathematical Knowledge in Childhood*

Sternberg/Ben-Zeev (Eds.) *The Nature of Mathematical Thinking*

Stylianou/Blanton/Knuth (Eds.) *Teaching and Learning Proof Across the Grades: A K-16 Perspective*

Watson *Statistical Literacy at School: Growth and Goals*

Watson/Mason *Mathematics as a Constructive Activity: Learners Generating Examples*

Wilcox/Lanier (Eds.) *Using Assessment to Reshape Mathematics Teaching: A Casebook for Teachers and Teacher Educators, Curriculum and Staff Development Specialists*

Wood/Nelson/Warfield (Eds.) *Beyond Classical Pedagogy: Teaching Elementary School Mathematics*

Zaskis/Campbell (Eds.) *Number Theory in Mathematics Education: Perspectives and Prospects*

Culturally Responsive Mathematics Education

Edited by

Brian Greer

Swapna Mukhopadhyay

Arthur B. Powell

Sharon Nelson-Barber

NEW YORK AND LONDON

First published 2009
by Routledge
711 Third Ave, New York, NY 10016

Simultaneously published in the UK
by Routledge
2 Park Square, Milton Park, Abingdon, Oxon OX14 4RN

Routledge is an imprint of the Taylor & Francis Group, an informa business

Typeset in Minion by EvS Communication Networx, Inc.

Library of Congress Cataloging in Publication Data
Culturally responsive mathematics education / edited by Brian Greer ... [et al.].
p. cm. — (Studies in mathematical thinking and learning)
1. Mathematics—Study and teaching. 2. Multicultural education—United States. 3. Education and state--United States. I. Greer, Brian.
QA13.C85 2009
510.71—dc22
2008046099

ISBN 10: 0-8058-6263-3 (hbk)
ISBN 10: 0-8058-6264-1 (pbk)
ISBN 10: 0-203-87994-5 (ebk)

ISBN 13: 978-0-8058-6263-8 (hbk)
ISBN 13: 978-0-8058-6264-5 (pbk)
ISBN 13: 978-0-203-87994-8 (ebk)

Contents

Part II Teaching and Learning

Foreword

UBIRATAN D'AMBROSIO

It gives me much pleasure to write a foreword for this book, which is highly distinctive among those treating the current scenario of mathematics education. It addresses the most crucial issues of education, particularly the political dimension of mathematics education, against the background of governmental efforts to improve achievement in school mathematics. The editors have organized the contents in an exemplary way, putting together valued contributions from some of the most distinguished mathematics educators concerned with the social issues involved in mathematics education. And this gives me the opportunity to reflect upon my own ideas, which I feel are so close to those of several of the contributors.

The main focus is an analysis of the political dimension of the call for a cultural perspective on mathematics education. To restore cultural dignity is, unquestionably, a matter of political action, but many critics claim that looking for political correctness in mathematics education is going too far. It is difficult to deny that mathematics, like education in general, is an arm of political and ideological systems. What can one say if one proposes a pedagogical practice that aims at eliminating belligerence, arrogance, intolerance, discrimination, inequity, bigotry, and hatred, and it is labeled as going too far? Is it questionable to use such negatively emotive terms when discussing mathematics? The discussion relies on a deeper examination of the historical and epistemological bases of mathematics as well as the (largely invisible) formatting of modern society by mathematics. However, both the historiography and philosophy of mathematics have been very conservative and one-sided. Historical, epistemological, and pedagogical issues are related. These considerations have obvious implications for mathematics education.

It is clear that traditional teaching of mathematics is not satisfactory. Testing has come to dominate traditional teaching. Regrettably, few discuss what testing tells us about proficiency in other than a superficial sense. Yet the system keeps applying tests. The results are alarming. Coercive measures to "tighten" teaching, hoping to get better results in tests and assessments are socially questionable. Countries that are models of traditional teaching and are proud of their systems face destabilizing confrontations with their youth.

Vulnerability to institutional disruption is the great threat to civilization. This is seen in governance, in social disequilibrium, in production, marketing, and consumption and, above all, in continuing, intense disputes over territory and resources. Gas, oil, and, of growing importance, water are the issues in these disputes. The environment is a battleground for all kinds of interests. Greed is clearly the motivation for this bleak scenario, and there is a clear threat to peace. And, as always, greed is rewarded. Besides human lives, the great loss is that of the cultural dignity of the survivors. Human cultural dignity, when it is referred to, is the object of a token discourse. This is my main concern about the future of civilization. We may lose the little we have achieved in respect and solidarity, in our struggle for the satisfaction, with dignity, of material and cultural needs of every human being, in every society in every corner of the world.

Do mathematics and mathematics education have anything to do with this scenario? It seems to be a comfortable posture in our profession to claim that better achievement in mathematics education will contribute to a good solution for these critical issues. It is a false claim that improving sameness is the answer to the vulnerability to disruption of civilization. I believe that restrictive and authoritarian measures simply lead to worsening effects. I believe that sameness may contribute to disaster.

Paraphrasing Russell and Einstein in the Pugwash Manifesto of 1955, I say that we have to learn to think in a new way. We have to learn to ask ourselves, not what steps can be taken to improve achievement in education, but rather what steps can be taken to achieve human cultural dignity through education.

I am convinced that mathematics broadly conceived, and consequently mathematics education, can be a most effective instrument to achieve social and cultural responsibility, and high levels of creativity.

Cultural dignity is the foundation of a new way of thinking that is aimed at establishing a planetary civilization. It can be achieved only if it is based in an ethics of respect for diversity, solidarity with difference, and cooperation with others. This ethics clearly results from recognition of the inevitability of difference. No two individuals are the same. Without others who are obviously different, the individual is doomed to extinction. We, as individuals, groups, societies, and cultures, need and depend on others who are obviously different, and need to overcome the feeling of dominance of one individual, group, society, or culture over another. Respect, solidarity and cooperation with difference are what I call the ethics of diversity, essential for the elimination of belligerence, arrogance, intolerance, discrimination, inequity, bigotry, and hatred.

I insist that mathematics and mathematics education have everything to do with this ethical necessity. History tells us that sameness, like fundamentalism, lacks the creativity to counter vulnerability to disruption.

This conclusion is particularly true in education, particularly mathematics education. If we blindly persevere with the obsolete, the uninteresting, and the useless, we will not avoid their rejection by new generations. When we focus on individual dignity, recognize the knowledge and intellectual activity of each individual and of her or his culture, we are preparing fertile ground on which to build new knowledge and practices.

In mathematics and mathematics education, the important step is to accept other ways of knowing and other forms of mathematical activity. The history of mathematics, when we focus on the dynamics of cultural encounters, shows that mathematics is, effectively, mankind's worldwide, transcultural endeavor in the search for survival and transcendence. Only a limited and biased view of history tells us that this search is the privilege of a specific culture. Instead, without any doubt, it is the result of the dynamics of cultural encounters. It is preposterous to claim that an individual, group, society, or culture has exclusive ownership of the truth.

This is clearly seen in the religions, in the arts, and especially in the sciences. They are accepted and regarded as absolute values by groups of individuals, by communities, by nations, by religious sects. Fundamentalism can be defined through a paraphrase of the great Indian philosopher Sri Aurobindo (1872–1950):

> For Western philosophy, a fixed intellectual belief is the most important part of a cult, it is the essence of its meaning and what distinguishes it from others. Thus, creeds are formulated and make true or false a religion, a philosophy, a history, or a science according to the agreement with the creed of their followers.

It is an important step in education to recognize that all forms of knowledge, and mathematics is no exception, have limitations. So, it is natural to continually search for new communicative and analytic instruments. That is what the history of mathematics tells us. Every advance in mathematics is related to overcoming difficulties in doing or explaining something, in some cases within mathematics itself. The advancement of knowledge and understanding of mathematics, once the ground is fertile, is a matter of motivation. This has much more to do with the overall goals and objectives of mathematics education. Why deny ethnomathematics, which is clearly alive in the professions, in communities, in extant cultures, and in cultural history? Who is afraid of it?

Ethnomathematics belongs to every class and context. It is undeniable that mathematics is the imprint of modern civilization, but this recognition does not mean that it is necessary for all members of a society to be skilled in academic mathematics, which is mostly irrelevant for the average person. However, it is relevant for all to acquire the communicative, analytic, and material instruments that are literacy, numeracy, and technoracy. These abilities and dispositions are essential if the individual is to attain full citizenship, and mathematics education makes essential contributions to that role. These are not skills in a narrow technical sense, but critical tools. Ethnomathematics is a step toward the critical acquisition of these instruments.

As we prepare future school teachers, it is appropriate to present to them one or two ethnomathematics (preferably one historical and one extant), teach methodology of inquiry and some theoretical reflection on ethnomathematics (historical, social, political, methodological). Surely, the ethnomathematics presented to prospective teachers will not be that encountered by the teacher in her or his practice. Methodology of inquiry is needed because future teachers will have to learn from their students. Future teachers must be culturally responsive.

Modern civilization is imposed on the entire planet through economics, politics, technology, and knowledge systems. In other words, the imposition occurs through shared knowledge (science and technology) and compatible behavior (international laws and codes of public conduct) supported by a system of values. The supporting values of modern civilization are essential: rigor in discourse; precision in time and space; increasingly strict etiquette, codes, and social stratification.

For example, there is universal acceptance of calendars and time regulated by the Greenwich standard. Every country honors international IDs, such as passports, and controls their space through the use of visas. Nation-states reach an accommodation on issues, however imperfect the accommodation may be, by the use of treaties. The role of supranational organizations is of increasing importance in the 21st century.

These values, particularly rigor, precision, strict and exclusive codes are organized as domains of knowledge—disciplines—which have been structured and epistemologically delimited since the 17th and 18th centuries. Disciplines are characterized by precise epistemological and normative specificities, represented by systems of codes, and precision in language. They are closed in their methods and objectives. Metaphorically, we may think of disciplines as cages: it is not possible to leave the cage because the codes (the bars) prevent it. The search for knowledge is limited to what is inside the cage. Creativity is restricted by the bars of the cage. Thus, from inside the cage, it is not possible to know the color of the external painting.

In the spirit of this metaphor, I see disciplines as "encaged" knowledge. Methods and results are specific to deal with well-defined questions, with specific language, style, and codes, formulated inside the cages. Encounters among disciplines are the juxtaposition of epistemological cages. We may easily be transferred from one cage to another one nearby. This is practiced in schools through the daily schedule. From 07:00 to 08:00 you are in the "cage" of algebra, from 08:00 to 09:00 you move to the "cage" of social sciences, and so on.

In the 19th century, we saw the emergence of the concept of interdisciplinarity. If we use the cage metaphor, this is like opening doors of communication between cages and allowing the bird to pass from one to another. Essentially, it is like building a larger cage. Interdisciplinary regimes develop their own specific methods and results to deal with well-defined questions. Indeed, they become new disciplines, such as physicochemistry, biochemistry, and others. Creativity is limited to well-posed questions that are proposed inside these enlarged cages. What is going on outside, subjected to an incredible degree of complexity, does not belong to the reflections inside these enlarged cages.

The proposal of interdisciplinary studies is, metaphorically, the abolishment of all cages. Inquiry and search must be open in quest and in methods. This is the quintessence of creativity.

I have always been in quest of a worldwide civilization, in which future generations can be free of fear and humiliation, with no place for bigotry, arrogance, and inequity and in which peace prevails. I subordinate my teaching and scholarship to the fulfillment of this quest. I believe mathematics, conceived in a much broader way, is a most efficient instrument to achieve my ideal. The search for a broader conception of mathematics and for the appropriate mathematics education led me to look for a transcultural and transdisciplinary approach to mathematics. This quest asks for a reconceptualization of rigor that relies on openness, coherence, and respect.

Although not explicitly dealing with these issues that I have raised, I see in this book many discussions and examples which support the daring and boldness of my ideas.

The book is organized in two sections, the first of which deals with foundations and backgrounds and the second more directly with the teaching and learning of mathematics. Each section includes chapters by renowned mathematics educators covering the most important issues in the sociology of mathematics education. The table of contents reveals the richness of the selection.

This book is an effective addition to the field, being a great contribution for everyone concerned with education. Among the mixed feelings and reactions toward governmental measures from many community and professional groups, some strongly supporting, others strongly objecting to these measures, an open and deep discussion of all the issues involved is not only welcome, but necessary. Otherwise, the support and objection may be based only on emotive arguments. Thus, I heartily welcome this book.

In emphasizing culture so centrally in all the chapters, the authors have shown a clear perception of what is central. In contrast to many books that look at mathematics from a point of view internal to the discipline, the authors have a broad perspective of why mathematics is important as a liberating intellectual force in our society, instead of being merely another instrument favoring inequity, arrogance, and bigotry.

The book is of interest to everyone concerned with education. Because mathematics is the most critical among all the school subjects, every discussion, proposal, and educational measure has mathematics at its center. Hence, besides the obvious audience of mathematics educators, teachers, and students of mathematics, the book will also be of interest to administrators, community and group leaders, and the educated public in general. Interest in this book is not limited to concerned individuals in the United States. The problems facing mathematics education and the suggestions of the authors are not specific to that country, but affect every part of the world.

Acknowledgments

This book grew out of a 2004 conference with the same title: *Culturally Responsive Mathematics Education*. The success of both the conference and its culmination as a book were made possible by many people. Starting from the conceptualization of ideas and execution of the process, we thank Elisabeth Swanson, Montana State University and PI of CLT-W for her encouragement and enduring support. Various other members of CLT-W and other CLTs played a strong role in building a community that grappled with the ideas of culturally responsive mathematics and inspired us. Our thanks go to all of them who worked with us at odd hours—in making the conference a success and, finally, the book project completed.

Our special thanks go to Alan Schoenfeld, the series editor. His thoughtful mentorship and encouragement from his first opening of the book proposal to the final frantic days of preparing the manuscript have been a key to completion of the project. He has been the kind of mentor that all should have.

We express our deep gratitude to Naomi Silverman at Lawrence Erlbaum and then Catherine Bernard at Routledge. They have supported us beyond their role of editor—encouraging us from the stage of developing a proposal through various logistical steps that often seemed daunting.

Our deep gratitude is always for Ubiratan D'Ambrosio, a champion for giving voice to the silent "others" and a fearless intellectual leader who not only supported the project but also helped us in realizing how to stand up for a cause in which we believe so strongly.

Of course, our heartfelt thanks go to our collaborating authors without whom this book would not have been completed. They provided us with stimulating ideas and gave us all a chance to have an intellectual pow-wow. Thank you for having trust and faith in us in seeing the project through to completion.

As always, big thanks go to the family members and colleagues who supported the authors and the editors in getting the book completed. Without you, the book would have suffered.

In appreciation and in solidarity

Brian Greer
Swapna Mukhopadhyay
Arthur B. Powell
Sharon Nelson-Barber

Introduction

BRIAN GREER, SWAPNA MUKHOPADHYAY,
SHARON NELSON-BARBER, AND ARTHUR B. POWELL

The idea of culturally responsive education (Gay, 2000; Ladson-Billings, 1995; Villegas & Lucas, 2002) is widely understood but, so the familiar argument goes, isn't mathematics, and more particularly the teaching of mathematics, culture-free?

We believe this book provides reasons to re-evaluate that belief. Even the nature of mathematics as a purely formal system is subject to debate (e.g., Hersh, 2006). But mathematics is more than a universal abstract system. To invoke an analogy, it is recognized that there is a human activity called architecture that includes academic and vernacular forms, and has aesthetic, spiritual, and functional purposes. Nobody would suggest that architecture is a culture-free discipline or deny the appropriateness of using the term *architecture* to describe Mayan pyramids or the temples of Petra.

Mathematics is comprised of a diversity of practices that make it as historically, culturally, socially, and politically situated as any other human activity. It is grounded in human interactions with the environment and with one another, in the solving of practical problems and the human desire to transcend matters of simple survival, in universal human traits such as the use of physical and mental tools, the decorative impulse, and pleasure in intellectual play. Over millennia, academic mathematics has evolved from these origins, and continues to evolve, as a very special kind of cultural activity. But academic mathematics is only one, albeit a very special case, of the many forms of mathematical practice.

In many respects, the field of mathematics education has become much more humanistic in recent years. The early influences on the field were predominantly mathematics itself and cognitive psychology. With the emergence of an emphasis on mathematics education, as well as mathematics itself, being situated in human life, the range of disciplines to which mathematics educators turn has been broadened to include the history and philosophy of mathematics, ethnomathematics, linguistics, anthropology, sociology, even psychoanalysis. The political context of mathematics education, certainly within the United States, is also becoming increasingly apparent. Recognizing the need for culturally responsive mathematics education fits squarely within these movements.

The origin of this book was a conference[1] in November 2004, at the headquarters of the National Science Foundation in Arlington, Virginia. It was an initiative of the Center for Learning and Teaching–West, on the subject that became the title of this book. The conference brought together both major figures from the field and graduate students. It included many of the main scholars and activists who have been working for social justice for minorities within mathematics education, and it also included scholars with backgrounds in history, sociology, and philosophy of mathematics.

It should be acknowledged that the focus of the conference and of the book is narrow in certain important respects. First, it is concerned almost exclusively with the United States, and almost all of the authors are from the United States, yet many of the themes apply in many other multicultural societies. Within the United States, it is narrowly focused on four ethnic groups—Native Americans, African Americans, Latinos/as, and the White, English-speaking "mainstream." That focus fails to take into account many other ethnicities within the United States, most notably the vast range of Asians or the increasing prevalence of mixed ethnicities. In all cases, we emphasize that culturally responsive teaching goes beyond trying to make connections with the students' personal cultures to make it clear that academic mathematics is the product of many cultures and that mathematical practices are pan cultural. There is very little explicit discussion within the book about class or about gender. Of course, the specific choices made about what to concentrate on by no means imply that we consider these other aspects unimportant.

A very significant aspect of the social/political reality of the United States may be conveyed by three numbers:

Year in which the White population of the United States is projected to be in the minority: 2042
Year in which the White population of U.S. public schools is projected to be in the minority: 2023
Proportion of White teachers in U.S. schools: 83%

These figures lend urgency to the question posed by Gay (chapter 8 this volume), namely:

> How can middle-class, monolingual European-American math teachers work better with students who are predominately of color, attend schools in poor urban communities, and are often multilingual? (p. 189)

In the face of this demographic reality, the performance of U.S. students, as measured, for example, in international comparison studies, is acknowledged to be weak and shows little sign of improving. When students of different ethnic groups are compared within the United States, the differences in test scores between White students and those of other ethnicities—African American, Latino/a, Native American—remain scarcely diminished over several decades. The response to these results, and with an eye on the advances of economic competitors (Gutstein, chapter 6 this volume) has been to put in place coercive measures which are intended to force improvement (see D'Ambrosio's foreword), but show no signs of doing so.

A counterargument, which is a leitmotif throughout this book, is that improving mathematics education is a human problem and a political problem. It requires a collective will to devote the necessary resources and to reduce the resource gaps in funding, provision of the best teachers, textbooks, and facilities and opportunities to learn (Nasir & Cobb, 2007). And it requires a radical shift in the teaching of mathematics to make it more engaging for all children, and more related to their lived experience.

The United States faces a complex matrix of political, social, and economic problems that both impact, and present a challenge to, education. Among contemporary developments that exercise those involved in education are: demographic trends (Villegas & Lucas, 2002, Ch. 1); de facto resegregation (Kozol, 2005); the cultural misalignment between student and teacher populations, continuing resource gaps (Berliner, 2005); failure to "close the achievement gaps" (Kloosterman & Lester, 2004); increasing evidence of the flawed conception and execution of the No Child Left Behind (NCLB) legislation, especially in relation to the pernicious effects of high-stakes testing (Nichols & Berliner, 2007; Valenzuela, 2005).

Further, these contemporary concerns must be seen from a historical perspective in which U.S. education has been marked by cultural oppression, a situation that has by no means ended. Speaking of the 1970s, Cole (2003) wrote:

> We worked then, as now, in an environment that routinely turned difference into deficit and that held up unexamined, ethnocentric, biases as the criterion against which to judge, and design programs for, those who did not fit the dominant ideology of then-and-still dominant social groups in American society. Our common enemy, then, as now, was the social creation of social inequality. Our common goal was the creation of an effective, human alternative to dominant disciplinary practices that would make diversity a resource for human development and not a problem. (p. 1)

These developments, which affect all aspects of education, have specific, and often particularly strong, impacts on mathematics education. The prominence of high-stakes testing in mathematics affords perhaps the clearest example.

The book is divided into two sections. The first section reflects our belief that the discussion of culturally relevant mathematics education must be situated within historical, cultural, social, and political contexts.

Frank Swetz has written many of the best books on the history of mathematics in many cultures (e.g., Swetz, 1994, 2002). In his chapter, through a wealth of examples spanning multiple cultures (with many of which he has first-hand experience) and across thousands of years, he amply illustrates his declaration that "history shows that no aspect of mathematics is free from cultural influences" (p. 38).

The chapter by Paul Ernest reflects a major shift in the philosophy of mathematics, one in which he has been very influential, particularly in making connections with mathematics education (e.g., Ernest, 1998). Until comparatively recently, philosophy of mathematics was predominantly preoccupied with "foundations." In recent years, a "new philosophy of mathematics" has been developed which is much more concerned with academic mathematics as a social and cultural construction (e.g., Restivo, 1993).

The next chapter, by Swapna Mukhopadhyay, Arthur Powell, and Marilyn Frankenstein, shows how the perspective of ethnomathematics is supremely relevant to culturally responsive mathematics education. They confront the influence of Eurocentrism in perceptions of the nature and history of mathematics, and the implications of its influence for mathematics education (Powell & Frankenstein, 1997).

Jim Barta and Mary Brenner continue the theme of ethnomathematics which D'Ambrosio (1997, p. 13) described as "on the borderline between the history of mathematics and cultural anthropology" with a consideration of the contributions that an anthropological perspective brings to mathematics education. They describe numerous projects in which mathematics educators are striving to make connections with the cultural practices and identities of indigenous groups (cf. Lipka, Yanez, Andrew-Ihrke, & Adam, chapter 11 this volume).

The chapter by Judit Moschkovich and Sharon Nelson-Barber reflects the crucial importance of forms of language, both vernacular and technical, in the mathematics classroom. In particular, they show the complexity of bilingualism, and argue that languages other than English represent a resource rather than a problem (e.g. Moschkovich, 2007).

Mathematics education has become politicized to an unprecedented degree. Eric Gutstein analyzes how the perceived threats to U.S. economic and other forms of dominance have led to calls for improvement in mathematics (and science) education. Gutstein argues that behind the egalitarian rhetoric of "mathematics for all," the effects of policies being implemented will not be to the advantage of class and ethnic groups that are already disadvantaged. He also debunks myths about the percentages of jobs in the future requiring high levels of mathematical and technical expertise.

The final chapter of the first section, by Dalton Miller-Jones and Brian Greer, concerns assessment, which has become the main element in political communication about mathematics education. In considering assessment from the perspective of communication, they present a stark contrast between assessment viewed as a means for social engineering and assessment as an ongoing part of instruction whereby teachers gain the deepest understanding of what students know and can do, and use this knowledge to guide their teaching. From the latter perspective, and viewing education as being, above all, about personal interactions, the relevance of cultural diversity is obvious.

The chapters in the second section more directly address issues of teaching/learning. Geneva Gay, who has written a classic on culturally responsive education (Gay, 2000), considers how that perspective applies specifically to mathematics education. She emphasizes a point also made by Miller-Jones and Greer that beyond content knowledge and pedagogical content knowledge, teachers need cultural knowledge or, to put it more simply, they need to know their students.

Danny Martin and Ebony McGee write about the experience of "doing mathematics while black." Relating to Gutstein's (2006) Freirean perspective of "reading and writing the world with mathematics," that is, striving not just for social justice in mathematics education, but also *through* mathematics education, they declare (p. 208) that "mathematics education that is committed to anything else is irrelevant for African-American children."

Bob Moses has applied his experiences as a leader in the drive to register African-American voters in Mississippi in the 1960s to the problems of access to educational and economic access for disadvantaged students, an access that he characterizes as a civil right (Moses & Cobb, 2001). In the chapter with Mary West and Frank Davis, he considers what is involved in bridging from students' lived experience to abstract mathematics, using the example of the property of arithmetic that $a + (-b) = a - b$. (A great mathematics educator, Bob Davis, once commented that you really understand addition when you understand that you can add a negative quantity.)

The next two chapters, in different ways, represent attempts to form a bridge between cultures in the development of curriculum materials that honor Native-American cultures. Jerry Lipka has been working with the Yupik people of Alaska for more than two decades with exemplary cultural respect. In their chapter, Lipka, Yanez, Andrew-Ihrke, and Adam describe their development of curriculum materials that bridge school mathematics and Yupik life, and present evidence of the efficacy of these materials.

Ron Eglash has a particular interest in finding mathematical themes within cultural artifacts (e.g., Eglash, 1999). In his chapter here, he describes a fascinating blending of cultures in the form of computer design software that allows exploration of the cultural activity of beading, and shows how the nature of that activity and forms of mathematical expression interact. By analyzing themes in American Indian cultures and in European mathematics (especially Descartes) he also raises intriguing questions about possible universal themes in mathematics that are grounded in environmental properties of the world common to all humankind.

Two papers address issues of identity facing Latino/as in the United States in relation to their perceptions of mathematics and mathematics education. As a teacher trainer, Julia Aguirre writes from a very personal perspective about her attempts to prepare teachers to teach for equity and social justice. She uses the framework suggested by Gutstein (2006) that aims for a balance among "classical knowledge" (academic mathematics), "cultural knowledge," and "critical knowledge."

Marta Civil and Beatriz Quintos address the very important issue of parental involvement in mathematics education, specifically through a description of a program that brings Latina mothers back into mathematics education to the benefit of themselves and their children. They argue (p. 321) that "a fundamental component for establishing a culturally responsive education is a dialogue that breaks down the hierarchical and hegemonic practices that often characterize parental involvement in U.S. schools, particularly in low income, minoritized communities."

Finally, Mark Davis, Shandy Hauk, and Paul Latiolais contend that the ideas discussed throughout this book are not limited to K-12 mathematics education, but have resonances also at the tertiary level. They describe common views among college professors about how they teach and the degree to which this is influenced by considerations of cultural responsiveness, and they present two examples of existing courses that are culturally responsive, with a discussion of the documented outcomes. They close by making recommendations to improve the educational environment for students and instructors through the lens of culturally responsive pedagogy.

As the above brief descriptions of the chapters indicate, the authors of this book, including many of the most important leaders in the cause of equity and social justice in and through mathematics education, avoid what Ubi D'Ambrosio calls "the trap of the same." Above all, they see education as primarily about personal relationships between students and teachers. In comments that are even more relevant today, Kilpatrick (1981) declared that: "The improvement of mathematics education is not a technological problem; it is a human problem" (p. 28).

Nobody would deny that mathematics education in the United States, and the society within which it is situated, are in need of improvement. We offer this book as a pointer to changes that will be part of the solution.

Note

1. This conference was supported by The Center for Learning and Teaching in the West (National Science Foundation Award #0119786) Montana State University.

References

Berliner, D. (2005). Our impoverished view of educational reform. *TC Record*. Retrieved from http://www.tcrecord.org/

Cole, M. (2003). Culture, technology, and development: In memory of Jan Hawkins. *Mind, Culture, and Activity, 10*(1), 1–2.

D'Ambrosio, U. (1997). Where does ethnomathematics stand nowadays? *For the Learning of Mathematics, 17*(2), 13–17.

Eglash, R. (1999). *African fractals.* New Brunswick, NJ: Rutgers University Press.

Ernest, P. (1998). *Social constructivism as a philosophy of mathematics.* Albany, NY: SUNY Press.

Gay, G. (2000). *Culturally responsive teaching: Theory, research, and practice.* New York: Teachers College Press.

Gutstein, E. (2006). *Reading and writing the world with mathematics.* New York: Routledge.

Hersh, R. (Ed.). (2006). *18 unconventional essays on the nature of mathematics.* New York: Springer.

Kilpatrick, J. (1981). The reasonable ineffectiveness of research in mathematics education. *For the Learning of Mathematics, 2*(2), 22–29.

Kloosterman, P., & Lester, F. K., Jr. (2004). *Results and interpretations of the 1990–2000 mathematics assessments of the National Assessment of Educational Progress.* Reston, VA: National Council of Teachers of Mathematics.

Kozol, J. (2005). *The shame of the nation: The restoration of apartheid schooling in America.* New York: Crown.

Ladson-Billings, G. (1995). But that's just good teaching! A case for culturally relevant pedagogy. *Theory into Practice, 34,* 159–165.

Moschkovich, J. N. (2007). Bilingual mathematics learners: How views of language, bilingual learners, and mathematical communication impact instruction. In N. Nasir & P. Cobb (Eds.), *Diversity, equity, and access to mathematical ideas* (pp. 89–104). New York: Teachers College Press.

Moses, R. P., & Cobb, C.E. (2001). *Radical equations: Math literacy and civil rights.* Boston: Beacon Press.

Nasir, N., & Cobb, P. (Eds.). (2007). *Diversity, equity, and access to mathematical ideas.* New York: Teachers College Press.

Nichols, S. L., & Berliner, D.C. (2007). *Collateral damage: How high-stakes testing corrupts America's schools.* Cambridge, MA: Harvard Education Press.

Powell, A. B., & Frankenstein, M. (2002, August 5–7). Paulo Freire's contribution to an epistemology of ethnomathematics. In *Proceedings of the Second International Congress on Ethnomathematics,* Ouro Pert, Minas Gerais: Universidade Federal de Ouro Preto.

Restivo, S. (1993). The social life of mathematics. In S. Restivo, J. P. Van Bendegem, & R. Fischer (Eds.), *Math worlds: Philosophical and social studies of mathematics and mathematics education* (pp. 247–278). Albany, NY: SUNY Press.

Swetz, F. (1994). *From five fingers to infinity.* Chicago: Open Court.

Swetz, F. (2002). *Legacy of the Luoshu.* Chicago: Open Court.

Valenzuela, A. (2005). (Ed.). *Leaving children behind: How "Texas-style" accountability fails Latino youth.* Albany, NY: SUNY Press.

Villegas, A. M., & Lucas, T. (2002). *Educating culturally responsive teachers.* Albany, NY: SUNY Press.

I
Foundations and Backgrounds

1
Culture and the Development of Mathematics
An Historical Perspective

FRANK J. SWETZ

History as a record of human achievement can tell us many things. It can relate what we've accomplished, isolate prerequisites, and in a sense, indicate how we have arrived at our present state of being. The history of a specific intellectual activity, such as mathematics, can do the same. It can answer many questions, such as, When did this mathematics come into being? How was it used? Who was responsible for it? But history is more than a quiz game, more than merely an accumulation of facts, names, and chronologies. Any substantial investigation of the history of mathematics should also seek to reveal and understand the forces and conditions that shape, nurture, and sustain mathematical thinking: How do humans perceive mathematical reality? Why do certain mathematical concepts come into being? What factors affect the transcendence of mathematics from a purely utilitarian activity to an abstract object of speculation and conjecture? As individuals move from the realm of self to the collective embrace of larger social groups, constraints are imposed on their perceptions of reality. They are indoctrinated into the rituals, beliefs, and traditions of the group. In the case of mathematics, a child is born with certain basic inherent mathematical capacities. Research has revealed that a newborn infant has a number sense and can discriminate and identify the number of objects in a visual array up to about four and perceives space in a topological manner; that is, identifying and understanding such spatial properties as connectedness and continuity (Butterworth, 1999; Dehaene, 1997; Van Loosbrock & Smitsman, 1990). As these basic mathematical abilities evolve, they and their expressions are modified by a series of internally and externally applied filters. Personal sensory experience is shaped by particular physical environments. Certainly, a child living in a dense jungle will develop different spatial perceptions from a peer living in a desert or on a Pacific atoll (Bishop, 1979). Quite simply, they will experience and see the "world" differently as their worlds are different. An individual's sensory perceptions are readily modified by cultural constraints imposed by the immediate family, clan, or tribe and "traditions." Further, consuming societal constraints allow for larger, approved social interactions, which bring economic and political considerations into play. Finally, even as a pure intellectual activity abstractly manipulated, mathematics, to be officially recognized, must adhere to formal systems of analysis and expression established by the mathematics community. In this hierarchy of influences, very early on and persistently thereafter, cultural constraints form a foundation upon which higher levels of conceptual interactions must build. It has been said that "culture makes a person what they are," so too, with mathematics, culture has played a long role in its development (Saxe, 1991). Let us now attempt to examine this relationship between culture and mathematics.

Defining the Task

Epigraphical records of human endeavors only extend back in history for about 3,000 years, a mere fraction of the time period humans have inhabited the earth. In attempting to understand our ancestors' actions before this time we must rely on conjecture and speculation. In their attempt to do this mathematically, historians must rely on the work of anthropologists, linguists, psychologists, educators, and sociologists and their own experience. These disciplines tell us something of how a people might have lived, functioned, and thought. Ongoing research is revealing how ancient peoples, formerly called "savage" or "primitive," were neither. At least for the last 30 millenniums, they had well-developed brains, were efficient innovators, functioned within complex social structures, possessed aesthetic sensibilities, and followed coherent systems of ritual and beliefs. The discovery and examination of a well-preserved Neolithic hunter on the Italian-Austrian border in 1991 further affirmed the similarities between our distant ancestors and us (Fowler, 2000). I will refer to such people who have no written history and lived or live in a preindustrial society, close to nature, as *traditional people.* Using the information supplied by scientific observers of today's existing traditional peoples we are able to project back traits, practices, and beliefs that our ancestors who lived in a similar manner might have experienced. Thus, using information on the traditional societies of today, we can obtain valuable insights on the approximate behavior of our distant ancestors (Sizer, 1991). In a similar but reverse manner, knowledge of the social and cultural interactions of the contemporary world can assist in interpreting and understanding past historical movements and developments. However, such transitional retrospection must be carefully applied lest the reviewer "see" mathematics where none is being exhibited. The mathematics must not be "ours" but theirs. The manifestation of mathematics must be justified as being possessed by the subject rather than imagined by the reviewer. Of course such retrospection raises relevant and valuable questions in our case: What is mathematics? Is it the ability to weave a basket or is it the ability to purposefully decorate that basket with geometric patterns involving parallelism and the concept of similarity? For this discussion, let us define mathematical activity as a conscious, systematic effort, a demonstration of an internalized concept that deals with the quantification and partitioning of objects and space in the environment. This definition then gives rise to various specific categories of activities that can more easily be recognized and commented upon:

- Enumeration
- Measurement
- Employment of geometric forms and relationships

From each category specific phenomena can be identified and examined more closely: number words, units of measure, decorative geometric patterns, and so on.

As for the cultural dimension of mathematics, this will be considered the "natural mathematics" of a people, that is, the mathematics they evolve, in isolation from external, dominating human influences, to survive and thrive in their particular environments. Sometimes this natural mathematics has been referred to as "cultural mathematics" or "ethnomathematics." This latter term has been coined by Ubiratan D'Ambrosio, a Brazilian mathematics educator, in his attempts to come to an understanding of the role of culture in mathematical understanding, teaching, and learning (D'Ambrosio, 1985). His conception of ethnomathematics is closely related to the natural mathematics we will examine in that it is the mathematical beliefs, practices, and traditions accumulated within a primary human grouping such as a family, clan, or tribe bereft of the formal educational intervention of a comprehensive society. It is how a people collectively work out mathematics for themselves (Ascher, 2002). Their methods may be judged inefficient by outside standards but such judgments are irrelevant. Nor should the concept of natural mathematics be solely relegated to preliterate or preindustrial societies. Methods and concepts of natural mathematics can evolve in children's games, work tasks, or neighborhood practices. Mathematics is a cultural phenomenon. It reflects the culture it serves and, in turn, is shaped by that culture. Cultural trends in mathematics are constantly evolving.

A Cultural Understanding of Enumeration

One of the basic mathematical activities of a people is to count, that is, to recognize cardinality as a property of a set and to communicate that cardinality with a number word or gesture. Technically, counting involves the establishment of a one-to-one correspondence between a set of objects and a sequential set of words or symbols designating numbers. These definitions are formal definitions that associate counting with enumeration—the assigning of number names (words) to a specify quantity, a sequential coding. They also allow for a use of written symbols, numerals, or physical gestures—two fingers extended to communicate "twoness." But does counting have to involve an outward expression? Can it be a completely internalized conceptualization based on recognition of difference other that cardinality? For example, when a mother is asked how many children she has, she will frequently answer by naming them: 'There's Alice, Sara, and Mark." She has answered the question in a more personal manner than by merely saying "three." She has identified each child by name and in so doing also conveyed the sex of the child and cardinality of the set of her children. Note, in this case, she has used a one-to-one correspondence. This is an example of qualitative counting where one knows the objects of concern so personally that cardinality as a descriptor is irrelevant. This explanation may sound strange but this concept of qualitative counting provides an understanding of the development of number words and systems. Anthropologists, particularly early in the 20th century, often reported how "primitive people" lacked a number sense and did not know how to count. For example, A. C. Haddon, reporting on his observations among the western tribes of the Torres Straits (1890), noted they had no written language and a limited counting system. Their counting words were:

1. *urapun*
2. *okosa*
3. *okosa-urapun*
4. *okosa-okosa*
5. *okosa-okosa-urapun*
6. *okosa-okosa-okosa*

Everything greater than six was termed *ras*. This example of limited number recognition and ability was repeated well into the 20th century, often by noted scholars in the history of mathematics. Citing the research of Levi L. Conant (1863), David Eugene Smith, the American pioneer in the history of mathematics, made such a mistake (Smith, 1958, p. 7). However, his colleague, John Dewey (1896), found much fault with Conant's conclusions. Such biases were perpetuated by early European ethnographic studies. Anthropology was a new field of study and its followers were attracted to Darwin's theories of social evolution. For the Victorians, it was the time of realizing "the White man's burden"; that is, the civilizing of the savage. In 1863, John Crawford, President of the Ethnological Society of London, devised a "scale of civilization" whereby cultures of the world were ranked according to the extent of their number vocabulary. Such a theory ignores cultural and societal priorities. Why should a people have an extensive number system? What do they wish to count? These are questions that must be considered when discussing counting abilities. In the sense that we usually understand it, counting is an abstract process dependent on pattern recognition and ordering. A systematic number sequence or code is devised and memorized. It depends on the use of a base, a convenient reference grouping. The decimal system we employ has a base 10. More perceptive research and experience has shown that traditional peoples rely on a mixture of qualitative and quantitative counting. For the most part, their world is limited in possessions—they know their possessions and the individuals around them. My own discovery of this fact came when I was living among the Iban people of Sarawak on the island of Borneo. Pigs are a source of food and a prized possession. In making polite conversation with an old woman, I asked how many pigs she owned. My query was met with a shrug. Pressing on, I counted for her in Malay, a mutually understandable language, and hoped for a corresponding sign of recognition. There was none! Aha, I thought, now I have experienced the aborigine's inability to count. But then she brought me outside among the pigs lying around the longhouse and pointed to her particular pigs, all eight of them. She knew them as individuals and as a group. The cardinality, number of, the set was unimportant. In almost all cultures, there are words for *one* and *two*, quantities that hold particular psychological significance. One represents self, the individual, being, and existence; two represents "other," contention, and competition. Philosophical and mystical systems have been devised on this principle of duality: male, female designation for objects, such as the Chinese cosmological worldview based on *yin-yang*. One is the builder of numbers, a creator; each successive number is numerically arrived at by adding one. Early cultures recognized this relationship, in fact the ancient Greeks and Chinese did not consider, one, itself, as a number but rather the builder of numbers. It is interesting that in 1889 when the Italian mathematician, Giuseppe Peano (1843–1930), formalized a theory for the mathematical construction of the counting numbers, he used one as the builder of the set. Shortly beyond the use of "one" and "two," for the needs of higher quantification, traditional people resort to qualitative counting. Usually this vocabulary is richer and more informative than mere number names. Often the words themselves imply a cardinality whose familiarity is obtained by experience. For example, in the English language, we use the word *pair* to indicate a grouping of two when referring to certain objects such as shoes, socks, or bookends. But two people become "a couple," two game birds "a brace," and two oxen "a yoke." Consider some available words to describe a collection of people: a *gathering*; a *crowd*; a *mob*; an *audience*; a *congregation*. All these words indicate cardinality greater than two but they also bear a certain nuance: a crowd is bigger than a gathering. Further, they describe the group in some manner: a mob is agitated; a congregation is a gathering for worship; and an audience is prepared to listen. So each word is a busy and multifaceted means of communication. Similar examples can be found in many cultures. Laplanders have 40 words for snow and in the Ukraine there are 20 words to describe a man's mustache, an indicator of male vanity.

So too with our ancestors, they probably used multipurpose words that conveyed cardinality (number) and also carried a qualitative dimension. Further, traditional people often employ special classes of adjectival modifiers that enhance their enumerative associations. Such words are known as numerical classifiers. Vestiges of such modifiers are found in early Arabic, Greek, Hebrew, and Sanskrit and some are still used today in China, Japan, Southeast Asia, and in Oceanic languages (Denny, 1979; Omar, 1972). For example, in the Malay language, the word for long sticklike objects would be preceded by the adjective *batang* and small round objects by *biji*:

sebatang rokok se:	one; *batang*: long, thin: *rokok*: cigarette
duabiji telur dua:	two; *biji*: small, round; *telur*: eggs

It has been reported that the Dioi people of Southern China employ the use of 55 numerical classifiers. The addition of such modifiers in language usage results in the production of concise, efficient descriptive/enumerative phrases. Such refinements of the categorization process and the relationships obtained lend themselves to the tasks of mathematical thinking.

All evidence indicates that the human counting process proceeded from the concrete, the use of counters (pebbles, fingers, sticks, etc.), to the semiabstract, the use of tally marks, to the abstract formal systems of symbols and words to describe numbers (Flegg, 1987). The verbalization of number concepts came late in this process. But even the use of verbalization does not guarantee the existence of an abstract number sense devoid of concrete connections. For example, at the turn of the 19th century, it was discovered that the Thimshian/Tsimshian people of British Columbia possessed seven counting systems, each devised for a different purpose; one for the counting of flat objects and animals; one for round objects and time; one for men; one for long objects and trees; one for canoes and, finally, one for counting when no particular object is referenced (Datzig, 1954, p. 6). Certainly the Thimshian/Tsimshian had a well-developed number vocabulary but they had not really abstracted the concept of number from concrete situations. Existing artifacts such as the 30,000-year-old Vestonice Wolf Bone found in the former Czechoslovakia testify to the use of notched sequences, tally marks, to record numerical counts (Absolon, 1937). Many present-day cultures still record numerical data on notched sticks or knotted cords. With such a recording technique, time considerations and efficiency would warrant the invention of convenient grouping symbols in the tallying/counting process.

Historically, the first recognizable grouping, or limit to counting, occurred at four. Physical counting on the hand focused on the fingers (*digiti*). The thumb, not being a finger, was ignored. Many early units of measure were based on the width of a hand (i.e., four fingers), for example: the Greek and Egyptian *ell* equaled six hand widths or 24 fingers and the Roman *pes,* foot, equaled four *palmae* or 16 digits (Høyrup, 1994). A vestige of this practice remains in the measuring of the height of a horse in "hands" of four inches each. While "oneness" and "twoness" are mental constructs arising from the consciousness of "me" and "other," three, four, and beyond require personal concrete experiences. Of all the counting numbers only one, two, three, and four serve as reflective adjectives, that is, they depend on the gender and plurality of the noun they are modifying (Menninger, 1969, pp. 18–24). Such adjectives are intimately bound to the noun they modify and reflect on the traditions of qualitative counting. The number four and the concept of "fourness" have retained special status in Western traditions.

But the techniques of finger counting eventually included all the appendages of the hand, which resulted in a counting grouping of fives. The Vestonice bone exhibited tally groupings by fives. Etymological vestiges of this association can be found in many languages: in Sanskrit the word for five is *panca* which also means hand; similarly with *piat*, five in Russian. In English, our word *five* derives from the same etymological base as the word *fist*. "Hand counting," that is, counting on one's fingers, has been done in almost all cultures. The Chinese bead abacus still in use today organizes its groupings by fives. This grouping around which a number system is formed is called a base for the system. Conventions of two-hand counting and cultural dominance of ruling empires such as ancient India and China eventually resulted in the wide dissemination and eventual establishment of the decimal, base 10, system.

Thus, in using cultural influences from existing peoples, one can judiciously speculate that our distant ancestors, in learning how to count, employed a limited discrete number vocabulary and supplemented it with a rich variety of "many" words. Such vocabularies were focused on what they believed was important. It is apparent that as a society grows and obtains more sophisticated needs, number vocabularies and their accompanying numerals become more extensive and complex. An extensive, precise number vocabulary is necessary when communication is remote, impersonal, and over a distance.

Even when formal number systems were developed, cultural influences continued to shape and modify them. In early number systems words or symbols for very large numbers either did not exist or were mystical abstract devices associated with religious beliefs and rituals. The Egyptians, among their hieroglyphic numerals, had a symbol for a "million," a pictogram of a seated man with his arms thrown up in amazement at the magnitude he represents. One of the few evidences we have of the use of this numeral is in the text of a stele describing a king's victory over an enemy and the numbers of his captives. Obviously, a hollow boast! The Romans had ruled the greatest empire of the ancient world, yet did they possess a numeral for a million? Pliny, the historian of the ancient world, tells his readers (100 CE) that the Romans had no number higher than 100,000 (Menninger, 1969, p. 44)! How often has a person seen a million of anything? A meaningful learning experience for school children is to collect a million objects such as pennies or bottle caps, to appreciate the magnitude of that number. As societies developed with commercial and economic needs, larger and larger numbers and quantitative measures are required and devised. For example, in the contemporary world, nanosecond, 10^{-10} sec, and gigaton, 10^{15} gm, measure speed and destructive power and are terms not known or needed a century ago!

The Cultural Evolution of the Hindu–Arabic Numerals

The common numeration system used today is a base 10 positional system with Sino-Hindu-Arabic origins. It is generally referred to as the Hindu-Arabic numeral system. After the fall of the Roman Empire many Roman institutions and practices lived on in Europe. One such practice was a use of the Roman number system and its numerals. Hindu-Arabic numerals found their way into Europe around AD 1000. The new strange counting system was adopted by merchants and the new numbers, in Italian, were known as *figura mercantesca,* mercantile figures, in contrast to the Roman *figura imperiale,* imperial figures (Swetz, 2002). Following Roman practices, computing was accomplished by the moving of counters; that is, tokens on a counting table with ruled columns and rows that helped establish numerical place value. For several reasons, some cultural, full acceptance of the new numerals and their accompanying written computing algorithms would be several centuries in coming.

In general, the European Middle Ages were a rather numberless period in human history: a use of numbers was limited to select segments of the population: merchants, clergy, computers, and a few academics. The Greeks had divided mathematics into two divisions: *arithmetica,* a philosophical study of numbers and their properties worthy of a scholar, and *logistica,* the mundane manipulation of numbers by tradesmen and merchants. The stigma followed mathematics into medieval Europe. Even in official documents of the time any use of number was rather vague. A 12th century description of London denotes the existence of a large variety of structures such as fortifications, mills, wells, and noble residences, and yet avoided enumerating any of them. Extant literary sources from this period are acutely devoid of a use of numbers. Written descriptions of time, distance, value, and quantity were most often presented without a use of numerical modifiers. Phrases such as *a little longer*, *a few miles*, and *many* or *multitude* were considered sufficient to indicate the writer's intent (Murry, 1978). Number associated with the supernatural (*arithmetica*) through the disciplines of theology, philosophy, astrology, and alchemy obscured its function as a measure and indicator of quantity. The resurrection of a moneyed economy and the rise of mercantile activity beginning in about the 11th century began to change this climate and fostered the import of the Hindu-Arabic numerals (Swetz, 1987). The new symbols were viewed with great suspicion because they were both foreign and pagan.

The culture of the Christian church impacted heavily on mathematical and scientific expression during the European Middle Ages. Its doctrines and practices promoted an intellectual humility based on an adherence to simplicity, scripture, and symmetry. During its rise to power, the Church condemned the pagan theories of the Greeks and Romans including those that involved number whose mysticism was associated with the Devil. It took St. Augustine (AD 354–430) to reconcile numbers and scripture and sanction the rise of a Christian numerology, eventually to be known as *arithmology.* In commenting upon the special status of the number six, the perfect number in Pythagorean theory, Augustine associated it with the six days of creation, commenting:

> We must not despise the source of numbers, which in many passages of the Holy Scripture, is found to be of eminent service to the careful interpreter. Neither has it been without reason numbered among God's praises, "thou has ordered all things in number, and measure and weight." (Augustine, 1871–1876, p. 73)

Churchmen now relied on numbers to help instill and reinforce doctrine. For example, the French Monk, Honorius of Antun (ca. AD 1100) divided the Ten Commandments into two sections: the first three commandments reflected love of God in heart, mind, and soul; the other seven dealt with love of neighbor and represented a threefold soul working in conjunction with a fourfold body. In such a pervasive religious context, numbers were intended to appeal to the emotions rather than the intellect. For the common person, number remained a remote and mysterious entity, powerful portents associated with the unknown and other worldliness.

Some of the mathematical concepts that came with these new numerals also caused problems. The formation of the decimal system first entailed counting numbers: 1, 2, 3… which would also be employed to designate groups of: 10, 100, 1,000, and so on. In a numeral, positional arrangement of digits had significance—various visual schemes were employed to teach this principle. A new member soon joined these new numerals, a circular, empty symbol, "zero" which served as an empty placeholder. This was a symbol to represent nothing, which to many seemed like a contradiction. Computers who operated the counting tables had intuitive concepts of both place value and zero—place value was incorporated into the positions of tokens on the table and an empty space indicated that no number occupied it, that is, zero. In their mind, zero was qualitatively defined, it was nothing, and in the written script of the Hindu-Arabic numerals it was enclosed by a symbol. As late as the 15th century, zero as a number was still held in contention, as a French writer of the time noted in ridicule: "Just as the rag doll wanted to be an eagle, the donkey a lion, and the monkey a queen, the *cifra* [zero] put on airs and pretended to be a digit" (Menninger, 1969, p. 422).

Eventually and begrudgingly, it was accepted into the family of numbers. At the other extreme, large numbers whose use was driven by commercial and political needs were also late comers. Use of a million appeared in the 13th century; a billion emerged as a concept in the 16th century but had little quantitative meaning until the 1914–1918 World War where it recorded financial losses. A trillion only took on meaning in the latter 20th century where it began recording the U.S. national debt.

Common fractions expressed by a numerator and denominator also took their place in usage among the new numerals. This conception of such fractions to denote parts of a unit had begun in China as a vertical array of two numbers: "the mother" above and the "son" below (Li & Du, 1987). Hindus emulated this technique of expressing fractions and it passed into the Islamic world where the order was reversed and a bar was added. This is the form that entered Europe, introduced mainly in the writings of Leonardo of Pisa (1202). European resistance to the notation of this system of fractions rested in convention and the practices of craftsmen and artisans where each occupation (carpenters, boat builders, coopers, stonemasons, etc.), had its own system of fractional measurement and notation. They would use these restricted names for a particular fraction rather than adhere to a more rational numerical system. For example, the Romans devised a system of fractional weights based on the *pondo*, pound, by dividing the pound into 12 parts or *unce*. Thus one *unce* equaled 1/12th of a pound but, at the same time, each division had a special name. Merchants used the names rather than the numerical designator, avoiding arithmetical complications. In specifying his needs, a merchant might require a *semis*, rather than requesting a half or 6/12th of a pound, similarly a *bes* would measure eight *unicae* or 2/3 of a pound. In a sense, the culture of the trade guilds controlled fractions. A French stonemason would employ a different measurement for the same length used by an English stonemason. Each guild held firm to its own systems of measurement. Even merchants, the patrons of this new numeration system, balked at its fractional notation. As a result of this practice, systems of measurement, particularly interregional, resulted in much confusion. For example, in the 13th century, 100 *salme* of wine from Scalea in southern Italy, upon import to Tunis, became 95 *mezzarioles* but another Calabria wine of 100 *salme* imported to the same city corresponded to 82 *mezzarioles*. A *centenaro* of hazelnuts from Naples was measured between 150 and 150 *cantari* in Tunis and 145 *cantari* in the nearby city of Bougie (Lopez, 1969). As late as the 17th century, a traveler in Europe found that the measure of a pound weight was regionally specified by 391 different units and that even the length of a foot bore contention, being indicated by 282 unlike units. Societal pressures, political considerations, and royal decrees would be needed to sort this situation out. It would really take the formation of nation-states and international agreements to arrive at unified systems of measurement.

Ways of measurement and approximation are extremely personal and culture bound. The jungle dwelling people of Southeast Asia measure the girth of trees by hugging them, the grasp of the hug, *sepemeluk*, being a unit of measure; distance can be reckoned by the *setapak* or monkey's pace; volume can be determined by a *cupak*, half an empty coconut shell filled with a substance. When I was a child, my mother would see if a pair of socks fit my feet by wrapping a sock about my fist. (This was the time before stretch socks fit all sizes). If the sock circled my fist, it fit my foot. In the Philippines, mothers test the size of a pair of pants for their child by wrapping the waist band around the child's neck. If it circles the neck, the pants fit the waist. In many cultures, children are considered to be old enough to attend school if they can reach over their head with their right hand and touch their left ear. Almost all contemporary units of measure bear cultural origins, particularly origins associated with the human body: the finger, the hand, the arm, the foot, and other parts of the human anatomy. Fingers, as counting and computing devices have served as computers in almost every culture. The term *digit* in English designates a finger and a numeral. Even today people from diverse cultures and regions of the world still rely on their fingers to communicate quantity to a stranger who does not speak their language.

The Mystery of Numbers

Number beliefs, the superstitions associated with various numbers, are purely cultural manifestations. While numbers and counting were derived for utilitarian purposes, numbers are powerful descriptors and carry a psychological appeal and mystique giving rise to a body of number lore and ritual. All cultures possess some particular number beliefs. For example, in the Western world, if one asks a person to choose a special or "lucky" number, seven would probably prevail. Seven is considered a lucky number. Why is this? There are seven days in a week. (Mathematically speaking, five would be a better choice as five is a divisor of 365, the number of days in the year.) A cat has seven lives. If one breaks a mirror one is said to be destined to have seven years of bad luck. In the Middle Ages, a popular belief was that seven demons plagued man giving him maladies ranging from headaches to impotency. A handkerchief tied in seven knots "binding up the demons" became a talisman to ward off their effects. Seven as a special number has occupied the human psyche for thousands of years. The Gilgamesh Epic of Babylonia mentions seven winds, seven spirits of a storm, seven diseases, and seven regions of the underworld entered by seven doors bound by seven seals. The reverence for the number seven was adopted into Judaic-Christian tradition: the Lord rested on the seventh day; the walls of Jericho fell after being circumvented seven times by seven priests; Jesus cast out seven demons. The power of seven results from our ancestors viewing the night skies and speculating on the movement they observed nightly: only seven objects can be observed with the naked eye to traverse fixed paths. For our ancestors these became "seven wandering gods": Venus, Mars, Saturn, Jupiter, the Sun, the Moon, and Mercury. This tradition is reflected in names for some of our days: Sunday, Saturday [Saturn day], and Monday [Moon day]. Similar culturally derived theories provide special status for many numbers—Western literature treats the number four in a special manner: up through the Middle Ages, it was believed that there were four elements from which all things were created; there were four humors that controlled human health; there were four winds. The Chinese are attracted to the number five: the metaphysics of Wuxing depended on five transformations and five was an auspicious number upon which to organize categories, the Chinese employed over 100 such listings based on five (Ho, 1985, p. 21).

Traditional Ways of Viewing and Conceptualizing Space

Let us start with a person. How do you orientate yourself in the world? A standing person is aware of four basic directions: front, behind, to one side, to the other side. Most people view their immediate space container as a rectangle. This awareness gives rise to four directions and the "four corners of the Earth." Ask a person in the United States what these four directions are and you will be told "north, south, east, and west." Ask a Chinese how many directions there are and the response will be five: "south, north, east, west, and here" the point where the person stands. They provide a reference point as one would establish an origin for a real number graph. This fact can be interpreted as a demonstration of more precise spatial thinking. Other cultures, for example the Zuni peoples of the American Southwest, employ the five directions of the Chinese and two more: up and down—providing an orientation in three-dimensional space. Their perception and involvement with space is more acute than their Anglo neighbors. Four basic orientations can also be viewed as formal boundaries for space, giving rise to an architecture based on the use of rectangles: houses, village walls, and street layouts. Space was usually viewed as a property of the object in question: a person, a house, or a village. It was conceived of as a container defined by the contained. Excavations indicate that almost all ancient peoples who built their houses of mud or stone chose a rectangular form. Of course, the economy of shared walls between dwellings may have been a factor. This rectangular method of construction, rectangular houses, within a rectangular security wall, mediated for rectangular street or lane systems and the popularity of a grid layout for a city. Ancient human centers such as Mohenjo-daro in the Indus Valley, Babylonia in the Tigris-Euphrates plains, the cities of the Inca in Mesoamerica, or the Hopi cliff dwellings of the American Southwest, all relied on rectangular grid layouts. Before the Christian era, rectangular systems of map coordinates were employed by the Babylonians and Chinese. Rectangular referencing systems were used in the decoration of Egyptian tombs and employed by Italian Renaissance painters. A small grid covering a sketch was used to reference a large grid on a large surface and the drawing could be transferred from the sketch to the painting employing a correspondence of grids. Thus, in the Western world, a cultural preference for rectangular orientation had a long history foreshadowed by the mathematical innovation of graphing functions on a rectangular coordinate system that is usually credited to the French mathematician and philosopher, René Descartes (1596–1650).

Individuals may also view their *lebensraum*, or living space, by turning 360°. They look "around." Their line of vision, domination, and area of awareness is a region defined by a circle. Such a figure can be more easily formalized by extending a taut cord from a peg and tracing out the path constrained by the cord. This figure depends on centrality; a center dictates the existence of a circle. The center controls the circle. Psychologically, this concept can be projected to an individual egocentrism or a political leader or, in the modern world, the influence of corporate power. The circle is a smooth curve always changing direction. Its beginning and end are mysteriously one, always changing but always remaining the same. The shape can be associated with the moon and the sun (gods?) and their cyclic behavior. Cultures incorporated cyclic progressions into their beliefs and rituals: a cycle of death and rebirth for plants, animals, and humans. A ring worn on one's finger designates fidelity. Reincarnation became a central focus of Hinduism and Buddhism. For the Chinese, the rise and fall of imperial dynasties was marked by cyclic behavior. The circle supplied a cosmogram for them representing the universe, with China and the emperor at the center. The ancient Chinese believed they were the center of the universe; they occupied the Middle Kingdom, *Chung kuo*, mediators between Heaven and the barbarians (i.e., non-Chinese). This exalted self-appointed positioning produced a severe xenophobia which would repeatedly hinder China's relationship to the outside world and other cultures.

The circle and its properties had great psychological/metaphysical appeal to traditional peoples and even extended into the European Middle Ages where religious mystics such as the German Friar, Nicholas of Cusa (1401–1464) likened God to an infinite circle while also being its generator and center. Later, one of the greatest thinkers of the Enlightenment, Gottfried Wilhelm Leibniz (1646–1716) was also attracted to this geometric analogy for God. Of course, early human experience discovered that a circle was the most efficient way to enclose a space and insure a maximum interior area with a minimum use of materials to construct a boundary. For a living structure, a hemisphere supplied the optimum volume. Even today, in many places in Africa, circular walled houses and corrals are still popular. The Inuit or Eskimos build their snow igloos on this principle. The Native Americans of North America held the circle in great spiritual esteem. The Osage people who lived on the plains always set up their camps in a circle because they believed it reflected the cosmos at large. Half the tribe resided within the northern half of the circle representing Heaven while the remaining half lived in the southern region representing Earth. Thus, Heaven and Earth were united within the circle of the camp. The base of each teepee was staked in a circle. The Zuni envisioned life as a circle with a dot in it, possibly representing individual existence. Death was the circle, with the interior region filled. The poignant lament of the Sioux Chief Black Elk on the demise of his reservation-bound people notes their reliance on the circle:

> You have noticed that everything an Indian does is in a circle, and that is because the Power of the World always works in a circle, and everything tries to be round.... But the Waischus [White men] have put us in square boxes. Our power is gone and we are dying, for the power is not with us anymore. (Neihardt, 1972, pp. 198–199)

The contemporary Bari people of northern Colombia are traditional rain forest dwellers (Brown, 1987; Lizairalde & Beckerman, 1982). Their world is circular:

they live in a round communal house organized around a central hearth; place their hammocks in a concentric circle; and plant their gardens in rings about the community house. All orientations and activities take place within this circular world. When anthropologists gave a Bari woman a photograph upside down, she did not reorient it but viewed it and correctly interpreted it as given. Further perceptual experimentation confirmed that the Bari do not view space in a rectangular manner, as Westerners do, but rather employ a system of polar coordinates. Similarly, research conducted on sub-Saharan African children indicates difficulties in visual perception and interpretation of isometric drawings and illustrations (Hudson, 1960; Mitchelmore, 1980; Omari, 1975; Poole, 1970). One rationale offered for this phenomenon is conditioning to a "non-carpentered" (few right angles) environment. A viable research question is: Has this trait been passed down to African Americans? Visual perception and interpretation are very much culture bound (Segall, 1966)!

The psychological appeal of both the straight line and circle permeated Greek geometrical thinking. A circle in its orbit prescribed a perfect geometrical shape: harmonious, possessing infinite rotational symmetries about its origin; rotated about its plane, the circle became a sphere, the most perfectly conceived of all three-dimensional objects. The Greek, Aristotelian, model of the universe became a set of nested, crystalline spheres upon whose great circles the planets spin their orbits about the central, immobile Earth. Built upon human centralism, this model of the universe exhibited balance, symmetry, and proportion and gave rise to the concept of the "music of the spheres." The whirling of the planets in their circular orbits caused a resonance of different frequencies within the glass spheres. If the whirling was as it should be the vibrations resulted in a subliminal harmony, "white music" if you will; but if the planets were out of line their music resulted in discord and resulted in discomfort and agitation among its human audience. Even when mathematical theories were formulated to describe planetary motion, they conformed to cultural beliefs. New heavenly theories and mathematical corrections were arrived at but the theory of symmetric geocentrism survived. This pattern of pleasing aesthetics was broken by the work of Nicholas Copernicus (1473–1543) who advocated a solarcentric or heliocentric universe. Finally, Johannes Kepler (1571–1630), relying on careful data collection and analysis, determined that the planets revolved in elliptic orbits in a heliocentric system. Scientific research overcame cultural convention. But it must be noted that despite this eventual accomplishment, both Copernicus and Kepler labored long to uphold and refine the classical Greek model, the cultural theory, they had inherited.

As natural scientists investigated and debated the movement of bodies in space, the power of the circle was displaced further. For example, the trajectory of a projectile in a gravitational field was envisioned in the classical mode as being composed of straight lines and a circular arc. Experimental investigations by Galileo Galilei (1564–1642) shattered this myth, the trajectory was a parabola, and resulted in a paradigm shift in geometrical thinking and spatial appreciation.

Investigation into the mathematical thinking of traditional people also reveals an appreciation of the concept of perpendicularity. In observing nature, early humans realized that plants and trees grow perpendicular to the surface of the Earth and that a supporting pole for a structure to be effective must stand straight up, that is, be perpendicular to its base (Harris, 1987). An arrow on the string of a bow must be set perpendicular to the string to achieve motion. This principle was further utilized in the telling of time whereby a straight rod, gnomon, was set perpendicular into the ground and the position and length of its sun-projected shadow noted. This information supplied a measure of time, particularly marking the solstices of the year. More formal efforts at such astronomical observations and measurements can be witnessed by the testimony of such stone structures as Stonehenge on Salisbury Plain in England or the Bighorn Medicine Wheel found in the mountains of Wyoming in the United States. This realization of the recognition and utilization of the relationships of perpendicularity and the early ability at "shadow reckoning" has led historians of mathematics to revise their Pythagorean centered theories. For at least 2,000 years, the Greek philosopher Pythagoras (ca. 585–500 BCE) was credited with the derivation of the formula known as the Pythagorean theorem which supplies a relationship between the three sides of a right triangle. It is now conceded that knowledge of this relationship was known well before the time of the Greeks. The Babylonian cuneiform tablet (ca. 2000 BCE) from Susa, known now by its museum catalog number as Plimpton 322, testifies that the ancient Babylonians knew and used the "Pythagorean Theorem" (Robson, 2002). Similarly, the Chinese knew and used this relationship centuries before the Greeks received their recognition for it (Swetz, 1977). Builders of the Egyptian pyramids and the sacrificial altars of ancient India had their "trade secrets" of the right triangle. This "builder's knowledge" arrived at by hands-on experience provided a cultural mathematics in many trades, a knowledge that often resisted its revelation. For example, there is a dearth of information on the use of formal geometry in medieval Europe; however, the testimony in the design and structures of Gothic cathedrals indicates that much geometry remained as "builder's secrets." The tracery or ornamental stonework that forms the frame of cathedral windows exhibits a creative use of circular arcs and a high degree of geometric design skill. Yet we possess almost no information on the mathematical techniques employed.

A culturally contrived conception of space concerns the "measurement of area." Most traditional people maintain gardens, thus, a reasonable question regarding area is, "How big is your garden?" In Zambia, answers include specifying how many anthills it contains to how many baskets of groundnuts (peanuts) can be planted in it (Careccio, 1970). Alan Bishop often relates his conversation with a Papuan, New Guinea schoolboy who was studying area in school. The boy knew that the area of a rectangle, the shape of his home garden, was computed using *school mathematics* as (length × width); however, at home, the garden was measured by (length + width). Which method was better? Both these examples from Zambia and New Guinea pass when they are subjected to rigorous mathematical analysis as to what makes a good measure of area. Their mathematics is not necessarily less correct than our mathematics.

Extant pottery designs and weavings of ancient peoples reveal a familiarity with, and use of angles, similarity, and the concept of parallelism. Even sophisticated designs such as spirals were adopted into their artwork. Our ancestors were avid observers of nature with keen aesthetic senses. They copied and innovated on the geometric patterns their world supplied.

Culture as an Intervening Force in Mathematical Development

We have seen how culture has played a role in mathematical thinking and the development of specific mathematics concepts and practices. Culture still played a mediating role in development as more complex social structures formed: the village, the city, the kingdom, and the nation-state. Now it was joined with other influences such as the political, economic, educational, and religious, that would shape and guide the course of the societies in question. At times, there would be tensions where culture would clash with other forces that were establishing societal priorities. Culture represents the popular will as to what is important at a particular time. As culture changes, this perception of societal importance and priorities also changes. In human history, there have been dramatic episodes of change in mathematical thinking and development. Many factors influenced these turning points but in each change a cultural dimension can be isolated. We will now look at several paradigm shifts in mathematical development and attempt to discern the cultural component or components for that change.

There are several turning points in Western history when the human world outlook changed, when perceptions of reality became different, and there were changes in the accompanying modes of action: intellectual, philosophical, and aesthetic. Perhaps the most dramatic and far reaching of these changes, in the European context, is designated by what is commonly referred to as "the Renaissance," the "rebirth of Western civilization." Many theories have been put forth to explain just why this movement took place in the West when it did; and why then did the European powers move to dominate the rest of the world (Diamond, 1999). Alfred Crosby (1997) offers one of the most intriguing and relevant theories on the subject in his book *The Measure of Reality: Quantification and Western Society*. For Crosby, the use of number, measure, and quantification, that is, mathematics, allowed Western people to make a quantum jump in development and by doing so, propelled the West into a position where it could dominate the other peoples of the world. More specifically, he believes that Europeans acquired a *mentalité*, a unique mentality, a worldview, that in large part was shaped by a recognition and utilization of quantification, a use of number. This is a fascinating thesis that must be explored further. What role did culture have in the rise of this new number awareness and use?

After the fall of the Roman Empire and the resulting loss of its control of taxes, road systems, legal structure, and a moneyed economy, much of Europe retreated into farmsteads and isolated hamlets dependent on agriculture for survival. Two institutions possessing authority rose to fill the void. First, the Catholic Church imposed doctrines and practices to be followed that turned its followers away from earthly concerns and focused on the saving of their souls and the attainment of Heavenly rewards. Second, the institution of feudalism arose, service to a lord or protector for the guarantee of physical protection from foreign invaders and marauding bandits. Both of these institutions greatly diminished personal initiative and responsibility and established a social hierarchy composed of three classes: the lords or masters, aristocracy; the clergy, spiritual/intellectual leaders; and the peasants or serfs. The peasants at the bottom of this scale had two groups above them who controlled their lives and directed them in carrying out most daily affairs. With the rise of the Carolingian dynasty (613+) some central authority and social order was returned to Europe. Despite sporadic warfare, agricultural production increased and living conditions improved. Increased economic prosperity saw a rise of towns accompanied by a demand for trades. The peasants now had power bases: their civic identity within a town and their professional identity, association with a trade guild, with which to confront their controlling authorities. One group emerged with particular strength amongst the guilds: the merchants. The merchants, individually and as a class, began to accumulate wealth. This wealth was in two forms, the first being knowledge. The merchants were the extensive travelers of this period and they brought back information about foreign places and practices and adopted those practices which they considered innovative for business purposes (remember Marco Polo?). The second form was financial, and this literally bought them power. Merchant guilds financed royal projects, including wars, and assisted the Church in its building and expansion efforts. Kings and Popes became indebted to the merchant class. Further, wealth allowed for the formation of a new aristocracy. Social position and influence now could be bought.

Two traumatic events now further altered this climate of social transition: the impact of the Black Death (1347–1352) and the Hundred Years War (1337–1453). The Black Death (bubonic plague) raged over Europe for five years, decimating the population and disrupting the social structure. In total, it is estimated that the population of Europe was reduced by one third. The Hundred Years War between England and France, which also included the Low Countries, devastated a large region of Europe. Civil order broke down. The war was marked by lawlessness and atrocities, the brunt of which was borne by the peasants. France and England nearly went bankrupt supporting their military endeavors.

The impact of this death and destruction radically changed the survivors' world outlook. The Catholic Church lost prestige, spiritual authority, and its leadership role over the people. Its spiritual interventions had not eased the people's pain nor saved their lives. For many, the Church was deemed an ineffective communicator with God, even priests and bishops fell to the scourge of the plague. Antireligious sentiment became prevalent. Neither could civic authority, when it existed, alleviate the situation. Kings and their royal entourages were also powerless in the face of the sweeping disease and further, they precipitated destructive wars that devastated the landscape. The resulting shortage of manpower increased the economic worth of the survivors. Displaced peasants flocked to the depleted cities and urban centers, asserting their importance in the growth of commerce and economics. Regional and national identities began to emerge. A use of local languages replaced the scholastic Latin. Individuals experienced an increase in self-estimation and moved forward with a new confidence. This is the cultural force that rose initially in the Italian city-states, such as Pisa, Florence, and Venice and spread to the rest of Europe. Traditional authority was questioned and degraded. Individuals, craftsmen, guilds, and city-states asserted themselves. This assertion, this aggressive self-confidence is perhaps the *mentalité* Crosby was attempting to isolate or comment upon in his book. It is unique to Western Europe at this time. The new mentality spawned a new world outlook in which man took a firmer control of his destiny, challenging institutions formerly held sacrosanct. This control was expressed in many ways, the rise of experimental science, a blossoming of literature and art, and a revitalization of mathematical thinking. This revision of mathematics was led and supported by the merchant class who realized that the Hindu-Arabic numerals and their algorithmic arithmetic lent itself to efficient record keeping and accounting. The *logistica* of the ancient Greeks now carried less of a stigma; one could be wealthy, famous, and powerful by using mathematics. With a greater dependence on and confidence in the use of numbers, the accompanying fields of measurement and quantification became more precise. Boundaries for capitalist ventures, geographical exploration, and scientific and philosophical investigation expanded. A sense of unlimited opportunity existed. This atmosphere was graphically captured by the new art forms of the period that depended on a use of geometric perspective that employed a vanishing point at infinity. In a sense, these Renaissance innovators are saying that we can see from here to there, a distant point harboring opportunities. This culture of self-assurance and awareness of worldly opportunities fostered an aggressive spirit that eventually resulted in movements of imperial and colonial expansionism. This new world stance can be best appreciated by viewing portraits of this period which feature individuals who stare defiantly outward. These individuals were usually merchants. The West sought to conquer the rest of the world. The cultural attitudes that saw the rise of a merchant sponsored mathematical revival in Renaissance Europe also set some cultural benchmarks for other mathematical movements and developments.

In the latter half of the 20th century, much concern was expressed about the lack of female participation in mathematics and mathematical professions. This issue was particularly prevalent in North America and was an offshoot of the feminist movement that questioned the constrained position of women in society (Fennema, 1976). Many divergent theories appeared to explain this avoidance of mathematical involvement. They ranged from the mundane, "They just don't like mathematics!" to the complex physiological analysis of brain architecture and hormone function. One of the most telling conclusions of this period is that

"Mathematics is an aggressive activity best suited to males" which points us back to the spirit and culture of the European Renaissance. As our examination of the period has shown, the moving force in the use and advancement of mathematics was the merchant class, particularly the merchants of the Italian city states. The mathematicians and reckoning masters of this period were intimately involved with trade and commerce. Merchants were men. The vicissitudes of the occupation: long sea voyages and abiding in foreign countries often under hardship conditions warranted male participation. A similar comparison would be that of a sailor in the 13th century—one would not expect a woman to be a sailor. High-born women of this period were also kept secluded, haremlike, isolated from the cares and challenges of this world. Thus the culture of the time mediated against women participating in mathematics. This, of course, was reflected in available education—reckoning schools, while they trained sons of merchants, did not take female pupils. Unfortunately, these practices and biases continued even when the nature of mathematics and its uses entailed fewer hardships and became more favorable to women. Thus the 20th/21st century dearth of women in the mathematical profession can be traced to the cultural priorities of Renaissance Europe.

Another interesting question arises as to the time and place of mathematical advancement: Why did mathematical activity in China, which was far superior to European accomplishments up until about the 14th century, falter and go into a state of decline just when Western mathematics was advancing? Indeed, if one examines the scope and caliber of early Chinese mathematical accomplishments, it is impressive: an early (300 BCE) proficiency with a decimal numeration system including a use of fractions; accurate root extraction processes; the ability to solve systems of linear equation including indeterminant and higher order polynomial equations; and an understanding of negative numbers. Chinese mathematical references such as the *Jiuzang suanshu* (The Nine Chapters of the Mathematical Art) (ca. AD 100) established mathematical techniques for solving the problems that arose in running an empire, such as taxation, construction, and labor allotments, and were adopted throughout Asia. But within the Chinese curriculum and examination system, mathematics was not considered an important subject. For the Chinese, it was a *logistica*, a minor technique, needed to run the empire and attend to the needs of the Bureau of Astronomy, whose calculations determined the ritual calendar of the Empire. The most important subjects for scholarly pursuit were calligraphy, poetry, music, and literature, activities that promoted the spiritual harmony of China, and through it insured the political harmony of its peoples. This sense of harmony, universal balance, permeated all Chinese philosophical, metaphysical, and intellectual activities. It was given dynamic form in the theories of Yin-yang and Wuxing and sanctioned in the writings of ancient masters such as Confucius. It was felt that the welfare of the Empire rested in the hands of humanistic trained literati. The functioning of Chinese society depended on social and heavenly harmony. Nothing could be allowed to disrupt the perceived state of societal harmony (Swetz, 1996). In 1600, the Jesuits penetrated China and established a Mission in Peking (Beijing). As evangelists of their Christian faith they attracted little attention, but as conveyors of outside scientific knowledge, they were welcomed into the Imperial Court. Matteo Ricci, working with the court scholar Xu Guangqi, translated the first six books of Euclid's *Elements* into Chinese. This was the first time the Chinese experienced a mathematical system formulated in a logical-deductive manner. The Jesuits also involved themselves in calendar reorganization and scientific work, including the casting of cannons. While the Chinese were passive to nature, Westerners stressed scientific observation and experimentation, intellectual movements that were then in vogue in Europe. Court officials became uneasy, the harmony of thought, the harmony of life, and the harmony of the Empire were being threatened by this foreign barbarian knowledge. China's cultural chauvinism and xenophobia took over. Led by Court conservatives—Daoists and Neo-Confucians—the ruling Qing government instituted a closed-door policy forbidding further foreign contact. Foreigners were expelled and external travel and communication ceased. Chinese mathematics remained in a state of stagnation and depreciation. This isolation would only be broken by the intrusion of foreign gunboats at the beginning of the 18th century. Modern Chinese governments, particularly the communist governments, have worked hard to change cultural attitudes toward mathematics and science.

The Imposition of Alien Mathematical Culture

Cultural norms and attitudes are incorporated into the formation of a society. Most often these norms represent the beliefs and traditions of an intellectual or political ruling elite. They become part of the educational values transmitted by that society and are thus formally perpetuated. A good participant or citizen in the society will be expected to reflect those cultural values. But what if the cultural values an individual holds differ from those of the society he or she resides in? Tensions evolve and some accommodations must be sought. In the case of mathematics, culture often expresses itself in the often heard classroom questions: What is this stuff good for? When am I going to use it? As we have seen, each culture focuses on what it believes is important and forms appropriate concepts and vocabularies around that belief. There are several classical examples where mathematics has been introduced across cultural boundaries with unsatisfactory results (for the implementer). Let us examine two of these historical endeavors: the imposition of American mathematics curricula into the Philippine Islands in the wake of the Spanish American War (1898); and the introduction of Western "modern mathematics" into the countries of Africa in the 1960s.

With its victory in the Spanish American War, the United States found itself in an awkward position: it was now an imperial power with no policies or experience in administering colonial holdings. Policies were quickly established on an "ad hoc" basis. They were pragmatic and influenced by the dominant ideological theme of the era, the promotion of democracy. Existing colonial powers such as Great Britain and France were "carrying the White man's burden" of civilizing their charges; that is, by bringing Christianity to their colonial people along with a basic legal system, an educational system, and some selected features of European life, such as hygiene, medicine, and communication, that would both benefit the populace and ease the chores of administration. America at the close of the 19th century was experiencing a period of exuberant jingoism and self-satisfaction. Democracy, independence, and freedom as known in America were extolled as desirable societal attributes. These would be the cultural virtues the United States would attempt to foster in the Philippines.

In its initial efforts to restore societal order, the U.S. Army found the Filipinos eager for educational opportunities. They wanted schools reopened. Under the Spanish occupation, education of the populace was minimal and directed at teaching Catholicism and the Spanish language. Little civic or vocational education took place. The American military authorities began operating schools with soldiers as teachers. Soon they found themselves supervising a system of a thousand functioning schools. They attempted to resurrect the previous Spanish system but found it impossible under existing circumstances; and then set forth to establish a new educational system (Swetz, 1999). This system would be free, comprehensive, and secular, serve Filipino expectations and promote American democratic ideals. For various practical reasons, the language of instruction was to be English, for which a thousand American teachers were requested. Now, the function of the U.S. military in general educational activities may seem strange but, at this time, it made sense (Gates, 1973). The initial victory over the Spanish did not end the fighting in the Philippines. An extensive and prolonged guerilla war was waged against the occupying Americans by Filipinos who sought complete independence and freedom from foreign domination, no matter how benevolent. Operating schools brought the military closer to the people to "win their hearts and minds" and further, the U.S. Army had staffed schools designed specifically for the Native American population. The most famous of these "noble experiments" was established in Carlisle, Pennsylvania, the Carlisle Indian Industrial School (1879–1918) (Landis, 2006). Such schools were intended to deculturize the Indians and turn them into *useful* citizens: "to kill the Indian and save the man"—not a very different objective from that intended for the Filipinos. Soldier-teachers stressed "character building" in their teaching, characteristics that they believed would contribute to a "democratic way of life": honesty, attention to duty, self-discipline, acceptance of moral responsibility. To this, the civilian teachers added the further goals of overcoming an inherited Spanish distaste for manual labor; overcoming the existing peasant mentality of servitude; and improving the sheltered, dependent position of women in society. America was going to import *its culture* of independence and self-reliance, the cornerstones of Democracy, to the Philippines.

In January 1901, a civilian Commission headed by William Howard Taft published its guidelines for a new system of Filipino education. This system closely followed the recommendations set by the military. A civilian Superintendent of Education was appointed and American teachers recruited and brought to the Philippines. At first, American mathematics texts were imported and used in the schools, books such as Heath's *Primary Arithmetics* and Wentworth's *Arithmetics*. However, the books' illustrations featuring White, Anglo images and the mathematical problems set out were alien and in conflict with the Filipino milieu. A new Filipino-centered series was edited by Mabel Bonsall and her teachers at the Philippine Normal School and was put into effect in 1905. Its text, illustrations, and problem situations all attempted to instill American democratic goals. Enumeration was illustrated by objects from the Filipino milieu such as mangoes, lady's fans, and palm trees. Local measures of capacity were introduced and used: the *chupa* and *ganta*. Illustrations depicted barefoot peasants involved in productive work: loading carts with water jars, herding pigs, building walls, and so on. Problems express the themes of past exploitation and the need for reforms. For example, in a section, "Philippine Farming—the Tenant" a problem scenario illustrates past injustices:

> 1. Pedro is a tenant on Mr. Santos' farm. He rented 4 hectares of rice land. After the cutting is paid for, Mr. Santos is to have for the use of the land one half of what rice is left, and Pedro will take the other half for himself. If 45 cavans grow on each hectare, and one sixth is given for cutting, how many cavans will the cutters get? How much will be left? What will be Mr. Savans' share? What will be Pedro's share? (Bonsall, 1905, p. 55)

Subsequent problems further illustrate Pedro's plight. He initially earned 75 cavans of rice for a year's work. Then a series of debts must be repaid to Mr. Santos. When the problem series is worked through and the computations are completed, it is found that at the end of a year Pedro will owe Mr. Santos P28.50 and that since this debt carries over to the following year, he will never get out of debt to Mr. Santos. The following section in this text is entitled "The Independent Farmer." It then contrasts earnings and rewards under free enterprise. Other themes promulgated in the mathematics series stress the necessity of saving money, thrift, hygiene, and the use of modern farming techniques.

By 1904, almost all of the primary mathematics instruction was carried out by Filipino teachers under American supervision. Gradually, Filipino authors assumed the tasks of textbook revision and writing. The year 1923 saw a Filipino revision of Bonsall's series. The new books reflected Mabel Bonsall's content and methodology; however, cultural directions in the material had been changed. Peasant work ethic had been minimized; family situations now depicted well-dressed people—men wearing suits and ties in formal domestic situations. These situations illustrated the lifestyle of the *gente ilustrada,* the ruling class, and the real aspirations of the Filipino people. Some practices of democracy were still advocated in the mathematics curriculum. But Filipinos rejected the concept of individualism in favor of collective cooperation and the subjection of the individual to the group, that is, the family or clan. The authoritarian nature of Filipino society remained unchallenged; a veneer of machismo dominated the society. Women's roles did not appreciably change and land reform remained, and remains today, a socioeconomic problem that plagues the Philippines.

The American efforts at social engineering in the Philippines bore little fruit. Efforts of early administrators and teachers were sincere and well intentioned. They offered what they thought best for their "little brown brothers." However, in doing this, they imposed alien cultural objectives, better suited to Midwestern American life than the tropical island existence of the diverse peoples of the Philippines. Even today, the self-professed cultural identity of the Filipino people remains confused.

Throughout the 20th century, much concern was focused on the content of mathematics curricula and the form of its teaching. International and national commissions and reports suggested reforms directed at securing better civic participation in a modern, technological-based society. Cold war tensions between the United States and the Soviet Union came to the forefront with the launching of the Soviet Sputnik in 1957. It was felt that Soviet superiority in mathematics and science was in the main part responsible for this "space victory." Radical reforms in mathematics teaching and learning were needed to counter this threat to our national security. The National Science Foundation (NSF), a government agency established to promote scientific development, stepped up efforts to encourage and support needed reforms. One of the first projects funded by the NSF under this effort was a reformulation and rewriting of the school mathematics curriculum. The School Mathematics Study Group (SMSG) took on this charge and produced a textbook series advocating a teaching of "new mathematics." The SMSG was dominated by university professors remote from the realities of the common school classroom. The new math produced was formalistic, abstract, and stressed precise thinking demonstrated by a use of precise terminology; thus a distinction was drawn between the word *number*, which represented a mental concept and the word *numeral* which represented a symbol for a number ("You don't write numbers on your paper, you write numerals!") An emphasis on correct vocabulary was advocated. In the formation of this mathematics content, little consideration was given to teaching methodology and the realities of the school classroom. One might say there was a clash of cultures between the SMSG culture of reform and the existing culture of mathematics teaching and learning. Debate and confusion reigned over the new math movement. One of the most vocal critics of this time, one who recognized this cultural clash was Morris Klein, respected applied mathematician and mathematical historian. Klein expressed his concerns in several books, perhaps the most relevant of which was *Why Johnnie Can't Add* (1973) but the reforms were put into place and the face of American mathematics education changed.

At this same period of time, the United States was waging a campaign in developing countries to win their alliance to Western ideals, notably those advocated by the United States. Through the U.S. State Department and the U.S. Agency for International Development (USAID), projects were organized and funds dispersed for their international projects. One of these projects was a six-week conference held in Accra, Ghana in 1961 to discuss the reform of African mathematics teaching. The conference was organized by Jerrold Zacharias, a professor of physics at MIT and attended by British and American mathematics educators and their African counterparts from the English-speaking countries. The overseas visitors brought the newest and best of their mathematics and it was soon agreed upon "that the work of curriculum reform in mathematics in the USA and Britain was sufficiently advanced to make a possible contribution to African education" (Swetz, 1975). The British reforms lay in their School Mathematics Program (SMP). Thus, SMSG and SMP curriculum and teaching outlooks would be brought to Africa. This latest effort to relieve "the White man's burden" became known as the African Mathematics Project (AMP). The project started in earnest in July 1962 under the aegis of Educational Services, Inc., later to become the Educational Development Corporation (EDC), Newton, Massachusetts, with the financial backing of USAID and the Ford Foundation. It remained under the leadership of Zacharias. At that time, a writing workshop hosted 54 educators, 24 of whom represented African countries. The workshop was held in Entebbe, Uganda and for many years this reform effort bore the popular name "the Entebbe Project." The American participants arrived with SMSG in their pockets. Eventually, such writing workshops resulted in the production of 60 volumes, both student and teacher texts. Ten African countries began classroom trials of the new math. In turn, the British began their own writing projects based on their SMP experiences: the Joint Mathematics Project (JMP), was begun in West Africa and the East African School Mathematics Project (EASMP) in East Africa.

In 1969, a committee of mathematicians and educators representing the American Conference Board of Mathematical Sciences visited Africa and reviewed the work of AMP. While praising some aspects of the work, the Committee also raised questions concerning the program's goal, methods, and general effectiveness. Local educators had difficulty in reading and understanding the books. In truth, most of the new material was taught by foreign, English-speaking volunteers: the U.S. Peace Corps and the British Voluntary Service Overseas. The "idea of proof" was particularly alien and the value of "terminological precision" came into question. The new materials were especially devoid of practical problems. As a result of such concerns, EDC in 1970 embarked on a revision phase of the materials, drawing on more local expertise.

It seems that in this bland adoption of Western experimental curriculum into an African situation, no consideration was given to the cultural and socioeconomic impact. When USAID officials were questioned on Jerrold Zacharias's experience and expertise involving education in poor, developing, countries, they responded that his association with MIT was sufficient. Apparently, the aura of MIT's excellence in science and mathematics was omnipotent! This was an example of educational imperialism at its worst! Available research findings on mathematical teaching and learning in the developing world were ignored. For example, B.W. King, commenting on his experiences in Papua, New Guinea (King, 1970) offered constructive suggestions concerning mathematics curriculum design:

> We make arithmetic more difficult for them [indigenous people] if we must teach them all the customary details on set theory first, or even insist on their accepting the foundation of number in the concept of cardinal number, instead of the concept of ordinal number. Ordinal numbers are more familiar to most traditional indigenous societies. (p. 57)

Most telling at this time was the criticism directed at AMP by Ed Begle, leading American mathematics educator and the director of the SMSG project:

> Many countries are asking not only the U.S., but also others of the affluent countries, for assistance in improving their mathematics education programs. Having looked into a number of attempts to honor these requests, I am convinced that failure to study the cultural milieu of the proposed reforms has often resulted in a serious waste of time, effort and money. (Begle, 1969, p. 241)

The AMP effort officially ended in 1976. Millions of dollars and thousands of work hours were expended on a questionable effort that was ill-conceived from the beginning. African students brought up on an oral tradition had difficulty with textbook-bound instruction. Their concepts of number, space, and logical and quantitative relationships differed from those of their Western counterparts. Vocabulary skills were extremely limited in both teachers and students. In most African languages, new words, often with much conceptual difficulty, had to be invented to accommodate the AMP materials. A textbook bound method of instruction could not be supported in poor countries. In much of the world, individual student textbooks are a luxury. A team investigating the impact of AMP on rural schools asked a headmaster if his school was involved with the new math. "Indeed!" he answered and led them to his office, where a set of unused AMP books were proudly displayed in a locked, glass fronted, bookcase—a shrine to progressiveness for the school.

This effort at cross-cultural curriculum adoption, in its failure, should serve as a warning for future efforts to import mathematical curriculum across cultural, national, and even regional boundaries. What are the cultural implications? What are the pedagogical implications? What are the socioeconomic complications of such an adoption? These are all questions whose answers must be seriously considered before any such action takes place. In light of this fact, it is indeed disturbing to realize that the use of large scale international mathematics and science achievement comparisons in recent years has resulted in attempts to import mathematics curriculum and teaching methods to solve student performance difficulties. In particular, the Trends in International Mathematics and Science Study (TIMSS), in its data analysis for 2003 testing, reported that the small island nation of Singapore emerged as the top performer (TIMSS, 2003). Its students did very well in mathematics, outperforming the representatives of 46 other countries. As a result of this assessment, several countries are now attempting to emulate Singapore by adopting its curricula and teaching methods. Beware!

Implications for Teaching and Learning

One of the offshoots of the New Math movement of the 1960s was the identification of the "culturally deprived child." This offensive and self-serving phrase was soon dismissed and replaced by the equally misguided theory that the learning of mathematics is "culture-free." It is hoped that the discussion up to this point will dispel this myth. Certainly, the role of culture in mathematics learning and teaching is important but how does one accommodate it? As more and more societies become truly multicultural, how should their educational systems respond to the challenge? With its early immigrant history, the United States served as a model for "melting pot" accommodation. Its schools bore the brunt of indoctrinating the newcomers into the traditions and skills of a useful citizen. As noted by Henry Ward Beecher, a 19th century social reformer and respected orator:

> The common schools are the stomachs of the country in which all people that come to us are assimilated within a generation. When a lion eats an ox, the lion does not become an ox but the ox becomes a lion. (quoted in Landis, 2006)

Perhaps Beecher's words were appropriate for his times, but in contemporary American society the belly of the beast does not rest easy. Cultural interactions are complex and accommodation often difficult. The most recent wave of immigrants to the United States and Western Europe are better educated than their predecessors, more politically savvy, and less inclined to discard their cultural attachments. The analogy of the melting pot no longer fits and should be replaced by that of a salad where each ingredient retains its identity but contributes to the whole. Seldom can accommodation be directed to "a culture," as the existence of any pure culture is questionable. What social planners and educators must face is a meshing of a variety of cultural inputs: The ethnic or racial culture of the individual; the influence of the family; their community and neighborhood (socioeconomic); the school; learning; the classroom; and the national society at large. For a high school student studying mathematics, add to this list the hormonal driven culture of adolescence and the culture of mathematics and, indeed, there is a cultural maelstrom fraught with possible tensions and conflicts.

The issue of mathematics as a cultural system within itself is often ignored but lies at the crux of attempting to understand the interactions, cultural or otherwise, between mathematics and its teaching/learning. This theory of mathematics as a cultural construction was enunciated by Raymond Wilder (1896–1982) in his lectures and writing (Smorynski, 1983; Wilder, 1968, 1981). Mathematics has a history, a literature, a special spoken and written language, traditions, and a social hierarchy based on accomplishment. At times, mathematics has even been described as a language. During the New Math movement, the need for the use of precise mathematical language was stressed. Researchers have often noted the strong connection between language and mathematics (Vygotsky, 1962; Wertsch, 1985). The manipulations of words and grammatical structures are instrumental in the formation of cognitive schemes; that is, how we think about and organize new knowledge in our minds. If the logic of our language and thought does not fit the logic of mathematics, there will be learning difficulties. Eleanor Orr, building upon research and her teaching of African Americans has noted strong negative connections between the use of Black English and student performance in mathematics and science (Orr, 1987). Despite support from such social commentators as Bill Cosby (Cosby, 2004), Orr's findings and recommendations have not been deemed "politically correct" and, unfortunately, have made little educational impact.

Any discussion of culture and mathematics performance should identify cultural traits that seem to promote mathematics learning. In the past 17 International Mathematical Olympiads, the annual world's championship competition for secondary school students in mathematics, the Chinese have reaped first place honors 13 times. Teams from the United States, representing our best math students, have been dominated by large numbers of Asian-Americans students, a disproportional representation for our society that only contains a 4.2% minority of Asians. Further, Scholastic Assessment Test (SAT) scores indicated that Asian Americans significantly outperform all other students in mathematics (National Center for Educational Statistics [NCES], 2002, p. 152).

In brief, most Asian students who have been socialized into a modern educational system do well in mathematics. The majority of these high performers come from Chinese, Korean, and Vietnamese backgrounds with Confucian traditions that promote education. Although there might be yet undetermined cognitive traits that allow these students as a group to do well, investigations indicate that their advantage lies in attitude and motivation (Butterfield, 1990; Chen & Stevenson, 1995; Hirschman, & Wong, 1986; Stevenson, Lee, & Stigler, 1986). In general, it is found that Asian-American students:

- Believe that the path to personal advancement lies in education as indicated in the Vietnamese saying, "If you don't study, you will never become anything. If you study, you will become what you wish" (Butterfield, 1990).
- Think their fate lies in their own hands and that success depends on

hard work. "If you try hard enough, you can make a piece of iron into a needle."
- Have strong parental support and guidance in their studies.

Quite simply, Asian students work harder and actively seek out more advanced studies. SAT statistics (NCES, 2002) show that AP calculus enrollments were 44% Asian American, 28% Caucasian, and 14% African American. For physics, the figures were 65% Asian American, 52% Caucasian, and 41% African American. In the Asian community reinforcement for education is strong! There are situations where African Americans are taunted by their peers for becoming "too White"; Hispanics are taunted for being "too Anglo" for attempting to excel in school, situations which would be unheard of amongst Asians.

Whereas, Caucasian students, when polled, credit "talent" or a "good teacher" for mathematics success, Asians answer "hard work." In growing up in a multicultural neighborhood of New York City, I knew another ethnic group, self-disciplined and highly motivated, who also did well in mathematics, the Jews. The joke about the Jewish Mother that always makes a point to refer to her "son/daughter, the doctor" or "the lawyer," is extremely telling and indicates high aspiration, parental pride and support, and a resulting motivation similar to that demonstrated by the Asian community. Another varying cultural trait important for learning and cognitive development is that of memorizing, or rather memory training, directed at the retention of selected information (Beran, 2004). If these factors for success, associated with ethnic or racial pride, can be instilled in lesser performing social groups then the climate of educational performance in the United States would radically improve.

Some Final Thoughts

Culture helps conceive of, formulate, and sustain mathematical concepts. It affects the way we use mathematics, think about, and teach mathematics. History shows that no aspect of mathematical involvement is free from cultural influences. The development and use of mathematics by a society is a primary example. It is the culture of a group that initially decides what is important for that group. This importance is abstracted into concepts which set mental priorities. Quite simply, a person will think about and act upon what he or she personally considers important. This limited importance can then be transformed into a larger societal priority. Attitude reflects the culture it represents. Far too often in the teaching of mathematics, a greater emphasis is placed on cognitive aspects of the subject rather than on its affective impact. If children are not interested in or attracted to mathematics, if they do not consider it important, they will not study it effectively. We do not learn what we do not want to learn! Where possible, mathematics and its teaching should reflect its historical and cultural background. Such an association personalizes mathematics. If one has a particular cultural connection to mathematics, it is meaningful and may become a source of pride, even empowerment. Jamie Escalante, an East Los Angeles mathematics teacher, inspired his inner city Latino students by informing them that their ancestors, the Maya of South America, developed their own system of mathematics; and they invented and used a "zero" well before Anglos appeared on their continent. Escalante's students went on to perform well in AP calculus work, a previously unimagined achievement (Mathews, 1988). Further, the realization that many cultures and peoples contributed to the development of mathematics highlights its universal appeal and importance. Mathematics is certainly a human endeavor, marked by mistakes and dead ends but built up by continuing effort, resulting in a series of successes. Yes, in mathematics, to err is human! By studying and doing work in mathematics, one is joining a long tradition.

References

Absolon, K. (1937, October 2). The world's earliest portrait—30,000 years old. *Illustrated London News,* pp. 550–553.

Ascher, M. (2002). *Mathematics elsewhere: An exploration of ideas across culture.* Princeton, NJ: Princeton University Press.

Augustine, Saint (1872). *The works of Aurelius Augustine* (Vol. 9, M. Dods, Trans.). Edinburgh, UK: T & T Clark.

Begle, E. (1969). The role of research in the improvement of mathematics education. *Educational Studies in Mathematics, 2,* 233–244.

Beran, M. (2004). In defense on memorization. *City Journal.* Retrieved August 24, 2008, from http://www.city-journal.org/html/14_3_defense_memorization.html

Bishop, A. J. (1979). Visualising and mathematics in a pre-technological culture. *Educational Studies in Mathematics, 10,* 135–146.

Bishop, A. J. (1990). Western mathematics: The secret weapon of cultural imperialism. *Race & Class, 32,* 51–65.

Bonsall, M. (1905). *Primary arithmetic, Parts I and II.* Manila, Philippines: World Book.

Brown, N. (1987). The rainforest: A special report. *Research Penn State, 8,* 18–29.

Butterfield, F. (1990, January 21). Why they excel. *Parade Magazine,* pp. 4–6.

Butterworth, B. (1999). *What counts: How every brain is hardwired for math.* New York: Free Press.

Careccio, J. (1970). Mathematical heritage of Zambia. *Arithmetic Teacher, 17,* 391–395.

Chen, C., & Stevenson, H. (1995). Motivation and mathematics achievement: A comparative study of Asian-American, Caucasian-American, and East Asian high school students. *Child Development, 66,* 1215–1234.

Conant, L.L. (1896). *The number concept: Its origin and development.* New York: Macmillan.

Cosby, W. (2004). *Dr. Bill Cosby speaks at the 50th Anniversary commemoration of the Brown vs Topeka Board of Education Supreme Court Decision.* Transcript of June 7, 2004 lecture at Howard University, Washington, D.C. Retrieved August 24, 2008, from http://www.eightcitiesmap.com/transcript_bc.htm

Crawford, J. (1863). On the numerals as evidence of the progress of civilization, *Transactions of the Ethnological Society of London, 2,* 84–111.

Crosby, A. W. (1997). *The measure of reality: Quantification and western society 1250–1600.* Cambridge, UK: Cambridge University Press.

D'Ambrosio, U. (1985). Ethnomathematics and its place in the history and pedagogy of mathematics. *For the Learning of Mathematics, 5,* 44–48.

Datzig, T. (1954). *Number: The language of science.* New York: Macmillan.

Dehaene, S. (1997). *The number sense: How the mind creates mathematics.* New York: Oxford University Press.

Denny, P. J. (1979). Semantic analysis of selected Japanese numerical classifiers for units. *Linguistics, 17*, 317–335.

Dewey, J. (1896). [Review of] The number concept: Its origin and development by Levi L. Conant. *Psychological Review, 3*, 326–329.

Diamond, J. (1999). *Guns, germs and steel: The fate of human societies.* New York: Norton.

Fennema, E. (1976, February 22–23). *Sex related differences in mathematics learning: Myths, realities and related factors.* Paper presented at American Association for Advancement of Science, Boston, MA.

Flegg, G. (1987). *Number through the ages.* London: Macmillan.

Fowler, B. (2000). *Iceman: Uncovering the life and times of a prehistoric man.* Chicago: University of Chicago Press.

Gates, J. G. (1973). *Schoolbooks and krags: The United States army in the Philippines, 1898–1902.* Westport, CT: Greenwood Press.

Guberman, S. (1999). Cultural aspects of children's mathematics knowledge. In J. V. Copley (Ed.), *Mathematics in the early years* (pp. 30–36). Reston, VA: National Council of Teachers of Mathematics.

Haddon, A. C. (1890). The ethnography of the western tribes of the Torres Straits. *Journal of the Anthropological Institute of Great Britain and Ireland, 19*, 297–437.

Harris, J. (1987). Australian aboriginal and islander mathematics. *Australian Aboriginal Studies, 2*, 29–37.

Hirschman, C., & Wong, M. G. (1986). The extraordinary educational attainment of Asian Americans: A search for historical evidence and explanations, *Social Forces, 65*, 1–27.

Ho, P. Y. (1985). *Li, qi and shu: An introduction to science and civilization in China.* Hong Kong: Hong Kong University Press.

Høyrup, J. (1994). *In measure, number and weight.* Albany, NY: SUNY Press.

Hudson, W (1960). Pictorial depth perception in sub-cultural groups in Africa. *The Journal of Social Psychology, 52*, 183–208.

Joseph, G. G. (1991). *The crest of the peacock: Non European roots of mathematics.* London: Penguin.

King, B. W. (1970). Objectives in mathematics: Why teach set theory? *Papua New Guinea Journal of Education, 6*, 54–66.

Klein, M. (1973). *Why Johnny can't add: The failure of the new math.* New York: St. Martin's Press. Retrieved August 24, 2008, from http://www.marco-learningsystems.com/pages/kline/johnny.html

Landis, B. (2006). *Carlisle Indian Industrial School (1879–1918).* Retrieved August 24, 2008, from http://home.epix.net/~landis/

Li, Y., & Du, S. (1987). *Chinese mathematics: A concise history* (J. Crosley & A. Lum, Trans.). Oxford, UK: Clarendon Press.

Lopez, R. S. (1969). Stars and spices: The earliest Italian manual of commercial practice. In D. Herlihy, R. S. Lopez, & V. Slessarev (Eds.), *Economy, society and government in medieval Italy* (pp. 35–42). Kent, Ohio: Kent State University Press.

Mathews, J. (1988). *Esconlante: The best teacher in America.* New York: Henry Holt.

Menninger, K. (1969). *Number words and number symbols: A cultural history of numbers.* Cambridge, MA: MIT Press.

Mitchelmore, M. (1980). Three-dimensional geometrical drawing in three cultures. *Educational Studies in Mathematics, 11*, 205–216.

Murry, A. (1978). *Reason and society in the middle ages.* Oxford, UK: Clarendon Press.

National Center for Educational Statistics (NCES). (2002). *Digest of educational statistics 2001.* Retrieved August 24, 2008, from http://nces.ed.gov/Pubsearch/pubsinfo.asp?pubid=2002130

Neihardt, J. (1972). *Black Elk speaks: Being the life story of a holy man of the Oglala Sioux.* Lincoln: University of Nebraska Press.

Omar, A. (1972). Numeral classifiers in Malay and Iban. *Anthropological Linguistics, 14*, 86–97.

Omari, I. (1975). Developmental order of spatial concepts among schoolchildren in Tanzania. *Journal of Cross-Cultural Psychology, 1*, 444–456.

Orr, E. W. (1987). *Twice as less: Black English and performance of black students in mathematics and science.* New York: Norton.

Peano, G. (1889). *Arithmetics principia, nova methodo exposita.* Rome: Augustae Taurinorum.

Poole, H. (1970). Restructuring the perceptual world of African children. *Teacher Education in New Countries, 10,* 165–175.

Robson, E. (2002). Words and pictures: New light on Plimpton 322. In M. Anderson, V. Katz, & R. Wilson (Eds.), *Sherlock Holmes in Babylonia* (pp. 14–26). Washington, D.C.: The Mathematical Association of America.

Saxe, G. (1991). *Culture and cognitive development: Studies in mathematical understanding.* Mahwah, NJ: Erlbaum.

Segal, M. (1966). *The influence of culture on visual perception.* New York: Bobbs-Merrill.

Sizer, W. (1991). Mathematical notions in preliterate societies. *The Mathematical Intelligencer, 13,* 53–60.

Smith, D. E. (1958). *History of mathematics* (Vols 1 & 2). New York: Dover. (Original work published 1923)

Smorynski, C. (1983). Mathematics as a cultural system. *The Mathematical Intelligencer, 5,* 9–15.

Stevenson, H, Lee, S. Y., & Stigler, J. (1986). Mathematics achievement of Chinese, Japanese, and American children. *Science, 231,* 693–699.

Swetz, F. J. (1975). Mathematics curricular reform in less-developed nations: An issue of concern. *Journal of Developing Areas, 10,* 3–14.

Swetz, F. J. (1977). *Was Pythagoras Chinese? An examination of right triangle theory in ancient China.* University Park, PA: Penn State Press.

Swetz, F. J. (1987). *Capitalism and arithmetic: The new math of the 15th century.* Chicago: Open Court.

Swetz, F. J. (1996). Enigmas of Chinese mathematics. In R. Callinger (Ed.), *Vita mathematica: Historical research and integration with teaching* (pp. 87–97). Washington, D.C.: Mathematical Association of America.

Swetz, F. J. (1999). Mathematics for social change: United States experience in the Philippines, 1898–1925, *Bulletin of the American Historical Collection Foundation,* 27, 61–80.

Swetz, F. J. (2002). Figura mercantesco: Merchants and the evolution of a number concept in the latter middle ages. In J. Contreni & S. Casciani (Eds.), *Word, image, number: Communication in the middle ages* (pp 391–412). Florence, Italy: SISMEL.

Trends in International Mathematics and Science Study. (TIMSS). (2003). Retrieved August 24, 2008, from http://timss.bc.edu/timss2003.html

Van Loosbrock, E., & Smitsman, A. W. (1990). Visual perception on numerosity in infancy. *Developmental psychology, 26,* 916–922.

Vygotsky, L. S. (1962). *Thought and language.* Cambridge, MA: MIT Press.

Wertsch, J. V. (1985). *Culture, communication and cognition: Vygotskian perspectives.* Cambridge, UK: Cambridge University Press.

Wilder, R. (1968). *Mathematical concepts: An elementary study.* New York: Wiley.

Wilder, R. (1981). *Mathematics as a cultural system.* Oxford, UK: Pergamon.

2
New Philosophy of Mathematics
Implications for Mathematics Education

PAUL ERNEST

The New Philosophy of Mathematics

In the past 50 years a new philosophy of mathematics has been emerging (Hersh, 2006). This movement foregrounds a new set of issues and concerns for the philosophy of mathematics, and consequently results in new implications for mathematics education. In this chapter after an initial analysis I shall outline some of these novel implications.

Traditional perspectives in the philosophy of mathematics have tended to focus on two main questions: What are the objects of mathematics? and What is the foundation for the certainty of mathematical knowledge? Traditional approaches to these questions articulate their answers with reference to some extramundane location or reality. The objects of mathematics are described as abstract, Platonic objects, existing in some possibly objective world, such as Popper's (1979) World 3, and the certainty of mathematical knowledge is also ascribed to its timeless, superhuman objectivity. Newer approaches to the philosophy of mathematics have engaged in what Restivo (1993) has aptly termed *the Promethean task of bringing mathematics to earth;* that is, accounting for mathematics in terms of the shared social, cultural, and material reality inhabited by human beings, not looking for answers in some alternative universe.

The new philosophy of mathematics emphasizes a number of novel and hitherto neglected aspects of mathematics as philosophically relevant. This includes the following innovations.

First, there is a new focus on the professional practices of mathematicians in their researches, both in their invention/discovery of new mathematical knowledge, and in their interactions with the objects of mathematics (Corfield, 2003; Davis & Hersh, 1980; Lakatos, 1963–1964, 1976; Polya, 1945).

Second, there is a new recognition of the central significance of its historical and social contexts for the nature of mathematics and for its philosophical problems (Gillies, 1992; Kitcher, 1984; Lakatos, 1963–1964, 1976).

Third, a new semiotic view of mathematical objects is emerging that sees them in terms of signs with cultural uses and meanings and in terms of human conceptions, rather than as abstract objects in some ideal Platonic realm (Ernest, 1998, 2008; Rotman, 1993).

Fourth, there is a reconceptualization of mathematical knowledge as a cultural human construction, which although unlikely to be significantly wrong is nevertheless corrigible and continually undergoing revision and reconstruction, and which is constitutionally incapable of revealing truths about the world (Kline, 1980; Lakatos, 1976; Tymoczko, 1986). However, ironically, because the invention of mathematics is often inspired by real world problems and situations, mathematics is supremely effective at modeling aspects of the world.

Fifth, a broader view of the philosophy of mathematics is emerging that includes the relevance of a range of traditionally excluded dimensions such as: culture, values, and social responsibility; applications of mathematics and their effectiveness in science, technology, and other realms of knowledge and social functioning; and the learning of mathematics, its role in the transmission of mathematical knowledge, and in the formation of individual mathematicians (Ernest, 1991, 1998; Restivo, Bemdege, Van, & Fischer, 1993; Skovsmose, 1994).

These novel emphases in the new philosophy of mathematics, that have resulted in it sometimes being referred to as postmodern (Ernest, 1998), lead to a number of consequences for mathematics education.

Implications for Mathematics Education: The Mechanisms and Relationships

To explore the implications that the new philosophy of mathematics might have for mathematics education it is first necessary to clarify the meaning of the term *implication*. Logical implication is a relation that holds between the antecedent and consequent in a logically valid inference. However, a discussion of the implications of the new philosophy of mathematics for mathematics education is not an exploration of the logically necessary correlation of a given philosophy of mathematics and specifics concerning mathematics education. Instead, I wish to explore the actual, empirically observed, as well as the potential influences or impacts of a philosophy of mathematics on the teaching and learning of mathematics. This is to be based on the consonances or resonances between philosophies and pedagogical/curricular positions, and these are looser relationships than implication in any strict sense.

In addition, to clarify these patterns of influence it is necessary to distinguish a number of different but related objects. In particular, the term *philosophy of mathematics* is used with both strict and loose meanings. The strict sense is the philosophy of mathematics as an academic discipline in itself. The loose sense concerns a range of views, perceptions, or images of mathematics. I shall term the first of these an *academic philosophy of mathematics*. This is a philosophically formulated and academically acceptable position stated as a set of claims about the nature of mathematics, concerning mathematical objects, mathematical knowledge, and the relationship of some or all of these within the discipline of mathematics and with the social context of mathematics. Within its area of focus this needs to be fully and explicitly formulated in writings acceptable in principle within scholarly circles. It addresses technical philosophical issues concerning the ontology, epistemology, or the application of some other branch of philosophy to mathematical issues. An academic philosophy of mathematics is a position from which it is possible to address or settle specific and precise questions and claims about mathematics from an academic perspective. It is intended for a narrow and specialist audience made up of philosophers, and it is represented in publications such as the Oxford University Press book series on the philosophy of mathematics and papers in the journal *Philosophia Mathematica*.

The academic literature documents a number of different academic philosophies of mathematics that includes: realism, Platonism, empiricism, formalism, logicism, intuitionism, conventionalism, fallibilism (including quasi-empiricism) and social constructivism. Some of these can be loosely grouped together and described as traditional philosophies of mathematics because of their shared absolutism, including realism, Platonism, formalism, and logicism. Others, including fallibilism, quasi-empiricism, humanism, and social constructivism can be seen as loosely forming a coalition of fallibilist or "new" philosophies of mathematics. The remaining schools are not so easy to classify with some, like intuitionism, inclining toward absolutism in some of its formulations, and others, including empiricism and conventionalism, closer to fallibilism.

Table 2.1 (adapted from Ernest, 2004), illustrates some differences between the traditional (also called absolutist) and the new (also called fallibilist) philosophies of mathematics. They are contrasted according to their accounts of a number of features, namely their positions on mathematical knowledge, the nature of mathematics, the relations of knowledge areas, values and mathematics, the relationship between mathematics and (everyday) reality, the nature of mathematical objects, and the structure of knowledge in mathematics.

Aspects of the traditional absolutist philosophies of mathematics summarized in the table can be inferred from the formalism espoused by Hilbert (1925/1964), the logicism proposed by Frege (1893/1964) and Russell (1919), and in the logical positivism of Ayer (1946) and others. Although controversial and subject to critiques by supporters of the new philosophies of mathematics, these remain well-established and defensible traditional views in the philosophy of mathematics. Likewise, Table 2.1 shows selected aspects of the new philosophies of mathematics which can be inferred from the work of Ernest (1998), Hersh (1997, 2006), Kitcher (1984), Lakatos (1963–1964, 1976, 1978), Tymoczko (1986), Wittgenstein (1953, 1956/1978) and others. These have been named fallibilist philosophies following the terminology of Lakatos (1963–1964, 1976). They are controversial modern

Table 2.1 Positions in the Philosophy of Mathematics

Aspect	Traditional (Absolutist) Philosophies of Mathematics	New (Fallibilist) Philosophies of Mathematics
Mathematical knowledge:	Certain truth; Objective, super-human, asocial, acultural, apolitical and absolute	Socially, culturally constructed and politically situated; Corrigible and eternally revisable knowledge (since humans are its makers and validators)
Nature of mathematics	Body of abstract knowledge	Knowledge, inquiry and the underlying human institutions. (Both the processes and products of human inquiry)
Relations of knowledge areas	Isolated and discrete knowledge, different in kind from all others (*analytic a priori* knowledge)	Joined up with and inseparable from other areas of knowledge
Values position	Neutral and value-free, Context independent	Value-laden but in 'objectivised' form, Context dependent
Relationship between mathematics and reality	Truths from an ideal objective realm that are unreasonably (miraculously) effective in applications to empirical reality	Constructed systems and models inspired by and abstracted from human practices and problem situations (hence highly applicable)
Nature of mathematical objects	Abstract objects in Platonic realm of Ideals	Socially constructed signs with social and individual meanings
Structure of knowledge in mathematics	Rigid, fixed hierarchy (metaphors: skyscraper, Eiffel Tower)	Fluid structures, forming and reforming (metaphors: icebergs, forest)

perspectives within the philosophy of mathematics, and the controversy between the traditional and these new philosophies is far from settled.

The second and looser sense in which the term *philosophy of mathematics* is sometimes used is what I term an *image of mathematics*. This is quite different from an academic philosophy for it is a view, perception, or informal account of mathematics as a discipline and area of enquiry. It is a system of beliefs or views which may only be partly expressed as well as being partly made up of tacit inferences, assumptions, and beliefs about the nature of mathematics. It constitutes part of a belief system or even part of an ideology (Ernest, 1991). Images of mathematics can vary greatly from the knowledgeable, elaborate, and well-articulated systems of belief about mathematics held by well-informed mathematicians, scientists, or philosophers of mathematics, to the rudimentary perceptions held by elementary school children and many members of the public. An image of mathematics is thus a set of beliefs about the nature of mathematics held by individuals or groups, although it can also be represented in written accounts directed at nonspecialist readers.

There have been a number of studies of the image of mathematics held by the public (Cockcroft, 1982; Lim, 1999; Rensaa, 2006; Sewell, 1981) and adult students

(Buerk, 1982; Buxton, 1981), including working groups on the public image of mathematics and mathematicians at the quadrennial International Congress on Mathematical Education. These and other studies have revealed the widespread presence of the traditional popular image of mathematics summarized in Table 2.2 (based on a table in Ernest, 2004).

The traditional popular image of mathematics as illustrated in the second column of Table 2.1 is one of difficultly and remoteness from the concerns, interests, and capabilities of the majority of population. Although a small minority of successful students and practitioners of mathematics are attracted by elements of this image, for a much larger group this is a negative view of mathematics that has arisen through negative aspects of their encounter with mathematics and its image, and which has turned them off mathematics. Consequently, for many the traditional image is associated with negative attitudes to mathematics.

Table 2.2 contrasts this traditional image with a humanistic image of mathematics (3rd column). Elements of this humanistic image have been identified among the public but results suggests that it is not as widely held as the traditional image (Lim, 1999). Primarily this is a positive image, and one that is promoted by progressive or reform-oriented developments in mathematics education. Where

Table 2.2 Contrasting Popular Images of Maths

Aspect	Traditional Image	Humanistic Image
Approachability	Difficult, forbidding	Approachable and accessible
Human dimension	Cold, neutral, abstract and impersonal	Human and personal
Social context	Abstract tools applied in advanced societies	Concepts and methods embedded in all of human history and societies
Key elements	Theoretical abstract theories	Practical problem solving and conceptual tools
Applications	Not part of 'real' (pure) mathematics. Applications work by coincidence or because mathematics describes the necessary structure of universe	Mathematics is grounded in applications providing both inspiration for its concepts and utility through modeling
Procedures and methods	Ultra-rational, strictly following fixed rules	Creative and flexible uses of knowledge to solve problems
Focus	Only interested in right answers and objective facts	Concerned with processes of personal inquiry and understanding
Problem solutions	Only one right answer exists for each task	Problems have multiple solution methods and multiple answers
Source of correctness	Experts have all the answers	Anyone should be able to solve problems and check answers
Ownership	Accessible only to gifted, stereotypically male, minority	Accessible to all and responsible to all

observed, the humanistic image is typically the adjunct of positive attitudes to mathematics (Ernest 1988; Thompson, 1984).

Comparing Tables 2.1 and 2.2, it appears that, at least on the surface, there is a strong analogy between the positions illustrated. Traditional absolutist philosophies of mathematics appear sympathetic to and to resonate with the traditional image of mathematics. Both portray mathematics as inaccessible and beyond the world of ordinary humanity, a subject that is abstract and separated from the world of everyday experience and other areas of study. Further, the absolutism and certainty of traditional philosophies fit with the idea in the traditional popular image that solving mathematical problems is about following determinate rules to reach the unique right answers.

Similarly, the emphasis of the new philosophy of mathematics on the centrality of the processes of human inquiry to mathematics is explicitly shared by the humanistic perspective, and both of these views also emphasize the inseparability of mathematics from other areas of knowledge, problem solving, and human activity.

Despite the strong resonances and sympathies between absolutist philosophies and traditional public images of mathematics, on the one hand, and between the new philosophies and humanistic images of mathematics, on the other, there are no logically necessary connections between them. In practice a traditional philosopher of mathematics might well say she or he believes in the humanistic image of mathematics, especially in the educational domain, but for technical reasons concerning epistemology or ontology subscribes to an absolutist philosophy of mathematics. This might describe the position of mathematicians Barnard and Saunders (1994), given their student-centered views on teaching combined with their adherence to a traditional philosophy of mathematics.

Analogously, a subscriber to one of the new philosophies of mathematics might argue that although mathematical knowledge is fallible or a contingent social construction, so long as it remains accepted in its present form by the mathematical community it is fixed and should be transmitted to learners in this way, and that questions of school mathematics are uniquely decidable as right or wrong with reference to its conventional corpus of knowledge. In a word, for this person the traditional public image of mathematics is the one that is most suitable for schooling. It is conceivable that this descriptor would have fitted Imre Lakatos (1976), given his combination of radical theories and a bombastic personal style, despite his critique of authoritarianism in mathematics and education.

Having offered this caveat, the question remains, what is the link between philosophies of mathematics and the image of mathematics envisaged for the teaching and learning of mathematics? In Ernest (1991) I develop an interdisciplinary model of educational and teacher ideologies that suggests that educational philosophies, including an image of school mathematics—what it should be like, from this perspective—arise from a whole complex of interrelated beliefs. According to this model, it is not just a personal philosophy of mathematics but this in conjunction with a personal epistemology, sets of values and educational aims, and theories of the child and of society that forms the basis for the philosophy of mathematics education. Thus my claim is that there are further elements of belief and ideology, of which a personal philosophy of mathematics is just one part, that are linked to an individual's or group's view of mathematics for education. Clearly, while such a model may provide a more complete explanation for the observed links and preferences, neither this model nor any further elaboration of it can provide the basis for *logically* derived consequences in this domain.

In considering the impact of both philosophies and images of mathematics in the educational system it is important to distinguish different curriculum manifestations. There are three manifestations usually distinguished, the planned, implemented, and the attained curriculum (Robitaille & Garden, 1989). The first of these is the intended curriculum as represented in documentary plans. This can be nationally or state specified, regional or school based or even the teacher's own plans. A more refined analysis could look at the relationships between these different types of plans, but for the present discussion these are just different specifications of the first manifestation, the planned curriculum. Second, there is the implemented curriculum. This is the curriculum as it is taught in the classroom. What is planned and what is offered need not be the same, since curriculum plans must be selected from, interpreted, and turned into practice by the teacher. Furthermore, the constraints of the social context of teaching—including time, resources, teacher orientations and knowledge, and social expectations of the milieu, including teachers, students, and parents—may all have an impact on the implementation of the planned curriculum. Third, there is the knowledge and other outcomes as actually acquired or successfully achieved by learners, the attained curriculum. This is yet again different, for learners must interpret and make sense of their learning experiences in their own idiosyncratic and not entirely predictable ways. So the "transmission" of the mathematics curriculum is like a game of Chinese whispers, with unintended and unpredictable transformations on route to learner outcomes.

Images of mathematics can be identified in and associated with each of these manifestations. The planned curriculum may include an explicit statement of an intended image of mathematics. This would indicate how mathematics as a whole is envisaged, and how it is intended it should be presented and experienced. Not all specifications of the planned mathematics curriculum include such an overt, intended image of mathematics. However, a detailed mathematics curriculum plan can also be read between the lines for what has been termed the "hidden" curriculum (Apple, 1979). Since the planned curriculum is represented by a set of documents it is clear that unintended contents, and in particular, a covert image of mathematics, might be identified by careful textual analysis, just as critics can identify hidden themes or meanings in fiction writings and in films. For example, a mathematics curriculum that emphasizes the mastery of arithmetical algorithms and the repetitive practice of arithmetic skills and low-level, routine problem solving, where each task has a unique right answer, may very well help to instill a traditional image of mathematics. If the style is also abstract and impersonal with examples unrelated or unrealistically related to students' own lives and experiences, this image, similar to that characterized in Table 2.2, will very likely be reinforced. As was mentioned above, such outcomes associated with a traditional algorithmic approach to the teaching and learning of mathematics have been widely observed (Boaler, 1997; Kouba & McDonald, 1987; Preston, 1975).

Table 2.3 lists the different images of mathematics that can be located at the three different manifestations of the mathematics curriculum, and the research methods that are used in identifying them.

Many examples of the importance of these distinctions for the mathematics classroom can be given. For example, the intended curriculum as taught in the classroom might stress the integration of knowledge and the importance of links with other subjects. But the division of the school timetable and school day, and the structure of the planned curriculum might contradict this and give the idea—via the hidden curriculum manifested in the classroom—that mathematics is diffuse and divided into small disconnected chunks. The teacher may be very enthusiastic and intend that students should develop positive attitudes to mathematics, but the unintended outcome of various factors such as pressure to cover the syllabus for examinations might result in less positive attitudes being acquired. What this demonstrates is that the image of mathematics embodied in the planned curriculum is not simply transformed into the image of mathematics implicit in classroom practice, for there are a number of intervening factors and processes. These include the beliefs and personal philosophy of mathematics of the teacher, which may or may not be consonant with that in the curriculum plans, as well as the various constraints imposed by the social context and the institution of schooling. Similarly, the image of mathematics implicit in classroom practice, bearing in mind that the complexity of practice may embody several inconsistent images, may not correspond very closely to the images of mathematics

Table 2.3 Images of Mathematics in Different Manifestations of the Mathematics Curriculum

Curriculum Dimension	Type of Image of Mathematics	Research Methods for Its Discovery
Intended Curriculum (embodied in documentary curriculum plans)	1. Overt, intended image of mathematics explicitly given in formal curriculum plans 2. Covert, hidden image of mathematics identified in curriculum documents	Analysis of planned curriculum documents
Implemented Curriculum (enacted in classroom practice)	Image of mathematics as publicly enacted or represented in classroom activities and practices	Observation of classroom processes and activities
Attained Curriculum (acquired by students)	Private image of mathematics as developed or acquired by students	Investigation of student attitudes and beliefs

developed by students. The latter will vary across the range of individuals and will build on the idiosyncratic personal images of mathematics that students arrive with. These in turn will be based on students' previous experiences in school, influenced by the views of mathematics expressed in the home and in their peer group discussions, or represented in the broadcast media.

What I describe, albeit in simplified terms, are the complex interrelationships between philosophies of mathematics, and at several levels, images of mathematics, beliefs about mathematics, and associated attitudes to mathematics. These relationships are not all top-down, for the images of and attitudes to mathematics developed by students will impact on the way mathematics is communicated in the classroom; that is, the enacted image of mathematics, as well as the public image of mathematics. Through affecting the beliefs of university students it will not only be a major contributor to their image of mathematics, but also to their choice of the particular philosophy of mathematics to which they subscribe.

Implications for Mathematics Education: The Ideas and Contents

As described above, the new philosophy of mathematics emphasizes a number of novel and hitherto neglected features pertaining to mathematics as philosophically relevant. In this section I explore four of them as well as their significance for the teaching and learning of mathematics. First, what happens when mathematical knowledge is reconceptualized as a socially constructed human invention? Second, what are the implications of the new attention that is being directed toward mathematical practices and the research activities of mathematicians? Third, what emerges from taking historical and contextual perspectives of mathematics as a social construction. Fourth, what does it mean to see mathematics as value laden and with social responsibility? It turns out that there is a fair bit of overlap between the answers to these questions and their educational implications.

Mathematical Knowledge as a Socially Constructed Human Invention

Traditional "absolutist" philosophies of mathematics view mathematics as an objective, absolute, certain and incorrigible body of knowledge, which rests on the firm foundations of deductive logic. From that perspective it is timeless, although we may discover new theories and truths to add, it is superhuman and ahistorical, for the history of mathematics is irrelevant to the nature and justification of mathematical knowledge, and it is pure, isolated, both value- and culture-free knowledge that happens to be useful because of its universal validity.

The new philosophy of mathematics rejects absolutism as being based on the false hope of finding absolute and eternally incorrigible foundations for mathematical knowledge. Due to a range of profound philosophical and technical problems, including Gödel's (1931/1967) incompleteness theorems, it is accepted that such foundations cannot be provided (Davis & Hersh, 1980; Ernest,

1998; Kitcher, 1984; Lakatos, 1976; Tiles, 1991; Tymoczko, 1986). However, the "loss of certainty" involved (Kline, 1980) does not represent a diminution in our knowledge. Rather it represents an increase in our metaknowledge about mathematics, just as in modern physics the uncertainties and limitations to our knowing are revealed by general relativity and quantum theory.

The new fallibilist philosophy reveals mathematics as human, corrigible, historical, and forever changing. Mathematical knowledge is fallible and eternally open to revision, both in terms of its proofs and its concepts. Mathematics appears timeless and flawless, because although humanly created, every trace of human effort and activity (and value-ladenness) is expunged from the final printed version. Mathematics, like a restaurant, has both a front and a back (Goffman, 1971; Hersh, 1988). In the front, the perfect finished mathematical dishes are served to the public. Here the illusion of absolute mathematics is preserved, but in the back, mathematicians cook up new knowledge amid mess, uncertainty, chaos, and all the inescapably human features of knowledge creation. Fallibilism admits both of these realms. Both the processes and the products of mathematics need to be considered as an essential part of the discipline. For accuracy the false image of overall perfection must be dropped (Davis, 1972).

One of the innovations associated with fallibilism is thus a reconceptualized view of the nature of mathematics. It is no longer seen as defined by a body of pure and abstract knowledge which exists in some superhuman, objective realm (the World 3 of Popper, 1979). Instead mathematics is associated with sets of social practices, each with its history, persons, institutions and social locations, symbolic forms, purposes, and power relations. Thus academic research mathematics is one such practice—or rather a multiplicity of shifting, interconnected practices. Likewise ethnomathematics and school mathematics are also distinct sets of multiple practices. These are intimately bound up together, because the symbolic productions of one practice are recontextualized and reproduced in another (Dowling, 1988). Fallibilism acknowledges that not only is academic mathematics utilized in a variety of applied practices, but also that both ethnomathematics and school mathematics have been appropriated and recontextualized in academic mathematical practices. For example, mathematics first emerged as a discipline through scribal training in numeration and arithmetic late in the fourth millennium BCE: "the creation of mathematics in Sumer was specifically a product of that school institution which was able to create knowledge, to create the tools whereby to formulate and transmit knowledge, and to systematize knowledge" (Høyrup, 1980, p. 45).

What does fallibilism mean for mathematics education? Its leading proponent, Imre Lakatos, rails against the "deductivist" style of advanced mathematics texts and teaching that inverts the order of discovery to present mathematical theories in a tidy but ultimately inhuman way.

> In deductivist style, all propositions are true and all inferences valid. Mathematics is presented as an ever-increasing set of eternal immutable

> truths. Counterexamples, refutations, criticism cannot possible enter. An authoritarian air is secured for the subject.... It has not yet been sufficiently realized that present mathematical and scientific education is a hotbed of authoritarianism and is the worst enemy of independent and critical thought. (Lakatos, 1976, pp. 142–143)

The traditional school image of mathematics as something fixed with only one right answer, right method, or preferred model cannot be sustained when the tentative, socially constructed nature of mathematics is acknowledged. It legitimates a move away from an authoritarian imposed body of mathematical knowledge to one that is brought to life and applied through cooperative coinquiry. Recognizing that mathematical concepts and methods have been created to solve real and pressing problems—enigmas and puzzles as well as everyday problems—requires that mathematics be taught in context, unless a major contradiction is to be countenanced. Reducing school mathematics to nothing but algorithmic thinking represents a major falsification of the nature of mathematics. And as Lakatos says, it supports unreasoning authoritarianism, rather than developing critical, independent, and yes—even democratic—ways of thinking and being. I shall enlarge on this theme below (see section on "Mathematics as Value-Laden and with Social Responsibility").

One outcome is to foreground the import of the applications, models, and problems used in school mathematics. How mathematical activities are expressed, the kinds of cultural assumptions, the cultural contexts and experiences they refer to—and whether such tasks include or alienate African-American, Latino/a, Native-American, and other minority students through these cultural references—is clearly vital from the perspective of a culturally responsive mathematics curriculum. From the perspective of a fallibilist philosophy of mathematics and a humanistic image of school mathematics it can no longer be argued—as it was from traditional perspectives—that such cultural references and their social impacts are immaterial to and irrelevant to the nature of mathematics. Reconceptualizing mathematics as a cultural construct no longer permits such flights from social responsibility.

Mathematical Practice and the Research Activities of Mathematicians

Traditional philosophies of mathematics have foregrounded the character and properties of readymade mathematical knowledge—theorems, proofs, and theories—and backgrounded mathematical activity as being purely incidental to these matters. New philosophies of mathematics, since the time of Wittgenstein (1953), Polanyi (1958), and Lakatos (1963–1964) have regarded mathematical practice and the research activities of mathematicians as being central to the character and constitution of mathematical knowledge. Wittgenstein focused on the nature of proof and the concept of "following a rule," and showed that in complex reasoning it is never fully explicit and objectively defined. In all cases, following a rule in mathematics or logic does not involve logical compulsion. Instead it is based on the tacit or conscious decision to accept the rules of a "language game" which are grounded in preexisting social "forms of life." Thus there are always elements of informed human choice and decision making in following the rules in mathematics, especially the higher level rules.[1]

Polanyi (1958) showed that all knowledge and knowing in science, including mathematics, has an ineliminable tacit dimension. In other words, mathematical theorems, proofs, and theories do not contain complete expositions of mathematical knowledge. To make sense and to be understood they need to be supplemented with mathematicians' tacit knowledge. This parallels the hidden tacit dimension long recognized as being ineliminably present in all linguistic understanding.

Lakatos (1963–1964, 1976) showed that mathematical knowledge—including both concepts and proofs—is never static, but undergoes radical changes over time. Thus, mathematical knowledge, like that in science, never achieves a final form but is always corrigible and revisable. These pioneers led the way to a new understanding of mathematics, an understanding that foregrounds the practices of mathematicians in making or finding new mathematical knowledge, placing this alongside and inseparable from the nature of mathematical knowledge itself.

Starting with Polya (1945), who was a key inspiration for Lakatos's philosophy of mathematics, there has been increased attention to the methodology of mathematics. This is the theory of mathematical practice, encompassing the rules, strategies, and problem solving activities engaged in by mathematicians in the invention or discovery of new mathematical knowledge. Although some small attention to problem solving in mathematics education precedes the developments in the new philosophy of mathematics (e.g., Brownell, 1942), the 1970s and 1980s saw the emergence of a new thrust in the teaching and learning of mathematics more directly attributable to the new philosophy of mathematics. This is the emergence of the problem solving and problem posing movements. A number of North American mathematics educators, such as Dawson (1969, 1971), explicitly drew out the implications of Lakatos's philosophy of mathematics for investigative and problem orientated mathematics teaching. The National Council of Teachers of Mathematics (1980) issued its *An Agenda for Action* that explicitly put problem solving as the number one priority for school mathematics. More radically, a number of mathematics educators (e.g., Brown & Walter, 1983), championed the inclusion of open ended problem posing and solving, in order to parallel the research practices of mathematicians. These approaches were subsequently endorsed in the National Council of Teachers of Mathematics' (1989) promotion of "mathematical power," encompassing both the posing and the solving of problems.

Overall, it can be said that the emphasis of the new philosophy of mathematics on the importance of mathematical practices and the research activities of mathematicians has led to a shift in mathematical pedagogy towards open ended problem posing and solving and modeling work, especially in teacher education programs. Although there remains a gap between the endorsement of these practices and their classroom take up, most mathematics educators and teacher educators would now argue for their importance, alongside more traditional pedagogies, for the development of mathematical capabilities, confidence and appreciation.

The Historical and Contextual Aspects of Mathematics as a Cultural and Social Construction

For hundreds if not thousands of years, scholars have studied the history of mathematics (see Swetz, chapter 1 this volume) in parallel to but separate from the philosophy of mathematics. But the new philosophy of mathematics adopts the position that the two are constitutionally inseparable.[2] Mathematics is constructed through its development located in various specific historical, geographical, cultural, and social contexts. Through failure to acknowledge this, the philosophy of mathematics risks becoming an empty language game. Paraphrasing Kant, Lakatos (1976) says "the history of mathematics, lacking the guidance of philosophy has become *blind*, while the philosophy of mathematics turning its back on the most intriguing phenomena in the history of mathematics, has become *empty*" (p. 2). Lakatos argues that mathematical development is embedded in history and there is a specific historical methodology at work, the Logic of Mathematical Discovery. This is a dialectical sociocultural mechanism through which the concepts and theorems of mathematics develop, illustrated by Lakatos with detailed case studies in the history of topology and analysis. In Ernest (1998) I extend Lakatos's argument and propose a Generalized Logic of Mathematical Discovery to account for the development of problems, methods, theories, and the underlying ideas of proof in a similar fashion. As a cultural construct mathematics is more like an endless relay race with runners passing on the baton or beacon of knowledge, than it is like a novel, the work of a single author beavering away in splendid isolation in an attic room.

Kitcher (1984) adds a further dimension to the historico-cultural basis of mathematics. In particular, he shows the role of mathematical authorities, such as teachers, in communicating and providing epistemological warrants for mathematical knowledge at both the disciplinary and the didactic levels. Authorities provide the warrants for mathematical assertions, which then later become warranted for an individual by reason or some similar process.

Davis and Hersh (1980, 1988) further elaborate on the insights of Lakatos. Their unique contribution is to demonstrate the dual cultural nature of mathematics, how it has both an inner and outer aspect. Whereas previous scholars have emphasized the import of the internal history of mathematics, these authors demonstrate that mathematics permeates and shapes all aspects of social and cultural life, and is in turn shaped by social forces.[3] Their position is important because it transcends the pure–applied and academic–folk mathematics boundaries and shows that mathematical activity is universal, multicultural, and that the philosophy of mathematics cannot be divorced entirely from the social and cultural contexts of use of mathematics.

Although such insights can be found in part in the history of mathematics (Høyrup, 1994; Joseph, 1991; Kline, 1980; Szabo, 1978), cultural studies of mathematics (Bishop, 1988; MacKenzie, 1981; Wilder 1981), semiotics of mathematics (Ernest, 2006; Rotman, 1993), sociology of mathematics (Bloor, 1991; Fisher, 1966; Restivo, 1992), anthropology of mathematics (Crump, 1992; Pinxten, 1987), and ethnomathematics (Ascher, 1991; D'Ambrosio, 1991; Gerdes, 1996; Zaslavsky, 1973), they are new to the philosophy of mathematics and have unique impact there. For the new philosophy of mathematics argues not only that mathematics has a wide social, cultural, and historical footprint, but that these dimensions are implicated in the very nature of mathematics—its "essence" if you like. Both the epistemology and ontology of mathematics emerge from its social construction, across the diverse cultures and civilizations of humankind. Every society in the past and present has its own modes of informal mathematical thinking, and it is these that give rise to, as well as benefiting from, the modern discipline of mathematics. Thus ethnomathematics is not just an "add-on" to mathematics, but an essential part of it, both in the past and present. Mathematics consists of more than just abstract knowledge representations and includes a broad range of human activities and knowledge-based practices. The new philosophy of mathematics greatly expands the boundaries to the human activities and knowledge that legitimately fall under the title of "mathematics."

Overall, the reconceptualization of mathematical knowledge as a cultural and social construction demystifies the concepts, results, proofs, methods, and theories of mathematics and sees them not as something extrahuman imposed upon humanity, but as something created and shaped by human concerns, interests, powers of reasoning, and historical and social practices. Mathematical thinking is something created and developed by all peoples, whether in Africa, Asia, all of the Americas, Oceania, or Europe. Globalization in the form of cultural transmission has spread many of the local developments worldwide, whether it be Indian numerals and zero, Mid-Eastern place value, or Arabic algebra—now utilized worldwide—or African counting systems and geometric patterns used in European and North American schools to show the broad multicultural footprint of mathematics.

A culturally responsive mathematics education needs to acknowledge the pan-human origins and presence of mathematics in all of its diverse forms. The myth, long foisted by traditional texts and philosophies, that mathematics is a European creation, needs to be refuted (see next section). Essential elements of mathematics derive from non-European cultures, like zero (India and Central/South America), place value (Middle East and India), geometry (North Africa as well as Greece), and algebra (Islamic civilization in North Africa/Spain and Middle East). Incorporating elements of the history of mathematics into school mathematics enables all students, including minority students, to feel a pride in the contributions of their ancestors as well as an ownership of mathematics. This is further fostered through the choice of problems and applications relevant to student interests and experiences as discussed above.

Mathematics as Value-Laden and with Social Responsibility

Traditional (absolutist) philosophies of mathematics assert that mathematics is objective and free of ethical, human, and any other values (despite its long association with war). Mathematics is viewed as value-neutral, concerned only with structures, processes, and the relationships of ideal objects, which can be described in purely logical language. Although mathematicians may have preferences, values, and interests reflected in their activities, choices, and even in the genesis of mathematics, according to this view, mathematical knowledge once validated is objective and neutral, based solely on logic. Pure reasoning and proof discriminate between truth and falsehood, correct and incorrect proofs, valid and invalid arguments. Neither fear nor favor nor values affect the court of objective reason. Hence, the argument goes, mathematical knowledge is value-neutral.

In contrast, the (fallibilist) view of the new philosophy of mathematics is that the cultural values, preferences, and interests of the social groups involved in the formation, elaboration, and validation of mathematical knowledge cannot be so easily factored out and discounted. The values that shape mathematics are neither subjective nor necessary consequences of the subject, but lie in-between. They are the values, both overt and covert, of the social groups and contexts in which mathematics is made. Even the most rigorous and objectively presented results of mathematics embody a set of values and a cultural perspective. However, part of the ideology and mystique of traditional mathematics and philosophy of mathematics is to hide the role of humans in mathematics, which renders the values of mathematics invisible. Through a refusal to admit any acknowledgment of the role of humans and cultures in mathematics all discussion of the values of mathematics is delegitimized within mathematics.[4]

So what are the values of mathematics? Examination of what counts as legitimate mathematical knowledge reveals the valuing of the abstract over the concrete, formal over informal, objective over subjective, justification over discovery, rationality over intuition, reason over emotion, generality over particularity, and theory over practice. These values work through the traditional definition of the field, and only that which satisfies these values is admitted as bona fide mathematics; and anything that does not is rejected as inadmissible (Ernest, 1991, 1998; Harding, 1991). Thus warranted mathematical propositions and their proofs are legitimate mathematics, but the rules demarcating the boundary of the discipline are positioned outside it, so that no discussion of these values is possible within mathematics. Once metarules are established in this way, mathematics can be regarded as value-free. In fact, the values lie behind the choice of the norms and rules. By concealing the underpinning values, absolutism makes them virtually unchallengeable. It legitimates only the formal level of discourse as mathematics (i.e., axiomatic theories, not metamathematical discussion), and hence it relegates the issue of values to a realm which is definitionally outside of the discipline (Rotman, 1993).

Nevertheless, overt or covert values can still be identified in mathematics underlying the choice of problems posed and pursued, and the features of proofs, concepts, and theories that are valorized. Deeper still, values underpin the conventions, methodologies, and constraints that limit the nature of mathematical activity and bound what is acceptable in mathematics (Kitcher, 1984). These values are perhaps most evident in the norms that regulate mathematical activity and the acceptance of mathematical knowledge. At times of innovation or revolution in mathematics, the values and norms of mathematics become most evident when there are explicit conflicts and disagreements in the underlying values. Consider the historical resistance to innovations such as negative numbers, complex numbers, abstract algebra, non-Euclidean geometries, and Cantor's set theory. At root the conflicts were over what was to be admitted and valued as legitimate, and what was to be rejected as spurious. The standards of theory evaluation involved were based on metalevel criteria, norms, and values (Dunmore, 1992). Since these criteria and norms change over the course of the history of ideas, they show that the values of mathematics are human in origin, and not imposed or acquired from some timeless source.

Human interests and values play a significant part in the choices of mathematical problems, methods of solution, the concepts and notations constructed in the process, and the criteria for evaluating and judging the resulting mathematical creations and knowledge. Mathematicians choose which of infinitely many possible definitions and theorems are worth pursuing, and any act of choice is an act of valuation. The current upsurge of computer-related mathematics represents a large scale shift of interests and values linked with cultural, material, and technological developments, and it is ultimately manifested in the production of certain types of knowledge (Steen, 1988). The values and interests involved also essentially form, shape, and validate that knowledge too, and are not merely an accidental feature of its production. Even what counts as an acceptable proof has been permanently changed by contingent technological developments such as the presence of computers on mathematicians' desks (De Millo, Lipton, & Perlis, 1979; Tymoczko, 1979).

Once conceded, this means mathematics cannot be coherently viewed as independent of social and cultural concerns, and the consequences of its social location and cultural embedding must be faced. If the direction of mathematical research is a function of historical interests and values as much as inner forces and logical drives, mathematicians cannot claim that the outcomes are inevitable, and hence free from human interests and values. Mathematical development is a function of intellectual labor, and its creators and appliers are moral beings engaged in voluntary actions. Mathematicians may fail to anticipate the consequences of the mathematical developments in which they participate, but this does not absolve them of responsibility. Mathematics needs to be recognized as a socially responsible discipline just as much as science and technology.

One of the positive values embedded in mathematics is that of democracy. In principle, mathematics is a highly democratic rational discipline in which knowledge is accepted or rejected on the basis of logic, not authority. Potentially, anyone can propose or criticize mathematical knowledge using reason alone, and social standing, wealth or reputation are immaterial to the acceptability of mathematical proposals. However, this claim is subject to two caveats. First, mathematicians with a good reputation are more likely to have their voices heard, and second, to be taken seriously, new knowledge submissions need to be formulated in keeping with the stylistic and rhetorical norms of the mathematics community.

The democratic character of mathematics is no surprise given the origins of proof in the open dialogues of Ancient Greece. As a consequence of these values, mathematics is a tool for democracy in the hands of every educated citizen. For mathematical knowledge provides anybody with a means of evaluating every numerical and financial calculation in terms of the correctness of the underlying mathematical reasoning (see Gutstein, chapter 6 in this volume). If these capabilities are extended to the ability to critically understand the uses and applications of mathematics across a variety of social contexts, then a further tool for democracy has been placed in the hands of citizens: critical mathematical literacy (Ernest, 1991; Skovsmose, 1994).

Given that the new philosophy of mathematics acknowledges the value-laden nature of mathematics, and its social responsibility, what does this mean for the teaching and learning of mathematics? Because education concerns the welfare and treatment of other persons, especially the young, it means that additional responsibility accrues to mathematics and its social institutions to ensure that its role in educating the young is a responsible and socially just one. In particular, mathematics must not be allowed to be distorted or partial to the values or interests of particular social groups, even if historically they have had a dominant role in controlling the discipline. There is an extensive literature treating criticisms of this sort, concerning gender and race in mathematics education. It has been argued that White European-origin males have dominated mathematics and science in modern times, and the androcentric values of this group have been attributed to knowledge itself (Ernest, 1991, 1995; Shan & Bailey, 1991; Walkerdine, 1988, 1997). Any distortions in the nature and presentation of mathematics are not an inevitable consequence of the discipline itself, but of some of the values and interests embedded in or associated with it. It is the mission of a just mathematics education to rebalance school mathematics to overcome such distortions.

One such distortion is the mathematics-centeredness of much of the school curriculum concerned with the formation and production of mathematicians. Since less than one in a thousand go on to become research mathematicians, letting the needs of this tiny minority dominate the mathematical education of the remainder of the population leads to both ethical and utilitarian problems. The needs of these two groups are not the same, and so a properly differentiated school mathematics curriculum is needed to accommodate students' different aptitudes, attainments, interests, and ambitions. Such differentiation must depend on balanced educational and social judgments rather than on mathematicians' views and values. This dilemma is not an idle one, because this issue, together with philosophical differences about the nature of mathematics, lie at the heart of the Math Wars raging over the control of the curriculum in the United States (see Sal Restivo's chapter in this volume).

Another distortion is Eurocentrism in the history of mathematics and the images of mathematics in society and throughout education. Many histories of mathematics, such as Eves (1953), promote a simplified Eurocentric view of its development. Typically such accounts identify Mesopotamia and Egypt as the sites of preliminary work that provided the raw materials for mathematics. Based on this the flame of "real" mathematics was lit by the Ancient Greeks, kept alight by the Arabs during the Dark Ages, until it was passed on like an Olympic torch, and blazed anew in modern Europe and her cultural dependencies. This, in a nutshell, is the view of history transmitted by many texts. There are at least two ways in which such accounts are wrong. First, all civilizations have had a sophisticated mathematical basis, and culturally embedded mathematics (ethnomathematics) is to be found in all cultures, covering every continent of the globe. Second, major contributions have been made that do not fit into the Eurocentric scheme. For example, what is probably the single most important conceptual innovation in the history of mathematics was made in India with the invention of the decimal place value system with zero. Less well known is the ground-breaking work on infinite series conducted in Kerala, in southern India. Over a hundred years before Europe caught up, many of the key results attributed to and named after the great mathematicians Gregory, Maclaurin, Taylor, Wallis, Newton, Leibniz, and Euler had already been discovered (Almeida & Joseph, 2004; Joseph, 1991; Pearce, n.d.). Another example is the Arab invention of algebra, which provides the all important language and conceptual basis for modern mathematics. Each of these examples, and many more, demonstrate the falsity of the Eurocentric history of mathematics described above.

Bernal (1987) has argued that during the past two hundred years or so, Ancient Greece has been "talked up" as the starting point of modern European thought, and the "Afroasiatic Roots of Classical Civilisation" have been neglected, discarded, and denied as part of the imperialistic European project to dominate the world materially and to assert its cultural superiority. Against this backdrop it is not surprising that mathematics has been seen as the product of European mathematicians. However, there is now a widespread literature supporting the thesis that mathematics has been misrepresented in a Eurocentric way, including Almeida and Joseph (2004), Joseph (1991), Powell and Frankenstein (1997), and Pearce (n.d.). This has important consequences for peoples of non-European origin. For the implied racist view that non-European societies are primitive, and their peoples intellectually inferior, is shown to be false. The corrected history of mathematics shows that all peoples are entitled to take a pride in the contributions of their cultures to modern scientific ideas and developments.

Mathematics already contains the seed values from which to grow a just and socially responsible school curriculum. The democratic aspect of mathematics—present in the rational basis of mathematical results and assertions—requires the development of an informed critical faculty in students, able to question the basis for assertions and construct rational justifications for them. Such capabilities have a greater significance than just being important in the teaching and learning of mathematics. For informed critical capabilities are also a vital part of democratic citizenship. While other aspects of schooling also contribute to developing citizens able to participate in and sustain modern democracies, mathematics education has a special role to play. Its learning outcomes should include critically understanding the uses of mathematics in society: to identify, interpret, evaluate, and critique the mathematics embedded in social, commercial, and political systems and claims, from advertisements, such as in the financial sector, to government and interest-group pronouncements. Mathematics is very widely used to express and support claims and its use lends an authority to advertisements, reports, and press releases. Every citizen in modern society needs to be able to analyze, question, critique, and understand the limits of validity of such uses, and where necessary reject spurious or misleading claims. This need is both to protect the rights and interests of citizens themselves, and also to protect the more vulnerable in society, unable to do this for themselves. Ultimately, such a capability is a vital bulwark in protecting democracy and the values of a humanistic and civilized society (e.g., Ernest, 2001; Frankenstein, 1989; Skovsmose, 1994; Gutstein chapter 6 in this volume).

Notes

1. Clearly, purely algorithmic rules can be specified completely for mechanical implementation in fully formalized languages. This was Turing's (1936) great insight, building on Gödel's (1931/1967) arithmetization of logic, which led to the birth and success of digital computing.
2. This parallels analogous developments outside of the field such as by Foucault (1972) and Hacking (2002), evidenced in the titles of their books: The *Archaeology of Knowledge* and *Historical Ontology*.
3. Niss (1983) and Skovsmose (1994) refer to the formatting power of mathematics whereby mathematics based systems embedded in society structure modern life in many key aspects, but often in ways that are invisible.
4. Ironically, the objectivization and dehumanization of mathematics that leads to the denial that any values are involved is, in fact, the reflection of a set of values for mathematics.

References

Almeida, D. F., & Joseph, G. G. (2004). Eurocentrism in the history of mathematics: The case of the Kerala School. *Race & Class, 45*, 5–59.

Apple, M. W. (1979). *Ideology and curriculum.* London: Routledge & Kegan Paul.

Ascher, M. (1991). *Ethnomathematics: A multicultural view of mathematical ideas.* Pacific Grove, CA: Brooks/Cole.

Ayer, A. J. (1946). *Language, truth and logic.* London: Gollancz.

Barnard, T., & Saunders, P. (1994, December 28). Is school mathematics in crisis? *The Guardian*, p. 18.

Bernal, M. (1987). *Black Athena, The Afroasiatic roots of classical civilization* (Vol. 1). London: Free Association Books.

Bishop, A. J. (1988). *Mathematical enculturation: A cultural perspective on mathematics education.* Dordrecht, The Netherlands: Kluwer.

Bloor, D. (1991). *Knowledge and social imagery* (2nd ed.). Chicago: University of Chicago Press.

Boaler, J. (1997). *Experiencing school mathematics: Teaching styles, sex and setting.* Buckingham, UK: Open University Press.

Brown, S. I., & Walter, M. (1983). *The art of problem posing.* Philadelphia, PA: The Franklin Institute Press.

Brownell, W. A. (1942). Problem solving. *The psychology of learning* (41st National Society for the Study of Education Yearbook, Part II). Chicago: NSSE.

Buerk, D. (1982). An experience with some able women who avoid mathematics. *For the Learning of Mathematics, 3,* 19–24.

Buxton, L. (1981). *Do you panic about maths? Coping with maths anxiety.* London: Heinemann Educational Books.

Cockcroft, W. H. (Chair). (1982). *Mathematics counts* (Report of the Committee of Inquiry on the Teaching of Mathematics). London: Her Majesty's Stationery Office.

Corfield, D. (2003) *Towards a philosophy of real mathematics.* Cambridge, UK: Cambridge University Press.

Crump, T. (1992). *The anthropology of numbers.* Cambridge, UK: Cambridge University Press.

D'Ambrosio, U. (1991). Ethnomathematics and its place in the history and pedagogy of mathematics. In M. Harris (Ed.), *Schools, mathematics and work* (pp. 15–25). London: Falmer.

Davis, P. J. (1972). Fidelity in mathematical discourse: Is one and one really two? *American Mathematical Monthly, 79,* 252–263.

Davis, P. J., & Hersh, R. (1980). *The mathematical experience.* Boston: Birkhauser.

Davis, P. J., & Hersh, R. (1988). *Descartes' dream.* London: Penguin Books.

Dawson, A. J. (1969). *The implications of the work of Popper, Polya, and Lakatos for a model of mathematics instruction.* Unpublished doctoral dissertation, University of Alberta, Alberta, Canada.

Dawson, A. J. (1971). A fallibilistic model for instruction. *Journal of Structural Learning, 3,* 1–19.

De Millo A., Lipton R. J., & Perlis, A. J. (1979). Social processes and proofs of theorems and programs. *Communications of the ACM, 22,* 271–280.

Dowling, P. (1988). The contextualising of mathematics: Towards a theoretical map. In M. Harris (Ed.), *Schools, mathematics and work* (pp. 92–120). London: Falmer Press.

Dunmore, C. (1992). Meta-level revolutions in mathematics. In D. A. Gillies (Ed.), *Revolutions in mathematics* (pp. 209–225). Oxford, UK: Clarendon Press.

Ernest, P. (1988). The attitudes and practices of student teachers of primary school mathematics. In A. Borbas (Ed.), *Proceedings of 12th International Conference on the Psychology of Mathematics Education* (Vol. 1, pp. 288–295). Veszprem, Hungary: OOK.

Ernest, P. (1991). *The philosophy of mathematics education.* London: Falmer Press.

Ernest, P. (1995). Values, gender and images of mathematics: A philosophical perspective. *International Journal for Mathematical Education in Science and Technology, 26,* 449–462.

Ernest, P. (1998). *Social constructivism as a philosophy of mathematics.* Albany, NY: SUNY Press.

Ernest, P. (2001). Critical mathematics education. In P. Gates (Ed.), *Issues in mathematics teaching* (pp. 277–293). London: Routledge/Falmer.

Ernest, P. (2004). *Mathematics and gender: The nature of mathematics and equal opportunities.* Exeter, UK: University of Exeter Press.

Ernest, P. (2006). A semiotic perspective of mathematical activity: The case of number. *Educational Studies in Mathematics, 61,* 67–101.

Ernest, P. (2008). Towards a semiotics of mathematical text (Part I). *For the Learning of Mathematics, 28*(1), 2–8.

Eves, H. (1953). *An introduction to the history of mathematics.* New York: Holt, Rinehart & Winston.

Fisher, C. S. (1966). The death of a mathematical theory: A study in the sociology of knowledge. *Archive for History of Exact Sciences, 3*, 137–159.

Foucault, M. (1972). *The archaeology of knowledge*. London: Tavistock.

Frankenstein, M. (1989). *Relearning mathematics: A different third R—Radical maths*. London: Free Association Books

Frege, G. (1964). *The basic laws of arithmetic* (M. Furth, Trans. & Ed.). Berkeley: University of California Press.

Gerdes, P. (1996). Ethnomathematics and mathematics education. In A. J. Bishop, K. Clements, C. Keitel, J. Kilpatrick, & C. Laborder (Eds.), *International handbook of research in mathematics education* (Vol. 2, pp. 909–943). Dordrecht, The Netherlands: Kluwer.

Gillies, D. A. (Ed.). (1992). *Revolutions in mathematics*. Oxford, UK: Clarendon Press.

Gödel, K. (1967). Über formal unentscheidbare Sätze der Principia Mathematica und verwandter Systeme I [Concerning a formal analysis of the incompleteness theorems of the Principia Mathematica and related systems, I]. In J. van Heijenoort (Trans. & Ed.), *From Frege to Gödel: A source book in mathematical logic* (pp. 592–617). Cambridge, MA: Harvard University Press. (Original work published 1931)

Goffman, E. (1971). *The presentation of self in everyday life*. London: Penguin.

Hacking, I. (2002). *Historical ontology*. Cambridge, MA: Harvard University Press.

Harding, S. (1991). *Whose science? Whose knowledge?* Milton Keynes, UK: Open University Press.

Hersh, R. (1988, August). *Mathematics has a front and a back*. Paper presented at Sixth International Congress of Mathematics Education, Budapest, Hungary.

Hersh, R. (1997). *What is mathematics, really?* London: Jonathon Cape.

Hersh, R. (Ed.). (2006). *18 unconventional essays on the nature of mathematics*. New York: Springer.

Hilbert, D. (1964). On the infinite. In P. Benacerraf & H. Putnam (Trans, & Eds.), *Philosophy of mathematics: Selected* readings (pp. 134–151). Englewood Cliffs, NJ: Prentice-Hall. (Original work published 1925)

Høyrup, J. (1980). Influences of institutionalized mathematics teaching on the development and organisation of mathematical thought in the pre-modern period. . In J. Fauvel & J. Gray (Eds.), *The history of mathematics: A reader* (pp. 43–45). London: Macmillan.

Høyrup, J. (1994). *In measure, number, and weight*. Albany, NY: SUNY Press.

Joseph, G. G. (1991). *Crest of the peacock: The non-European roots of mathematics*. London: I. B. Tauris.

Kitcher, P. (1984). *The nature of mathematical knowledge*. New York: Oxford University Press.

Kline, M. (1980). *Mathematics: The loss of certainty*. Oxford: Oxford University Press.

Kouba, V., & McDonald, J. L. (1987). Students' perceptions of mathematics as a domain. In J. C. Bergeron, N. Herscovics, & C. Kieran (Eds.), *Proceedings of PME 11 Conference* (Vol.1, pp. 106–112). Montreal: University of Montreal.

Lakatos, I. (1963–1964). Proofs and refutations. *British Journal for the Philosophy of Science, 14*, 1–25, 120–139, 221–243, 296–342.

Lakatos, I. (1976). *Proofs and refutations*. Cambridge, UK: Cambridge University Press.

Lakatos, I. (1978). *Philosophical papers* (Vols. 1 & 2). Cambridge, UK: Cambridge University Press.

Lim, C. S. (1999). *The public image of mathematics: A cross-cultural comparison study*. Unpublished doctoral dissertation, University of Exeter, Exeter, UK.

MacKenzie, D. (1981). *Statistics in Britain, 1865–1930*. Edinburgh: University of Edinburgh Press.

National Council of Teachers of Mathematics. (1980). *An agenda for action*. Reston: VA: Author.

National Council of Teachers of Mathematics. (1989). *Curriculum and evaluation standards for school mathematics*. Reston, VA: Author.

Niss, M. (1983). Mathematics education for the "Automatical Society." In R. Schaper (Ed.), *Hochschuldidaktik der Mathematik* [Teaching high school math] (pp. 43–61). Alsbach-Bergstrasse, Germany: Leuchtturm-Verlag.

Pearce, I. G. (n.d.). *Indian mathematics: Redressing the balance*. Retrieved November 18, 2005, from http://www-history.mcs.st-andrews.ac.uk/history/Projects/Pearce/index.html

Pinxten, R. (1987). *Towards a Navajo Indian geometry*. Ghent, Belgium: Kultuur, Kennis en Integratie (Communication and Cognition).

Polanyi, M. (1958). *Personal knowledge*. London: Routledge & Kegan Paul.

Polya, G. (1945). *How to solve it*. Princeton, NJ: Princeton University Press.

Popper, K. R. (1979). *Objective knowledge* (Rev. ed.). Oxford, UK: Oxford University Press.

Powell, A. B., & Frankenstein, M. (Eds.). (1997). *Ethnomathematics: Challenging Eurocentrism in mathematics education*. Albany, NY: SUNY Press.

Preston, M. (1975). *The measurement of affective behaviour in C.S.E. mathematics* (Psychology of Mathematics Education Series). London: Centre for Science Education, Chelsea College.

Rensaa, R. J. (2006). The image of a mathematician. *Philosophy of Mathematics Education Journal, 19*. Retrieved January 29, 2007, from http://www.people.ex.ac.uk/PErnest/

Restivo, S. (1992). *Mathematics in society and history*. Dordrecht, The Netherlands: Kluwer.

Restivo, S. (1993). The Promethean task of bringing mathematics to Earth. In S. Restivo, J. P. Van Bendegem, & R. Fischer, R. (Eds.), *Math worlds: Philosophical and social studies of mathematics and mathematics education* (pp. 3–17). Albany, NY: SUNY Press.

Restivo, S., Bendegem, J. P. Van, & Fischer, R. (Eds.). (1993). *Math worlds: Philosophical and social studies of mathematics and mathematics education*. Albany, NY: SUNY Press.

Robitaille, D. F., & Garden, R. A. (Eds.). (1989). *The IEA study of mathematics:Vol. 2. Contexts and outcomes of school mathematics*. Oxford, UK: Pergamon.

Rotman, B. (1993). *Ad infinitum... The ghost in Turing's machine: Taking God out of mathematics and putting the body back in—An essay in corporeal semiotics*. Stanford, CA: Stanford University Press.

Russell, B. (1919). *Introduction to mathematical philosophy*. London: Allen & Unwin.

Sewell, B. (1981). *Use of mathematics by adults in daily life*. Leicester, UK: Advisory Council for Adult and Continuing Education.

Shan, S., & Bailey, P. (1991). *Multiple factors: Classroom mathematics for equality and justice*. Stoke-on-Trent, UK: Trentham Books.

Skovsmose, O. (1994). *Towards a philosophy of critical mathematics education*. Dordrecht, The Netherlands: Kluwer.

Steen, L. A. (1988). The science of patterns. *Science, 240*(4852), 611–616.

Szabo, A. (1978). *The beginnings of Greek mathematics*. Dordrecht, The Netherlands: Reidel.

Thompson, A. G. (1984). The relationship of teachers' conceptions of mathematics and mathematics teaching to instructional practice. *Educational Studies in Mathematics, 15*, 105–127.

Tiles, M. (1991). *Mathematics and the image of reason*. London: Routledge.

Turing, A. M. (1936). On computable numbers, with an application to the Entscheidungsproblem. *Proceedings of London Mathematical Society, 42* (Series 2), 230–265.

Tymoczko, T. (1979). The four-color problem and its philosophical significance. *The Journal of Philosophy, 76*, 57–83.

Tymoczko, T. (Ed.). (1986). *New directions in the philosophy of mathematics*. Boston: Birkhauser.

Walkerdine, V. (1988). *The mastery of reason*. London: Routledge.

Walkerdine, V. (1997). *Counting girls out* (Rev. ed.). London: Falmer Press.

Wilder R. L. (1981). *Mathematics as a cultural system*. Oxford: Pergamon Press.

Wittgenstein, L. (1953). *Philosophical investigations*. Oxford: Blackwell.

Wittgenstein, L. (1978). *Remarks on the foundations of mathematics* (Rev. ed.). Cambridge, MA: MIT Press. (Original work published 1956)

Zaslavsky, C. (1973). *Africa counts*. Boston: Prindle, Weber & Schmidt.

3
An Ethnomathematical Perspective on Culturally Responsive Mathematics Education

SWAPNA MUKHOPADHYAY, ARTHUR B. POWELL, AND MARILYN FRANKENSTEIN

All good teachers respect their students. This includes listening to and learning from their students. In this case, all cultural backgrounds will be honored. But, since mathematics has traditionally been taught from a very narrow perspective, the serious contributions of most cultures and other groupings of people have been ignored or trivialized in teacher education, resulting in omissions from mathematics education curricula that can have the consequence of devaluing and disrespecting many students' cultural backgrounds. In this chapter, we propose that an ethnomathematical perspective can enrich mathematics curricula in ways that promote cultural responsiveness in mathematics education.

Culturally responsive teaching, founded on mutual respect, is validating in the following respects (Gay, 2000):

- It acknowledges the legitimacy of the cultural heritages of different ethnic groups, both as legacies that affect students' dispositions, attitudes, and approaches to learning and as worthy content to be taught in the formal curriculum.
- It builds bridges of meaningfulness between home and school experiences as well as between academic abstractions and lived sociocultural realities.
- It uses a wide variety of instructional strategies that are connected to different learning styles.
- It teaches students to know and praise their own and each others' cultural heritages.

- It incorporates multicultural information, resources, and materials in all the subjects and skills routinely taught in schools. (p. 29)

Among the other characteristics Gay attributes to culturally responsive teaching are that it is empowering, transformative, and emancipatory. Ladson-Billings (1995) defines the criteria for culturally responsive teaching as:

(a) students must experience academic success;
(b) students must develop and/or maintain cultural competence; and
(c) students must develop a critical consciousness through which they challenge that status quo of the current social order. (p. 160)

Though the need has always been present, the rapidly changing demographics in American schools, has made the discussion of culturally responsive teaching more prevalent in the professional discourse within the mathematics education community. For example, in 2023, by the recent projection of the U.S. Census Bureau, using current racial classifications, White children in schools will be the minority; by 2042, it is projected that White people will be less than half of the U.S. population (U.S. Census Bureau, 2008). Yet the latest figures show that 83% of public school teachers are White (National Center for Education Statistics, 2006) and that 40% of schools have no non-White teachers (Howard, 2006). Further, a large measure of de facto resegregation has happened (Kozol, 2005).

But the traditional mathematics curriculum can make it hard to realize a culturally responsive pedagogy. That curriculum is too narrowly focused on the technical aspects of mathematics, ignoring many cultural contributions, and ignoring any debate over the uses of mathematics in our world. Skovsmose (2005, pp. 100–101) has elaborated on the theme of D'Ambrosio (1994, p. 443) that human use of mathematics is capable of both horrors and wonders. We enjoy being able to fly to distant parts of the world to visit colleagues, attend conferences, and experience the diversity of the world and its inhabitants. We are delighted to have the tools that computers offer for our writing, for access to information, and for communication. Of course, it is necessary to have a new generation of mathematics researchers who will advance the field, and a cadre of applied mathematicians, scientists, engineers, and inventors to harness the power of mathematics for advances that improve the lives of humankind. But we simultaneously need to examine critically what Skovsmose (2005) calls "the heroic picture of mathematics education as a main vehicle for technological development" (p. 5).

It is vital, as D'Ambrosio has eloquently and passionately expressed, to bring a moral sense to what is done with the power of mathematics. Historically, there has been a close link between mathematics and the making of war and, unfortunately, that is becoming closer, and with more horrific results. Further, as, for example, Frankenstein (e.g., in press) has amply illustrated, mathematics has too often been implicated in exploitation of people for profit, and generally for dehumanized and mechanistic forms of control. Thus, the myth and comfort of the assumption of neutrality of mathematics as a human activity are not sustainable. Mathematicians and mathematics educators must face their ethical responsibilities (D'Ambrosio, 2003):

> It is clear that Mathematics is well integrated into the technological, industrial, military, economic and political systems and that Mathematics has been relying on these systems for the material bases of its continuing progress. It is important to look into the role of mathematicians and mathematics educators in the evolution of mankind.... It is appropriate to ask what the *most universal mode of thought*—Mathematics—has to do with the *most universal problem*—survival with dignity.
>
> I believe that to find the relation between these two universals is an inescapable result of the claim of the universality of Mathematics. Consequently, as mathematicians and mathematics educators, we have to reflect upon our personal role in reversing the situation. (p. 235, emphasis added)

Thus, rather than mathematics narrowly and divisively serving nationalistic and competitive interests (Gutstein, chapter 6, this volume), D'Ambrosio offers a vision of mathematics in the service of humankind.

In this chapter, we argue that the theoretical framework of ethnomathematics first articulated by D'Ambrosio is a useful way of thinking about creating more culturally responsive mathematics classrooms. We first outline the historical development of this relatively young and still evolving field of ethnomathematics. As argued by D'Ambrosio in the Foreword to this volume, ethnomathematics struggles to escape sameness and epistemological cages. We do, however, suggest parallels and resonances with many other theoretical positions that have emerged within (mathematics) education, and with liberatory movements.

We then discuss how the ethnomathematical stance can promote cultural responsiveness toward students and their communities. We review the challenges to the traditional mathematics curricula ethnomathematics poses, focusing on how ethnomathematics challenges Eurocentrism in the characterization of mathematics; how ethnomathematics challenges what counts as mathematical knowledge; and how ethnomathematics challenges the disconnections between mathematics education and social and political change. Further we will show how addressing these challenges create a culturally responsive teaching.

Theoretical Evolution of Ethnomathematics

Ubiratan D'Ambrosio is recognized as the intellectual father of ethnomathematics, which he described as: "the mathematics which is practiced among identifiable cultural groups, such as national-tribal societies, labor groups, children of a certain age bracket, professional classes, and so on" (1985, p. 45). Later on he further elaborated it as "on the borderline between the history of mathematics and cultural anthropology" (1997, p. 13). As such it clearly has many connections with other disciplines, particularly with anthropological investigations, such as Pinxten's work among the Navajo (Pinxten, van Dooren, & Harvey, 1983). D'Ambrosio (2006, pp. 7–8) refers to the German philosopher Spengler, who declared that there is no single mathematics, but rather many mathematics. Spengler was also singled out by the sociologist Bloor (1976, p. 95) as "one of the few writers who challenges the self-evident 'fact' that mathematics is universal and invariant" (cited in Restivo, 1993, p. 250). Restivo also draws attention to affinities between Spengler and Wittgenstein who might also be claimed as a precursor of ethnomathematics on account of, in particular, his emphasis on practices and forms of life.

There are a number of fundamental principles underpinning an ethnomathematical perspective, including respect for the "other" and the intellectual achievements of all, thus striving to undo the reality that, as observed by Freire and Macedo (1987, p. 122), "the intellectual activity of those without power is always characterized as non-intellectual" (see D'Ambrosio's Foreword to this volume).

Above all, ethnomathematics draws attention to mathematics as a human activity. Ethnomathematics draws attention to the long, complex, and multicultural intellectual and social history of mathematics, which, as in all disciplines, remains always open to evolution. Mathematics as a discipline is grounded in cultural practices (Swetz, chapter 1 this volume), the solving of practical problems, and universal aspects of human nature such as the decorative impulse (Mukhopadhyay, 2009), a delight in intellectual play, coping with survival but also seeking to transcend the day-to-day practicalities of living (D'Ambrosio, Foreword to this volume).

Resonating with the quotation from Spengler above, rather than thinking of mathematics as a single entity whose essence—while debated—is believed to exist in some Platonic sense, from the ethnomathematical perspective mathematics comprises a diversity of mathematical practices, of which academic mathematics is one. An important question in thinking about culturally responsive mathematics teaching is to what extent mathematics-as-a-school-subject should take more account of the diversity of mathematical practices rather than, as hitherto, being dominated by the practices of mathematics-as-the-academic-discipline.

From the ethnomathematical perspective, mathematical practices exist both in cultures which have clearly labeled mathematical practices, such as among engineers and academic mathematicians, and *also* among cultures which have no activity labeled as "mathematics" or people labeled as "mathematicians." Barton (2008) makes a useful distinction between a QRS-system, defined as "a system for dealing with quantitative, relational, or spatial aspects of human experience"(p. 10) and NUC mathematics (near-universal, conventional mathematics). The former allows practices within societies with no concept of "mathematics" to be analyzed and described from a mathematical standpoint. Consider also cultural groups and individuals within our own society that, from the outsider's perspective, do mathematics, yet do not recognize or label their activity as such. There is a suggestive parallel with the aesthetic appreciation of artifacts from cultures that do not refer to "art" or "artists" as categories and with "outsider art" in our own culture.

However, the term *ethnomathematics* (by analogy with "ethnomusicology," for example), and the fact that many of the early studies were concerned with the mathematics of indigenous peoples, has led to a rather widespread misconception that ethnomathematics is concerned *only* with "others," "exotic," non-Western, nonliterate, "underdeveloped" people. However, the conceptualization of ethnomathematics from D'Ambrosio (1985), as discussed earlier, makes it clear that the concept is more inclusive.

The scope of ethnomathematics, accordingly, spans at least the following broad categories:

1. Studies and analyses of the mathematics of social groups in all areas of the world, including areas underappreciated for their contributions to mathematical knowledge: Africa (e.g., Gerdes, 1986, 1988, 1995; Lumpkin, 1983; Powell & Temple, 2001, 2002; Zaslavsky, 1973); Latin America (e.g. Ferreira, 1997; Knijnik, 1997; and see D'Ambrosio, 2006 for a list of theses and dissertations); and, indigenous groups in the Americas (e.g., Bazin, 2006; Mukhopadhyay, 2009; Pinxten et al., 1983).
2. Mathematics in out-of-school contexts (Lave, 1988), including "street mathematics" (Nunes, Schlieman, & Carraher, 1993); and, the mathematics of activities traditionally associated with women (e.g., Fasheh's, 2002 comments on his mother's work cited below; Harris, 1997).
3. Uncovering the contributions of many cultures to academic mathematics (Joseph, 1991; Powell & Frankenstein, 1997) and thereby combating the Eurocentric narrative of the history of its development.
4. Attending to how social, cultural, and political contexts influence the development and dissemination of mathematics, countering a history of mathematics predominantly written in terms of intellectual achievements of individuals. For example, Struik (1997), an eminent mathematician and historian of mathematics, indicated how a particular perspective—dialectical materialism—decisively influenced Marx's theoretical ideas on the foundation of the calculus (and see Gerdes, 1985, 2008; Powell, 1986). In our terms, the interpretation of calculus by Marx (1983) represents the ethnomathematical production of a specific cultural group—dialectical materialists—defined by a philosophical and ideological perspective. On a larger scale, the story of the development of probability and statistics is intricately interwoven with analysis of social phenomena, views of the nature of humankind, and much else, as has been painstakingly documented and analyzed by Hacking (1975, 1990).

5. Highlighting and interrogating the practices within mainstream academic mathematics. As a form of ethnomathematics, academic mathematics has characteristics that make it special, as suggested by Greer (1996):

> Important features of academic mathematics that differentiate it from localized mathematical activities and practices include the length and complexity of its historical development, the multiplicity of cultures that have contributed to that development, the degree of recording and communication and thereby criticism and negotiation of meaning [among] mathematicians...the technological advances that have generated problems stimulating new mathematics, the creation and codification of abstract mathematics, and...the degree of reflection on the nature of mathematics. (p. 188)

An important example of a growing literature in which scholars, including mathematicians, reflect on what it is to do mathematics is the book *The Mathematical Experience* by Davis and Hersh (1981). In a later book, the same authors (Davis & Hersh, 1986) took a critical stance toward the increasing mathematizations of aspects of social life.

6. The particular practices of school mathematics. From the perspective of a situated theory of learning, Lave (1993) states that:

> ...math in school is situated practice: school is the site of children's everyday activity. If school activities differ from the activities children and adults engage in elsewhere, the view of schooling must be revised accordingly; it is a site of specialized everyday activity—not a privileged site where universal knowledge is acquired. (p. 81)

As implied by the final two elements listed above, from our perspective, ethnomathematics is not proposed, as is often believed, as an alternative to either academic mathematics or to school mathematics which can be characterized as particular manifestations of essential responses of cultural entities to their perceived needs.

The formulation of ethnomathematics, as a relatively young theoretical position, is by no means tightly defined and continues to evolve. D'Ambrosio's own writings show considerable development, complexity, connections, and multifacetedness. Further, different self-identified ethnomathematicians have clearly contrasting perspectives; for example, see Barton's (1996) analysis of the disciplinary spaces spanned by D'Ambrosio, Gerdes, and Ascher.

Ethnomathematics has strong resonances with many theoretical movements within psychology and other social sciences, the history and philosophy of mathematics, and mathematics education, notably situated cognition and the notion of communities of practice, cultural historical activity theory, and multicultural education (Banks, 2006). Ethnomathematics also connects deeply with critical and political liberatory movements such as Freirean (Frankenstein & Powell, 1994); postcolonialism, subaltern studies (Apple & Buras, 2006); and the emergent group of critical mathematics educators (e.g., Frankenstein, 1983; Skovsmose, 1994; and see Vithal, 2003, ch.1, for a useful overview).

Ethnomathematics falls squarely within the fundamental emphasis on characterizing mathematics as a human activity, related to the concern of many mathematics educators that school mathematics does not connect with people's lives, exemplified by this declaration from Fasheh (2000): "I cannot subscribe to a system that ignores the lives and ways of living of the social majorities in the world; a system that ignores their ways of living, knowing and making sense of the world" (p. 5).

Throughout its short history as an area of practice and research, ethnomathematics has generated considerable controversy and resistance, in at least three respects. It questions the dominant Eurocentric narrative of the history of mathematics as a discipline, and as such has incurred criticism from some mathematicians. Second, the implications of ethnomathematics for mathematics education threaten the dominance of mathematics-as-school-subject by mathematics-as-the-academic-discipline—to put it provocatively, the view that the paramount reason for teaching mathematics in schools is the reproduction of academic mathematicians. Third, for us, ethnomathematics has an explicitly political character, so it encounters resistance from those who want to cling to the myth of the neutrality of knowledge. As an extreme case, Eglash (1997) refers to an attitude that "any tie to 'political' motivations is described as an inherent defect, a loss of scholarly status, and thus...ethnomathematics can be eliminated out of hand" (p. 88).

Critical concerns are by no means limited to reactionary mathematicians and educators. Vithal (2003) describes how an ethnomathematical perspective was used in South Africa as a supporting justification for separate and unequal educational provision during the Apartheid era. Atweh and Clarkson (2001, pp. 86–87) describe interchanges at an ICME Regional Collaboration conference at which Clements (1995, p. 3) said that "Over the past 20 years I have often had cause to reflect that it is Western educators who were responsible not only for getting their own mathematics teacher education equation wrong, but also for passing on their errors to education systems around the world" (cf. Swetz, chapter 1 this volume). Yet, at the same conference, the president of the African Mathematical Union (Kuku, 1995, p. 407), "warned against the overemphasis on culturally oriented curriculum for developing countries that act against their ability to progress and compete in an increasingly globalized world" (Atweh & Clarkson, 2001, p. 87) and similar comments were made by a mathematics educator from Malaysia. There is clearly a complex tension here, which has echoes within the United States.

We agree that an ethnomathematics curriculum used uncritically can indeed lead to disempowerment. However, addressing the challenges a *critical* ethnomathematics curriculum poses to the mainstream mathematics curriculum can instead empower students, through broadening, not narrowing their knowledge of mathematics; through inspiring their participation and creativity in contributing to the development of mathematical knowledge, and, for teachers, through the creation of a culturally responsive teaching. The latter is the focus of this chapter, and will be specifically developed below.

Addressing the Challenges Posed by Ethnomathematics

Some of the challenges to be addressed include: challenging the Eurocentric narrative; challenging what counts as knowledge in school mathematics; and challenging the disconnection between mathematics education and social and political change.

Challenging the Eurocentric Narrative to Promote Culturally Responsive Mathematics Teaching

Powell and Frankenstein (1997) introduced their edited book on ethnomathematics by discussing the arbitrariness of the construct *Europe* and associated terms such as *European*—with ramifications that continue into categorization of ethnic groups in the present-day United States. (Likewise, we find problematic the widespread usage of the term *Western mathematics*, and prefer the term *academic mathematics*.) In terms of development of civilization in that part of the world, a more meaningful region is the Mediterranean basin rather than the simplistic results of looking at a world map and calling some unclearly delineated geographical region on that map "Europe."

The geographic constructs underpinning military and mercantile colonization extended also—and perhaps in the long run, with even deeper consequences—to intellectual colonization. The question of the superiority of "Western civilization" has been debated on the history front of the Culture Wars (Nash, Crabtree, & Dunn, 2000), and anyone living today in the United States can hardly fail to be aware of such claims. According to Diaz (2002):

> The understanding of what is "human" and what should be regarded as "development" has taken—in a comparative view of world history—a specific [turn] since the coming up of the "Invention of Man" towards the end of the sixteenth century, and of the subsequent hegemonic construction of the [alien], subaltern (non-European) other. The consequence has been the steady marginalization, separation and sub-ordination of difference and diversity of the world-wise existing human and cultural experience and its multifaceted expressions. This domination structure has as its correlates the privileging and selective imposition of reduced cognitive structures, of one-sided interpretation patterns, of restricted scientific and technical solutions, and of monolinguistic habits. (p. 205)

Arguably the most extreme expression of Eurocentrism among traditional histories of mathematics is the following, from Kline (1953):

> ... [mathematics] finally secured a firm grip on life in the highly congenial soil of Greece and waxed strongly for a short period.... With the decline of Greek civilization, the plant remained dormant for a thousand years.... When the plant was transported to Europe proper and once more imbedded in fertile soil. (pp. 9–10)

Contrast this view with Joseph's (1991, p. 10) version of the lines of intercultural exchanges in the "Dark Ages" (note the loaded nature of that term) between the 5th and 15th centuries AD (Kline's dormant thousand years). The spread of ideas from the Hellenistic world through Sicily to Western Europe is linked with the mathematics of India and China through the nodes of Toledo and Cordoba in Spain, Cairo in Egypt, Baghdad in Iraq, and Jund-i-Shapur in Persia (modern Iran).

There have, increasingly, been significant intellectual challenges to this Eurocentric worldview. One of the areas of ethnomathematics delineated above, for example, reviews disputation over the controversial question of just how "European" the mathematics developed in Egypt (part of Africa) was, and deconstructs efforts to portray pre-Greek mathematics as "merely practical" and unsystematized (Powell & Frankenstein, 1997). As another example, Almeida and Joseph (2007) have researched the development of significant elements of the calculus in the Kerala School of mathematics during the 14th to 16th centuries. Moreover, they have conjectured that communications between Kerala and Europe were sufficient for this knowledge to have been shared. While this is controversial, they also suggest that accounts that downplay the possibility of the Keralite work contributing to the development of calculus are motivated by the desire to protect the claims of precedence of Newton and Leibnitz.

Political and cultural domination were inseparably linked (Bishop, 1990). Zaslavsky (1973, p. 131) commented "it is incredible that African games were actually discouraged by the colonial education authorities in favor of ludo, snakes-and-ladders, and similar games of European origin." For this reason, ethnomathematicians with a political sense are not just interested in the mathematics of, say, Angolan sand drawings and their use in story-telling, but also in the politics of imperialism that arrested the development of this cultural tradition, and discounted the mathematical activity involved in creating these drawings. Likewise, beyond studying the incredible mathematics built into the pyramids, it is important to expose the Eurocentrism embedded in various descriptions of that mathematics.

The most obvious way to challenge the Eurocentric narrative is to offer a counternarrative. As discussed above, scholars have addressed the contributions of non-European cultures to academic mathematics (Joseph, 1991; Powell & Frankenstein, 1997) and also the history of colonization in which intellectual domination was a partner of military and religious domination (Bishop, 1990). In spite of this scholarship, and with an inevitable lag, perhaps, the Eurocentric myth continues to pervade school mathematics education in more or less subtle and more or less hidden ways. A simple, but potent, case is the assignment of intellectual credit in such familiar labels as "Pythagoras's Theorem" and "Pascal's Triangle" despite evidence of precedent knowledge of the former in many cultures (Gerdes, 1988) and the latter in China (Swetz, 1994). A teacher teaching mathematics in an American school today may well have taken, as part of her or his training, a course on the history of mathematics following more or less the line of Kline cited above.

From our perspective, it is necessary, therefore, to be conscious of, and counter, such beliefs as these: that the academic mathematics taught in schools worldwide was created solely by (male) Europeans and diffused to the periphery; that mathematical knowledge exists outside of and is unaffected by culture; and that only a narrow part of human activity is mathematical and, moreover, worthy of serious contemplation as "legitimate" mathematics.

The obvious counter to such influences is to make students aware of a more balanced account through historical information. A straightforward example would be to point out that the Chinese had estimations for the value of π that were both more accurate and centuries in advance of what Europeans achieved (Swetz, 1994). A more extended example would be to make clear the importance of the Arabic culture during the "Dark Ages" (the term itself is loaded) to the development of algebra. Another example would be to trace the origins of the concept of zero to its ancient Egyptian, Indian, and Mayan roots.

We also argue that, beyond the intellectual history of academic mathematics (often the history of great [male] individuals), attention should be given to ways in which mathematics is culturally embedded and the roles that mathematics-in-action plays in contemporary society (Skovsmose, 2005). Moreover, we contend that it is important to teach about the intellectual history that has created the Eurocentric myth. We believe that a truly culturally responsive teaching needs to go further than correcting the record—truly culturally responsive teaching needs to understand why the record is wrong, and how that wrong record is culturally disrespectful and disempowering. More generally, all students should have some knowledge of the history of education as a tool of oppression in the United States, a history that is by no means over (e.g., Lomawaima, 1999; Martin & McGee, chapter 9 this volume; Valenzuela, 1999).

Challenging What Counts as Knowledge in School Mathematics to Promote Culturally Responsive Mathematics Teaching

> In the 1970s, while I was working in schools and universities in the West Bank region (in Palestine) and trying to make sense out of math, science, and knowledge, I "discovered" that what I was looking for has been next

> to me, in my own home: my mother's math and knowledge. She was a seamstress. Women would bring to her rectangular pieces of cloth in the morning; she would take few measures with colored chalk; by noon each rectangular piece is cut into 30 small pieces; and by the evening these scattered pieces are connected to form a new and beautiful whole. If this is not math, I don't know what math is. The fact that I could not see it for 35 years made me realize the power of language in what we see and what we don't. Her knowledge was embedded in life (like salt in food) in a way that made it invisible to me as an educated and literate person. I was trained to see things through official language and professional categories. *In a very true sense, I discovered that my mother was illiterate in relation to my type of knowledge, but I was illiterate in terms of her type of understanding and knowledge.* (Fasheh, 2002, emphasis in original)

A defining tenet of ethnomathematics is its openness to acknowledging as mathematical knowledge and mathematical practices elements of people's lives outside the academy, in cultures that have been denigrated, at various times, by terms such as *primitive, underdeveloped, nonliterate,* and in the practical intelligence of people in our own society (as beautifully described in essays and short stories by Primo Levi, for example—*The Monkey's Wrench* (1986)—including women, as illustrated in the quotation above (and see Gerdes, 1995; Harris, 1997).

Much of the most salient work in ethnomathematics is concerned with revealing the mathematics embedded in artifacts and practices of other cultures. In "unfreezing" such "frozen mathematics" (Gerdes, 1986), ethnomathematicians are sensitive to the dangers of interpreting such cultural products through their own cultural lenses, dangers to which anthropologists have become increasingly alert.

D'Ambrosio (1997) argues that mathematics appears different in different cultural contexts:

> Much of the research in Ethnomathematics today has been directed at uncovering small achievements and practices in non-Western cultures that resemble Western mathematics. Western mathematics remains the standard of rationality. It is even suggested that if other cultures had a few more centuries of development, they might reach higher stages of rationality! The key issue, which seems to be omitted from most developments of Ethnomathematics, is that mathematical developments in other cultures follow different tracks of intellectual inquiry, hold different concepts of truth, different sets of values, different visions of the self, of the Other, of mankind [sic] of nature and the planet, and of the cosmos. All these visions belong together and cannot be isolated from each other. (p. 15)

So this central tenet of ethnomathematics is that beyond academic mathematics there lies a wealth of human activity that should be acknowledged as mathematical—historical and contemporary mathematical knowledge and practices of all peoples.

Many reasons may be given why instruction should be respectful of students' cultures. It has been pointed out (Zehr, 2008) that there is scant research providing evidence that such instruction affects student achievement, but there are many grounds for rejecting the proposal for that reason alone, teaching that includes the contributions of all cultures to mathematics should not be promoted. In the first place, lack of research is not a sufficient reason for refusing to take actions that have a high plausibility level of being appropriate. This case is one of many of the most important questions in mathematics education that are as much a matter of values as of "hard" evidence. Moreover, it is a legitimate question to ask why the research is so limited. Further, there is a cluster of clarifications needed around such issues as: What kind of instruction? What forms of evaluation of the effects are to be used? Similar issues have been posed by Schoenfeld (2006) in relation to the What Works Clearinghouse. According to Tharp (cited by Zehr, 2008, p. 8) a number of studies show "culture-based education systematically produces greater student engagement, greater parental involvement, better attendance rates, lower dropout rates, better graduation rates, and general satisfaction of all participants, as opposed to a standard, traditional program based on mainstream models." Many of these indications of positive outcomes are much more difficult to quantify than test scores. Further, the only reasonable evaluation of an instructional program of this sort would span a considerable number of years.

According to Zehr, the U.S. Department of Education's Institute of Educational Sciences has funded only one program of research to study the effects of culture-based education other than on language, and that is the work of Lipka and his group (Lipka, Yanez, Andrew-Ihrke, & Adam, chapter 11 this volume). The effects of Lipka's program have indeed been shown in test scores, but, from our perspective there are much more important aspects of his research, notably the very long commitment in time, the exemplary and respect in cooperating with the Yup'ik people, especially the elders, and the authenticity of the activities that form the basis of the curricular units that have been developed (for other examples, see Barta & Brenner, chapter 4 this volume).

In particular, in paying attention to the cultural embeddedness of the activities, Lipka's work is in contrast to superficial references in mathematics classrooms to Native- American culture (Barta & Brenner, this volume, make a similar point). For example, it has become rather fashionable to use various Native-American "games" with a probabilistic element in teaching probability in school, with no attempt to understand the cultural matrix from which these activities have been detached, in which the notions of individual competition, winning and losing, do not play a role.

There are two problematic issues with this kind of cultural-based teaching that can be answered by a *critical* application of these ideas. Readers will question what to do with classes of students from various cultural backgrounds, and whether, in any case, it would be limiting students' horizons to learn only their particular cultures' contributions to mathematics. But, we are not recommending that students only narrowly learn the mathematics of their own culture, and we are not advocating a narrow definition of culture that ignores each individual's simultaneous participation in many different cultures (i.e., Yup'ik, gender, age cohort, school, and so on). We would recommend that mathematics instruction start from the points of cultural familiarity, brought out in the curriculum in a deep way connected with the entire context of intellectual activities of the particular culture. But, we also recommend that all students learn about the mathematical contributions of various cultures, including the "current academic math" culture.

Challenging the Disconnections between Mathematics Education and Social and Political Change to Promote Culturally Responsive Mathematics Teaching

For us as well as for others such as D'Ambrosio, Gerdes, and Knijnik, a critical (and in the field of mathematics, a controversial) approach to ethnomathematics includes challenging the "neutrality" of mathematics education and insisting that we are activist educators, committed to finding ways to contribute to struggles for social justice through our educational work (see also Zinn, 1997). We contend that no academic discipline is neutral. As Profreidt (1980) points out, in most educational settings there exists

> ... a silly neutralism in which teachers believe they are just presenting facts and avoiding opinions or value statements. They avoid value statements because...they do not believe that such statements are susceptible to rational inquiry and verification. Of course, in practice they are transmitting a set of values, but one which is not identified as such, and hence is not open to critical inquiry. (p. 477)

And, we contend that the central purpose of an education is to contribute to the development of our collective world, in the direction of more justice. Freire (1972) made clear that "reflection without action is sheer verbalism, 'armchair revolution', whereas action without reflection is 'pure activism', that is action for action's sake" (p. 41). The title of Gutstein's (2006) book, *Reading and Writing the World with Mathematics*, underlines this by emphasizing Freire's call to go beyond understanding (reading) the social and political environment in which one lives to taking action (writing) to change it (see also Gutstein, chapter 6 this volume).

In mathematics instruction and in mathematics education research, the tendency to view education as neutral, and unconnected to action for change, can be particularly strong. Skovsmose (2005) notes that, "the community of mathematics education manifests an ignorance of social, political and cultural aspects in the lives of students" (p. 3). He cites Apple (1995) who said that, "In the process of individualizing its view of students, it [mathematics education] has lost any serious sense of the social structures and race, gender and class relations that form these individuals" (p. 331). Ethnomathematicians have been prominent among those critical mathematics educators working to break the myths of neutrality and objectivity and turn a critical lens toward the activity system of research in mathematics education (Valero & Zevenbergen, 2004).

We argue here that ignoring these connections disrespects students, and treats their learning in isolation from their roles as citizens, where they need to use the knowledge gained in their education to contribute to the development of their societies. Tate (1995) provides an example of students using mathematics in the course of political action within their own community. The students, in a predominantly African-American urban middle school, identified the large number of liquor stores near their school as a problem, developed a plan to move them away, and carried out that plan by various direct actions, including lobbying the state senate. Mathematical modeling was an important tool in this campaign. The students analyzed the local tax and other codes that led to financial advantages for the liquor stores and reconstructed this incentive system to protect their school community. As Tate (1995) comments:

> This required the students to think about mathematics as a way to model their reality.... Percentages, decimals, and fractions became more than isolated numbers as the students tried to mathematically manipulate these different, yet related, symbol systems and to link them to real problem solving and decision making. (p. 170)

Another compelling example is how students in a New York middle school used mathematics to document, analyze, and take action to confront the overcrowding in their school (Turner & Strawhun, 2006).

These two examples suggest a general strategy, that teachers and students together could experience the power of mathematics and their own agency through the use of modeling tools to critique and act upon their own educational circumstances. Likewise, students in underresourced schools (or, indeed, overresourced schools) could study data bearing on the local manifestations of inequity in school funding.

Conclusion

We recognize the tension in arguing that the priorities and nature of mathematics education are in need of deep critique, while recognizing at the same time that real students, here and now, need access to the educational and economic opportunities in which mathematics is so tightly implicated (Moses & Cobb, 2001).

Enhancing the Mathematics Curriculum through Culturally Responsive Teaching

Macedo, in a dialogue with Freire, stated that:

> On the one hand, students have to become literate about their histories, experiences, and the culture of their immediate environments. On the other hand, they must also appropriate those codes and cultures of the dominant spheres so they can transcend their own environments. (Freire & Macedo, 1987, p. 47)

Gutstein (2006) advocates a balance between three forms of mathematical practice, which he labels Classical Knowledge, Community Knowledge, and Critical Knowledge. We agree with this approach, although we would use a different label for "classical" referring to it more contextually as "current traditional, globalized academic" mathematics. This approach does not "water down" the "real" math curriculum, but rather "thickens" and strengthens math curricula. Advocates of ethnomathematics should not be afraid of the "Where's the math?" question.

An ethnomathematical position deepens studies within traditional topics from the mathematics curriculum. For example, Powell and Temple (2004), as an integral part of their curriculum, teach students how to solve equations with *more* analysis of the process and *more* effectively by using knowledge of the Ancient Egyptians. In so doing, they avoid trivializing that ancient knowledge, mentioning it as a 5-minute after-thought to the "real" mathematics lesson. Instead, Powell and Temple translate the ancient mathematical knowledge from the Ahmose Papyrus into relevant activities for their current students. In so doing, they are not behaving very differently from those mathematics educators who are inspired by Euclid's Elements. The difference is that they are more inclusive and aware of the contributions and intellectual achievements of many cultures other than those recognized in the Eurocentric narrative about the history of mathematics ideas and forms of reasoning.

Beyond this more enlightened view of the history and development of mathematics, ethnomathematics also valorizes other forms of mathematical knowledge, expertise, and practices. Moreover, in relation to a critical stance toward the activity system of teaching and learning mathematics, we are not just advocating exploring what nonacademic knowledge the students already bring to the learning situation—such as the funds of knowledge in their families and communities (Gonzalez, Moll, & Amanti, 2005). Rather, we are invested in challenging and extending the students' ideas, adding context and political awareness, recognizing the teachers' often broader knowledge base and the responsibilities of educator-activists to build upon and to challenge students' ethnomathematical knowledge. Youngman (1986) suggested that Freire's uncritical faith in the people "makes him ambivalent about saying outright that educators can have a theoretical understanding *superior* to that of the learners and which is, in fact, the indispensable condition of the development of critical consciousness" (p. 179). It is important, therefore, to listen to students' themes, but also to organize them using our critical and theoretical frameworks, and re-present them as problems challenging students' perceptions. It is also important, as teachers, to suggest themes that may not occur to our students, themes we judge are important in shattering commonly held myths about the structure of society and knowledge that interfere with the development of critical consciousness.

A good example, showing the teacher building on the knowledge of the students, but not ignoring the teacher's deeper understanding of the larger political issues that arise from his student's mathematical practices, is a study of the "Animal Lottery" that was done in Brazil. This (illegal) activity "is part of Brazilian folklore and is played all over the country" (Nobre, 1989, p. 175). Nobre describes three stages of the work:

1. Exchanging information about the game, including the students informing the teacher about "the mysticism and the popular beliefs that involve the game" (p. 176).
2. Mathematization of the odds.
3. Interpretation where the activities expanded the student ideas so that they concluded that it is the owners of the business who profit, and became aware of the political ramifications of the associated corruption and unfairness.

Nobre's final comment is important: "Having the mathematical elements to understand society in his hands, the student begins to see society with other eyes, thus being able to interfere with it and ceasing to be just a spectator" (p. 177). This is the type of culturally responsive teaching we are advocating. A *critical* ethnomathematical perspective will uncover the mathematics in this lottery and connect it clearly with the mathematics of those who currently have power, so as not to disempower the students, but rather to show the students how they are already engaging in mathematical practices that are connected to academic mathematics. A *critical* ethnomathematical perspective will continue explorations with the students so that they see the larger economic picture involved in the lottery and can discuss their analysis of its fairness. A *critical* interdisciplinary perspective will add to the mathematics lesson more data about lotteries that could allow students to engage in a deeper examination of the allocation of economic resources.

References

Almeida, D. F., & Joseph, G. G. (2007, June). Kerala mathematics and its possible transmission to Europe. *Philosophy of Mathematics Education Journal, 20* Retrieved August 27, 2008, from http://www.people.ex.ac.uk/PErnest/pome20/index.htm

Apple, M. W. (1995). Taking power seriously: New directions in equity in mathematics education and beyond. In W. G. Secada, E. Fennema, & B. Adajian (Eds.), *New directions for equity in mathematics education* (pp. 329–348). Cambridge, UK: Cambridge University Press.

Apple, M. W., & Buras, K. L. (2006). *The subaltern speak.* New York: Routledge.

Atweh, B., & Clarkson, P. (2001). Internationalization and globalization of mathematics education: Towards an agenda for research/action. In B. Atweh, H. Forgasz, & B. Nebres (Eds.), *Sociocultural research on mathematics education: An international perspective* (pp. 77–94). Mahwah, NJ: Erlbaum.

Banks, J. A. (2006). *Race, culture, and education: The selected works of James A. Banks.* New York: Routledge.

Barton, B. (1996). Making sense of ethnomathematics: Ethnomathematics is making sense. *Educational Studies in Mathematics, 31,* 201–233.

Barton, B. (2008). *The language of mathematics.* New York: Springer.

Bazin, M. (2006). *Ethnomathematics with and for indigenous people.* Unpublished manuscript.

Bishop, A. J. (1990). Western mathematics: The secret weapon of cultural imperialism. *Race and Class, 32*(2), 51–65.

Bloor, D. (1976). *Knowledge and social imagery.* London: Routledge & Kegan Paul.

Clements, K. (1995). Restructuring mathematics teacher education: Overcoming the barriers of elitism and separatism. In R. Hunting, G. Fitzsimons, P. Clarkson, & A. J. Bishop (Eds.), *Regional collaboration in mathematics education* (pp. 1–10). Melbourne, Australia: Monash University.

D'Ambrosio, U. (1985). Ethnomathematics and its place in the history and pedagogy of mathematics. *For the Learning of Mathematics, 5*(1), 44–48.

D'Ambrosio, U. (1994). Cultural framing of mathematics teaching and learning. In R. Biehler, R. W. Scholz, R. Strasser, & B. Winkelmann (Eds.), *Didactics of mathematics as a scientific discipline* (pp. 443–455). Dordrecht, The Netherlands: Kluwer.

D'Ambrosio, U. (1997). Where does ethnomathematics stand nowadays? *For the Learning of Mathematics. 17*(2), 13–17.

D'Ambrosio, U. (2003, December). The role of mathematics in building up a democratic society. In B. L. Madison & L. A. Steen (Eds.), *Quantitative literacy: Why numeracy matters for schools and colleges: Proceedings of National Forum on Quantitative Literacy, National Academy of Sciences, Washington, DC.* Princeton, NJ: National Council on Education and the Disciplines.

D'Ambrosio, U. (2006). *Ethnomathematics: Link between tradition and modernity.* Rotterdam, The Netherlands: Sense.

Davis, P. J., & Hersh, R. (1981). *The mathematical experience.* Boston: Birkhauser.

Davis, P. J., & Hersh, R. (1986). *Descartes' dream.* Brighton, UK: Harvester.

Diaz, P. V. (2002). Human development in history and society: Multi-perspectivity of perceptions and diversity of linguistic expressions. In S. C. Agarkar & V. D. Lale (Eds.), *Science, technology and mathematics education for human development: Proceedings of the CASTME-UNESCO-HBSCE International Conference, Goa, India* (Vol. 2, pp. 205–214). Mumbai, India: Homi Bhabha Centre for Science Education/Tata Institute of Fundamental Research.

Eglash, R. (1997). When math worlds collide: Intention and invention in ethnomathematics. *Science, Technology, & Human Values, 22*(1), 79–97.

Fasheh, M. (2000, September). *The trouble with knowledge.* Paper presented at a global dialogue on "Building Learning Societies—Knowledge, Information and Human Development," Hanover, Germany. Retrieved August 27, 2008 from http://www.swaraj.org/shikshantar/resources_fasheh.html

Fasheh, M. (2002, September 9–10). *How to eradicate illiteracy without eradicating illiterates?* Paper presented at the UNESCO round table on "Literacy as Freedom." The International Literacy Day, UNESCO, Paris. Retrieved January 1, 2009, from http://www.almoultaga.com/munir.aspx

Ferreira, M. K. L. (1997). When 1+1≠2: Making mathematics in central Brazil. *American Ethnologist, 24,* 132–147.

Frankenstein, M. (1983). Critical mathematics education: An application of Paulo Freire's epistemology. *Journal of Education, 165*(4), 315–340.

Frankenstein, M. (in press). Developing a critical mathematical numeracy through real-life word problems. In L. Verschaffel, B. Greer, W. van Dooren, & S. Mukhopadhyay (Eds.), *Words and worlds: Modelling verbal descriptions of situations*. Rotterdam, The Netherlands: Sense.
Frankenstein, M., & Powell, A. B. (1994) Toward liberating mathematics: Paulo Freire's epistemoloty and ethnomathematics. In P. McLaren & C. Lankshear (Eds.), *The politics of liberation: Paths from Freire* (pp. 74–99). London: Routledge.
Freire, P. (1972). *Pedagogy of the oppressed*. Harmondsworth, UK: Penguin.
Freire, P., & Macedo, D. (1987). *Literacy: Reading the word and the world*. South Hadley, MA: Bergen & Garvey.
Gay, G. (2000). *Culturally responsive teaching: Theory, research, and practice*. New York: Teachers College Press.
Gerdes, P. (1985). *Marx demystifies calculus*. (B. Lumpkin, Trans). Minneapolis: MEP. (Original work published 1983)
Gerdes, P. (1986). How to recognize hidden geometrical thinking: A contribution to the development of anthropological mathematics. *For the Learning of Mathematics, 6*, 10–12, 17.
Gerdes, P. (1988). A widespread decorative motif and the Pythagorean theorem. *For the Learning of Mathematics, 8*(1), 35–39.
Gerdes, P. (1995). *Women and geometry in southern Africa: Some suggestions for further research, on women and mathematics*. Maputo, Moçambique: Ethnomathematics Research Project, Universidade Pedagógica Moçambique.
Gerdes, P. (2008). *Os manuscritos filosófico-matemáticos de Karl Marx sobre o cálculo diferencial: Uma introdução*: Lulu. [Karl Marx's philosophic-mathematical manuscripts about the differencial of mathematics and calculus: An introduction]. Morrisville, NC: Lulu.com.
Gonzalez, N., Moll, L. C., & Amanti, C. (Eds.). (2005). *Funds of knowledge: Theorizing practices in households, communities, and classrooms*. Mahwah, NJ: Erlbaum.
Greer, B. (1996). Theories of mathematics education: The role of cognitive analyses. In L. P. Steffe, P. Nesher, P. Cobb, G. A. Goldin, & B. Greer (Eds.), *Theories of mathematical learning* (pp. 179–196). Mahwah, NJ: Erlbaum.
Gutstein, E. (2006). *Reading and writing the world with mathematics: A pedagogy for social justice*. New York: Routledge.
Hacking, I. (1975). *The emergence of probability*. Cambridge, UK: Cambridge University Press.
Hacking, I. (1990). *The taming of chance*. Cambridge, UK: Cambridge University Press.
Harris, M. (1997). *Common threads: Women, mathematics and work*. Stoke-on-Trent, UK: Trentham Books.
Howard, G. (2006). *We can't teach what we don't know*. New York: Teachers College Press.
Joseph, G. G. (1991). *The crest of the peacock: Non-European roots of mathematics*. London: Penguin.
Kline, M. (1953). *Mathematics in western culture*. New York: Oxford.
Knijnik, G. (1997). An ethnomathematical approach in mathematical education: A matter of political power. In A. B. Powell & M. Frankenstein (Eds.), *Ethnomathematics: Challenging Eurocentrism in mathematics education* (pp. 403–410). Albany, NY: SUNY Press.
Kozol, J. (2005). *The shame of the nation: The restoration of Apartheid schooling in America*. New York: Crown.
Kuku, A. (1995). Mathematics education in Africa in relation to other countries. In R. Hunting, G. Fitzsimons, P. Clarkson, & A. J. Bishop (Eds.), *Regional collaboration in mathematics education* (pp. 403–423). Melbourne, Australia: Monash University.
Ladson-Billings, G. (1995). But that's just good teaching! A case for culturally relevant pedagogy. *Theory into Practice, 34*, 159–165.
Lave, J. (1988). *Cognition in practice: Mind, mathematics, and culture in everyday life*. New York: Cambridge University Press.
Lave, J. (1993). Word problems: A microcosm of theories of learning. In P. Light & G. Butterworth (Eds.), *Context and cognition: Ways of learning and knowing* (pp. 74–92). Hillsdale, NJ: Erlbaum.
Levi, P. (1986). *The monkey's wrench* (W. Weaver, Trans.). New York: Summit Books.

Lomawaima, K. T. (1999). An unnatural history of American Indian education. In K. G. Swisher & J. W. Tippeconnic, III (Eds.), *Next steps: Research and practice to advance Indian education* (pp. 3–31). Charleston, WV: Clearinghouse of Rural Education and Small Schools.

Lumpkin, B. (1983). Africa in the mainstream of mathematics history. In I. V. Sertima (Ed.), *Blacks in science: Ancient and modern* (pp. 100–109). New Brunswick, NJ: Transaction.

Moses, R. P., & Cobb, C. E. (2001). *Radical equations: Civil rights from Mississippi to the Algebra Project.* Boston: Beacon Press.

Mukhopadhyay, S. (2009). The decorative impulse: Ethnomathematics and Tlingit basketry. *ZDM, 41,* 117.

Nash, G. B. Crabtree, C., & Dunn, R. E. (2000). *History on trial: Culture wars and teaching of the past.* New York: Vintage.

National Center for Education Statistics, U.S. Department of Education. (2006). Schools and staffing survey, Public School Teacher Data File, 2003–04 Retrieved August 27, 2008, from. http://nces.ed.gov/surveys/sass/tables/state_2004_18.asp#f2

Nobre, S. R. (1989). The ethnomathematics of the most popular lottery in Brazil: The "Animal Lottery." In C. Keitel, P. Damerow, A. Bishop, & P. Gerdes (Eds.), *Mathematics, education, and society* (pp. 175–177). Paris: UNESCO.

Nunes, T., Schliemann, A. D., & Carraher, D. W. (1993). *Street mathematics and school mathematics.* Cambridge, UK: Cambridge University Press.

Pinxten, R., van Dooren, I., & Harvey, F. (1983). *The anthropology of space: Explorations into the natural philosophy and semantics of the Navajo.* Philadelphia: University of Philadelphia Press.

Powell, A. B. (1986). Marx and mathematics in Mozambique. *Science and Nature, 7/8,* 119–123.

Powell, A. B., & Frankenstein, M. (2002, August 5–7). Paulo Freire's contribution to an epistemology of ethnomathematics. In *Proceedings of the Second International Congress on Ethnomathematics* Ouro Preto, Minas Gerais, Brazil: Universidade Federal de Ouro Preto.

Powell, A. B., & Frankenstein, M. (1997). *Ethnomathematics: Challenging Eurocentrism in mathematics education.* Albany, NY: SUNY Press.

Powell, A. B., & Temple, O. L. (2001). Seeding ethnomathematics with *oware*: *Sankofa. Teaching Children Mathematics, 7*(6), 369–375.

Powell, A. B., & Temple, O. L. (2002, August 5–7.). Bridging past and present: Ethnomathematics, the Ahmose Mathematical Papyrus, and urban students. In *Proceedings of the Second International Congress on Ethnomathematics.* Ouro Preto, Minas Gerais, Brazil: Universidade Federal de Ouro Preto.

Powell, A. B., & Temple, O. L. (2004). Construindo pontes entre passado e presente: etnomatemática, o papiro matemático de Ahmose e estudantes urbanos [Bridging past and present: Ethnomathematics, the Ahmose Mathematical Papyrus, and urban students]. In J. P. M. Ribeiro, M. D. C. S. Domite, & R. Ferreira (Eds.), *Etnomatemática: papel, valor e significado* [Ethnomathematics: Role, value, and significance] (pp. 267–284). São Paulo, Brazil: Zouk.

Profreidt, W. (1980). Socialist criticisms of education in the United States: Problems and possibilities. *Harvard Educational Review, 50*(4), 467–480.

Restivo, S. (1993). The social life of mathematics. In S. Restivo, J. P. Van Bendegem, & R. Fischer (Eds.), *Math worlds: Philosophical and social studies of mathematics and mathematics education* (pp. 247–278). Albany, NY: State University of New York Press.

Schoenfeld, A. H. (2006). What doesn't work: The challenge and failure of the What Works Clearinghouse to conduct meaningful reviews of studies of mathematics curricula. *Educational Researcher, 35,* 13–21.

Skovsmose, O. (1994). *Towards a philosophy of critical mathematics education.* Dordrecht, The Netherlands: Kluwer.

Skovsmose, O. (2005). *Travelling through education: Uncertainty, mathematics, responsibility.* Rotterdam, The Netherlands: Sense.

Struik, D. J. (1997). Marx and mathematics. In A. B. Powell & M. Frankenstein (Eds.), *Ethnomathematics: Challenging eurocentrism in mathematics education* (pp. 173–192). Albany, NY: SUNY Press.

Swetz, F. (1994). *From five fingers to infinity.* Chicago: Open Court.

Tate, W. F. (1995). Returning to the root: A culturally relevant approach to mathematics pedagogy. *Theory into Practice*, *34*, 166–173.

Turner, E. E., & Strawhun, B. T. (2006). With math, it's like you have more defense. In E. Gutstein & B. Peterson (Eds.), *Rethinking mathematics* (pp. 81–89). Milwaukee, WI: Rethinking Schools.

U.S. Census Bureau News (2008, August 14). An older and more diverse nation by midcentury. Retrieved August 15, 2008, from http://www.census.gov/Press-Release/www/releases/archives/population/012496.html

Valenzuela, A. (1999). *Subtractive schooling: U.S.-Mexican youth and the politics of caring.* Albany, NY: SUNY Press.

Valero, P., & Zevenbergen, R. (Eds.). (2004). *Researching the socio-political dimensions of mathematics education.* Dordrecht, The Netherlands: Kluwer.

Vithal, R. (2003). *In search of pedagogy of conflict and dialogue for mathematics education.* Dordrecht, The Netherlands: Kluwer.

Youngman, F. (1986). *Adult education and socialist pedagogy*. London: Croom Helm.

Zaslavsky, C. (1973). *Africa counts: Number and pattern in African culture.* Boston: Prindle, Weber & Schmidt.

Zehr, M. A. (2008). Evidence of culture-based teaching called thin. *Education Week, 27*(17), 8.

Zinn, H. (1997). The uses of scholarship. In *The Zinn reader: Writings on disobedience and democracy* (pp. 499–507). New York: Seven Stories Press.

4

Seeing With Many Eyes

Connections Between Anthropology and Mathematics

JIM BARTA AND MARY E. BRENNER

> When I was in school, teachers never discussed my people and certainly not in math class. Although most of my classmates were just like me, teachers did not tell stories of our people. I grew up thinking that there was something wrong with my people and me. As a child, I thought our people did not know anything about mathematics and seldom used it. (S. Reeder, personal communication, June 25, 1997)

Understanding and describing the diverse manifestations of the human condition is at the heart of the science known as anthropology (Lévi-Strauss, 1985). Behaviors such as language use, communication systems, wedding and funerary rituals, religious or spiritual beliefs, or articles of use such as tools and artifacts are examined to help illuminate similar and distinguishing characteristics between and among human populations. Anthropology provides a detailed and complex view of the human species and its development causing many to question the long-held idea of cultural progression from "primitive" to "advanced."

Implicit in any discussion of anthropology is the role of culture, a concept that has become quite contested both within the field of anthropology as well as more generally (e.g., Borofsky, Barth, Shweder, Rodseth, & Stolzenberg, 2001; Fox & King, 2002). Lévi-Strauss wrote that the term *culture* "signified particular life styles that are not transmissible, that can be grasped only as concrete products—skills, customs, folkways, institutions, beliefs, rather than virtual capacities and that correspond to observable values instead of truths or presumed truths" (Lévi-Strauss, 1985, p. 26), stressing that culture is not a set of capabilities or truths but a set of values. Barth (2002) stressed that culture is discernable as both actions and thoughts that vary between individuals because it is created and used by "situated persons with purposes, acting in complex life situations"

(p. 32). Within ethnomathematics and in this paper, the aspects of culture that are considered include the cognitive aspects of mathematics, how mathematics is used, and the values that are attached to mathematics within the lives of different groups of people who might share an ethnic tradition, an occupation, or who are merely engaged in joint activity for particular purposes.

There are many contributions anthropologists may provide in the educational context. These include but are not limited to: acting as consultants providing ideas that may cause a fuller understanding of human educational behaviors; helping educators to better perceive education as a process of enculturation; providing ongoing research particularly in areas of cross-cultural settings; and sharing as instructors themselves helping others to understand the role and influence of myriad cultural assumptions embedded in the educational process (Spindler, 2000). The "aim is to create cultural awareness, which is perhaps even more important than the self-awareness in the teacher's sphere of activity and which is pedagogically much more attainable" (Spindler, 2000, p. 70).

Anthropology as a discipline is among many on which mathematics education draws. From an educational perspective, the field of anthropology has been instrumental in causing scholars and practitioners to carefully consider the interactions of and motivations for people who gather to provide teaching and promote learning. Phil Jackson (1990) uses ethnographic techniques in his seminal description of the implications of the classroom, and describes the "life" which occurs for students and helps to shape and influence their intellectual, emotional, and social development. Berlak and Berlak (1981), using the lens of the anthropologist, describe the enculturation of social roles for students, which they learn through obligatory educational experiences in school as enacted by instructional practice and curricular intervention. A critical examination of what occurs in the social and educational development of students in schools could not occur without ethnographic methods, which originated in the field of anthropology.

The similarities and contrasts illuminated between the disciplines of anthropology and education can be very enlightening. Spindler (2000) suggested that in using anthropological perspectives to examine the role and influence of culture in teaching and learning, we create forms of cultural therapy where we can learn to step back from the personal and societal bias inherent in any cultural perspective to consider the motivations and implications of someone who does the same thing differently from "us." The focus of the therapy centers on the culture of the teachers and the bias that may be inherent in their relationships with those they teach. As educators, such perspective taking broadens our view of "the others," helping us realize in many ways that we are more similar than different and that in the diversity lies the beauty and intrigue of our human ways. From "making the strange familiar," where differences in human behaviors are seen as social interactions used to complete the same task or which serve the same purpose, to "making the familiar strange," we are challenged to deepen our awareness of how our seemingly universal activities, beliefs, and practices are actually shaped and enacted in the culture(s) in which we are enculturated (Spindler, 2000, pp. 367–368). As educators, little else could be more important than for us to deeply understand how our narrow vision of culture, bias, prejudice, and discrimination all creep consciously or unconsciously into the subject matter we present, the pedagogy we implement, and what we fail to do to minimize or eliminate them from our instruction.

The field of anthropology has had a dramatic effect on how we today understand what takes place in schools. Anthropology allows us to more deeply examine the multiple dynamics involved as humans learn in the educational settings society creates. The subject of mathematics in particular has benefited from the use of anthropological techniques as educators have become more cognizant of the role of culture in its teaching and learning.

Using research techniques designed and developed through anthropological studies since the early 1980s, a new science of ethnomathematics has been born. *Ethnomathematics* is the term used to describe a people's mathematical contributions in society, and reflects that the need for and use of mathematical techniques is linked to specific cultural contexts (Ascher, 2002; D'Ambrosio, 2001). A student of ethnomathematics must study in a range of subjects such as anthropology, sociology, psychology, linguistics, cognition, education, and mathematics. This wide array of disciplines contributes to the field of ethnomathematics and reflects the numerous intersections and relationships that exist between various bodies of knowledge, as well as helping to illustrate countless social and cultural applications. In this light, ethnomathematics is best understood as seeing with many eyes the mathematical complexity and beauty of ways of knowing and doing that offer the student detailed illustrations of how mathematics shape who we are, how we are, and the resulting applications and products of our human labors.

Ethnomathematics can be experienced as the intersection existing between anthropology, mathematics, and mathematics education. D'Ambrosio (1997) has noted that ethnomathematics "lies on the borderline between the history of mathematics and cultural anthropology" (p. 13). When he first wrote these words in 1985, he further went on to state that mathematicians and others had given little attention to the diverse mathematical practices of the world's peoples, but "there is a reasonable amount of literature on this by anthropologists" (p. 14). In subsequent years, ethnomathematics has grown as a field in its own right as demonstrated by edited volumes (e.g., Powell & Frankenstein, 1997), the application of enthnomathematics in educational practice (e.g., Bishop, 1988; Secada, 2000), and the organization of research groups such as the International Study Group on Ethnomathematics, along with this volume itself. Still, anthropological perspectives continue to be useful for informing the field of ethnomathematics as well as the contextualized use of ethnomathematics in educational contexts.

In turn, ethnomathematics provides a model for how anthropology can move beyond its boundaries as a discipline, as it challenges educators to reconceptualize the creation and use of mathematics in human practice across diverse cultures. Second, teachers who embrace an ethnomathematical perspective may further consider the impact of cultural infusion on the context in which they place their instruction and the pedagogy they follow.

Ethnomathematics provides a way to better understand the reciprocal nature of mathematics and culture, of how culture influences the way cultural communities implement mathematical applications, skills, and knowledge in solution to problems encountered daily, and how these culturally inspired responses reciprocally affect the way mathematics is conceived and applied in each particular group. It illustrates in dynamic fashion that cultural responses to living are witnessed through an anthropological perspective, where mathematical actions are considered as defining dimensions which shape the cultural communities to which one belongs. This starkly clear and beautiful personification of cultural behavior as it reflects the interplay between the application of human intelligence and one's enculturation is reflected in virtually every action or product. The work of the master weaver, potter, or woodworker, for example, reflects the personalized application of mathematical capabilities through their use.

Given that it is obvious that these "users" of mathematical ideas and skills possess the knowledge to apply it, why then do many consider themselves lacking in mathematical abilities when they describe their classroom experiences with mathematics? What creates this tension? How do contemporary classroom practices promote or restrict some students who may benefit from instruction where their cultural needs are considered and included in the classroom instruction? These are the issues to be further discussed; first by providing the foundational knowledge that explains the results of the intersection of anthropology and mathematics and later how culturally responsive mathematical classroom practices can be created and applied for our students.

Anthropology and Mathematics

Anthropology outlines three main perspectives for ethnomathematics and for those who want to apply it within their classrooms. (1) Mathematics is a cultural practice present in all societies, and all practice of mathematics is culturally situated. (2) The meaning of mathematics resides in the ways it is used within culturally meaningful practices and within specific contexts. (3) An ethnographic perspective enables teachers to understand the world from their students' perspectives, and thereby bridge between the ideas of different mathematical practices.

Anthropology is the social science that from its inception has seriously studied the diversity of human ways of living. Early ethnographies, typically of small and isolated communities, attempted to capture the entirety of a group's way of living. Within such descriptions, counting systems or games with a mathematical focus were mentioned as small components of the larger culture. Although the study of mathematical practices in the world's cultures has not been a major focus of anthropological research, the anthropological record substantiates that mathematics is most likely a universal cultural characteristic.

Since mathematics is not demarcated as a separate body of knowledge in many cultures, mathematics can be identified in the products and practices of different cultural traditions. For instance, Bishop (1988) identified six activities that embody mathematical ideas: counting, locating, measuring, designing, playing, and explaining. He described how each of these activities derives from the need that all persons have to interact with the environment and the others who coexist in their environment. Bishop noted that lists of cultural universals by anthropologists such as Murdock (1945) include relevant items such as calendars, numerals, and games, which fit with Bishop's own assertion about the ubiquitous nature of mathematical activities.

Just as cultures can be examined for their mathematical practices, the discipline of mathematics as found in the school curriculum and Western society can be analyzed as a cultural system and as the product of particular cultural traditions. As stated many years ago by the anthropologist Leslie White, "Mathematical truths exist in the cultural tradition into which an individual is born" (1949, p. 285), in contradistinction to the belief that mathematics is a universal truth. White's assertion that Western mathematics can be understood as a culturally based way of thinking (1947, 1949) was extended by the mathematician Wilder (1960, 1981) with examples from the history of mathematics and different branches of mathematics. These ideas have been extended through continuing analysis of the origins and culture of formal mathematics (Davis & Hersh, 1981; Kline, 1972; Lakoff & Nuñez, 2000. Thus, as Bishop (1988) argued, learning formal mathematics is a process of enculturation because it has its own symbolic technology and values that arose to meet particular societal needs. Understanding the mathematics of other cultures can also enhance one's understanding of the mathematics students learn in school because all are forms of cultural practice.

More recently, some anthropologists have turned from examining "traditional" cultures to studying contemporary society and the everyday activities in which mathematics are used. An example is the work of Lave, Murtaugh, and de la Rocha (de la Rocha, 1985; Lave, 1988; Lave, Murtaugh, & de la Rocha, 1984; Murtaugh, 1985) in which they examined the shopping, dieting, and cooking activities of middle-class American adults. Although the participants in their studies had the tools of formal mathematics available to them from school, their use of mathematics for practical purposes was quite different from school mathematics and perhaps even more effective. Many others have examined the mathematics in contemporary activities as diverse as candy selling in Brazil (Saxe, 1991), to carpet laying (Masingila, 1994), to automobile production work (Smith, 2002). Such research supports Bishop's contention that mathematics can be found in many different activities and may not even be perceived by the actors as an example of mathematics per se. Furthermore, less formalized mathematical practice is not a characteristic of less developed or nonliterate traditions, but a feature of human life wherever it may occur.

Ethnomathematics has both extended and deepened the work done by anthropologists. Often anthropologists are not concerned enough to discern the complexity of mathematics inherent in many cultural practices and instead have simply focused on the basic systems of arithmetic and counting. Partnerships, between anthropologists and mathematicians (e.g., Ascher & Ascher, 1981), or between mathematicians working from anthropological descriptions or with anthropological methods (Ascher, 2002; Eglash, Bennett, O'Donnell, Jennings, & Cintorino, 2006; Zalavsky, 1973), have revealed the mathematics inherent in cultural activities or "frozen" in the artifacts produced by diverse peoples (Gerdes, 1988). With their focus on mathematics, practitioners of ethnomathematics are actively documenting the richness of mathematics throughout the world as described in the reviews of D'Ambrosio (2006) and Gerdes (1997).

For students and teachers of mathematics, the cultural nature of mathematics means that all communities and cultures have a corpus of mathematical practices which can be discerned and studied. Some information is available in the ethnographic record of societies as the descriptions of cultural practices in the areas identified by Bishop (1988), while ethnomathematicians have described a wider variety of mathematic practices that can serve as resources for teachers. Everyday life is also a source for understanding mathematical concepts. Ethnomathematic practice can be seen as a method used to discern the mathematics that have been used by people in the creation of the material culture (Gerdes, 1988; Were, 2003), or in their everyday discourse (Walkerdine, 1988), as well as in the documentation of mathematical practices. The examples in this chapter demonstrate how ethnomathematics is productively used in classrooms.

In addition to documenting the diversity of human cultures and mathematical practices, the field of anthropology has research methods and theories that can be used to better understand how humans learn and conceptualize mathematics. Ethnographic research in education has been characterized as having a focus on context; and as using an interpretive lens to understand the meanings that are ascribed to schools and other learning situations by the participants. Traditionally, however, cognition and learning have been the purview of other disciplines, primarily psychology. Thus cognition and context have been treated as separate domains of research, thereby limiting understanding, for instance, of how educational innovation can improve learning (Jacob, 1997) or how classroom dynamics and culture enhance or inhibit the learning of mathematics (Eisenhart, 1988). Both Jacob and Eisenhart argued that through long term participation in the contexts where cognition and learning occur, as in the anthropological tradition, researchers can come to understand the ways in which meaning is created. This understanding of cognition applies to the study of how mathematics is both used and contextualized. Although it is important to remember that mathematics can be considered a system of knowledge, the nature of this knowledge is often seen in how people use it for a particular purpose.

As a result of her research on "everyday" mathematics in Liberia with tailors (Lave, 1977) and in the United States with middle-class adults (Lave, 1988), Lave challenged the widely held belief that arithmetic (and by implication mathematics) is a general skill that is taught in school and then directly applied in many contexts. Rather, cognition, including mathematical cognition, is "socially organized and quintessentially social in its very existence, its formation, and its ongoing character" (Lave, 1988, p. 177). For instance, tailors gave change in money transactions in ways that made the mathematics visible to the customer, rather than applying perhaps more efficient place value arithmetic, although Lave's research showed they were equally able to calculate exchanges of standard algorithms. Similarly, grocery shoppers used a variety of proportional reasoning strategies to decide which purchase was a best buy, but these did not entail computation with fractions (Murtaugh, 1985). Rather, shoppers used features of the products to make comparisons that produced accurate decisions.

A more recent example is seen in the work of Ferreira in central Brazil. In this context social values about the exchange of goods transcend simple arithmetic computations. Thus giving away something does not mean ending up with less, as is the case with an arithmetic word problem about subtraction. Ferreira gave the example of this "dilemma" with the following problem: "I caught 10 fish last night and gave 3 of them to my brother. How many fish do I have now?" (Ferreira, 1997 p. 141). Rather than being an example of subtraction, several of her informants saw this as an addition problem with the answer of 13. Their reasoning was that when something is given away, the receiver has a future obligation to reciprocate, thus increasing the number of fish one will "have." Since reciprocity includes a variety of considerations that transcend simple quantitative equivalences, the numerical answer to a problem can vary depending upon the circumstances according to Ferreira's informants. Thus multiple forms of mathematics are involved in solving problems. Ferreira noted that mathematics as taught in school was frequently used as a tool to exploit the Indians, and thus embodied a conflict between local cultural values and capitalist concerns with material profit. In this particular locale, who you are and who you are dealing with influence how you use mathematics. Mathematics in practice becomes an issue of identity as well as a cognitive process.

Some aspects of culturally embedded mathematical knowledge are amenable to formal description, but do not fully capture the mathematical competencies of the people who use that knowledge. The number systems of many cultures have been described and coded in terms of their complexity (Chrisomalis, 2004), but the resulting typologies do not capture the cognitive work that is done with such systems. Reed and Lave (1979) were among the first researchers to explore the ways in which number systems with a different base system were used for solving arithmetic problems. The Vai and Gola traditional number systems used base 5 and 20, and some (but not all aspects of the base system) were used by informants to solve arithmetic problems. Some number systems such as the Yoruba system as described by Verran (2001) were extremely complex in that they include not just a variety of bases, but subtractive and multiplicative relationships. While such an account supports relativist claims that "other" mathematics is not necessarily simpler, Verran (2001) claims that her own description misses essential aspects of Yoruba numerical understanding. By studying the "ritual of gesture," that accompanied the use of Yoruba numbers, Verran came to understand that the system had a totally different conceptualization of unities/multiplicities and that the gestures, at times, indicated numerical conceptualization as vectors rather than groupings.

The understandings gained by Ferreira (1997), Lave (1977, 1988), Verran (2001), and others derive from the ethnographic stance of interviewing, living with, and participating in the mathematical practices of people in order to "understand mathematical problem solving *in the same way* as their subjects" (Eisenhart, 1988, p. 110). Part of the challenge of such research is to preserve the contextual and cultural meaning of the mathematics while communicating to audiences from other cultures. For educators and their students, this suggests that using ethnomathematics in the classroom should include more than superficial features of different mathematical systems. Any mathematics is part of a larger knowledge system (Barnhardt & Kawagley, 2005) that determines the nature of the problems to be solved as well as the methods to be used. When such instruction is omitted as is typical in contemporary classrooms, tensions which may impede the learning of some students may arise. Students whose cultural identity is shaped through their enculturation in communities where worldviews are different and distinct from the Eurocentric view, which comprises the Western formalized system of school, must often struggle to interact with a system of education where the philosophical and pedagogical foundations of their cultural traditions are disrespected or completely ignored.

Aikenhead (1998) suggests that the school subjects, such as mathematics and science, actually reflect subcultures of the dominant Western society and that their teaching is an attempt at transmitting specific subculture information to students (p. 87). Students who are not naturally enculturated in the ways of the dominant culture must learn to "cross the border" between school culture and school science (Aikenhead, 1998). Negotiating this border can be problematic for such students, as described by Solomon (1998):

> Science is a strict knowledge culture prescribing the meanings of words, experimental design, the form of explanations, and even the methods of publication of its practitioners. For our students it is a whole new world of thought. Coming to feel comfortable within this new territory is, for most of our young students, as long and slow a process as joining a new tribe might be. To make it even more difficult, the students find that while they learn, their own culture of everyday life and meaning continues to intrude on every side. (p. 171)

In such an environment active learning, healthy growth, and optimal development may become difficult or even unattainable.

Curricular Examples and Cross-Cultural Implications

The use of cultural references and examples in mathematics classrooms increases as teachers begin to see the value of framing the mathematics they teach in a context with which the students are familiar (Lipka, 1998). Such integrations work to validate local knowledge and mathematical applications implemented within the student's community that are typically omitted from curricular inclusion. Gerdes (1988) warns of the harmful effects that may result when educators selectively create divisions between daily life events and what is taught in school. D'Ambrosio contends that mathematical applications and "ways of knowing," which students naturally obtain when entering schools, or what are known as "spontaneous matheracies," can be devalued, overwhelmed, and supplanted by the decontexualized and depersonalized "learned matheracies" of a typical school curriculum (D'Ambrosio, 1985). When students are not allowed, or encouraged, to coconstruct mathematical knowledge they run the risk of discounting who they are and what they know. Furthermore, they may grow to lose interest in learning mathematics or question their ability to be successful in using mathematical skills (Kamii & Dominick, 1998).

Numerous examples exist of teachers who contextualize their mathematics instruction by connecting mathematics and culture, several of which will herein be described. One should note that such instruction is much more than a superficial attempt to enliven instruction; rather, it indicates the complex nature of teaching and learning itself. This instruction that integrates ethnomathematical dimensions reflects a shift in the educational status quo which typically occurs in the mathematics classroom and calls for a discussion of challenging political issues of power such as "whose" way of math is it, and how are "they" being represented in the mathematical instruction.

The artifacts, traditions, and behaviors of a learning community are obvious components of instruction, but subtle pedagogic techniques are included which attune to the natural learning styles and tendencies of those present. School, as a vital aspect of everyday life rather than a separate reality, begins to incorporate those very activities, which are often overlooked and undervalued by emphasizing them within the instruction. Such efforts help to scaffold the instruction, not merely in the activities described, but also by including less obvious yet equally important values, traditions, and cultural nuances of those who are familiar with the activities portrayed in each community.

Learning from Elders

Jerry Lipka and colleagues have been working with Yup'ik elders in southwest Alaska for several decades to develop mathematics curriculum based on elders' knowledge (Lipka, 1998). Everyday and seasonal tasks form the basis upon which these math modules have developed. Elders and the Math in a Cultural Context (MCC) team worked together participating in activities like building a fish rack, star navigating, basket weaving, picking berries, and egging (to name a few). The outcome of this collaboration is a set of supplementary math modules for elementary school students used throughout Alaska. The modules infuse local cultural knowledge in a variety of ways from story knifing where elder women teach young girls necessary cultural knowledge, through stories told and pictures drawn in the tundra soil, to expert-apprentice modeling and Yup'ik ways of counting.

Recent research on the effect of this culturally situated instruction indicates statistically significant results for Yup'ik students, other indigenous students, and students living in Alaska's cities.

Finding Our Way

Star navigation is helping researcher and curriculum developer Engblom-Bradley (2006) find her way as she explores techniques to help the teachers and students with whom she works to better learn the math they study. Similar to the efforts of Lipka, Engblom-Bradley (2006) works with an elder, Fred George, who possesses a lifetime of knowledge of how to travel and survive on the tundra. Reflective of instruction in many indigenous communities, the knowledge is gained through actual application to the information shared. Traditional navigation involves keen awareness of environmental conditions, landmarks, and the positions and movements of stars in the sky. Mathematical connections include time telling, calendrics, angles and their measures, and modular math. Engblom-Bradley (2006) has created student instruction on the Suite of Cultural Situated Design Tools where students apply their newly learned knowledge to tell the month and time of night as well as orient themselves to the cardinal directions.

Reclaiming Identities

In Los Altos, Chiapas, Mexico, Hirsch-Dubin worked with the Maya Tzotzil community members, elected school leadership, teachers, and students at a local autonomous school over a four-year term (2000–2003) to rediscover their indigenous knowledge that historical influences and contemporary instructional practices had marginalized and deemphasized. Learning mathematics was not separated from a focus on developing an active voice in self-determination and consensus building among the participants, which the contemporary state curriculum did not provide. Teachers involved in this project were named "knowledge promoters" to indicate the vital collaborative role they played in deciding what and how things were to be taught.

Hirsch-Dubin, together with promoters, initiated instruction through study of the ancient Mayan numeration system. This included deciphering the base 20 system and learning and using the three symbols (a shell for zero, dot for one, and bar for five) to practice operations and to name values of numbers. Further investigations centered on the mathematics of agricultural practices where historic traditions, such as praying before planting, and in relation to times set by the ancient Mayan calendar were compared with contemporary and recently introduced "scientific" farming methods. The new methods tend to disregard traditional practices and planting times and encourage the use of new hybrid seed varieties rather than using traditional seed types grown in the past millennium.

Knowledge of traditional measurement systems described by promoters was gathered and shared with students learning math skills in the context of determining the size of a cornfield or measuring patterns and designs created by weavers constructing textiles for use in daily applications. Throughout the instructional interactions, promoters and students were challenged to compare and contrast how Mayan mathematics relates to the European-centered mathematics typically taught, and how knowing the mathematical practices of one's people validates one's culture and allows for a greater voice in determining the direction of the teaching and authenticates who owns the knowledge. Hirsch-Dubin relates, "This work with Mayan ethnomathematicians at this autonomous school in Los Altos of Chiapas indicates that the struggle to regain knowledge removed by over 500 years of colonial practices, takes years to overturn. Important inroads are being made but need to be deepened in the future." (P. Hirsch-Dubin, personal communication, July 2006).

Renewing Resources

Indian Summer was the name given to a six-year project implemented by high school science teacher, Ed Galindo, to help his students acquire necessary mathematics, science, technology, and research instruction. Galindo strove to do this within a cultural and environmental context while working to reintroduce endangered salmon and steelhead into lifeless rivers where the Shoshone-Bannock people once fished in the wilderness of what is now central Idaho (Galindo & Barta, 2001).

Students incorporated their study of mathematics (as it related to topics including ecology, chemistry, water science, and environmental education) and applied concepts typically learned in the school classroom to experiment with their fish recovery project along the Salmon River basins. Additionally, the students were taught the value of preserving habitat as they studied problems which result from people estranging themselves from the "circle of life."

A key focus of the project centered on research aiming to see if student efforts using wilderness streamside incubators could hatch and successfully release up to 60,000 hatchery spawned fish, and if those fish would make the 2,400 mile, four-year return trip, to the Pacific Ocean. Shoshone-Bannock elders supplemented the academic instruction with knowledge of traditional ceremonies and prayers for interacting with the fish. The project merged traditional learning with the most contemporary technology, including data being relayed from the incubators to school labs via communication satellite systems.

Preliminary data suggest that the project was successful with the incubated eggs, resulting in a survival rate equal to that raised in a typical hatchery. Time will tell if there are sufficient numbers of returning fish to renew and revitalize these "dead" rivers and streams. Students gained a deeper awareness of their cultural identities and the impact they have on their world as they combined traditional beliefs and values with modern techniques and tools.

Expanding Cultures

African cornrow hair braiding, a popular hairstyle among a number of African Americans (Eglash et al., 2006), set the context for study and experiences specifically designed to reflect interests among students of inner city schools and other areas with large African-American student populations. Photos students took of themselves or of friends modeling various braiding styles served as the model in which complex geometric concepts involving aspects of fractal geometry were presented.

Eglash and colleagues have constructed an online suite of culturally situated design tools where students can learn mathematical concepts as they use the tools to describe their various hairstyles in both visual and mathematical terms.

Students were challenged to consider whether stylists capable of such skill in braiding were mathematicians. Eglash et al. report (2006) that some students insisted that they had been using mathematics throughout but had just not considered the skill as being mathematical. Others suggested that unconscious intuition was practiced, but that the computer graphic tool use was simply an enjoyable way to learn. Students considered the changes that occurred when certain variables were altered; furthermore, they were encouraged to use the graphic tools to design their own patterns. Even those students who, in more traditional classes, were reported as unmotivated became seemingly engrossed in creating patterns that illustrated a particular topic or image of personal importance. Eglash et al., in considering the experience a success, suggest that the "fundamental goal for design tools is to empower the students' sense of ownership over math and computing" (p. 351). They continue,

> It seems less a question of ethnic pride than one of context and motivation: given a chance to incorporate some agency into their encounter—to creatively improvise with these cultural materials—these students often find it fascinating. It is not simply a matter of using a static, pre-formed identity to "lure" students into doing math or computing. (p. 351)

The ethnomathematical goal is to create a culture-enriched computational medium that offers students new opportunities in identity self-construction. These opportunities will provide the students with critical tools and perspectives needed for both social and technical domains, as well as the interrelationships between the two (Eglash et al., 2006. p. 358).

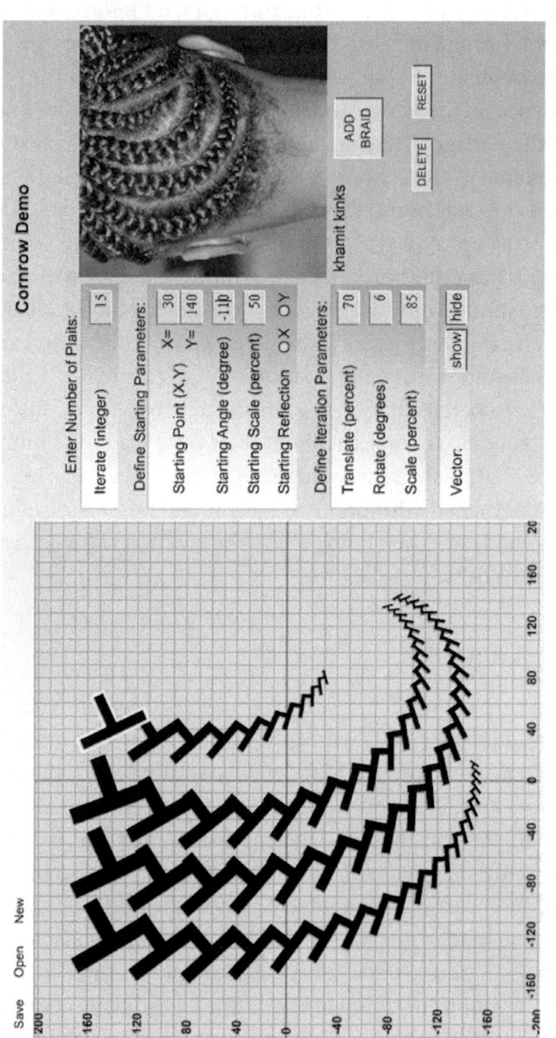

Figure 4.1 Cornrow curves: At right an original hair style selected by the student, at left the student's simulation, generated by the parameters in the center control panel.

Mathematical Empowerment

Knijik (1998) discusses in her research how ethnomathematics and political struggles in the development of educational efforts by teachers, students, parents, peasants, and technicians of a Brazilian "Landless Peoples Movement" improve their social, economic, and instructional situations. Documented are the efforts of people who are striving for social justice through land reform, which is currently brought about through increased education. Knijik describes the inclusion of local knowledge in the developing curriculum and reports on the reciprocal nature of this influence on the school and its students along with the "knowledge produced during the pedagogical process pouring out from the school space" (1998, p. 188). Students of the school in a small settlement in southern Brazil studied debt records to understand the mathematics of loans and rates of interest. Students debated implications of family debt and proposed solutions for minimizing or eliminating this burden. Furthermore, students, with the help of agrarian specialists, studied optimal ways to farm the land in order to receive the most return on their investments. These empowering efforts increased their understanding and use of various mathematical principles, and further deepened their awareness of the social situations in which they live. This transformative process did more than help them learn about their people and the multitude of challenges they face. Rather, their knowledge is helping to develop a new generation of farmers strengthened with political insight and possessing educational capabilities, which will foster their being able to better direct and determine the outcomes of their own lives.

Recalling Traditional Ways

> I often reflect on this experience. It was an amazing opportunity for me to learn as I observed John Bear's teaching. There existed so much modeling of ideas that permeated all of his pedagogy, something very important for me to better understand as I work with in-service and preservice teachers that need to be aware that their pedagogy needs to be inclusive of local pedagogy. John's interactions with the students were also personal and meaningful. He and I particularly appreciated how the students engaged in the tasks and began to rely on what they had immediately available, which is a reference to using body parts for measurement. One particular case stands out where a young girl trying to assure that horizontally placed lodge pole braces were parallel used the distance from her elbow to her closed fist, which then became the "standard" measurement for parallel. This was exciting to watch, the mathematics coming to life in these experiences for school children. (Shockey, personal communication, 2006)

At a middle school encampment in the fall of 2004, nearly 140 students and teachers came together to learn about the traditional housing construction used by their ancestors, the Wabanaki. The site selected for the gathering was on land where the Wabanaki have lived for centuries in what is now part of southern Maine.

The goal of the two-week long activity (Shockey, personal communication, 2005) was to immerse local Native and non-Native students in learning traditional Wabanaki house building techniques while integrating stories and legends, mathematics, science, and social studies. John Bear Mitchell, the Associate Director for the Wabanaki Center at the University of Maine, shared traditional knowledge he had learned throughout his life from the Elders who had guided and taught him in building a Wabanaki Wigwam, a hemispherical lodge constructed with local natural materials. The instruction reflected a number of traditional instructional practices which relied heavily on group cooperation as Mitchell first demonstrated a skill, answered any questions, and then encouraged students to apply their newly learned skills while he guided and supported their efforts.

Students actively participated in applying the ancestral engineering techniques used by their people in building the lodges and secondary buildings and items to be found in any traditional village. Wabanaki ways of knowing were integrated in the activities and discussions along with the seamless incorporation of mathematical concepts and applications. Students oriented the lodge doorways to the east to capture the first rays of the sun. Discoveries were made as to the insulation qualities of certain grasses and the benefit of building in the round versus constructing square or rectangular homes of the same perimeter.

Initially, students and some teachers were skeptical that mathematics were present in these everyday activities. As students used parts of their bodies as measurement units or determined the angle at which lodge poles must be driven into the ground (before being bent toward the center and lashed together—poles set vertically could spring out dangerously when pressure is applied), they began to marvel at the fact that math was in everything. One teacher, after seeing yet another example of mathematics in application, was overheard to ask, "So math is there too?"—only to quickly add, "Make it stop!" (T. Shockey, personal communication, July 2006).

Together teachers and students learned about and participated not only in the construction of dwellings but also in the knowledge which had supported the people in the past. This reconnection of past and present entrenched and expanded an awareness of what it means to be Wabanaki and how such knowledge will serve as an asset to the individual and collective.

Building Upon Children's Thinking

A different approach to enhancing mathematics instruction is seen in the work of Brenner (1998a, 1998b) who combined ethnographic and cognitive research (Moschkovich & Brenner, 2000) to work with elementary teachers to improve instruction with Native Hawaiian children. Children at the Kamehameha School received instruction in Hawaiian language and culture as a regular part of their curriculum. In addition, instructional arrangements had been adapted to build upon the children's cultural practices of cooperation and individual responsibility. However, mathematics instruction still followed the traditional textbook topics, without great success. Teachers did not see the mathematical competencies that children brought from their homes and communities, and the children found their mathematics lessons irrelevant or frustrating. Brenner observed children in their homes and schools to discover how children used mathematics in their daily lives. She also interviewed children and administered specially designed written tests to uncover the children's skills as displayed in tasks similar to those outside of school and those typically required at school.

Brenner found that the children began school with good counting skills, an understanding of quantitative relationships, and a functional understanding of the money system. She also discovered that for many children quantitative vocabulary was more developed in Hawaiian Creole English (HCE), known locally as *pidgin*, than in the Standard English that was the exclusive language for mathematics in the classroom. Further, the presentation of certain topics such as using money as a model for the base 10 system was in clear conflict with the ways in which the children understood the mathematical relationships instantiated in money and the ways in which children used money in their everyday lives. At the same time, the textbook curriculum assumed that children had certain vocabulary and skills that were not in fact well developed in everyday activities. As a result, children came to devalue their own mathematical intuitions and disengaged from classroom instruction.

In cooperation with the teachers, and considering the constraints of typical classrooms, a number of principled changes were made in mathematics instruction. The goal was to build from children's strengths and to engage them in mathematical activities that were meaningful to them. The first change was to use HCE vocabulary as way to teach Standard English vocabulary in mathematics. The second change was to reorder the presentation of topics, beginning where the students had strengths rather than trying first to remediate "weaknesses." In kindergarten this meant beginning with counting and simple computation rather than vocabulary related to position and one-to-one correspondence. The third change was to incorporate more hands-on activities and to spend less time on workbook activities. Although this is in accord with the recommendations of reform mathematics, teachers sometimes worked from a deficiency model in which they felt they had to compensate for homes where books may not have been used by parents for teaching their children. The fourth change was to incorporate what the children saw as more authentic activities that required use of mathematics. For kindergarten children this meant including more games into the classroom, since games were popular in their homes. For second graders, this meant running a school store and practicing computation in the course of acting as cashier or checking the inventory of supplies.

In both kindergarten and second grade, these changes resulted in significantly improved test scores (Brenner, 1998a) as well as more smoothly functioning classrooms. The children became more active agents in their own learning and their competencies were more clearly apparent to the teachers. The teachers themselves began to initiate changes in their instruction outside of the research project. Most of the teachers themselves grew up speaking HCE and following the local style for cooking and other everyday activities. But such knowledge had been devalued in their own education and not seen as a resource for teaching. Thus teachers as well as students became freer of the "authority" of the textbook and began to incorporate their lived experience into the classroom.

Cross-Curricular Implications

The cross-curricular implications demonstrated in each of the described settings provide vivid illustrations for how important mathematical skills and concepts can be taught using cultural connections. The context of the setting influences not only what skills can be most appropriately accessed through their analysis but provides a guide for the selection and use of the most efficient culturally sensitive instruction.

Each of the examples of culturally situated mathematics instruction illustrates common threads in their application: (1) Teachers or promoters situate their instruction in lived experiences of those they teach resulting in increased cultural awareness. (2) Collaborative efforts are apparent as community experts and teachers team to share knowledge and experience of the culture and context thereby sharing more equally decisions involving what should be taught and how. (3) Empowerment and greater self-determination are emphasized, which helps those for whom the culturally responsive instruction has been developed to reclaim their created voices and knowledge.

Teachers as Promoters and Conveyors of Culture

Not all teachers are aware of the role culture plays in the education process or even see themselves as being cultural. In studies of teacher education students entering multicultural foundations courses, Brown (1998) and Lehman (1993) found that students project various stages of resistance. The stages reflected in phases of resistance were predicated on the degree of their previous cross-cultural experiences and were influenced by the individual's current worldview. Efforts to diminish resistance do not appear to affect everyone similarly because of personal variability, perceptions, and experience.

Value judgment changes are not static (West & Pines, 1985) but rather unpredictably incremental and seem to be related to the continuous reevaluation and modification of a person's existing frame of reference. Teacher training designed to examine self-concept, perception, and motivation may generate more receptive attitudes toward multicultural awareness and sensitivities (Fried, 1993; Lehman, 1993). Banks (1995) argues that such inquiry must include a study of individual history and how this relates to one's current beliefs and values.

Teachers must first come to understand their identity as members of various cultural communities if they are to become capable of understanding the necessity of teaching their students to identify their own place, purpose, and position as cultural members. Several years ago, during a workshop on cultural diversity, a teacher reacted to a presentation from a speaker (the first author) who had shared his reflections on being Mexican born and moving at an early age to the United States. The speaker described that during his formative years, his Spanish-speaking parents and grandparents taught him the values and traditions that sustained them in their lives. They helped him learn an identity, which made him proud and confident of his abilities even when those around him prejudged him. He had shared his insights into the values of his parents, which strengthened him during particular challenges in his life. The teacher, a middle-aged, Caucasian woman, who had always lived in the same area of the state where the majority of people around her shared a common ancestral heritage and practiced the dominant religion, was greatly moved by the powerful story of tenacity and persistence, and she confessed. "I wish I had a culture!"

Borba (1997) explains,

> A human is only seen in connection with the world. She/he cannot be seen without the world; neither can the world be seen without her/him. Moreover, the concept "human" and "world" themselves are intrinsically linked since both terms reflect meanings, which have been constructed by humans. Each human relates to other humans based on comprehensions: understanding existing meanings and making new meanings. Each person is always in a place in the world and living in a historical moment. (p. 262)

Teachers who do not consider their own cultural identities run the risk of not accepting and respecting the diversity in cultures displayed by their students. Whorf (1940) suggests as human beings we are enculturated by the codes, language, and values of those around us. Our community affiliations shape who we are as individuals because our participation in these communities helps to shape the cultural influences surrounding us. Whorf (1940,) stated,

> We dissect nature along lines laid down by our native languages. The categories and types that we isolate from the world of phenomena we do not find there because they stare every observer in the face; on the contrary, the world is presented in a kaleidoscopic flux of impressions which has to be organized by our minds—and this means largely by the linguistic systems in our minds. We cut nature up, organize it into concepts, and ascribe significances as we do, largely because we are parties to an agreement to organize it in this way—an agreement that holds throughout our speech community and is codified in the patterns of our language. The agreement is, of course, an implicit and unstated one, but its terms are absolutely

> obligatory; we cannot talk at all except by subscribing to the organization and classification of data, which the agreement decrees. (pp. 213–214)

So how do teachers become more aware of the cultures which surround them and use this understanding as the basis for making contextual instructional connections in the mathematics classroom? A model for instigating this shift in teacher perception and practice involves ethnographic techniques often used in anthropology. Using the six universals of human behavior (Bishop, 1988) involving mathematics, counting, measuring, locating, designing, explaining, and playing, educators can be taught to seek out and conduct semistructured mathematical/cultural interviews of cultural experts in their communities (see appendix A).

Knowledge gained from the experts illustrates deeper dimensions of the art, craft, or skill practiced in the community along with the inseparable beliefs and values inherent in the process. From this, teachers can develop instruction inclusive of local culture using the stepped model provided. Teachers can:

1. Interview experts/elders/cultural representatives who will describe a particular activity important to the cultural community and share not only content knowledge but also related beliefs, values, and traditions related to the doing of the activity. Such experts often maintain a special respect in the community and their words and presence can establish motivation as well as credibility for what will be taught.
2. Examine the knowledge gained for curricular connections to the core mathematical objectives or expected curricular standards. A list of possibilities is made and one or more mathematical principles/concepts to teach are selected.
3. Design a lesson or series of lessons around the selected principle or concept. The lesson, while focused on the mathematics to be learned can also include objectives to inform students of important cultural knowledge and practices. Information is presented using a variety of techniques but the main instructional emphasis should be on cooperative problem solving using materials/models and hands-on interaction. The context of the culturally relevant application provides additional opportunities to share and discuss the values, beliefs, and traditions inherent in application. Students should be encouraged to establish a personal understanding of what is studied and offer their newly gained knowledge/wisdom in circles of sharing during the activity.
4. Assess using performance-based techniques. Attitudinal as well as cognitive evaluations can be established. The process a student has exhibited in the completion of an activity will often be as good if not a better demonstration of learning as that of the final product. Primary in the learning is the degree to which the learner establishes personal meaning for use in life and for the benefit of the community.

An example of teachers learning to become more aware of the role of culture in education and how to better reflect community culture in their mathematics instruction follows (Barta & Orey, 2008). Teachers in Santa Avelina, a rural community of several thousand in the highlands of Guatemala, are learning to prepare lessons that incorporate local cultural situations, values, and traditions as they work with math specialists from HELPS International, a nonprofit organization based in Dallas. HELPS organizes volunteer teams to provide medical and educational assistance to rural indigenous villagers. The region, which is located in what is called the Ixil Triangle, is populated with people of Mayan descent who speak various Mayan dialects as well as Spanish and who maintain a number of practices of traditional Mayan life.

The landscape is dotted with small homes whose male occupants farm the surrounding hillsides to provide food for themselves and their family and when possible grow extra for sale at the weekly markets. Women, the traditional weavers of the community, create various multicolored textile items to be shaped into clothes or bags, straps, or wraps for personal use or for sale.

Education for children is encouraged but not mandatory and some children are obligated to work to help sustain the family economy. The government provides the existing Guatemalan State Core curriculum and commercial texts when available are written in Spanish. The state-provided curriculum is not responsive to or inclusive of the local Mayan languages, culture, or heritage.

The teachers of Santa Avelina have been receiving instruction (Barta & Orey, 2008) to better understand the role and influence of culture in the educational process through the HELPS in-services provided. Members of the community whose professions include farming, house building, weaving, and bicycle and small engine repair are interviewed by teachers to document where and how they use mathematical principles in their daily endeavors. This information serves as the basis for making connections to and providing a context for the mathematics taught at the school. Students, some of whom had begun to show disdain for their parents because of their inability to help them with their academic work, are being taught to value the skills and knowledge their parents possess (L. O'Neal, personal communication, June, 2006). The unintentional separation between school and community is disappearing, as parents are valued for their cultural knowledge and expertise. Teachers, formerly viewed as dispensers of academic knowledge, are now respected for their growing ability to contextualize the instruction using information and examples which demonstrate the beauty and dynamic of Ixil culture.

Conclusion

Readers have been provided multiple landscapes for seeing with many eyes the connections which evolve when comparing anthropology and mathematics. The role of culture as it influences the creation and application of mathematics in diverse communities is shown to balance the juxtapositional role mathematics plays in shaping those unique cultures. Together such interactions work to establish symmetry between purpose, place, and those people involved.

It is the hope of the authors that teachers will benefit from the insights and examples shared as a stimulus of change with those they instruct. It is possible that teachers who see themselves in this new light will realize how closely they physically represent and extend the interrelationship between anthropology and education and the critical role they play in helping students themselves see their mathematical potential and their responsibility for learning it well, clearly, and profoundly.

Appendix A

Date: ______________ Interviewer's Initials__________
Name of person interviewed ____
Title/Occupation ____

Please use these questions as a guide for your cultural interview. Consider it a conversation where you are trying to discover more about how this person uses mathematics specific to who they are and what they do. Not all questions listed will be necessarily appropriate for your particular interview. Please remember to add a short piece when you are done describing the insights you have gained. Try to question in all six categories.

Counting

How do you count things in what you do?
Special names for counting numbers?
Written symbols?
How did you describe "0"?
How did you describe "infinity"?
Are numbers represented using body parts or gestures?
Do you count in any special groups such as by 5s or 10s? Are certain things counted in groups?
Are large numbers used? How are large numbers described?
Do many numbers have any special significance?
What else can you do with your numbers besides count with them—subtract, multiply, divide?
Are fractions used?
Other?

Measurement

Do you use a particular kind of standard unit in what you do?
Do you use parts of the body as specific units?

Are specific tools used as measurement devices?
How are small things measured/described?
How are large things measured/described?
How are great distances measured/described?
How is rate/speed measured/described?
How is weight measured/described?
How is time (hours, minutes, etc.?) measured/described?
Is some sort of calendar used?
How is temperature measured/described?
How are perimeter, area, volume measured/described?
Other?

Locating

Are "maps" used?
How are things described spatially—their orientation in a particular place?
Left/right?
Up/down?
Above/below?
Depth/height?
Horizontal/vertical?
Cardinal directions?
Navigation?
Is sorting/classifying (of objects) used in any way?
Other?

Designing

What shapes are used for various purposes?
Names?
Spiritual significance of shapes?
Angles (square angle)?
What patterns are important and how are they constructed (tessellations)?
Designs for clothing, pottery, etc.?
Other?

Explaining

Are specific values recorded in any way; i.e., graphs?
How is wealth/prominence shown?
Other?

Playing

Are special games played and how? Special tokens used?
How are things scored?
Other?

Comments/Insights of Interviewer:

References

Aikenhead, G. (1998). Border crossing: Culture, school science and assimilation of students. In D. A. Roberts & L. Ostman (Eds.), *Problems of Meaning in Science Curriculum* (pp. 86–100). New York: Teachers College Press.

Ascher, M. (2002). *Mathematics elsewhere: An exploration of mathematics across cultures.* Princeton, NJ: Princeton University Press.

Ascher, M., & Ascher, R. (1981). *Code of the quipu: A study in media, mathematics, and culture.* Ann Arbor, MI: University of Michigan Press.

Banks, J. A. (1995). Multicultural education: Historical development, dimensions, and practice. In J. A. Banks & C. A. McGee Banks (Eds.), *Handbook of research on multicultural education* (pp. 3–24). New York: Simon & Schuster.

Barnhardt, R., & Kawagley, O. (2005). Indigenous knowledge systems and Alaska native ways of knowing. *Anthropology and Education Quarterly, 36*(1), 8–23.

Bar ta, J., & Orey, D. (2008). It takes a village: Culturally responsive professional development and creating professional learning communities in Guatemala. *Journal of Mathematics Education Leadership, 10.*

Barth, F. (2002). Toward a richer description and analysis of cultural phenomena. In R. G. Fox & B. J. King (Eds.), *Anthropology beyond culture* (pp. 23–36). New York: Berg.

Berlak, A., & Berlak, H. (1981). *Dilemmas of schooling: Teaching and social change.* New York: Methuen.

Bishop, A. (1988). *Mathematical enculturation: A cultural perspective on mathematics education.* Dordrecht, The Netherland: Kluwer.

Borba, M. (1997). Ethnomathematics and education. In A. B. Powell & M. Frankenstein (Eds.), *Ethnomathematics: Challenging Eurocentrism in mathematics education* (pp. 261–272). Albany, NY: SUNY.

Borofsky, R., Barth, F., Shweder, R. A., Rodseth, L., & Stolzenberg, N. M. (2001). WHEN: A conversation about culture. *American Anthropologist, 103*(3), 432–446.

Brenner, M. E. (1998a). Adding cognition to the formula for culturally relevant instruction in mathematics. *Anthropology and Education Quarterly, 29,* 214–244.

Brenner, M. E. (1998b). Meaning and money. *Educational Studies in Mathematics, 36,* 123–155.

Brown, E. L. (1998). The relevance of self-concept and instructional design in transforming Caucasian preservice teachers' monocultured world-views to multicultural perceptions and behaviors (Doctoral dissertation, The University of Akron). *Dissertation Abstracts International, 59,* 7, A2450.

Chrisomalis, S. (2004). A cognitive typology for numerical notation. *Cambridge Archaeological Journal, 14,* 37–52.

D'Ambrosio, U. (1985). Ethnomathematics and its place in the history and pedagogy of mathematics. *For the Learning of Mathematics, 5,* 44–48.

D'Ambrosio, U. (1997). Where does ethnomathematics stand nowadays? *For the Learning of Mathematics, 17,* 13–17.

D'Ambrosio, U. (2001). What is ethnomathematics, and how can it help children in schools? *Teaching Children Mathematics, 7,* 308–310.

D'Ambrosio, U. (2006). *Ethnomathematics: Link between tradition and modernity.* Rotterdam, The Netherlands: Sense.

Davis, P. J., & Hersh, R. (1981). *The mathematical experience.* Boston: Houghton Mifflin.

de la Rocha, O. (1985). The reorganization of arithmetic practice in the kitchen. *Anthropology & Education Quarterly, 16,* 193–198.

Eglash, R., Bennett, A., O'Donnell, C., Jennings, S., & Cintorino, M. (2006). Culturally situated design tools: Ethnocomputing from field site to classroom. *American Anthropologist, 108,* 347–362.

Eisenhart, M. A. (1988). The ethnographic research tradition and mathematics education research. *Journal for Research in Mathematics Education, 19,* 99–114.

Engblom-Bradley, C. (2006). Learning the Yup'ik way of navigation: Studying time, position, and direction. *Journal of Mathematics and Culture, 1*(1), 91–126.

Ferreira, M. K. L. (1997). When 1+1≠2: Making mathematics in central Brazil. *American Ethnologist, 24,* 132–147.

Fox, R. G., & King, B. J. (Eds.). (2002). *Anthropology beyond culture* (pp. 23–36). New York: Berg.

Fried, J. (1993). Bridging emotion and intellect: Classroom diversity in process. *College Teaching, 41*(4), 123–128.

Galindo, E., & Barta, J. (2001). Indian summer: A hands-on, feet wet approach to science education. *Winds of Change: American Indian Science and Engineering Society, 16*(4), 54–56.

Gerdes, P. (1988). On culture, geometrical thinking and mathematics education. *Educational Studies in Mathematics, 19,* 137–162.

Gerdes, P. (1997). Survey of current work in ethnomathematics. In A. B. Powell & M. Frankenstein (Eds.), *Ethnomathematics: Challenging Eurocentrism in mathematics education* (pp. 331–372). Albany, NY: SUNY Press.

Hirsch-Dubin, P. (2005). Evolution of a dream: The emergence of Mayan ethnomathematics and expressions of indigenous ways of knowing at a Mayan autonomous school in Chiapas, Mexico. Published Dissertation (ProQuest No. AAT 3190433). Retrieved August 20, 2006, from Dissertations and Theses database.

Jackson, P. W. (1990). *Life in classrooms.* New York: Teachers College Press.

Jacob, E. (1997). Context and cognition: Implications for educational innovators and anthropologists. *Anthropology and Education Quarterly, 28,* 3–21.

Kamii, C., & Dominick, A. (1998). The harmful effects of algorithms in grades 1–4. In L. J. Morrow & M. J. Kenney (Eds.), *The teaching and learning of algorithms in school mathematics:1998 yearbook* (pp. 130–140). Reston, VA: National Council of Teachers of Mathematics.

Kline, M. (1972). *Mathematical thought from ancient to modern times.* New York: Oxford University Press.

Knijnik, G. (1998) Ethnomathematics and political struggle. *ZDM Zentralblat fur didaktik der Mathematik, 30*(6), 188–194.

Lakoff, G., & Núñez, R. E. (2000). *Where mathematics comes from: How the embodied mind brings mathematics into being.* New York: Basic Books.

Lave, J. (1977). Cognitive consequences of traditional apprenticeship training in West Africa. *Anthropology and Education Quarterly, 8,* 177–180.

Lave, J. (1988). *Cognition in practice: Mind, mathematics and culture in everyday life.* New York: Cambridge University Press.

Lave, J., Murtaugh, M., & de la Rocha, O. (1984). The dialectic of arithmetic in grocery shopping. In B. Rogoff & J. Lave (Eds.), *Everyday cognition: Its development in social context* (pp. 67–94). Cambridge, MA: Harvard University Press.

Lehman, P. R. (1993). The emotional challenge of ethnic studies classes. *College Teaching, 40*(4), 134–137.

Lévi-Strauss, C. (1985). *The view from afar.* Chicago: Chicago University Press.

Lipka, J. (1998). Expanding curricular and pedagogical possibilities: Yup'ik-based mathematics, science, and literacy. In J. Lipka, with G. V. Mohatt & the Ciulistet Group (Eds.), *Transforming the culture of schools: Yup'ik Eskimo examples* (pp. 139–181). Mahwah, NJ: Erlbaum.

Masingila, J. O. (1994). Mathematics practice in carpet laying. *Anthropology and Education Quarterly, 25,* 430–462.

Moschkovich, J. & Brenner, M. E. (2000). Using a naturalistic lens on mathematics and science cognition and learning. In A. E. Kelly & R. Lesh (Eds.), *Research design in mathematics and science education* (pp. 457–486). Mahwah, NJ: Erlbaum.

Murdock, G. P. (1945). The common denominator of culture. In R. Linton (Ed.), *The science of man in the world crisis* (pp. 123–142). New York: Columbia University Press.

Murtaugh, M. (1985). The practice of arithmetic by American grocery shoppers. *Anthropology and Education Quarterly, 16*, 186–192.

Powell, A. B., & Frankenstein, M. (Eds.). (1997). *Ethnomathematics: Challenging Eurocentrism in mathematics education.* Albany, NY: SUNY Press.

Reed, H. J., & Lave, J. (1979). Arithmetic as a tool for investigating relations between culture and cognition. *American Ethnologist, 6*, 568–582.

Saxe, G. B. (1991). *Culture and cognitive development: Studies in mathematical understanding.* Hillsdale, NJ: Erlbaum.

Secada, W. G. (Ed.). (2000). *Perspectives on multiculturalism and gender equity* (Changing the Faces of Mathematics). Reston, VA: National Council of Teachers of Mathematics.

Shockey, T. (2005). Wabanaki Wigwams: Traditional knowledge through mathematics. *Winds of Change: American Indian Science and Engineering Society, 20* (2), 54–56.

Smith, J. P. III (2002). Everyday mathematical activity in automobile production work. In M. E. Brenner & J. N. Moschkovich (Eds.), *Everyday and academic mathematics in the classroom* (pp. 111–130). Reston, VA: National Council of Teachers of Mathematics.

Solomon, J. (1998). The science curricula of Europe and the notion of scientific culture. In D. A. Roberts & L. Ostman (Eds.), *Problems of meaning in science curriculum* (pp. 166–177). New York: Teachers College Press.

Spindler, G. (Ed.). (2000). *Fifty years of anthropology and education, 1950–2000: A Spindler anthology.* Mahwah, NJ: Erlbaum.

Verran, H. (2001). *Science and an African logic*. Chicago: University of Chicago.

Walkerdine, V. (1988). *The mastery of reason: Cognitive development and the production of rationality.* New York: Routledge.

Were, G. (2003). Objects of learning: Anthropological approach to mathematics education. *Journal of Material Culture*, 8, 25–44.

West, L., & Pines, A. L. (1985). Introduction. In L. West & A. L. Pines (Eds.), *Cognitive structure and conceptual change* (pp. 1–7). Orlando, FL: Academic Press.

White, L. (1957). The locus of mathematical reality: An anthropological footnote. *Philosophy of Science, 14*, 289–303.

White, L. (1949). *The science of culture.* New York: Farrar, Straus.

Whorf, B. L. (1940). Science and linguistics. *Technology Review, 42*(6), 229–231.

Wilder, R. L. (1960). Mathematics: A cultural phenomenon. In G. E. Dole & R. L. Carneiro (Eds.), *Essays in the science of culture: In honor of Leslie A. White* (pp. 471–485). New York: Crowell.

Wilder, R. L. (1981). *Mathematics as a cultural system.* New York: Pergamon Press.

Zaslavsky, C. (1973). *Africa counts.* Boston: Prindle, Weber, & Schmidt.

5
What Mathematics Teachers Need to Know about Culture and Language

JUDIT MOSCHKOVICH AND SHARON NELSON-BARBER

For some time now, school improvement efforts have been inextricably linked to the steady demographic shifts of our nation's student populations. With more and more students speaking home languages other than English and representing cultural traditions outside those of mainstream America, teachers now need more and better cultural and linguistic knowledge in order to teach effectively (Wong-Fillmore & Snow, 2000). In actuality, American society has long been diverse, but it is only in recent decades that large numbers of educators have recognized that education guided solely by Western European-American values and experiences (representing the dominant culture) is inappropriate or ineffective for many students.

The aim of this chapter is to discuss what mathematics teachers need to know about cultural and language practices that are germane to students' learning mathematics and to the design of mathematics instruction. Students whose cultural communities represent approaches to teaching, learning, and using language that differ from those of the mainstream demand relevant knowledge and understanding from teachers. In our exploration of cultural practices, we focus on research and practice within indigenous communities throughout the United States and the Pacific region. In our exploration of language, we focus on English learners, for whom successful instruction also depends upon specialized teacher knowledge and understanding.

At this juncture, four points must be emphasized:

1. Indigenous students who speak English are also likely to be bilingual or to speak a variety of English that is not the same as that used in school.[1]

2. English learners most often come from families whose cultural practices are different from those of the mainstream.
3. Language and culture are of a piece, in that language is a cultural resource and creation that reflects a culture's values, experience, and goals and is used to transmit them across generations. As Nieto (1999) says, "[T]he language, language variety, or dialect one speaks is culture made manifest" (p. 60). This is equally the case in the classroom, where the cultural practices and language (and a particular dialect of it) reign.
4. Perhaps the most powerful language differences lie at the intersection of language and culture. They have to do with the sociocultural aspects of language use—how children and adults are expected to participate in conversation, argument, discussion, story telling, explanation, or recounting of experience (Gee, 1996; Heath, 1983, 1986).

Many of the issues highlighted by a discussion of mathematics instruction and learning are in large part applicable to teaching in general. But mathematics is of special interest because it is so widely thought to be "free" of language and culture. In fact, because mathematics is a multisemiotic system, mathematical practices are highly dependent on natural language as well as other semiotic systems (Abedi, 2003; O'Halloran, 2005; Radford, Bardini, & Sabena, 2007; Sáenz-Ludlow & Presmeg, 2006; Schleppegrell, 2007); and ways of thinking mathematically are, like other ways of thinking, culturally situated (Lave, 1988; Lave & Wenger, 1991; Saxe, 1991; Solano-Flores & Nelson-Barber, 2001).

Meeting these demands for cultural and linguistic knowledge can be quite a challenge for teachers, given the generally inadequate preparation provided by teacher education programs for discerning and building upon linguistic and cultural differences in ways that result in enriched schooling experiences for students from routinely underserved groups (Nelson-Barber, 1999).

Teacher Knowledge

Knowledge about students' cultural and linguistic backgrounds may contribute to teachers' ability to establish the kinds of relationships with students that motivate them to succeed (cf., Nieto, 1996). However, deeper knowledge about the linguistic and cultural practices in students' communities is essential if teachers are to make connections between the content they are trying to teach and what their students already know (Trumbull, Nelson-Barber, & Mitchell, 2002). If, as cultural psychologists contend, the mind itself is forged in a cultural context (cf., Cole, 2002; Kozulin, 1998), to understand students' ways of knowing and learning, teachers need knowledge of the cultural practices within students' communities—especially practices related to communicating, interacting with adults and peers in groups, and constructing knowledge. General recognition that student cultural and linguistic backgrounds matter and that knowledge about them should be sought is relevant to the different kinds of classes that a teacher may have—relatively homogeneous (e.g., a reservation school), mixed (e.g., Latino/a, African American, European American), along with classes that are composed of students from numerous ethnolinguistic groups (e.g., "United Nations"), which are now evident in rural as well as large metropolitan areas. In the absence of such teacher knowledge, classrooms can be places where teachers' assumptions about students' experiences and approaches to learning (Spindler & Spindler, 2000) may combine with subtle, yet damaging, attitudes toward difference, which can serve to widen the distance between teacher and student and between student and school—reducing student engagement and learning (e.g., Nelson-Barber, 1999; Osterman, 2000; Valenzuela, 1999).

The need to communicate across differences in cultural and language practices is an everyday fact of life in today's bilingual and multilingual classrooms. Studies that describe how teachers and students in such classrooms communicate mathematical ideas reveal the complexity of these learning environments (Adler, 1998, 2001; Khisty, 1995, 2001; Khisty & Chval, 2002; Moschkovich, 1999a, 2000, 2002a; Setati, 1998; Setati & Adler, 2001). Teachers need to develop the capacity to see, hear, and build on students' own and varying mathematical ideas, some of which may be rooted in local knowledge systems and community practices (Moll & Gonzalez, 2004). They need to understand that students may use different national languages and dialects to express specialized, discipline-based knowledge, such as mathematics, differently, but that there are also differences across formal and informal language registers.[2]

It is equally important for teachers to be knowledgeable about the home and community practices that are integral to the multiple and hybrid styles of communication that children use in classrooms (Gutiérrez, Baquedano-Lopez, & Alvarez, 2001). Cultural differences in communication style will be apparent across all content areas of the curriculum. Students from some communities, for example various Asian (Ho, 1994; Ryu, 2004) or Latino/a (Greenfield, Quiroz, & Raeff, 2000) groups, may have been socialized to listen respectfully to adults. In contrast, students from other communities, in particular their dominant culture peers, may have been socialized to interact with adults more directly—even to question them (Greenfield et al., 2000; Snow, 1983). Students socialized in these very different ways can be expected to respond quite differently to classroom demands to participate. In other words, teachers need to know something about students' home, community, social, and cultural values and practices and how these may influence classroom interactions across all content areas. Even recognizing that there are such differences and that they are not deficits is an important step for a teacher who is teaching students from a cultural or linguistic community different from her own.

In the following sections, we discuss culture and language separately for the purpose of organizing the chapter and providing grounded examples in which the focus shifts to either language or culture. Nevertheless, readers should bear in mind that a shifting focus does not imply that these aspects of human activity can truly be understood independently of each other.

A Cultural Affirmation Approach to Difference

As a way to frame the many connections among language, culture, and mathematics learning/teaching, we use Brenner's (1998) three-dimensional framework, which reflects a "cultural affirmation approach." That is to say, practices and approaches to learning that are different from those of the dominant culture (reflected in schooling practices) are affirmed rather than denied. This framework identifies three areas central to ensuring that curricula and instructional practice are culturally relevant for students: *cultural content*, *social organization*, and *cognitive resources*.

As Brenner sees it, examining materials and instructional techniques for their *cultural content* can reveal the extent to which mathematical activities utilized in instruction relate to mathematical activities operating in local community practices, no matter what communities students come from. For instance, in an agricultural setting, mathematical concepts and operations can be taught as they pertain to crop planning, rotation, harvesting, and marketing. Where fishing and navigation are prominent, instruction can capitalize on community-based practices of predicting and measuring tides, calculating navigational routes, estimating the food yield of a catch, and the like.

Similarly, ensuring that classroom *social organization* takes into account a variety of possible roles, responsibilities, and communication styles and includes multiple and hybrid repertoires of practice (Gutiérrez & Rogoff, 2003) will more likely support comfortable and productive student participation. For example, one recent study in a second-grade classroom where immigrant Latino/a students predominated showed that when students were allowed to work cooperatively to learn "math facts," they performed better than when they were required to work independently on the same material (Rothstein-Fisch, Trumbull, Isaac, Daley, & Pérez, 2003). In a similar classroom, with immigrant Latino/a students, Isaac (1999) observed tensions within and between children when their teacher forced them to stop helping one another and to compete. Additional work among indigenous communities in Alaska (e.g., Ilutsik, 1994; Nelson-Barber & Dull, 1998) and in Micronesia (Nelson-Barber, 2001; Nelson-Barber, Trumbull, & Wenn, 2000) documented tendencies of students to gravitate toward cooperative rather than competitive ways of interacting (see also McDermott & Varenne, 2006). These studies are part of a body of research that seeks to understand the kinds of resources students bring from home and ways in which they apply to school relationships across cultures.

Classrooms that make use of the *cognitive resources* students bring from previous instruction and from home—a variety of ways of thinking used in their communities to solve problems—make the most of students' existing knowledge and lived experiences (Moll & Gonzalez, 2004). Language is one such cognitive resource, as are local systems for collecting and interpreting data (e.g., related to environmental changes, weather patterns), family systems for tracking the completion of work, and specialized local maps. Teachers' ability to recognize and appreciate students' particular cognitive resources ultimately has a bearing on how they interpret student talk and activity in the classroom. Awareness of other ways of thinking, constructing knowledge, and problem solving can yield insights into the cultural nature of "usual" school-based practices. As Bruner (1996) observed, "School curricula and classroom 'climates' always reflect inarticulate cultural values as well as explicit plans.... [T]he school can never be considered as culturally 'free standing'" (pp. 27–28).

A Caveat About Generalizations and Assumptions

At this point, we would like to share a few words of caution. First, tapping into students' content knowledge and problem-solving strategies does not translate to automatic understanding of students' epistemologies or the underlying socio-cultural practices (e.g., values, beliefs, experiences acquired as a member of a given community) that influence how students construct knowledge (Solano-Flores & Nelson-Barber, 2001). Second, we should not assume that communication styles and home cultural practices are homogeneous in any community, dominant or nondominant. Nasir and Cobb (2002) argue that "equity does not merely involve helping students reach higher standards set by the mainstream but instead is a matter of understanding diversity as a relation between the community of practice established in the math classroom and the other communities of practice of which students are a part" (p. 97). Gutiérrez, Baquedano-Lopez, and Alvarez (2001) describe language practices as "hybrid," meaning that they are based on more than one language or dialect. Gutiérrez and Rogoff (2003) caution us against ascribing cultural practices to individuals and instead propose we consider the repertoires of practice that any one individual has had access to. We cannot assume that *any* cultural group has "cultural uniformity or a set of harmonious and homogeneous shared practices" (González, 1995).

González (1995) decries perspectives that "have relegated notions of culture to observable surface markers of folklore, assuming that all members of a particular group share a normative, bounded, and integrated view of their culture" and suggests that "approaches to culture that take into account multiple perspectives can reorient educators to consider the everyday experiences of their students" (González, 1995, p. 237). Still, Brenner's three-part framework can be used as a broad guide for designing curricula, instruction, and assessments. It leads teachers to consider the complexity in what constitutes comfortable and productive participation for learners, as well as the multiple communication practices that students have experienced, both at home and in school.

What Do Mathematics Teachers Need to Know to Address Cultural Content, Social Organization, and Cognitive Resources?

Cultural Content

Connecting school mathematics with children's own experiences and intuitive knowledge has been an important theme in efforts to improve formal mathematics education (Lipka, Webster, Yanez, 2005; Trumbull, Nelson-Barber & Mitchell, 2002, among others). With today's call for higher standards of effectiveness in the classroom and greater teacher accountability, practitioners are finding that they need to become knowledgeable about their students' personal experiences, particularly as the research continues to demonstrate that factors of context and culture are powerful contributors to the ways in which students make sense of schooling (e.g., Barnhardt & Kawagley, 2005; Delpit, 1995; Ladson-Billings, 1994; Nelson-Barber, 2006; Gutiérrez & Rogoff, 2003; Solano-Flores & Nelson-Barber, 2001, Trumbull, Greenfield & Quiroz, 2004).

For example, though indigenous groups are distinctive one from another (i.e., consider the diversity of ecosystems among the Hopi of northeastern Arizona in comparison with the Makah of northwestern Washington state), it is a widespread practice among members of these groups to maintain extensive knowledge of the natural environment and deep spiritual connections to their land base. As a result, many indigenous students experience culturally embedded, community-based education from an early age. Elders and other community members educate their youth about the requisite cognitive tools that suit local purposes, such as the processing of plants and herbs for medicinal purposes (pharmacology), a lifestyle that successfully manages wildlife and habitats (conservation biology), or about how to rely on star formations to track the migratory patterns of buffalo or hunt on the tundra (celestial navigation). Using conceptions of environmental phenomena embodied in local ways of thinking, reasoning, and expression, community educators convey specialized *ethno*mathematics and *ethno*science knowledge that is implicit in the activities they carry out for practical purposes.

It is also the case that many tribal groups socialize their children to pursue balanced and harmonious lives—what the Diné (Navajo) characterize as achieving a state of *hozho*. Benally (1988) writes, "The individual is taught the interrelationship and interdependence of all things and how we must harmonize with them to maintain balance and harmony" in our lives (p. 10). According to Benally (1988), this integrated reality enfolds Navajo learners as they pursue a state of *hozho*. All knowledge is viewed with respect to its ability to draw one closer to this spirit of harmony. By contrast, "western organization of knowledge, with its fragmentation…and lack of connectedness, does not promote *hozho*" (p. 12). Here, it is evident that one cannot consider cultural "content" without also considering the epistemological framework that addresses the nature of "knowledge." What *is* knowledge? What is its purpose?

American Indian philosopher Vine Deloria, Jr. (1992) further defines this epistemological perspective when he explains that indigenous peoples understand new information and experience in terms of their full tapestry of continuous experience and contextualized knowledge. Rather than matching generalizations with new phenomena (a "Western" approach), Native people match their more specific body of information with the immediate event or experience. In other words, from an indigenous perspective: (1) the observer is not separate from the observed and (2) broad generalizations cannot be abstracted from experience and then used to explain new experiences. Aleut educator, Larry Merculieff (2004), explains that "separating the 'what' from the 'how' results in use of information out of context.… Cultural wisdom passed on to new generations can be understood and applied only to the degree the individual integrates this wisdom into everyday life and living" (p. 2). This distinctive approach to education is akin to Valenzuela's (1999) notion of "educación," which she characterizes as "a conceptually broader term than its English language cognate. It refers to the family's role of inculcating in children a sense of moral, social, and personal responsibility and serves as the foundation for all other learning" (p. 23).

Thus, an indigenous approach to "understanding" includes essential *ethical and historical dimensions* that situate knowledge in a context. A more complete approach to instruction—one relevant to many indigenous students—would include transformative dimensions, promoting an inquiring stance toward the content itself. Questions are needed that arise from taking ethical and historical standpoints, such as: What knowledge is important to the survival of our society, our earth? To what use will knowledge be put? What might be the effects of using knowledge in this way? Such questions need to be addressed in schools that serve indigenous communities. Moreover, "progress" may be conceived of more in spiritual and ethical terms than in terms of the growth of knowledge per se. As much as these principles affirm local values and epistemologies, they also bring forth elements that the "mainstream" could learn from and adopt.

Cognitive Resources and Social Organization

The ways of knowing acquired by children who populate today's diverse classrooms often represent values, beliefs, and perspectives specific to their cultural communities, and these resources, which are largely expressed in their preferences for thinking, observing, and (inter)acting, have great influence over their learning as well as how they approach schooling. Indigenous students whose life ways emphasize knowledge of the natural environment and whose groups maintain spiritual connections to their land base experience culturally embedded, community-based education from an early age. Thus it is quite useful to examine ways in which indigenous contextual concepts and cultural heritage practices influence how these students learn about the mathematics they encounter in school (Nelson-Barber, 2006).

Vygotskyian theorists posit that cultures create meaning from experience in different ways (cf., Vygotsky, 1978; Wertsch, Del Río, & Alvarez, 1995). Key factors that influence students' ways of learning and thus interact with the nature of schooling (Cole, 2002) include:

1. Their sociocultural setting (cf., Berger & Luckman, 1966; Whorf, 1956),
2. Their community's relationship with place and forms of place-based learning (Basso, 1996; Gladwin, 1970; Hutchins, 1996; Kana'iaupuni, 2004),
3. Patterns of interaction between individuals in the community (Au, 1980; Giglioli, 1972; Labov, 1972; Nelson-Barber, 1985), and
4. The manner in which all of these factors combine to structure learners' engagement in ethnomathematical heritage activities (cf., Lipka & Adams, 2004; Nelson-Barber, Trumbull, & Wenn, 2000) and eventually in formal education (Cazden, John, & Hymes, 1972; Lipka, 1998; Nelson-Barber, 2001, 2006).

Sociocultural setting and sense of physical place are two distinct, yet experientially interwoven, factors that together influence all knowledge construction and interactions within the community. The significance of place for many indigenous communities is deep and abiding. Research in place-based education also points to the meaning of place and its relevance to schooling across a range of cultural and geographic contexts (cf., Miller & Hahn, 1997; Rural School and Community Trust, 2000; Smith, 2002; see also, Cajete, 2001). Because place- and culture-based education derive from the particular local context of a cultural group or nation, one must understand the teaching and learning styles of such a group in order to orchestrate instruction and make accurate judgments about student learning and conceptual understanding (Delpit, 1995; Lipka, 1998; Steele, 1991).

Borba (1990) observes that the practices developed by different groups are likely to be more efficient for solving problems related to their own surroundings than are academic mathematical practices, because the solutions are tailored to the particular obstacles encountered by those groups. For example, the nature of a map that will be useful to a traveler going by foot through Arctic territory, in which physical features (including trail contour and visibility) change frequently because of weather effects, will be quite different from one useful to a traveler going by car on highways through the Midwest. The mapmaker in the first case will need to select environmental benchmarks that resist destruction or disguise by weather. As Greenfield (1997) points out, understanding this tailoring of information for real-world problem solving together with the epistemologies intrinsic to given cultures—the way groups construct knowledge and view the world—can help teachers avoid misjudgments about group member capabilities (cf., Baugh, 2000; Kopriva & Sexton, 1999; Meier, 2008). Cognitive resources, quite naturally, are likely to look different depending upon the communities of practice in which they originate.

Beyond a Single, "Western" Notion of Mathematical Knowing and Doing

So, if we understand that all cultural groups generate mathematical knowledge, we also understand that this knowledge may appear and be demonstrated very differently from one group to another. People from all communities see patterns in the natural world, create categories, and develop classification systems to organize daily life in these terms. For all groups, mathematical ideas are concerned with space, number, and logical relationships and with systems for organizing these elements (e.g., Bishop, 1988). However, the ways in which any community handles mathematical ideas will be both constrained and afforded by local needs, such as the need to organize social and kinship systems or devise effective approaches to navigation.

Moreover, these ethnomathematical constellations of ideas and systems of representing knowledge cannot be compared along any single linear, developmental scale, contrary to the way "western" texts on mathematics, for instance, have tended to represent "progress" in mathematical thinking (Ascher, 1991). This "Western" approach is situated in a worldview that posits discrete entities, quantities, and states. Natural phenomena are often analyzed out of context, "objectified"; and scientific "facts" are thought to be value-free, and determined through rigorous observation or experimentation. From this perspective, societies and their cognitive systems, such as science and mathematics, are viewed as moving inexorably toward more complex ("advanced" or "better") states. There is an expectation that what is to come will be better than what went before. Time is sequential and linear.

These taken-for-granted, features of Western thought run counter to the ways of knowing of many Indian cultures, where interrelationships, flux, observation, and evaluation in context, and a more circular view of time prevail (cf., Johnston, 2002, 2003; Nelson-Barber, LaFrance, Trumbull, & Aburto, 2005; Sapir, 1921; Whorf, 1956; Witherspoon, 1977). From a Navajo perspective, "the focus is on process, change is ever-present; interrelationship and motion are of primary significance. These incorporate and subsume space and time" (Ascher, 1991, p. 129). Space is not conceived of as separate from time and motion. Ascher (1991) offers the example of Inuit (living in Alaska) who travel great distances across a continually changing landscape of snow and ice, and who may find it more useful to note significant, unchanging aspects of a landscape (a hill, a ridge along a river, the configuration of a coastline) than to establish distance measures in standardized units. Community practices may tend toward valuing multiple perspectives rather than an ability to use specific units of measurement. Thus, when spatial boundaries are not independent of the processes of which they are a part, segmenting space in an "arbitrary and static way without accounting for flux over time is senseless" (Ascher, 1991, p. 129). A teacher who has been exposed to this very different perspective is more likely to understand the thinking of a student from such a community—or at least to stop short of judging this student's ways of thinking as defective.

As children learn their cultures' *theories* of language and cognition (Lancy, 1983), they learn what knowledge is important for what purposes and when and how it is acquired and displayed. The Western approach serves to obscure important social information in technical facts that purport to be value free. A more explicitly cross-cultural perspective would better equip educators to recognize the values embedded in Western mathematics and to identify the information and processes required to understand alternatives (Levidow, 1988), so that they can support the much needed bridging between multiple perspectives.

There is great potential when these multiple perspectives are identified and contribute to intentionally-structured, context-rich learning environments. Such learning environments can be designed to activate young indigenous learners' knowledge in ways that are meaningful to them and to begin to build links among multiple knowledge bases. A blanket approach to teaching all students is not likely to succeed. However, developing a flexible repertoire of approaches that respect and incorporate the epistemological and pedagogical foundations of different cultural traditions may hold the key to improved student outcomes.

What Do Mathematics Teachers Need to Know about the Cultural Nature of Language?

As a powerful cognitive resource, language is responsive to the intellectual and social needs of a community. Students learn not only the language (Spanish, English, etc.) of their home communities but also specific varieties of that language appropriate to various social settings. They may or may not learn the language or dialect that is privileged in the school they will first attend. As important as the *forms* of language that children learn are the *uses* of language modeled in their home communities and the ways people in various role groups (e.g., children, adults, males, females) are expected to use language (Heath, 1983, 1986). Is language used for story telling? Is it used for recounting experiences? Is it used for explaining natural phenomena? Is it used for entertaining? Are children expected to respond to questions? Are they encouraged to ask questions? Are they praised for listening politely?

These questions point to the importance of not only what one thinks of as the "language code" but also of the discourse practices in students' communities of origin. As young children, students will have appropriated notions of what constitutes a story, how one talks about a past event, how one explains a task (or, rather, does not explain it but demonstrates it), or how one engages in argument. Students who have been exposed to certain language practices, for example, may tend to turn all classroom discourse into personal narrative rather than use "accepted" expository forms to talk about science or mathematics (e.g., Trumbull, Diaz-Meza, & Hasan, 2000).

Sociolinguistic research tells us that teachers need much more understanding of these kinds of conventionalized expectations in children's language. They need to learn how to value and capitalize on student's particular linguistic skills and at the same time explicitly model and teach the discourse styles expected in most classrooms, where there are rules about who can talk when, about what, and in what manner, as well as predictable communication routines that get established early in the school year (Morine-Dershimer, 2006, p. 129). The research leaves little doubt that the ways of organizing discourse can either include or exclude students from participating, particularly young children or those otherwise not accustomed to classroom norms of communicating. Discourse mediates students' learning, and "[t]eacher management of verbal interaction processes can strongly influence who has an opportunity to learn, as well as what disciplinary knowledge and what social values are available to be learned" (Morine-Dershimer, 2006, p. 132).

The practice of incorporating students' own ways of using language into the classroom is now recognized as one aspect of the success of many elementary schools serving Latino/a students (for example, in Los Angeles, as described in Greenfield, Quiroz, & Raeff, 2000; Isaac, 1999; Rothstein-Fisch et al., 2003; Trumbull, Greenfield, & Quiroz, 2004). What are some of these ways of using language that instruction should build on? What are common language practices among students from nondominant language communities? We will use the case of bilingual mathematics learners to describe some of these practices in more detail.

What Do Mathematics Teachers Need to Know about Language and Bilingual Mathematics Learners?

In this section, we use examples from research with Spanish-speaking bilingual learners to describe what mathematics teachers need to know about bilingualism and about common language practices among bilingual mathematics learners (Moschkovich, 2007a, 2007b). Many conversations about "language" are clouded by the fact that there are multiple meanings for terms such as *language* and *bilingual*, meanings that sometimes are strongly tied to fundamental assumptions and attitudes about language and thinking. We will clarify our use of these terms. First, we distinguish between national languages (such as Spanish or Haitian Creole) and social languages used in particular settings (such as mathematics classrooms). We assume that understanding utterances and texts involves generating and negotiating meanings and interpretations. We also assume that these meanings and interpretations are situated in practices and communities, not individuals. And lastly, we assume that any speaker's competence is multifaceted: How a person uses language will depend on what is understood to be appropriate in a given social setting, and as such, linguistic knowledge is situated "not in the individual psyche but in a group's collective linguistic norms" (Hakuta & McLaughlin, 1996, p. 22).

Bilingualism

Definitions of bilingualism range from nativelike fluency in two languages, to alternating use of two languages (De Avila & Duncan, 1981), to belonging to a bilingual community (Valdés-Fallis, 1978). We ground ourselves in a definition that characterizes bilingualism as not only an individual but also a social and cultural phenomenon involving participation in language practices and communities: "...the product of a specific linguistic community that uses one of its languages for certain functions and the other for other functions or situations" (Valdés-Fallis, 1978, p. 4).[3]

"Bilingual" refers to a wide range of proficiencies in two languages, and modes (listening, writing, speaking, and reading). Current scholars studying bilingualism see "nativelike control of two or more languages" as an unrealistic definition that does not reflect evidence that the majority of bilinguals are rarely equally fluent in both languages: "Bilinguals acquire and use their languages for different purposes, in different domains of life, with different people. It is precisely because the needs and uses of the languages are usually quite different that bilinguals rarely develop equal fluency in their languages" (Grosjean, 1999, p. 285).

Grosjean proposes we shift from using the terms *monolingual* and *bilingual* as labels for *individuals* to using these as labels for the endpoints on a continuum of *modes*. Bilinguals make use of one language, the other language, or the two together as they move along a continuum from monolingual to bilingual *modes*:

> Researchers are now starting to view the bilingual not so much as the sum of two (or more) complete or incomplete monolinguals but rather as a specific and fully competent speaker-hearer who has developed a communicative competence that is equal, but different in nature, to that of the monolingual. (Grosjean, 1999, p. 285)

Whereas being bilingual in some languages and settings is a sign of education and cultural advantage, bilingualism in other languages or in other settings can be associated with poverty, lack of education, or imagined cultural disadvantages (De Avila & Duncan, 1981). For example, Latino/a bilinguals in the United States have a particular history as part of a language minority. Some bilingual Latinos/as came to the United States as immigrants, others are the descendants of immigrants, and still others never emigrated or immigrated anywhere but live in regions that were originally part of Mexico and later became part of the United States. In the United States, bilingualism is not always considered an asset. In particular, Spanish is not considered a high-status second language. Bilingual Latino/a learners in the United States, instead of being viewed as having additional language skills, have often been described in terms of deficiency models (Garcia & Gonzalez, 1995). No doubt in part because of this devaluing of Spanish as a heritage language, there is a pattern of language loss from one generation to another (Tse, 2001).

Common Language Practices among Bilingual Mathematics Learners

Two common language practices documented among bilingual learners are using two languages when carrying out arithmetic computation alone and during a conversation with another person. Bilingual mathematics learners sometimes use two languages during arithmetic computation and sometimes code-switch (alternate between two languages such as Spanish and English) during one conversation—or even within a single sentence (Gumperz, 1973). What can research tell mathematics teachers about these two practices?

Although there are no available studies documenting language switching during computation among children or adolescents, several experimental (and often cited) studies with adults concluded that adult bilinguals have a preferred language for carrying out simple arithmetic computation (usually the language they experienced during arithmetic instruction). For example, two studies conducted with adult U.S. Spanish speakers (Marsh & Maki, 1976; McLain & Huang, 1982) found that adult bilinguals performed arithmetic operations more rapidly in their preferred language than in their nonpreferred language. These studies suggested that adult bilinguals may be "slower" when using their nonpreferred language. However, the reported differences in response times were infinitesimal (about 0.2 seconds for average response times ranging between 2 and 3 seconds), and the small difference in response time disappeared if there was no switch from one language to another during the experiment. Even though these results apply to adults, one finding by McLain and Huang (1982) may be relevant to mathematics classrooms. This study showed that if bilingual adults were required to use only one of their languages, the "preferred language advantage" was eliminated. On the one hand, this finding suggests that classroom practices that allow bilingual students to choose the language they use for arithmetic computation in the classroom, rather than requiring them to change languages, may be beneficial to bilingual mathematics learners because such changes may impact response time. On the other hand, we need to remember that any reported differences in response times were minimal.

Because these studies focused on computation, they say little regarding language practices during more conceptual mathematical activity. What might be the role of translating arithmetic computation from one language to another while solving word problems? Unfortunately, there is little research available to answer this question. One possible source is a case study of a bilingual adult when solving arithmetic word problems (Qi, 1998). The case study described how she switched to her first language for simple arithmetic computation while solving word problems. The study concluded that while solving word problems, this adult's switches were swift and highly automatic and that language switching facilitated rather than inhibited solving word problems in the second language. There seems to be strong evidence suggesting that switching languages does not affect the quality of conceptual thinking (Cumming 1989, 1990 as cited in Qi, 1998).

The studies discussed above were conducted with adults, and it may well be that the effects of language choice during mathematical activity are different for younger learners. Assessment research on bilingual elementary students showed that on mathematics and science items of a similar level of difficulty, native speakers of Mandarin and Spanish performed better on some items in English and on others in their native language (Solano-Flores et al., 2001). This result suggests that bilingual students should be allowed to use both languages whenever possible. After all, their knowledge and their linguistic skills are distributed across two languages.

What does research say about the impact of bilingualism in general on mathematical thinking and problem solving? One researcher summarizing work on bilingualism and mathematical performance writes:

> The most generous interpretation that is consistent with the data is that bilingualism has no effect on mathematical problem solving, providing that language proficiency is at least adequate for understanding the problem. Even solutions in the weaker language are unhampered under certain conditions. (Bialystok, 2001, p. 203)

A crucial concern for assessment, then is to ensure that students understand the word problem. Or that the language of instruction and assessment includes access to learners' first language, so that all students, including those who are learning English, have an opportunity to be successful in mathematical problem solving (e.g., Durán, 1985; Lager, 2006).

Clearly problems and questions remain for future research studies to address before we can say more regarding what teachers need to know about teaching mathematics to English learners. How do English learners, particularly children, solve mathematics word problems in English when their second language proficiency is not adequate for understanding the problem? How can instruction support children who are learning English in developing the English proficiency they need to understand mathematics word problems written in English? What skills do mathematics learners (whether they are learning English or not) need to understand mathematics word problems as a genre? These are questions that require further empirical study before we can make research based recommendations for mathematics teachers of English learners.

A second common language practice among bilingual learners is code switching during conversations. What does research say about code switching? When a bilingual student inserts an English word or phrase into her Spanish conversation (or the other way around), does it mean she is linguistically deficient? Linguistic researchers say "no" (Genesee, 2002; Reyes, 2004). Code switching is, instead, a complex, rule governed, and systematic language practice. Although code switching has an improvised quality, it reflects "language choice" (Wei, Milroy, & Ching, 2000) and a speaker's understanding of a community's linguistic norms

(Zentella, 1997). As such, it should be distinguished from the language mixing that may take place early in the development of a new language (Bialystok, 2001). Researchers have concluded that "code switching is not an ad hoc mixture but subject to formal constraints and that for some communities it is precisely the ability to switch that distinguishes fluent bilinguals" (Zentella, 1981). Teachers, themselves, code switch at times in order to communicate effectively (Khisty, 1995, 2001; Zentella, 1981).

How, when, and why do children code switch? Sociolinguists have concluded that, overall, young bilinguals (beyond age 5) speak as they are spoken to. A bilingual child's choice of language seems to be most dependent on the person addressing him or her. The language ability and language choice of the person addressing a bilingual child are "recognized as the most significant variable to date in determining the child's language choice" (Zentella, 1981, p. 110).

The consistent conclusion that code switching is not a reflection of a low level of proficiency in a language or the inability to recall a word (Genesee, 2002; Valdés-Fallis, 1979) is relevant to bilingual mathematics learners. It may seem reasonable to conclude that uttering a word in language A in the middle of an utterance in language B means that the speaker does not know or cannot retrieve that word in language B. But teachers need to recognize that this is not, in fact, the best explanation of code switching. Because bilinguals use two languages depending on the interlocutor, domain, topic, role, and function, researchers in bilingualism caution us against using someone's code switching to make conclusions about their language proficiency, ability to recall a word, or knowledge of a particular technical term. Likewise, it is not warranted to draw simple conclusions about a student's mathematical proficiency on the basis of his or her code switching.

In summary, teachers need to be familiar with the findings from current research on bilingual learners. Nativelike control of two or more languages is an unrealistic definition of bilingualism that does not reflect evidence that the majority of bilinguals are rarely equally fluent in both languages. Teachers need to know and build on the fluencies their students bring rather than comparing bilinguals to monolinguals or focus on how bilingual students miss the mark in comparison to monolinguals. Because bilinguals have a wide range of proficiencies in two languages, teachers should not expect mathematics students to know mathematical terms in a first or second language unless they have had mathematics instruction in that language. Bilinguals have a wide range of proficiencies in modes (listening, writing, speaking, and reading) in their two languages. Teachers should not assume that proficiency in one mode implies proficiency in another mode and should provide mathematics assessment and instruction across all modes. Switching languages is not a sign of a deficiency. In fact, this skill is a complex cognitive and linguistic resource. Teachers should not imagine that switching languages is related to mathematical thinking or understanding in any simple way.

What Do Mathematics Teachers Need To Know about Mathematical Discourse?

Teachers need to not only understand bilingualism and the common language practices bilingual students are likely to engage in, they also need to understand what is entailed in communicating mathematically, also known as participating in "mathematical discourse." Current research in mathematics education describes how, as students are learning mathematics, they are also learning to participate in mathematical discourse (Cobb, Wood, & Yackel 1993; Forman, 1996; Moschkovich, 2002a, 2007c). The term *discourse* is another example of a term with multiple meanings. Some use the word *discourse* to refer to any unit of language longer than a sentence. Gee (1996) distinguishes between *discourse* and *Discourse*. In keeping with this distinction, we will use the term *Discourses*. Gee's definition of Discourses highlights how these are not just sequential speech or writing:

> A Discourse is a socially accepted association among ways of using language, other symbolic expressions, and "artifacts," of thinking, feeling, believing, valuing and acting that can be used to identify oneself as a member of a socially meaningful group or "social network," or to signal (that one is playing) a socially meaningful role. (p. 131)

As a start, mathematical Discourse involves the mathematics register. Halliday (1978) defines register as:

> ...a set of meanings that is appropriate to a particular function of language, together with the words and structures which express these meanings. We can refer to the "mathematics register," in the sense of the meanings that belong to the language of mathematics (the mathematical use of natural language, that is: not mathematics itself), and that a language must express [itself] if it is being used for mathematical purposes. (p. 195)

Researchers have described learning to communicate mathematically as, in part, sorting out differences in meanings of many terms and phrases that are used both in mathematical and everyday settings (Khisty, 1995; Moschkovich, 1996, 2002a, 2007c; Pimm, 1987). Since there are multiple meanings for the same term or phrase, as students learn mathematics they are learning to use these multiple meanings appropriately. Examples of multiple meanings are the meanings for the word *set* and the phrase *any number*, which, in a mathematics classroom, means "all numbers" (Pimm, 1987). But the mathematics register does not simply involve the meaning of single words or phrases, it also involves relational meanings between pairs of terms. Walkerdine (1988) contrasts the way that in school the opposite of "more" is assumed to be "less." In contrast, she documented how in British home settings, young children usually experienced the opposite of "more" as "no more." For example, if a child asked for more paper, she was likely to hear the response "there is no more paper" rather than a response using the term *less* (Walkerdine, 1988). Walkerdine thus documented how at home children paired up "more" with "no more" while at school the expectation was that the opposite of "more" would be "less."

What are mathematical Discourse practices?[4] In general, students communicate mathematically by making conjectures, presenting explanations, constructing argumentsabout mathematical objects, with mathematical content, and toward a mathematical point (Brenner, 1994). Participating in classroom mathematical Discourse practices involves much more than the use of technical language. We should not imagine that classroom discussions involve one single set of discourse practices that are (or are not) mathematical. In fact, we might imagine the classroom as a place where multiple Discourse practices meet.[5] Mathematical Discourse practices vary across different communities; for example, between research mathematicians and statisticians, elementary and secondary school teachers, or traditional and reform-oriented classrooms. Mathematical arguments can be presented for different purposes such as convincing, summarizing, or explaining. Mathematical Discourse practices also involve different genres such as algebraic proofs, geometric proofs, school algebra word problems, and presentations at conferences.

In general, particular modes of argument, such as precision, brevity, and logical coherence, are valued (Forman, 1996). Abstracting, generalizing, and searching for certainty are also highly valued practices in mathematical communities. The value of generalizing is reflected in common mathematical statements, such as "the angles of any triangle add up to 180 degrees," "parallel lines never meet," or "a + b will always equal b + a." Making claims is another important mathematical Discourse practice. What makes a claim mathematical is, in part, the attention paid to describing in detail when the claim applies and when it does not. Mathematical claims apply only to a precisely and explicitly defined set of situations as in the statement "multiplication makes a number bigger, except when multiplying by zero, one, or a number smaller than one." Many times claims are also tied to mathematical representations such as graphs, tables, or diagrams. Although less often considered, imagining is also a valued mathematical practice. Mathematical work often involves talking and writing about imagined things—such as infinity, zero, infinite lines, or lines that never meet—as well as visualizing shapes, objects, and relationships that may not exist in front of our eyes.

We should not confuse "mathematical" with "formal" or "textbook" definitions. Formal definitions and ways of talking are only one aspect of academic mathematical Discourse practices. Some of the characteristics summarized above may be particular to the end point of producing mathematics, such as making a presentation or publishing a proof, while others are characteristics of the discourse practices involved in the process of producing mathematics.

In general, when describing everyday and academic mathematical Discourse practices, it is important to avoid construing this as a dichotomous distinction (Moschkovich, 2007c). This distinction is not intended to be a tool to categorize utterances as originating in particular experiences. During mathematical discussions, students use multiple resources from their experiences both in and out of school. It is difficult, if not impossible, to use this distinction to describe the origin of student talk. It is not always possible to tell whether a student's competence in communicating mathematically originated in her everyday experiences or her school experiences. Similarly, we cannot identify whether the meaning for any given utterance originated in everyday or school activity.

The existence of multiple meanings and practices across everyday and math classroom settings has sometimes been described as creating obstacles in classroom mathematical discussions because students are often using colloquial meanings, while teachers (or other students) are using mathematical meanings. However, we should not assume that the everyday meanings and experiences are necessarily obstacles; they also provide resources for communicating mathematically. Everyday Discourse practices should not be seen only as obstacles to participation in academic mathematical Discourse. The origin of some mathematical Discourse practices may be everyday experiences and practices. Some aspects of everyday experiences can provide resources in the mathematics classroom, as we have suggested earlier in the chapter. Everyday experiences with natural phenomena can be resources for communicating mathematically. For example, climbing hills is an experience that can be a resource for describing the steepness of lines (Moschkovich, 1996). Other everyday experiences with natural phenomena also may provide resources for communicating mathematically.

In addition to experiences with natural phenomena, O'Connor (1999) proposes that students' mathematical arguments can be at least partly based on what she calls argument proto-forms:

> Experiential precursors (arguments outside of school, the provision of justification to parents and siblings, the struggle to name roles or objects in play) may provide the discourse 'protoforms' that students could potentially build upon in the mathematical domain. (O'Connor, 1999, p. 27)

What about vocabulary? We alluded to vocabulary early on in this discussion. While vocabulary is necessary, it is not sufficient. It must be clear by now that learning to communicate mathematically is not merely or primarily a matter of learning vocabulary. During discussions in mathematics classrooms students are also learning to describe patterns, make generalizations, and use representations to support their claims. The question is not whether students who are English learners should learn vocabulary but how instruction can best support them as they learn both vocabulary and mathematics.

Vocabulary drill and practice are not the most effective instructional practices for learning vocabulary. Instruction should provide opportunities for students to actively use mathematical language to communicate about and negotiate meaning for mathematical situations. Researchers who study vocabulary learning and teaching report that vocabulary acquisition occurs most successfully through instructional contexts that are language rich, actively involve students in using language, require both receptive and expressive understanding, and require students to use words in multiple ways over extended periods of time (Blachowicz & Fisher, 2000; Pressley, 2000). To develop written and oral communication skills students need to participate in negotiating meaning (Savignon, 1991) and in tasks that require output from students (Swain, 2001). Instruction should provide opportunities for students to actively use mathematical language to communicate about and negotiate meaning for mathematical situations. In sum, vocabulary instruction is necessary but not sufficient for supporting mathematical communication. Because mathematical Discourse practices are central to success in mathematics, teachers need to balance vocabulary instruction with modeling of and opportunities for student participation in mathematical Discourse practices.

Conclusion

We have outlined and described some of the important aspects of what mathematics teachers need to know about language and culture. Teachers need to have some knowledge of local communities, take a cultural affirmation approach to differences, and be careful of generalizations and assumptions about cultural or linguistic practices. Teachers also need to be aware of the cultural content of the lessons they teach, consider the cognitive resources provided by both community and discipline practices, and examine how the social organization of the classroom affords or constrains student participation in mathematical activities. Mathematics teachers who work in communities where students are bilingual or learning English also need to understand the nature of bilingualism, be aware of common language practices among bilingual students, and know that all students can participate in mathematical discourse, even as they are learning English.

Even a brief foray into the realm of culture, language, and mathematics teaching and learning illustrates the breadth, depth, and complexity of what teachers need to know to teach mathematics successfully with the range of students in today's classrooms. Few teachers have the opportunity to develop deep understandings of culture and language and each teacher cannot be expected to know everything about each and every cultural and linguistic aspect of their students' lives and experiences. However, teachers can be aware that there are differences and similarities among students, that some of these differences may be relevant for the classroom, and that some differences may be relevant for teaching and learning mathematics. Teachers can also value community knowledge and ways of using language and collaborate with colleagues and people in local communities to learn as much as possible about the students and families they serve. If they do even just one of these, they will be making great strides toward designing mathematics teaching that meets the needs of all their students.

Acknowledgments

The preparation of this paper was supported in part by a grant from the National Science Foundation to the Center for the Mathematics Education of Latinos/as (No. ESI-0424983) and to WestEd (DRL-0529639). The findings and opinions expressed here are those of the authors and do not necessarily reflect the views of the funding agency. We would also like to thank Elise Trumbull, Alisan Andrews, May Miller-Ricci, Nara Nayar, and William Zahner for their important collegial support.

Notes

1. Of course, many other students—such as African Americans and Appalachians—speak a home dialect that is different from the dialect privileged in the classroom. Associated with a different dialect are differences not only in pronunciation and grammar but also in *how* language is used in various social settings including school.
2. A language register is a variety of speech associated with a particular setting (e.g., religious setting, courtroom, social get-together, mathematics classroom).
3. In reality, this division may not be quite so neat and tidy.
4. Moschkovich (2007c) uses the phrase "Discourse practices" to emphasize that Discourse is not individual, static, or refers only to language. Instead, she assumes that Discourses are more than language, that meanings are multiple and situated, that Discourses occur in the context of practices, and that practices are tied to communities. Thus, mathematical Discourse practices are connected to multiple communities.
5. The labels used to refer to different mathematical Discourse practices, such as *everyday, professional, academic,* and *school,* can be misleading. The terms are complex and contested, and the categories are not mutually exclusive. "Professional mathematical discourse" refers to how mathematicians talk and act. "School mathematical discourse" refers to how students and teachers who are competent in school mathematics talk and act. For a more detailed discussion of multiple mathematical Discourse practices see Moschkovich (2002b, 2007c).

References

Abedi, J., (2003). *Impact of students' language background on content-based performance: Analyses of extant data* (Executive Summary. CSE Technical Report No. 603). Los Angeles: University of California, Center for the Study of Evaluation/National Center for Research on Evaluation, Standards, and Student Testing.

Adler, J. (1998). A language of teaching dilemmas: Unlocking the complex multilingual secondary mathematics classroom. *For the Learning of Mathematics, 18*(1), 24–33.

Adler, J. (2001). *Teaching mathematics in multilingual classrooms.* Dordrecht, The Netherlands: Kluwer.

Ascher, M. (1991). *Ethnomathematics: A multicultural view of mathematical ideas.* Pacific Grove, CA: Brooks/Cole.

Au, K. (1980). Participation structures in reading lessons: Analysis of a culturally appropriate instructional event. *Anthropology and Education Quarterly, 11*(2), 91–115.

Barnhardt, R., & Kawagley, A. (2005). Indigenous knowledge systems and Alaska Native ways of knowing. *Anthropology & Education Quarterly, 36*(1), 8–23.

Basso, K. (1996). *Wisdom sits in places: Landscape and language among the Western Apache.* Albuquerque: University of New Mexico Press.

Baugh, J. (2000). *Beyond ebonics.* New York: Oxford University Press.

Benally, H. (1988). Dine philosophy of learning. *Journal of Navajo Education, 6*(1), 10–13.

Berger, P., & Luckman, T. (1966). *The social construction of reality.* Garden City, NY: Anchor Books.

Bialystok, E. (2001). *Bilingualism in development: Language, literacy, and cognition.* Cambridge, UK: Cambridge University Press.

Bishop, A. (1988). *Mathematical enculturation: A cultural perspective on mathematics education.* Dordrecht, Netherlands: Kluwer.

Blachowicz, C., & Fisher, P. (2000). Vocabulary instruction. In M. Kamil, P. Mosenthal, P. D. Pearson, & R. Barr (Eds.), *Handbook of reading research* (Vol. 3, pp. 503–523). Mahwah, NJ: Erlbaum.

Borba, M. (1990). Ethnomathematics and education. *For the Learning of Mathematics, 10* (1), 39–42.

Brenner, M. (1994). A communication framework for mathematics: Exemplary instruction for culturally and linguistically diverse students. In B. McLeod (Ed.), *Language and Learning: Educating linguistically diverse students* (pp. 233–268). Albany: SUNY Press.

Brenner, M. E. (1998). Adding cognition to the formula for culturally relevant instruction in mathematics. *Anthropology and Education Quarterly, 29*(2), 213–244.

Bruner, J. S. (1996). *The culture of education.* Cambridge, MA: Harvard University Press.

Cajete, G. (2001). Indigenous education and ecology: Perspectives of an American Indian educator. In J. Grim (Ed.), *Indigenous traditions and ecology: The interbeing of cosmology and community* (pp. 619–638). Cambridge, MA: Harvard University Press.

Cazden, C., John, V., & Hymes, D. (Eds.). (1972). *Functions of language in the classroom.* New York: Teachers College Press.

Cobb, P., Wood, T., & Yackel, E. (1993). Discourse, mathematical thinking, and classroom practice. In E. Forman, N. Minick, & C. A. Stone (Eds.), *Contexts for learning: sociocultural dynamics in children's development* (pp. 91–119). New York: Oxford University Press.

Cole, M. (2002, November). *Cross-cultural and historical perspectives on the consequences of education.* Herbert Spencer Lecture on the future of education, Oxford University, Oxford, UK.

Cumming, A. (1989). Writing expertise and second language proficiency. *Language Learning, 39,* 89–141.

Cumming, A. (1990). Meta-linguistic and ideational thinking in second language composing. *Written Communication, 7,* 482–511.

De Avila, E., & Duncan S. (1981). Bilingualism and the metaset. In R. Durán (Ed.), *Latino language and communicative behavior* (pp. 337–354). Norwood, NJ: Ablex.

Delpit, L. (1995). *Other people's children.* New York: New Press.

Deloria, Jr., V. (1992). Ethnoscience and Indian realities. *Winds of Change, 7*(3) 12–18.

Durán, R. P. (1985). Influences of language skills on bilinguals' problem solving. In S. F. Chipman, J.W. Segal, & R. Glaser (Eds.), *Thinking and learning skills* (pp. 187–207). Hillsdale, NJ: Erlbaum.

Forman, E. (1996). Learning mathematics as participation in classroom practice: Implications of sociocultural theory for educational reform. In L. Steffe, P. Nesher, P. Cobb, G. Goldin, & B. Greer (Eds.), *Theories of mathematical learning* (pp. 115–130). Mahwah, NJ: Erlbaum.

Garcia, E., & Gonzalez, R. (1995). Issues in systemic reform for culturally and linguistically diverse students. *Teachers College Record, 96*(3), 418–431.

Gee, J. (1996). *Social linguistics and literacies: Ideology in discourses* (3rd ed.). London: Falmer Press.

Genesee, F. (2002). Portrait of the bilingual child. In V. Cook (Ed.), *Perspectives on the L2 user* (pp. 170–196). Clevedon, UK: Multilingual Matters.

Gigoli, P. (1972). *Language in social context.* New York: Penguin.

Gladwin, T. (1970). *East is a big bird: Navigation and logic on Puluwat Atoll.* Cambridge, MA: Harvard University Press.

González, N. (1995). Processual approaches to multicultural education. *Journal of Applied Behavioral Science, 31*(2), 234–244.

Greenfield, P. (1997). Culture as process: Empirical methods for cultural psychology. In J. W. Berry, Y. H. Pootinga, & J. Pandey (Eds.), *Handbook for cross-cultural psychology: Theory and method* (2nd ed., Vol. 1). Needham Heights, MA: Allyn Bacon.

Greenfield, P. M., Quiroz, B., & Raeff, C. (2000). Cross-cultural conflict and harmony in the social construction of the child. In S. Harkness, C. Raeff, & C. M. Super (Eds.), *Variability in the social construction of the child* (pp. 93–108) (New Directions in Child Development, No. 87). San Francisco: Jossey-Bass.

Grosjean, F. (1999). Individual bilingualism. In B. Spolsky (Ed.), *Concise encyclopedia of educational linguistics* (pp. 284–290). London: Elsevier.

Gumperz, J. J. (1973). The communicative competence of bilinguals: Some hypotheses and suggestions for research. *Language in Society, 1*(1), 143–154.

Gutiérrez, K., Baquedano-Lopez, P., & Alvarez, H. (2001). Literacy as hybridity: Moving beyond bilingualism in urban classrooms. In M. de la Luz Reyes & J. Halcon (Eds.), *The best for our children: Critical perspectives on literacy for Latino students* (pp. 122–141). New York: Teachers College Press.

Gutiérrez, K., & Rogoff, B. (2003). Cultural ways of learning: Individual traits or repertoires of practice? *Educational Researcher, 32*(5), 19–25.

Hakuta, K., & McLaughlin, B. (1996). Bilingualism and second language learning: Seven tensions that define research. In D. Berliner & R.C. Calfe (Eds.), *Handbook of educational psychology* (pp. 603–621). New York: Macmillan.

Halliday, M. A. K. (1978). Sociolinguistics aspects of mathematical education. In M. Halliday (Ed.), *Language as a social semiotic: The social interpretation of language and meaning* (pp. 194–204). London: University Park Press.

Heath, S. B. (1983). *Ways with words: Language, life, and work in communities and classrooms.* Cambridge, UK: Cambridge University Press.

Heath, S. B. (1986). Sociocultural contexts of language development. In *Beyond language: Social and cultural factors in schooling language minority students* (pp. 143–186). Los Angeles: Evaluation, Dissemination and Assessment Center, California State University, Los Angeles. (Developed by Bilingual Education Office, California State Department of Education, Sacramento)

Ho, D. Y. F. (1994). Cognitive socialization in Confucian heritage cultures. In P. M. Greenfield & R. R. Cocking (Eds.), *Cross-cultural routes of minority child development* (pp. 285–313). Mahwah, NJ: Erlbaum.

Hutchins, E. (1996). *Cognition in the wild.* Cambridge, MA: MIT Press.

Ilutsik, E. (1994). The funding of the Ciulislet: One teacher's journey. *Journal of American Indian Education, 33*(3), 6–13.

Isaac, A. R. (1999). *How teachers' cultural ideologies influence children's relations inside the classroom: The effects of a cultural awareness teacher training program in two classrooms.* Unpublished honors thesis, University of California, Los Angeles.

Johnston, A. (2002, November). *Building capacity: Ensuring evaluation findings contribute to program growth.* Paper presented at the annual meeting of the American Evaluation Association, Washington, D.C.

Johnston, A. (2003, June). *A Canadian First Nations approach to evaluation.* Paper presented at the annual meeting of the Canadian Evaluation Society, Vancouver, B.C.

Kana'iaupuni, S. (2004). Ka'akalai ku kanaka: A call for strengths-based approaches from a Native Hawaiian perspective, *Educational Researcher, 33*(9), 26–32.

Khisty, L. L. (1995). Making inequality: Issues of language and meanings in mathematics teaching with Hispanic students. In W. G. Secada, E. Fennema, & L. B. Adajian (Eds.), *New directions for equity in mathematics education* (pp. 279–297). New York: Cambridge University Press.

Khisty, L. (2001). Effective teachers of second language learners in mathematics. In *Proceedings of the 25th Conference of the International Group for the Psychology of Mathematics Education* (pp. 225–232). Utrecht, The Netherlands: The Freudenthal Institute, Utrecht University.

Khisty, L., & Chval, K. (2002). Pedagogic discourse and equity in mathematics: When teachers' talk matters. *Mathematics Education Research Journal, 14*(3), 154–168.

Kopriva, R., & Sexton, U. (1999). *Guide to scoring LEP student responses to open-ended science items.* Washington, D.C.: Council of Chief State School Officers.

Kozulin, A. (1998). *Psychological tools: A sociocultural approach to education.* Cambridge, MA: Harvard University Press.

Labov, W. (1972). *Language in the inner city: Studies in the Black English vernacular.* Philadelphia: University of Pennsylvania Press.

Ladson-Billings, G. (1994). *Dreamkeepers*. San Francisco: Jossey-Bass.

Lager, C. A. (2006). Types of mathematics-language reading interactions that unnecessarily hinder algebra learning and assessment. *Reading Psychology, 27*(2–3), 165–204.

Lancy, D. (1983). *Cross-cultural studies in cognition and mathematics*. New York: Academic Press.

Lave, J. (1988). *Cognition in practice: Mind, mathematics, and culture in everyday life*. New York: Cambridge University Press.

Lave, J., & Wenger, E. (1991). *Situated learning: Legitimate peripheral participation*. New York: Cambridge University Press.

Levidow, L. (1988). Non-western science, past and present. *Science as Culture, 3*, 101–117.

Lipka, J. (Ed.). (1998). *Transforming the culture of schools: Yup'ik Eskimo examples*. Mahwah, NJ: Erlbaum.

Lipka, J., & Adams, E. (2004). Culturally based math education as a way to improve Alaska Native students' math performance. *The Appalachian Collaborative Center for Learning, Assessment and Instruction in Mathematics Series*. Retrieved November 29, 2008, from http://acclaim-math.org/docs/working_papers/WP_20_Lipka_Adams.pdf

Lipka, J., Webster, J., & Yanez, E. (2005). Factors that affect Alaska Native students' mathematical performance, *Journal of American Indian Education. 44*(3), 1–8.

Marsh, L., & Maki, R. (1976). Efficiency of arithmetic operations in bilinguals as a function of language, *Memory and Cognition, 4*, 459–464.

McDermott, R., & Varenne, H. (2006). Reconstructing culture in educational research. In G. Spindler & L. Hammond (Eds.), *Innovations in educational ethnography: Theory, methods and results* (pp. 3–31). Mahwah, NJ: Erlbaum.

McLain, L., & Huang, J. (1982). Speed of simple arithmetic in bilinguals. *Memory and Cognition, 10*, 591–596.

Meier, T. (2008). *Black communications and learning to read*. New York: Erlbaum.

Merculieff, L. (2004). *The value and use of traditional knowledge and wisdom: Partnerships for the Bering Sea*. Anchorage: Alaska Native Science Commission. Unpublished manuscript.

Miller, B., & Hahn, K. (1997). *Finding their own place*. Charleston, WV: Clearinghouse on Rural Education and Small Schools.

Moll, L. C., & Gonzalez, N. (2004). Engaging life: A funds-of-knowledge approach to multicultural education. In J. Banks & C. A. McGee Banks (Eds.), *Handbook of research on multicultural education* (pp. 699–715). San Francisco: Jossey-Bass.

Morine-Dershimer, G. (2006). Classroom management and classroom discourse. In C.M. Evertson & C.S. Weinstein (Eds.), *Handbook of classroom management: Research, practice, and contemporary issues* (pp. 127–153). Mahwah, NJ: Erlbaum.

Moschkovich, J. N. (1996). Moving up and getting steeper: Negotiating shared descriptions of linear graphs. *The Journal of the Learning Sciences, 5*(3), 239–277.

Moschkovich, J. N. (1999a). Supporting the participation of English language learners in mathematical discussions. *For the Learning of Mathematics, 19*(1), 11–19.

Moschkovich, J. N. (1999b). Understanding the needs of Latino students in reform-oriented mathematics classrooms. In *Changing the faces of mathematics: Vol. 4. Perspectives on Latinos* (pp. 5–12). Reston, VA: NCTM.

Moschkovich, J. N. (2000). Learning mathematics in two languages: Moving from obstacles to resources. In W. Secada (Ed.), *Changing the Faces of Mathematics: Vol. 1. Perspectives on multiculturalism and gender equity* (pp. 85–93). Reston, VA: National Council of Teachers of Mathematics.

Moschkovich, J. N. (2002a). A situated and sociocultural perspective on bilingual mathematics learners [Special issue Diversity, Equity, and Mathematical Learning, N. Nassir & P. Cobb (Eds.)]. *Mathematical Thinking and Learning, 4*(2&3), 189–212.

Moschkovich, J. N. (2002b). An introduction to examining everyday and academic mathematical practices. In M. Brenner & J. Moschkovich (Eds.), *Everyday and academic mathematics: Implications for the classroom. Monographs of the Journal for Research in Mathematics Education, 11*, 1–11.

Moschkovich, J. N. (2007a). Bilingual mathematics learners: How views of language, bilingual learners, and mathematical communication impact instruction. In N. Nasir & P. Cobb (Eds.), *Diversity, equity, and access to mathematical ideas* (pp. 89–104). New York: Teachers College Press.

Moschkovich, J. N. (2007b). Using two languages when learning mathematics. *Educational Studies in Mathematics, 64,* 121–144.

Moschkovich, J. N. (2007c). Examining mathematical Discourse practices. *For The Learning of Mathematics, 27*(1), 24–30.

Nasir, N., & Cobb, P. (2002). Diversity, equity, and mathematical learning, *Mathematical thinking and learning* [Special issue on Diversity, Equity, and Mathematical Learning, N. Nassir & P. Cobb (Eds.)], *4*(2&3), 91–102.

Nelson-Barber, S. (1985). *Prosodic patterning in Pima English: Relevance for interethnic miscommunication.* Unpublished doctoral dissertation, Harvard University, Cambridge, MA.

Nelson-Barber, S. (1999). A better education for every child: The dilemma for teachers of culturally and linguistically diverse students. In N. Simms & A. Peralez (Eds.), *Including culturally and linguistically diverse students in standards-based reform: A report on McREL's Diversity Roundtable I* (pp. 4–21). Aurora, CO: Mid-Continent Regional Educational Laboratory.

Nelson-Barber, S. (2001). Exploring Pacific knowledge and classroom learning in Micronesia: The promise of "cultural considerations." In C. Park, A. Goodwin, & S. Lee (Eds.), *Research on the education of Asian and Pacific Americans* (pp. 41–54). Greenwich, CT: Information Age.

Nelson-Barber., S. (2006, July). Transformative approaches to mathematics and science education. Expert Panel on Pacific Education. Pacific Education Conference, Koror, Palau.

Nelson-Barber, S., & Dull, V. (1998). "Don't act like a teacher!" Images of effective teaching in a Yup'ik Eskimo classroom. In J. Lipka (Ed.), *Transforming the culture of schools: Yup'ik Eskimo examples* (pp. 91–105). Mahwah, NJ: Erlbaum.

Nelson-Barber, S., LaFrance, J., Trumbull, E., & Aburto, S. (2005). Promoting culturally reliable and valid evaluation practice. In S. Hood, R. Hopson, & H. Frierson (Eds.), *The role of culture and cultural context: A mandate for inclusion, the discovery of truth and understanding in evaluative theory and practice* (pp. 61–85). Greenwich, CT: Information Age.

Nelson-Barber, S., & Lipka, J. (2008). Rethinking the case for culture-based curriculum: Conditions that support improved mathematics performance in diverse classrooms. In M. Brisk (Ed.), *Language, culture and community in teacher education* (pp. 99–123). New York: Erlbaum.

Nelson-Barber, S., Trumbull, E., & Wenn, R. (2000). *The coconut wireless project: Sharing culturally responsive pedagogy through the worldwide web.* Honolulu: Pacific Resources for Education and Learning.

Nieto, S. (1996). *Affirming diversity: The sociopolitical context of multicultural education* (2nd ed.). White Plains, NY: Longman.

Nieto, S. (1999). *The light in their eyes: Creating multicultural learning communities.* New York: Teachers College.

O'Connor, M. C. (1999). Language socialization in the mathematics classroom. Discourse practices and mathematical thinking. In M. Lampert & M. Blunk (Eds.), *Talking Mathematics* (pp. 17–55). New York: Cambridge University Press.

O'Halloran, K. L. (2005). *Mathematical discourse: Language, symbolism and visual images.* New York: Continuum.

Osterman, K. F. (2000). Students' need for belonging in the school community. *Review of Educational Research, 70*(23), 323–367.

Pimm, D. (1987). *Speaking mathematically: Communication in mathematics classrooms.* London: Routledge.

Pressley, M. (2000). What should comprehension instruction be the instruction of? In M. Kamil, P. Mosenthal, P. D. Pearson, & R. Barr, (Eds.), *Handbook of reading research* (Vol. 3, pp. 545–561). Mahwah, NJ: Erlbaum.

Qi, D. S. (1998). An inquiry into language-switching in second language composing processes. *Canadian Modern Language Review, 54*(3), 413–435.

Radford, L., Bardini, C., & Sabena, C. (2007). Perceiving the general: The multisemiotic dimension of students' algebraic activity. *Journal for Research in Mathematics Education, 38*(5), 507–530.

Reyes, I. (2004). Functions of code switching in schoolchildren's conversations. *Bilingual Research Journal, 28*(1), 77–98.

Rothstein-Fisch, C., Trumbull, E., Isaac, A., Daley, C., & Pérez, A. (2003). When "helping someone else" is the right answer: Teachers bridge cultures in assessment. *Journal of Latinos and Education, 2*(3), 123–140.

Rural School and Community Trust. (2000). *Learning in place: Report of the Annenberg Rural Challenge Research and Evaluation Program.* Washington, D.C.: Author.

Ryu, J. (2004). The social adjustment of three, young, high-achieving Korean-English bilingual students in kindergarten. *Early Childhood Education Journal, 32*(3), 165–171.

Sáenz–Ludlow, A., & Presmeg, N. (2006). Guest editorial: Semiotic perspectives on learning mathematics and communicating mathematically. *Educational Studies in Mathematics, 61*(1), 1–10.

Sapir, E. (1921). *Language: An introduction to the study of speech.* New York: Harcourt Brace.

Savignon, S. (1991). Communicative language teaching: State of the art. *TESOL Quarterly, 25*(2), 261–277.

Saxe, G. (1991). *Culture and cognitive development: Studies in mathematical understanding.* Mahwah, NJ: Erlbaum.

Schleppegrell, M. (2007). The linguistic challenges of mathematics teaching and learning: A review. *Reading Writing Quarterly, 23*, 139–159.

Setati, M (1998). Code-switching and mathematical meaning in a senior primary class of second language learners. *For the Learning of Mathematics, 18*(1), 34–40.

Setati, M., & Adler, J. (2001). Between languages and discourses: Code switching practices in primary classrooms in South Africa. *Educational Studies in Mathematics, 43*, 243–269.

Smith, G. (2002). Place-based education: Learning to be where we are. *Phi Delta Kappan, 83*(8), 584–594.

Snow, C. (1983). Literacy and language: Relationships during the preschool years. *Harvard Educational Review, 53*, 165–189.

Solano-Flores, G., Lara, J., Sexton, U., & Navarrete, C. (2001). *Testing English language learners: A sampler of student responses to science and mathematics test items.* Washington, D.C.: Council of Chief State School Officers.

Solano-Flores, G., & Nelson-Barber, S. (2001). On the cultural validity of science assessments. *Journal of Research in Science Teaching, 38*, 1–21.

Spindler, G., & Spindler, L. (2000). *Fifty years of anthropology and education, 1950–2000: A Spindler anthology.* Mahwah. NJ: Erlbaum.

Steele, C. (1991, April). Race and the schooling of Black Americans. *The Atlantic Monthly*, pp. 68–76.

Swain, M. (2001). Integrating language and content teaching through collaborative tasks. *Canadian Modern Language Review, 58*(1), 44–63.

Trumbull, E., Diaz-Mesa, R., & Hasan, A. (2000, April). *Using cultural knowledge to inform literacy practices: Teacher innovations from the Bridging Cultures Project.* Paper presented at the annual meeting of the American Educational Research Association, New Orleans, LA.

Trumbull, E., Greenfield, P. M., & Quiroz, B. (2004). Cultural values in learning and education. In B. Williams (Ed.), *Closing the achievement gap: A vision for changing beliefs and practices* (2nd ed., pp. 67–98). Alexandria, VA: Association for Supervision and Curriculum Development.

Trumbull, E., Nelson-Barber, S., & Mitchell, J. (2002). Enhancing mathematics instruction for indigenous American students. In J. Hankes & G. Fast (Eds.), *Changing the faces of mathematics: Perspectives of indigenous people of North America* (pp. 1–18). Reston, VA: NCTM.

Tse, L. (2001). *Who don't they just learn English? Separating fact from fallacy in the U.S. language debate.* New York: Teachers College Press.

Valdés-Fallis, G. (1978). Code switching and the classroom teacher. *Language in education: Theory and practice* (Vol. 4). Wellington, VA: Center for Applied Linguistics.

Valdés-Fallis, G. (1979). Social interaction and code switching patterns: A case study of Spanish/English alternation. In G. D. Keller, R.V. Teichner, & S. Viera (Eds.), *Bilingualism in the bicentennial and beyond* (pp. 86–96). Jamaica, NY: Bilingualism Press.

Valenzuela, A. (1999). *Subtractive schooling: U.S.-Mexican youth and the politics of caring.* Albany, NY: State University of New York Press.

Vygotsky, L. (1978). *Mind in society: The development of higher psychological processes.* Cambridge, MA: Harvard University Press.

Walkerdine, V. (1988). *The mastery of reason: Cognitive development and the production of rationality.* New York: Routledge.

Wei, L., Milroy, L., & Ching, P. S. (2000). A two-step sociolinguistic analysis of code-switching and language choice: The example of a bilingual Chinese community in Britain. In L. Wei (Ed.), *The bilingualism reader* (pp. 188–209). London: Routledge.

Wertsch, J., Del Río, P., & Alvarez, A. (Eds.). (1995). *Sociocultural studies of mind.* New York: Cambridge University Press.

Whorf, B. (1956). *Language, thought and reality.* Cambridge, MA: Technology Press of MIT.

Witherspoon, G. (1977). *Language and art in the Navajo universe.* Ann Arbor: University of Michigan Press.

Wong-Fillmore, L., & Snow, C. (2000). *What teachers need to know about language.* Washington, D.C.: U.S. Department of Education, Office of Educational Research and Improvement.

Zentella, A. (1981). Tá bien. You could answer me en cualquier idioma: Puerto Rican code switching in bilingual classrooms. In R. Durán (Ed.), *Latino language and communicative behavior* (pp. 109–130). Norwood, NJ: Ablex.

Zentella, A. C. (1997). *Growing up bilingual: Puerto Rican children in New York.* Malden, MA: Blackwell.

6
The Politics of Mathematics Education in the United States
Dominant and Counter Agendas[1]

ERIC GUTSTEIN

> At present the United States faces no global rival. America's grand strategy should aim to preserve and extend this advantageous position as far into the future as possible. Project for a New American Century (2000, p. i)

The above quote succinctly summarizes the goal, if not the reality, of post-World War II (at least) U.S. administrations, as well as that of the financial and corporate elites in the country. However, the context of the quote is about "rebuilding America's defenses," and it refers to military rivals. As such, it may have neglected what U.S. capital and government now do consider to be genuine global rivals—but on the economic rather than the military front. These competitors include China, Russia, Brazil, India, Japan, South Korea, and the European Union, and depending on various trade agreements, industries, and other particularities, also include other nations. There is substantial contention between the United States and others for investment possibilities, markets, natural resources, tax breaks, cheap labor sources, and locales with lax environmental regulations. U.S. corporations, like those around the world, consistently vie with others for these opportunities, and economic competition is fierce. Trade skirmishes regularly take place in international arenas like the World Trade Organization. In addition, the United States uses to its advantage both the World Bank and International Monetary Fund, both of which it dominates by having the largest share of votes (by far), as well as a permanent seat on their governing boards (similar to permanent UN Security Council members). In short, global contention is omnipresent (Harvey, 2005).

The perceived threat and onslaught by economic rivals, however, has an envisioned solution, and this is where mathematics education comes in. Several influential groups in the United States have produced documents that locate science, mathematics, engineering, and technology (STEM) education as key to staving off the attack on the "advantageous position." This ultimately has significant implications for U.S. mathematics classrooms. In this chapter, I look at the way U.S. mathematics education is framed as a way to serve capital and to continue U.S. global dominance. I examine the arguments and how policies actualize them. I also explore the potential impact and implications for equity and social justice for students in urban schools, predominantly low-income African American and Latina/o youth.

However, although continuing U.S. supremacy represents a genuine concern for other countries, particularly to the global South and economically developing nations, that is only one side of the dialectic—because wherever there are dangers, there are also opportunities. These include educational projects that support students in critically analyzing and subsequently working to undermine U.S. policies that serve capital rather than the interests of humanity. A concrete example is *to use mathematics education as a weapon in the struggle for social justice*—that is, to involve K-12, urban, mathematics students as investigators of social reality and as advocates and actors for social change. Thus, while my main focus here is to analyze the politics of mathematics education writ large, in the second part of the chapter, I briefly examine the possibility for (and give a specific example of) mathematics education to oppose U.S. plans for global supremacy. My overall purpose is to contribute to understanding and developing a program to counter the dominant agenda.

My central argument is this: While the U.S. government and its corporate allies view global economic competition as a crisis and threat to their continued dominance, their proposed solution will benefit capital and not the majority of the U.S. people. The public discourse emanating from government and think tanks describes the crisis as affecting all U.S. residents, and the response is a publicly funded initiative with multiple prongs. A key plank is to use science, technology, engineering, and math education to boost productivity. U.S. students, reportedly underprepared and performing poorly in international assessments, are to learn more mathematics, science, and technology and become the professionals needed to answer the challenges from other countries. However, history shows that when U.S. productivity increases, the wealthiest benefit, not the majority. This program to channel public funding and students' talents into salvaging U.S. economic supremacy—in capital's interests—diametrically contrasts with educating youth to critique unjust relations of power and for democratic participation to change the world.

Second, the public discussion accompanying these plans portrays the future labor force composition as overwhelmingly one of "skilled, high-tech" workers, and hides the fact that the United States is—and will remain—a nation with close to half of its workers *not* needing postsecondary education. This project, rather than benefiting working-class and low-income students, often of color, who will become those workers, is intended for the few who will benefit from U.S. global economic dominance.

To clarify, I am not contesting that the U.S. economy has serious problems or that economic competition is real. My main point is that the proposals of the administration and capital serve only them, but in the long run, solutions benefiting the majority lie in cooperative economic relations based on genuine mutual respect among nations and real efforts for global sustainability. These include a true commitment to ending poverty, the elimination of the debt of economically developing countries, and the fostering of economic and political independence of nations and peoples. For the planet to survive, it is impossible for the U.S. to implement its "grand strategy" that situates it over the rest of the world.

A Nation At Risk, Yet Again

The specter of the United States as a second-rate economic power looms large in a string of recent, highly influential reports. One of the most important, *Rising Above the Gathering Storm*, was produced by a committee of the National Academies (2006). Beginning with its title, the report evoked a sense of foreboding and danger. It stated:

> Having reviewed trends in the United States and abroad, the committee is deeply concerned that the scientific and technological building blocks critical to our economic leadership are eroding at a time when many other nations are gathering strength...we are worried about the future prosperity of the United States.... This nation must prepare with great urgency to preserve its strategic and economic security. (p. 4)

The report outlined four sets of major recommendations concerning K-12 education, postsecondary education, research, and economic policy which are directed to policy makers, corporate heads, and government officials. Its position was: "Without a renewed effort to bolster the foundations of our competitiveness, we can expect to lose our privileged position. For the first time in generations, the nation's children could face poorer prospects than their parents and grandparents did" (p. 10).

Other equally gloomy reports with appropriately depressing titles include *The Looming Work Force Crisis* (National Association of Manufacturers, [NAM], 2005), *American's Perfect Storm* (Educational Testing Service, 2007), and *Tough Choices or Tough Times* (National Center on Education and the Economy [NCEE], 2007). The *Looming Work Force Crisis* reported that, "...below the seemingly calm surface an undercurrent of uncertainty is roiling the emotional waters for American workers. Rapid changes in technology and intense global competition—particularly from Asia—have fomented a gnawing anxiety about the future" (p. 1). With respect to the declining percentage of college degrees being awarded to U.S. students in the science, mathematics, and technology fields, compared to the increase reported for South Korea, Japan, and China, the report warned:

> By itself, this problematic trend should be enough to grab the attention of our nation's leaders and compel them to develop a comprehensive strategy for reinvigorating science and engineering education. Viewed in an international context, the facts should be downright frightening for policymakers. (p. 5)

Words sprinkled throughout the report aimed to capture the current state of our allegedly underprepared work force, vis-à-vis those of other nations, and suggest that the crisis is indeed imminently upon us. These descriptors included *woeful*, *unfortunate*, *troubling*, *disturbing*, and *alarming*! The document finished with the dire warning that:

> These troubling trends can lead our country down a path we do not want to take. Without an educated and highly skilled workforce to drive 21st century innovation, America's capacity to remain the world's most advanced economy is at risk. Other countries are moving fast to educate their workers and to innovate. If we do not implement a concerted national strategy to do the same, we risk America's future. (p. 10)

The Educational Testing Service (ETS) produced its own report, *America's Perfect Storm: Three Forces Changing Our Nation's Future* (ETS, 2007). The three factors creating the storm were "divergent skill distributions, a changing economy, and demographic trends" (p. 6). The report detailed various issues confronting the U.S. economy and nation as a whole, and it argued against those who believe that the rhetoric of crisis is overblown:

> Unlike the perfect storm chronicled in the novel written by Sebastian Junger, the forces behind this storm continue to gain strength, and calm seas are nowhere in sight. We can't hope to ride this one out. If we continue on our present heading and fail to take effective action, the storm will have a number of predictable and dire implications for future generations, with consequences that extend well beyond the economic realm to the ethos of our society. (p. 7)

The report authors did express concern with the "recent concentration of wealth and power that contrasts with the more broadly shared prosperity America experienced in the decades following World War II" (p. 26). But their broader worries were increased fragmentation and polarization of U.S. society along lines of race, social class, educational attainment, and immigration status.

Tough Choices or Tough Times (NCEE, 2007) also suggested that the United States as a whole would suffer if we do not innovate and transform our economy and educational system:

> If we continue on our current course, and the number of nations outpacing us in the education race continues to grow at its current rate, the American standard of living will steadily fall relative to those nations, rich and poor, that are doing a better job. If the gap gets to a certain—but unknowable—point, the world's investors will conclude that they can get a greater return on their funds elsewhere,[1] and it will be almost impossible to reverse course. Although it is possible to construct a scenario for improving our standard of living, the clear and present danger is that it will fall for most Americans. (p. 8)

In short, the flood of reports suggests that the situation is indeed perilous and that unless substantive steps are taken—soon, if not immediately—the situation may be out of control and the serious decline of the U.S. economy and its world standing may occur. And these reports were all written before the credit and subprime mortgage crises and recent U.S. economic downturn.

This concern about the deterioration of the U.S. economy is not new. An earlier alarm bell in the early 1980s was rung by the highly influential report, *A Nation at Risk: The Imperative for Educational Reform* (National Commission on Excellence in Education, 1983). Its primary purpose was to report on the state of U.S. education to then-Secretary of Education Bell and then-President Reagan, as well as to the U.S. people. The report explicitly linked the quality of the U.S. education system to its economic standing:

> ...the educational foundations of our society are presently being eroded by a rising tide of mediocrity that threatens our very future as a nation and a people. What was unimaginable a generation ago has begun to occur—others are matching and surpassing our educational attainments.... America's position in the world may once have been reasonably secure with only a few exceptionally well-trained men and women. It is no longer.... If only to keep and improve on the slim competitive edge we still retain in world markets, we must dedicate ourselves to the reform of our educational system for the benefit of all—old and young alike, affluent and poor, majority and minority. Learning is the indispensable investment required for success in the "information age" we are entering. (pp. 7–8)

That report significantly impacted the U.S. educational system and influenced the development of the National Council of Teachers of Mathematics (NCTM) *Curriculum and Evaluation Standards*, among other policy documents and proposals (NCTM, 1989). Although many of its recommendations were never implemented (e.g., that the federal government take a greater role in funding local educational efforts), and although some argued that the risk was "manufactured" (e.g., Berliner & Biddle, 1995), the specter that the U.S. educational system was "at risk" propelled forward the goals of "life-long learning" and of improving the educational system to meet the challenge of foreign competitors to the U.S. economy.

Today, this fear has reemerged with new vigor. The reports are filled with data purporting to show the material impact of the threat, including, but not limited to, educational issues. For example, from 1985 to 2000, the annual number of first-degree Chinese engineering graduates increased 161% to 207,500; in Japan, the number increased 42% to 103,200; and in South Korea, the increase was 140% to 56,500—while at the same time U.S. engineering graduates declined 20% to 59,500 (National Science Foundation, 2004). In 2005, IBM, that emblem of U.S. technological status, sold its personal computer business to Lenovo—a Chinese corporation. The reports also cited the U.S. trade imbalance with other countries as a serious problem. For example, in 2004, China bought $278 million of U.S. textile products while selling $14.6 billion worth to the U.S., or about 53 times as much as it purchased from the U.S. Finally, although some (e.g., Farrell & Rosenfeld, 2005) argue that non-U.S. engineers lack the technological competence of those in the United States—and thus U.S. firms are unlikely to offshore skilled work—nonetheless, U.S. corporations have increasingly relocated plants and services, especially those requiring less skilled workers, to the global South (e.g., call centers in the Philippines, Conde, 2006).

The Premises of U.S. Economic Decline and Salvation

Woven within the documents describing the decline of the U.S. economy are three key premises that together explain much of the direction of the Bush Administration's policy initiatives in STEM education. The first is that scientific and technological innovation have not only been the "engines" propelling the U.S. to its preeminent economic position since the end of World War II, but more importantly, hold the key to fending off foreign competition and continuing U.S. economic dominance vis-à-vis other countries. The U.S. Domestic Policy Council's (DPC, 2006) report stated, "America's economic strength and global leadership depend in large measure on our Nation's ability to generate and harness the latest in scientific and technological developments and to apply these developments to real world applications" (p. 1). The U.S. Department of Education's (2006a) document, *Answering the Challenge of a Changing World: Strengthening Education for the 21st Century,* claimed: "To Americans, innovation means much more than the latest gadget. It means creating a more productive, prosperous, mobile and healthy society" (p. 5). Without continued U.S. supremacy in technological innovation and invention, the notion is that the economy will slip and quality of life will worsen. As *Rising Above the Gathering Storm* (National Academies, 2006) suggested, "Without high-quality, knowledge-intensive jobs and the innovative enterprises that lead to discovery and new technology, our economy will suffer and our people will face a lower standard of living" (p. 3).

The second assertion is that the productivity and educational level of the U.S. workforce are not up to the demands of the high-technology economy that is needed to maintain U.S. economic superiority. Put succinctly by the National Association of Manufacturers (2005), "Unfortunately, there are troubling signs that the American workforce is not ready to meet innovation's challenge, and our position as leader of the global economy is threatened" (p. 2). These remarks are allegedly substantiated by data in the various reports giving the impression that almost every new job in the postindustrial United States will require highly skilled and educated workers. As Margaret Spellings, U.S. Secretary of Education said in Congressional testimony, "We know that 90 percent of the fastest-growing jobs require postsecondary education" (U.S. Department of Education, 2006f).

The third premise is that education—especially in mathematics, science, and technology—is the key to the necessary innovation and the solution to the "looming workforce crisis." The United States scores poorly on international educational assessment instruments in these areas relative to some Asian and European countries (e.g., on the *Program for International Student Assessment*). These, then, are key places on which to focus attention and, more importantly, substantive resources over the next 10 years. As the National Association of Manufacturers (2005), citing cross-national studies, wrote:

> In 1995, U.S. fourth graders ranked 12th against other nations when it came to mathematics competency. By the 8th grade their ranking dropped to 19th, below not only Asian students in countries such as Korea, Japan and Taiwan, but also below students in many Eastern European nations such as Bulgaria, the Czech Republic and Slovenia. (p. 4)

Although few claim an actual parallel to 1957, it is as if the Soviet Union just launched yet another Sputnik into the night skies, and the leader of the "free world" has to again respond by pouring massive resources into mathematics and science education (i.e., the National Defense Education Act of 1958). Indeed, Sputnik is actually invoked in several of the documents (Educational Testing Service, 2007; National Academies, 2006; National Association of Manufacturers, 2005; U.S. Department of Education, 2006a). Or, to bring it more up to date—because then, the perceived threat was the Soviet Union's military—the nation is "at risk" once again, but this time, of being a second-rate economic power.

The Solution? The American Competitiveness Initiative

> Billions of new competitors are challenging America's economic leadership. (U.S. Department of Education, 2006a, p. 4)

The American Competitiveness Initiative (ACI) is a central plank of the U.S. plan to meet and overcome this threat (U.S. Domestic Policy Council, 2006). Then-President Bush launched it in his 2006 State of the Union address, and it was partially codified in the America Competes Act (signed into law in August 2007). While the new law only authorized funding for 2008 to 2010 and thus was not as far reaching as the ACI itself (with a 10-year horizon that Bush stated he intended to pursue), nevertheless both the Act and the ACI are aptly named, ambitious undertakings. With a proposed investment of $136 billion over 10 years, the ACI represents a major attempt to shore up the U.S. position relative to economic competitors by enhancing workforce preparation, research and innovation, and education (U.S. Department of Education, 2006a). While extolling the virtues of the U.S. economy ("The American economy today is the envy of the world," U.S. Domestic Policy Council, 2006, p. 4), the documents describing the ACI sounded a warning similar to those in the reports I discuss above:

> While the US is supporting science at unprecedented levels, the rest of the world is not standing still. Following the successful US model, many countries are working hard to build their own innovation capacity by pouring resources into their scientific and technological infrastructure…the ability of foreign nations to compete with America in the increasingly integrated global economy is much greater. The enhanced innovation capacity of our economic competitors makes it increasingly important to make our own economy more flexible and responsive. (p. 5)

The ACI is driven by a vision of U.S. economic dominance and global preeminence in markets and technological innovation (U.S. Department of Education, 2006a; U.S. Domestic Policy Council, 2006). The problem is the "challenge of a changing world" (U.S. Department of Education, 2006a), one in which U.S. command of the global economy is no longer secure, and the answers are straightforward. The ACI proposes substantial government spending over a relatively brief period for education, research and development (e.g., for the National Science Foundation), and technological innovation, while tax cuts and immigration reform (for high-tech workers) are also on the agenda. The ACI provides money for new mathematics and science teachers, including for advanced placement classes, some grant support for college students and for workers to get retrained, and support for "research-based" mathematics curricula in middle and high schools, among other initiatives. The National Mathematics Advisory Panel (NMAP), a part of the ACI, has, as one of its purposes, to "evaluate empirically the effectiveness of various approaches to teaching math and science and to create a research base to improve instructional methods and materials" (U.S. Domestic Policy Council, 2006, p. 16). The range of initiatives is broad, from developing and initiating educational programs from elementary mathematics education up to university-level education, to making permanent the research and experimentation tax credit (at the cost of $86 billion to U.S. taxpayers) and increasing funding for various federal agencies. The program is relatively coherent and far reaching, and its purpose is evident: to save the U.S. economy from becoming surpassed by foreign competitors. All these components (and others) are to address the central problems of international competition as well as America's allegedly underprepared work force and the educational systems supporting it.

The ACI has other international implications. While substantial numbers of knowledge workers immigrated to the United States in the past, the ACI reflects post-September 11 border restrictions which have internal economic ramifications. Government spokespeople are concerned that fewer high-skilled workers with mathematical and scientific knowledge will come to the United States (applications are down), or stay if they do. Yet these highly educated immigrants historically have contributed substantially to the U.S. economy (as have immigrants across the spectrum; Fiscal Policy Institute, 2007). Thus, one ACI provision proposes revamping immigration policies to: "increase our ability to compete for and retain the best and brightest high-skilled workers [particularly in technological fields] from around the world by supporting comprehensive immigration reform that meets the needs of a growing economy" (U.S. Domestic Policy Council, 2006, p. 6). A background document for *Tough Choices or Tough Times* clearly expressed this view:

> …with IT salaries rising in both India and China, and restrictions on finding employment in the US, there is the growing risk that foreign students will take the lessons from their participation in cutting-edge research in US universities back to their home countries to support the growth of competitor firms there. There is also the risk that they would choose never to come to the US in the first place. (Troppe & Carlson, 2006, p. 79)

Unpacking the Initiative's Underlying Assumptions

The ACI specifically addresses the three central premises that relate to the current "crisis": the U.S. economy needs technological innovation for its salvation; the U.S. workforce is unprepared to meet the challenges; and mathematics and science education are key to the solution. In the ACI's vision, all three come together to solve the major problem of U.S. global competitiveness. To fully unpack these arguments and all their interconnections, and to deconstruct their ideological foundations, is beyond the scope of this chapter, but an important aspect that I analyze here is the relationship of premises two and three—that is, the workforce analyses and the role of mathematics education. I also discuss whom the ACI benefits.

The ACI platform makes STEM education an important focus and positions it as a central means of solving the problem of foreign competition:

> Education is the gateway to opportunity and the foundation of a knowledge-based, innovation-driven economy. For the US to maintain its global economic leadership, we must ensure a continuous supply of highly trained mathematicians, scientists, engineers, technicians, and scientific support staff as well as a scientifically, technically, and numerically literate population. (U.S. Domestic Policy Council, 2006, p. 15)

The specific issues are that the mathematical (and scientific/technological) knowledge of U.S. students is insufficient to fully develop the needed innovations and inventions to match those of the European Union, Asia, and other countries, and that U.S. students are lagging behind students in other nations on various cross-national assessments. The latter point has caused considerable consternation for U.S. policy makers, as I mention above. *Rising Above the Gathering Storm* (National Academies, 2006) cited the National Center for Education Statistics and stated, "Alarmingly, about one-third of the 4th graders and one-fifth of the 8th graders lacked the competence to perform even basic mathematical computations" (p. 12), and "U.S. 15-year-olds ranked 24th out of 40 countries that participated in a 2003 administration of the Program for International Student Assessment (PISA) examination, which assessed students' ability to apply mathematical concepts to real-world problems" (p. 12). The current discourse is that U.S. students are far behind where they need to be.

The other widely discussed aspect of the current situation is the requirements for new jobs. The prevailing assumption is that new jobs in the U.S. require new skills, which students presumably lack. Margaret Spelling, in commenting on new job requirements, said, "fewer than half of our students graduate from high school ready for college level math and science" (U.S. Department of Education, 2006f). Bill Gates (Gates Foundation, 2007) testified at a U.S. Senate committee hearing that:

> The US Department of Labor has projected that, in the decade ending in 2014, there will be over two million job openings in the United States in these fields [mathematics, computer science, engineering, and the physical sciences]. Yet in 2004, just 11 percent of all higher education degrees awarded in the US were in engineering, mathematics, and the physical sciences—a decline of about a third since 1960.

Statements like these underscore the worry about economic competitiveness and become part of an unquestioned assessment of the current, underprepared U.S. situation.

Problematizing the Work Force Data

However, the workforce data are more complex than what appears on the surface and in public statements. The U.S. Bureau of Labor Statistics (BLS) estimates complicate, if not directly contradict, Spellings' claim about the requirements for the fastest-growing jobs. Every two years, the BLS makes a 10-year projection of job growth based on many factors. Although these estimates are subject to economic swings (e.g., recessions), BLS analyses are useful for government economists and policy makers, and for my discussion here. The BLS classifies 753 specific jobs into 10 major occupational groups and also into 11 categories that capture the jobs' education/training requirements. They then further classify each job into six "educational attainment clusters," finally collapsed into three main educational clusters: "high graduate school or less," "some college," and

Table 6.1 Key Points on Workforce Data from this Section

1. Many of the fastest-growing jobs are in technical or professional fields.
2. Service sector jobs (including low-skilled ones) will also grow quickly.
3. The fastest growing jobs do not necessarily have high numerical growth and vice-versa.
4. Personal/home care aides (low-skill, very low pay) have very high projected numerical growth (389,000) and a very fast projected growth rate (50.6%).
5. Home health aides (low-skill, very low pay) have very high projected numerical growth (384,000) and a very fast projected growth rate (48.7%).
6. Of the 30 fastest growing jobs, personal/home care aides have the highest projected numerical growth, with home health aides immediately behind.
7. Registered nurses have the highest projected numerical growth (587,000), with retail salespersons (low-skill, low-pay) immediately behind (557,000).
8. Two thirds of the jobs with the highest numerical growth require short-term or moderate-term training (generally not college).
9. Close to half of all the jobs in 2016—71+ million—will be filled by workers with a high school diploma or less.

"bachelor's degree or higher" (BLS, 2008b). Their most recent report covered 2006 to 2016 and examined the 30 fastest growing jobs, the 30 with the largest numerical growth, trends for the 10 major occupational groups, and projections for educational attainment (Dohm & Shniper, 2007). It is important to distinguish between jobs with a fast *rate* of growth from those with high *numerical* growth. Table 6.1 summarizes this section's main points.

The BLS does project that many of the fastest-growing jobs are in technical and professional fields. For example, for the period from 2006 to 2016, they expect the subcategory "Computer and Mathematical Occupations" (professional jobs requiring postsecondary education such as actuaries, computer scientists, mathematicians, programmers, and software engineers) to increase by 24.8%, fastest among professional jobs (Dohm & Shniper, 2007). And the fastest growing individual job category (53.4%) is "network systems and data communication analysts." The BLS also projects that a larger proportion of jobs will require at least some college, although the increase is small (BLS, 2008b).

But this is only half of the story. The service sector, which includes many low-skilled jobs, will also experience fast growth as well as high numerical growth in certain industries. The job with the second fastest projected growth rate from 2006 to 2016, 50.6%, is that of "personal and home care aide"—a very low-paying, low-skill job—that requires only short-term, on-the-job training. The job description, as listed in the BLS's *Standard Occupational Classification System* (2000), is to "Assist elderly or disabled adults with daily living activities at the person's home or in a daytime non-residential facility. Duties performed at a place of residence may include keeping house (making beds, doing laundry, washing dishes) and preparing meals." Furthermore, while its growth rate is just slightly less than the fastest job (network systems/data communication analysts), the latter is projected to increase by 140,000 jobs, while personal/home care aides will increase by 389,000, close to three times as many.

The third fastest growing job is "home health aides," defined by the BLS (2000) as "[p]roviding routine, personal healthcare, such as bathing, dressing, or grooming, to elderly, convalescent, or disabled persons in the home of patients or in a residential care facility." Its projected growth rate is 48.7%, adding 384,000 jobs. Together, the numerical growth of personal/home care and home health aides *by themselves* account for one third of the growth of the 30 fastest growing jobs. The BLS classifies these two jobs as "very low paying," requiring "short-term, on-the-job training" (30 days or less) (Dohm & Shniper, 2007). And, most people currently doing this work have a high school education or less (BLS, 2006).

Furthermore, others of the 30 fastest growing jobs do not have large numerical growth, and some requiring postsecondary education have very small numerical growth. Forensic science technicians (a job that generally requires an associate degree) have a fast projected growth rate of 30.7% over the 2006 to 2016 period—but the BLS forecasts suggest only 4,000 additional jobs. Similarly, "makeup artists, theatrical and performance" has a fast growth rate (39.8%)—but the BLS expects it to grow by only 1,000 jobs.

This contrasts with many jobs that the BLS projects to grow more slowly but have both large numerical growth *and* substantially less educational requirements. The two jobs I mention above, personal/home care aides and home health aides are respectively ranked second and third in terms of growth rate, and sixth and seventh in terms of numerical growth. Of the 30 job categories with the highest projected numerical growth, the BLS classifies two thirds of the jobs themselves (5,383,000 of 8,101,000) as requiring short-term (less than 30 days) or moderate-term (up to one year) on-the-job training. Although some people in these jobs have education past high school, it is not generally required. And while these 30 include professional occupations such as college professors, elementary school teachers, accountants and auditors, software engineers, and computer system analysts, most are not. These are janitors and cleaners, wait staff, food preparation and serving workers (including fast food), home health aides, nursing aides, attendants and orderlies, laborers, security guards, and maids.

These data suggest some general conclusions about the future work force: By 2016, the United States will continue to have an economically polarized and educationally stratified work force rather than be a society of high-tech workers almost all needing postsecondary education and advanced degrees. Although there will be a slight shift (about 1%) from the "high school or less" category to that of the "bachelor's degree or more," *over 71 million jobs*, close to half of all jobs, will be filled by workers with at most a 12th-grade education—including millions who do not finish high school (Figure 6.1). Margaret Spellings' claim does have *some* validity—there are jobs with fast growth rates that require advanced schooling. In fact, the BLS concludes that the fastest numerical growth will be in jobs requiring a bachelor's degree or higher. However, the other, nondiscussed part of the story demands attention as well. The BLS (2008b) makes this clear:

Education cluster	Employment				Change			Total job openings due to growth and net replacements, 2006–16[1]	
	Number		Percent distribution		Number	Percent distribution	Percent	Number	Percent distribution
	2006	2016	2006	2016					
Total	150,620	166,220	100.0	100.0	15,600	100.0	10.4	50,732	100.0
High school graduate or less	66,365	71,484	44.1	43.0	5,119	32.8	7.7	21,656	42.7
Some college	46,229	51,074	30.7	30.7	4,845	31.1	10.5	15,534	30.6
Bachelor's degree or higher	38,026	43,663	25.2	26.3	5,637	36.1	14.8	13,542	26.7

1. Total job openings represent the sum of employment and net replacements. If employment change is negative, job openings due to growth are zero and total job openings equal net replacements.

Note. Detail may not equal total or 100 percent due to rounding.

Figure 6.1 Employment and job openings by education cluster, 2006–2016 (numbers in thousands). (U.S. Bureau of Labor Statistics, 2008b)

> . . .the projected change in employment for each of the 753 detailed occupations was assigned to the three educational attainment groups (high school or less, some college, and bachelor's or higher degree). Among these three groups, *jobs projected to be filled by workers with a high school degree or less will account for the largest share*, 43.0 percent, of all jobs in 2016. However, the jobs expected to be filled by those with a bachelor's or higher degree is expected to grow fastest at 14.8%. [emphasis added] (p. 3)

Close to half of all projected U.S. jobs in 2016—about 43%—will not require education past high school. Seventy-one million jobs is no small number. These jobs include, but are not limited to, ones often filled by immigrants, women, and people of color, and they are mainly low paying, which is common knowledge, as well as substantiated by government data. They include stock clerks, sewing machine operators, farmworkers, parking lot attendants, housekeepers and maids, fast food preparation workers, child care workers, receptionists, laborers, retail salespeople, home health care workers, wait staff, and custodial workers. These jobs often are unchallenging, unstimulating, and routinized. They rarely have health care, are usually nonunion, have few benefits, and require little formal education. And with the possible exception of the personal care occupations (child, elderly) provide little connection between the worker and the product of her or his labor—that lack is what Marx called "alienated labor."

The ACI—for Whom?

A key element of the ACI's framing, and of all the related reports, is that the U.S. people as a whole are in economic jeopardy because of foreign competition. It follows, then, that the ACI will benefit the whole country. The impression that almost all new jobs require advanced schooling and the data about the poor educational showing of U.S. students on international assessments further support the idea that the United States has a common, national problem. However, I argue here that the ACI is not intended to benefit the majority of the U.S. people, but rather to serve capital by strengthening corporate profits, increasing the wealth of the wealthy, and maintaining U.S. economic supremacy. Here I examine the question: Whom does the ACI benefit, and who is excluded? I also briefly address why the U.S. government presents the ACI as aiding the whole nation.

Analyzing Who Benefits The contention that increased productivity will boost the economic fortunes of the country obscures the history of who has actually benefited in the United States over the last 40 years as productivity grew—and by extension, who *will* benefit from the ACI. U.S. labor productivity rose (although at uneven rates) during this time period, while income inequality increased substantially—and the wealthiest overwhelmingly collected the riches. The *gini coefficient* is a one-number summary of income (or wealth) inequality; the larger the number, the larger is the income (wealth) inequality. The gini index ranges from 0.0 (perfect equality) to 1.0 (maximum inequality). The U.S. gini coefficient (in terms of income) has increased markedly since 1968 when it was 0.386. Ten years later, in 1978, it was 0.402; in 1988, it was 0.427; and in 1998, it was 0.456. By 2001, it had climbed to 0.466, and was 0.470 in 2006 (U.S. Census Bureau, 2007). Additionally, the ratio of mean U.S. CEO annual salary to that of a minimum wage worker was 51 to 1 in 1965, but by 2005, it had soared to 821 to 1 (Mishel, Bernstein, & Allegretto, 2007). During this period, wealth inequality also climbed (Wolff, 2002). In 2003, Edward Wolff, a well-known economist who studies wealth inequality, reported, "We [the U.S.] have had a fairly sharp increase in wealth inequality dating back to 1975 or 1976" and he added that the *wealth* gini index in 2003 was ".82, which is pretty close to the maximum level of inequality you can have" (Multinational Monitor, 2003)—far more unequal than income inequality.

In a carefully argued, detailed analysis that directly tied U.S. productivity to income distribution, Dew-Becker and Gordon (2005), stated that from 1966 till 2001, "*nobody below the 90th* [income] *percentile received the average rate of productivity growth*" [emphasis original] (p. 58). Where did the gains in productivity go? Their answer is that, "*only the top 10 percent of the income distribution enjoyed a growth rate of real wage and salary income equal to or above the average rate of economy-wide productivity growth*" [emphasis original] (abstract). They further point out that the skewing of income inequality is more pronounced as one gets richer:

> Another way to state our main results is that the *top 1 percent* of the income distribution accounted for 21.6 percent of real total income gains during 1966–2001 and 21.3 percent during the productivity revival period 1997–2001, again excluding capital gains. Still another and perhaps even more stunning way to describe our results is that the top one-tenth of one percent of the income distribution earned as much of the real 1997–2001 gain in wage and salary income, excluding nonlabor income, as the bottom 50 percent [emphasis in the original]. (p. 76)

In other words, during that period, the top 0.1% made as much as the bottom 50%—which is 500 times larger. Dew-Becker and Gordon further noted: "Not only have the bottom 90 percent of American workers failed to keep up with productivity growth, many have been harmed by it" (p. 77). If the past is any indication, the record of increased enrichment of the wealthy few and the impoverishment of the majority as a result of, or at least correlated to, increased economic productivity, points out whom the ACI will benefit.

The ACI's proposals for mathematics education also shed light on whom it will—and will not—benefit. The ACI calls for two new college scholarships (not only for mathematics): the *academic competitiveness* (AC) and *national SMART grants* (U.S. Department of Education, 2008). Since the money is to be spent to meet critical national needs, it follows that it goes only to those who can presumably help resolve the crisis. Thus, these programs are not for everyone (nor do they provide much money). The AC grants are for first and second-year college students. The guidelines stipulate that only young graduates, basically fresh out of high school, can apply, so older adults (often working class and of color) returning to school are ineligible. Students only qualify if they passed either two advanced placement exams (with a score of 3 or better) or *international baccalaureate* program exams (with a score of 4), or took a "rigorous" high school course of study. Rigor is defined at the state level but generally includes three years of mathematics (including an "advanced" class of Algebra II), three years of science (at least two years of biology, physics, or chemistry), four years of English, three years of social studies, and one year of foreign language. Students who have struggled or who had no opportunity to take "rigorous" courses, or those leading to advanced placement classes, are not eligible for the grants. In fact, *no* ACI money supports these students for college.

The SMART grants, for third and fourth-year college students, are even more restrictive. Only those majoring in a mathematical or scientific field (or in a "critical foreign language," including Farsi, Arabic, Chinese, Japanese, Russian, Korean, and Urdu) are eligible, and they must have a GPA of 3.0 or above. Sociology majors, for example, or again, students not achieving at a level deemed sufficiently useful for capital and U.S. competitive advantage cannot apply. Furthermore, the AC grants give only $750 maximum for first-year students and up to $1300 for sophomores (who must also have a 3.0 or better GPA). SMART grants increase the amount to $4,000 for seniors, under the evident presumption that students who have demonstrated their potential economic value to the nation are thus worthy of further and larger support.

The thrust of the grants and who gets them is clear. They are not for all students, and certainly not for those students who were profoundly *miseducated* (Woodson, 1933/1990) and received substandard educations—like many urban public school youth. For example, in 2004, the mean ACT score of Chicago students in neighborhood (i.e., nonselective enrollment) public high schools was 15.3 (Chicago Public Schools, 2005)—hardly enough to qualify for college. Students who went to schools with no advanced placement courses, international baccalaureate (IB) programs, or an insufficiently "rigorous" curriculum cannot apply. In Illinois, where I live, the state education board mandates less social studies and science than the AC or SMART grants require (Illinois State Board of Education, 2007), so a student with straight A's who followed the "basic" plan of her school is ineligible. Furthermore, although $750 is not trivial, it may not make enough difference to enable working-class and low-income students to attend college.

The ACI has other mathematics education initiatives, but none prepares teachers to support their students in learning to understand and change society and to participate in a democracy. Teachers need knowledge of sociopolitical contexts and students' lives, cultures, languages, experiences, and communities (Ladson-Billings, 1994, 1995). They also need to politically understand the struggles facing their students' communities and how to act in solidarity with them against oppressive conditions (Freire, 1970/1998a; 1998b). These knowledges, however, are totally absent from the ACI's plans.

On the contrary, the ACI argues that professionals' content knowledge is necessary, and it proposes an *adjunct teaching corps* who will presumably be excellent teachers because they know mathematics. Based on a recommendation from *Rising Above the Gathering Storm* (NA, 2006), the goal is to recruit and prepare some 30,000 mathematics and science professionals:

> While many scientists and engineers express an interest in teaching, traditional teacher certification programs are seen by many scientists and mathematicians as an unnecessary and unacceptable barrier to becoming a classroom teacher…anecdotal evidence does suggest that math and science majors and professionals are more likely to transition to careers in teaching if their teacher certification recognizes the training and experience they possess in their field. (U.S. Domestic Policy Council, 2006, p. 17)

It is remarkable to see a U.S.-government-produced document cite "anecdotal evidence" when the U.S. Department of Education's Institute of Education Sciences (IES) essentially acknowledged only "randomized, controlled, double-blind experiments" as evidence for "what works" in education (see the *What Works Clearinghouse,* IES, 2007). But that contradiction aside, most educators accept content knowledge as necessary—but insufficient to teach all students (Martin, 2007). Subject-matter expertise alone does not guarantee that individuals can teach appropriately, effectively, and respectfully, but the ACI's emphasis on it implies that the real goal is to develop future, technologically sophisticated innovators to help bail out the U.S. economy.

The ACI documents proclaim that it is intended for all students, but this rhetoric matches neither the reality of the workforce predictions nor the situation in urban schools. The U.S. Department of Education's (2006c) website claims: "The expansion of AP-IB programs will not only benefit students passing the AP exams, but will also serve as a mechanism to upgrade the entire high school curriculum so that other students benefit." However, in a tracked educational system and stratified labor market, it is not clear that the "entire" curriculum will be upgraded so that "other students benefit." The U.S. does not have jobs for a work force that is entirely "highly educated," and from capital's perspective, the 71 million low-skill workers who need a 12th grade education or less have little need to take AP tests because few will likely go to college, if even finish high school. The high-quality, college-preparatory education that *all* low-income students of color need to fully participate in a democratic society, and for which their communities have fought for over a century, has been systemically denied to them (Anderson, 1988; Getz, 1997). Capital has no use for such an educated mass of youth of color who might use their knowledge to rearrange the structural inequalities that oppress them (Freire & Macedo, 1987). A recent study showed that 25.8% of African American male public high school students in Chicago dropped out in the 2001 to 2002 school year (Greater Westtown Community Development Project, 2003). Extrapolating this to four years suggest that only approximately one third of the Black males entering high school in Chicago will graduate in four years—and that does not even account for those who leave during middle school or after eighth grade. These young men are slated, and in general, educated (Anyon, 1980), for those low-skilled jobs at best, but even that will be a challenge due to structural and institutional racism—Black unemployment rates are double those of whites (9.7% vs. 4.9% as of May 2008; BLS, 2008a).

Another ACI component is the National Mathematics Advisory Panel (NMAP), the purpose of which is to inform the Department of Education of successful mathematics programs to support the ACI's goals. The very first words of the charge to the NMAP are clear and consistent with the ACI: "In order to keep America competitive, support American talent and creativity, encourage innovation throughout the American economy…." Point number one of the executive order that created the NMAP stated that its role was to recommend, "[t]he critical skills and skill progressions for students to acquire competence in algebra and readiness for higher levels of mathematics" (U.S. Department of Education, 2006b, p. 3). The thrust for higher mathematics is for those who have the potential to remedy the economic crises forecast by *Rising Above the Gathering Storm* (National Academies, 2006) and other documents, but not for the 71 million low-skill workers projected for 2016.

Analyzing Why the ACI Claims to Be for All I argue above that a major ACI goal is to boost productivity for U.S. capital by educating more mathematically, scientifically, and technologically adept students who will then become professionals. Why, then, do its documents and proclamations proclaim that it is "for all?" There are at least three possible reasons: for legitimation, potential economic savings, and so-called "creaming the crop."

First, given that taxpayers are paying for the ACI, a U.S. administration cannot easily state that this major initiative supports the wealthy and the corporate elite. Instead, it poses the threat as a common danger to all: "Without high-quality, knowledge-intensive jobs and the innovative enterprises that lead to discovery and new technology, our economy will suffer and *our people will face a lower standard of living*" [emphasis added] (National Academies, 2007, p. 3). Throughout the reports I discuss here, the impression is clear that this national situation affects all U.S. people. When the documents frame the problem as, for example, losing control of global markets, they imply a negative impact on the people as a whole rather than the potential decline of U.S. corporate profits. There is no mention that "our people" already face a lower standard of living because of the growth of wealth and income inequality, and the U.S. government would find itself in an unsustainable position if it were to directly declare that. Also, the claim that 90% of the fastest-growing jobs require postsecondary education gives the impression that "everyone" needs to "upgrade" their knowledge and skills—and will consequently benefit—and should therefore support the initiatives. It would not be in capital's interest to explicitly state that over 40% of U.S. jobs now—and in 2016—will require a high school diploma at most.

Second, some data suggest that there may be some economic savings to the United States as a whole from increased education, but again, this would not necessarily benefit the majority any more than increased productivity. Education Secretary Spellings gave a 2005 speech in which she claimed, "The one million students who drop out of high school each year cost our nation more than $260 billion in lost wages, lost taxes, and lost productivity over their lifetimes," although the U.S. Department of Education gave no source for this statement nor analyzed where that money would go otherwise (2005). Other analyses suggest that more students completing college would boost productivity: "Boosting our college completion rate from 25 percent to 27.5 percent would yield a full one percent increase in real GDP per worker or about 125 billion for the overall economy" (Uhalde & Strohl, 2006, p. 12), but the authors also gave no data source. In yet another calculation, the U.S. Department of Education (2006d) stated, "Because high school graduates are less likely to commit crimes, increasing the high school completion rate by just 1% for all men ages 20 to 60 would reduce costs in the criminal justice system by as much as $1.4 billion per year." This latter argument may effectively play upon public fears that stem from, and in turn reproduce, the demonization of African American and Latino males who are disproportionately incarcerated, but again, one has no idea of the source of the statement.

From the standpoint of the competitiveness of U.S. capital, the ACI's proposed investment of $122 million for "training 70,000 new teachers and increasing the number of students achieving passing AP/IB scores to 700,000" (U.S. Domestic Policy Council, 2006, p. 18) is small indeed if it were to contribute to raising the college completion rate, reducing the high school dropout rate, and keeping the streets "safe." But regardless of the claim's veracity, if true, those who would profit from this investment would likely be the same economic beneficiaries of the ACI in general.

Third, "creaming the crop" relates to the idea that "they [schools] must develop a pool of technically adept and numerically literate Americans to ensure a continual supply of highly trained mathematicians, scientists and engineers" (U.S. Department of Education, 2006a, p. 9). The U.S. administration and the U.S. Department of Education are not so naïve as to believe that no potential future engineers, scientists, and mathematicians attend urban public schools (and certainly some individuals within government sincerely want to increase opportunity for low-income students of color). The U.S. Department of Education (2006e) stated, "It is crucial that middle school students who are significantly below grade level in math receive appropriate and effective interventions so that they will be prepared to take challenging math courses in high school"—to become those "highly trained" professionals. By widening the precollege "pipeline," those students who squeeze through may join the knowledge intelligentsia that capital needs if it is to pacify the "gathering storms." The obvious, and unstated, corollary is that for those who do not, there are always the 71 million low-skill jobs, if they are lucky.

In short, the ACI and its various components related to mathematics education aim to strengthen the U.S. hold on the global economy. To the extent that the ACI boosts innovation and productivity, the richest will benefit as they did in the past (Dew-Becker & Gordon, 2005), and the U.S. financial and corporate elite will be well served. Increasing opportunities for a few by focusing on the most-advantaged, highest-achieving students may help U.S. capital, but not those who will fill the low-skill, service sector jobs—disproportionately low-income students, students of color, and immigrants. The ACI does not support the majority of urban students, nor change the barriers that keep them from accessing opportunities. Nothing in it promotes education for democracy and critical literacies, or the development of sociopolitical consciousness, sense of social agency, and positive cultural and social identities of students in K-12 schools. Nothing in it advocates for the transformation to a more socially just planet.

An Alternative Framing: Mathematics Education as a Weapon in the Struggle for Social Justice

Although the ACI is intended to alleviate U.S. economic woes for the benefit of capital, and thus positions mathematics education as part of that larger plan, a different framing of mathematics education is possible—one that situates teaching and learning mathematics as a weapon in the struggle for social justice on a local, as well as global scale. Space prevents me from more fully discussing the possibilities here, but I provide an example from our work in an urban Chicago public school (see Gutstein, 2007, 2008) and draw out some implications.

The Greater Lawndale/Little Village School for Social Justice grew out of a community struggle for a new high school in an overcrowded, educationally underserved, Mexican immigrant community in Chicago (Russo, 2003; Stovall, 2005). The school building opened in Fall 2005 and has four small high schools, each with 350 to 400 students. Students are 70% of Mexican heritage, 30% from a neighboring African American community, and virtually all are low-income. The schools are "neighborhood attendance area" ones, meaning that any student living in the surrounding community can attend. Community members won the new building by waging a 19-day hunger strike in 2001, and the Greater Lawndale school took on the theme of social justice from that struggle. I was on the design team that developed the proposal and initial plan for that school. Since it opened, I have worked closely with students and supported the teachers as we developed and cotaught a mathematics curriculum oriented toward social justice. We also formed a student coresearch team that participates in data analysis and helps develop curriculum. In the 2006 to 2007 and 2007 to 2008 school years, these students made presentations about social justice mathematics at 12 regional or national education conferences (e.g., Gutstein, Blunt, et al., 2007). As I write this (September 2008), I work with the 80 or so seniors and the school's three mathematics teachers. I also teach one 12th grade mathematics class, focusing on social justice contexts.

A key element of the school's still evolving educational philosophy is to build on students' *community knowledge* (experiences, cultures, languages, and ways of seeing and understanding their lives and society) to support the development of their *classical knowledge* (or academic knowledge) and their *critical knowledge* (sociopolitical consciousness of their immediate lives as well as of broader contexts) (Gutstein, 2006, 2007). We also aim to support students' sense of themselves as actors capable of shaping history (Freire, 1970/1998a) and the development of strong cultural and social identities.

We started the 2007 to 2008 school year with a mathematics project about the criminalization of youth of color, specifically about the Jena 6. The Jena 6 are six African American male teenagers from Jena, Louisiana, a small town in the southern United States. In December 2006, they were initially charged with attempted murder in a schoolyard fight that developed out of a racist incident a few months earlier. The first of the six (Mychal Bell) was tried and convicted in June 2007 and was awaiting sentencing that September as we started the school year.

We did the project in the five 11th grade classes over two weeks. The focus question was: What was the probability that Mychal Bell's jury would be all white, if the jury selection process was truly random? In the United States, one is ostensibly tried by a "jury of one's peers," but there is no stipulation for what this means. No legal mandate exists that, for example, a person of color should be tried by other people of color, or even that someone of their race be on the jury. U.S. history is full of counter examples, including that of Mychal Bell, the first of the Jena 6 to be tried (and convicted)—by an all-white jury.

This focus problem is solvable in various ways, none of which our students knew. In 2000, the U.S. Census reported that Jena was approximately 85.6% white, and 14.4% people of color (mainly Black). We made some simplifying assumptions (e.g., using the number of adults in Jena as a proxy for potential jury members) and told students that they would have to "think like mathematicians" and make "mathematical generalizations." In particular, we explained that when mathematicians were confronted with a problem they did not know how to solve, they often scaled down the problem to a size which they could analyze and then generalized to the full problem. We treated the problem as one requiring combinatorics and approached it by finding the ratio of the number of 12-person combinations (i.e., a typical jury) of all the white Jena adults compared to the number of 12-person combinations of all Jena adults. Since students did not know how to find these (and we did not show them the $n\,C\,r$ function on their calculators), we started with a small problem of parallel structure and gradually built up to the full problem. They eventually developed the generalizations (*n C r* and *factorial(n)*) and solved the focus problem. Along the way, mathematics became an analytical tool and an entry point into deeper discussions of racism, justice, and criminalization of youth of color.

Projects like these have several purposes that align with our understanding of the goals of teaching and learning mathematics for social justice (Gutstein, 2006). First, students should develop a deeper capacity to critically understand social reality, both their immediate and broader contexts. We use Freire's (Freire & Macedo, 1987) term *reading the world* to capture the development of this sociopolitical consciousness. Understanding current issues, their historical roots, and how social movements produce change are all important components of students' learning. A second purpose is to support students' sense of social agency, or, again, in Freire's terms, to *write the world*. We understand that youth (like adults) take action in society as a gradual, developmental process. A third purpose is that students develop the mathematical competencies needed for access and opportunity, but also to read and write the world with mathematics. A question some might raise about critical mathematics pedagogy is whether students develop mathematical rigor, and we were mindful and intentional about that as we pushed students to think like mathematicians and develop mathematical generalizations.

Although this was to only be an 11th grade project, the 9th and 10th grade math teachers decided to also teach a simplified version, so all Greater Lawndale students learned about Jena. On Mychal Bell's scheduled sentencing day in September 2007, people protested around the country, including at a Black college in Chicago, which students only learned about that morning. Several 11th graders, both Black and Latina/o, demanded that the school charter a bus for the local rally. When the principal told them it was impossible, they were furious, organized a walkout, and held an impromptu demonstration of around 30 students on a nearby busy corner. Before the students walked out, the principal initiated an all-school assembly about Jena, and all three administrators noted that students had learned about the Jena 6 in mathematics classes. Thus, the school's mathematics program led the way in this particular politicization moment. And finally, the mathematics was challenging and rigorous, at least for the 11th graders who developed mathematical generalizations. In these ways, this project supported our multiple goals for teaching and learning mathematics for social justice.

I make no claim that projects like these, by themselves, in one school, are sufficient to answer the U.S. government's plans for mathematics education. However, I argue that creating an educational movement to challenge U.S. plans for global supremacy requires transformative models. There are teachers around the United States (and world) who are providing their students with the opportunities to read and write their world, and learn mathematics by so doing (Frankenstein, 1998; Gutiérrez, 2002; Gutstein & Peterson, 2005; Mukhopadhyay & Greer, 2001; Peterson, 1995; Turner & Font Strawhun, 2005). Along with other efforts now taking place in the United States for liberatory education (e.g., such as in other social justice schools around the country and as reported in *Rethinking Schools*), such examples become important ways to share lessons and move the process forward. Small projects become part of a larger social movement, both inside and outside school, and education is reframed for the purpose of fundamentally transforming society, from the bottom to the top, to end injustice in all forms.

Conclusion

The politics of mathematics education in the United States can only be understood by examining the larger sociopolitical context in which it resides. From the perspective of the U.S. ruling elite, the story is this: In the present moment, there is a genuine economic danger, from many nations. The poor showing of U.S. students on international mathematics and science assessments is a major concern precisely because other countries are rapidly developing their infrastructure and educational capacity to challenge U.S. economic dominance. The jobs needed to meet the threat will require technological competence and postsecondary education, but the workforce is woefully underprepared to meet the demands. U.S. productivity must be increased, by fueling and furthering scientific, mathematical, and technological innovation. And the key to getting that necessary innovation is to improve education in these fields, especially mathematics education. The "challenge of a changing world" is that the United States can no longer complacently rest on its laurels. It must act, quickly, or be consumed by the "looming crisis" and by the "perfect" and "rising storm" and suffer the consequences of a diminished lifestyle for its people.

The ACI is the appropriate vehicle to stem the tide. A "bold initiative," already partially enacted as law, it will stimulate research and development (through tax credits and increased funding), increase immigration of high-tech professionals, recruit technologically competent professionals as high school teachers, fund mathematically and scientifically oriented college students, and increase the number of students taking and passing advanced placement tests. Through the National Mathematics Advisory Panel, the ACI will find mathematics curricula at the elementary and middle school levels to prepare students for the all-important technical career paths that will lead the way to continued economic security and world dominance. The rising tide, put into place by the coordinated response to the national crisis, will then lift all boats.

Or so the tale goes. The story, however, looks quite different when viewed from another perspective. Improved education may lead to more innovation and therefore to increased productivity, but for whose benefit? The last 40 years of U.S. history has shown that productivity has increased, but most have seen little improvement. Real wages have stagnated. "The typical, or median, workers' hourly wage was just 8.9% higher in 2005 than in 1979, with almost all of the growth (7.7%) occurring from 1995–2000. In contrast, productivity has grown by 67% since 1979" (Economic Policy Institute, 2006). As numerous analysts have pointed out (Dew-Becker & Gordon, 2005; Krugman, 2004; Tabb, 2007;

Wolff, 2002), the growth in income and wealth has bypassed the majority of the U.S. people and has gone to the richest. The ACI, with the explicit purpose of maintaining and extending U.S. economic supremacy on the planet, will continue to serve the interests of capital and those who already have the most wealth.

As for workforce predictions and the changing nature of the U.S. occupational structure, the data are clear: 71 million low-skill, low-paying, low-education-requiring jobs are very much on the horizon, despite a slight decrease in the proportion of these jobs. Although the ACI rhetorically purports to assist all students, nothing in it explicitly supports low-income students of color in urban public schools except those who have managed to fight their way through obstacles to be on the mathematics/science professional trajectory—the occupational prospects for many of the rest point toward those 71 million jobs—if any job at all. The ACI has no meaningful support for "regular" students and scholarships only for those who can potentially add to the economy. It "leaves behind" most African American and Latina/o students and perpetuates and exacerbates the historical legacy of racism in the United States.

But the ACI and U.S. plans for supremacy do not go uncontested, both within schools and outside of them. People are engaged in projects like those set up at the Greater Lawndale school and others, and they are committed to supporting youth to be agents of change. In these spaces, students are learning to read and write the world with mathematics. The project about the Jena 6 is but one example. And alongside these and other educational efforts are social movements and political struggles against U.S. empire across the world. This work across the planet brings us hope. Freire (1994) described hope as "an ontological need" (p. 8), meaning, I believe, that hope is an integral part of being human. But Freire always related hope to the fight for a better life: "...hope needs practice in order to become historical concreteness...without the struggle, hope...dissipates, loses its bearings, and turns into hopelessness" (p. 7). Hope, for Freire, came not from faith but from an understanding of social agency and history, that human beings make the social world: "Just as...social reality exists not by chance, but as the product of human action, so it is not transformed by chance. If humankind produces social reality...then transforming that reality is an historical task, a task for humanity" (Freire, 1970/1998, p. 33).

The dominant program may be for a "new American century"—but it is with the hope that Freire named, grounded in the ongoing people's struggles for social justice, that mathematics education can play a role in developing and actualizing a counter agenda.

Acknowledgment

I wish to acknowledge students and teachers of the Greater Lawndale/Little Village School for Social Justice with whom I have worked, especially: Nikki Blunt, Patricia Buenrostro, George Carr, Matt Crye, Veronica González, Darnisha Hill, Phi Pham, Amparo Ramos, Jon Reitzel, Rogelio Rivéra, Rut Rodríguez, and

Joyce Sia, and also thanks to Brian Greer and Pauline Lipman for help on this manuscript and the overall analysis.

Note

1. Surprisingly, some of the policy documents are explicit that capital chases after maximum profits. The executive summary of *Rising Above the Gathering Storm* (National Academies, 2006) states, "We have already seen that capital, factories, and laboratories readily move wherever they are thought to have the greatest promise of return to investors" (p. 4), and, "Market forces are *already at work* moving jobs to countries with less costly, often better educated, highly motivated work forces and more friendly tax policies" (p. 10).

References

Anderson, J. (1988). *The education of Blacks in the south, 1860–1935.* Chapel Hill, NC: University of North Carolina Press.

Anyon, J. (1980). Social class and the hidden curriculum of work. *Journal of Education, 167,* 67–92.

Berliner, D. C., & Biddle, B. J. (1995). *The manufactured crisis.* Reading, MA: Addison-Wesley.

Chicago Public Schools. (2005). School test score and demographic reports. Retrieved March 31, 2005, from http://research.cps.k12.il.us/resweb/schoolqry

Conde, C. (2006, November 24). Erosion of English skills threatens growth in Philippines. *New York Times.* Retrieved August 15, 2008, from http://www.nytimes.com/2006/11/24/business/worldbusiness/24english.html

Dew-Becker, I., & Gordon, R. J. (September, 2005). *Where did the productivity growth go? Inflation dynamics and the distribution of income.* Paper presented at the 81st meeting of the Brookings Panel on Economic Activity, Washington, D.C.

Dohm, A., & Shniper, L. (2007). Occupational employment projections to 2016. *Monthly Labor Review Online, 130*(11), 86–125.

Economic Policy Institute. (2006). *Economic snapshots: CEO pay-to-minimum wage ratio soars.* Retrieved July 9, 2007, from http://www.epi.org/content.cfm/webfeatures_snapshots_20060627

Educational Testing Service. (2007). *America's perfect storm: Three forces changing our nation's future.* Princeton, NJ: Author.

Farrell, D., & Rosenfeld, J. (2005). *U.S. offshoring: Rethinking the response.* Washington, D.C.: McKinsey.

Fiscal Policy Institute. (2007). *Working for a better life: A profile of immigrants in the New York State economy.* New York: Author.

Frankenstein, M. (1998). Reading the world with math: Goals for a critical mathematical literacy curriculum. In E. Lee, D. Menkart, & M. Okazawa-Rey (Eds.), *Beyond heroes and holidays: A practical guide to K-12 anti-racist, multicultural education and staff development* (pp. 306–313). Washington, D.C.: Network of Educators on the Americas.

Freire, P. (1994). *Pedagogy of hope: Reliving Pedagogy of the Oppressed.* (R. R. Barr, Trans.). New York: Continuum.

Freire, P. (1998a). *Pedagogy of the oppressed.* (M. B. Ramos, Trans.). New York: Continuum. (Original work published 1970)

Freire, P. (1998b). *Teachers as cultural workers: Letters to those who dare teach.* (D. Macedo, D. Koike, & A. Oliveira, Trans.). Boulder, CO: Westview Press.

Freire, P., & Macedo, D. (1987). *Literacy: Reading the word and the world.* Westport, CT: Bergin & Garvey.

Gates Foundation. (2007, March 7). Written testimony by Bill Gates, cochair, U.S. Senate Committee Hearing. Retrieved December 2, 2008, from http://www.gatesfoundation.org/speeches-commentary/Pages/bill-gates-2007-senate-hearing.aspx

Getz, J. M. (1997). *Schools of their own: The education of Hispanos in New Mexico, 1850–1940*. Albuquerque, NM: University of New Mexico Press.
Greater West Town Community Development Project. (2003). *Chicago's dropout crisis: Continuing analysis of the dropout dilemma by gender and ethnicity*. Chicago: Author.
Gutiérrez, R. (2002). Beyond essentialism: The complexity of language in teaching mathematics to Latina/o students. *American Educational Research Journal, 39*, 1047–1088.
Gutstein, E. (2006). *Reading and writing the world with mathematics: Toward a pedagogy for social justice*. New York: Routledge.
Gutstein, E. (2007). Connecting community, critical, and classical knowledge in teaching mathematics for social justice. *The Montana Mathematics Enthusiast, Monograph 1*, 109–118.
Gutstein, E. (2008). Developing social justice mathematics curriculum from students' realities: A case of a Chicago public school. In W. Ayers, T. Quinn, & D. Stovall (Eds.), *The handbook of social justice in education* (pp. 690–698). Mahwah, NJ: Erlbaum.
Gutstein, E., Blunt, N., Buenrostro, P., González, V., Hill, D., Rivera, R., & Sia, I. J. (2007, April). *Developing social justice mathematics curriculum in a Chicago public school*. Paper presented at the annual meeting of the American Educational Research Association, Chicago.
Gutstein, E., & Peterson, B. (Eds.). (2005). *Rethinking mathematics: Teaching social justice by the numbers*. Milwaukee, WI: Rethinking Schools.
Harvey, D. (2005). *A brief history of neoliberalism*. Oxford, UK: Oxford University Press.
Illinois State Board of Education. (2007). *State graduation requirements*. Retrieved June 17, 2008, from http://www.isbe.net/news/pdf/grad_require.pdf
Institute of Education Sciences. (2007). *Elementary school math*. Retrieved November 22, 2007, from http://ies.ed.gov/ncee/wwc/reports/elementary_math/topic/
Krugman, P. (2004, January 4). The death of Horatio Alger. *The Nation*. Retrieved December 24, 2007, from http://www.thenation.com/doc/20040105/krugman
Ladson-Billings, G. (1994). *The dreamkeepers*. San Francisco: Jossey-Bass.
Ladson-Billings, G. (1995). Making mathematics meaningful in multicultural contexts. In W. G. Secada, E. Fennema, & L. B. Adajian (Eds.), *New directions for equity in mathematics education* (pp. 126–145). Cambridge, UK: Cambridge University Press.
Martin, D. (2007). Beyond missionaries or cannibals: Who should teach mathematics to African American children? *The High School Journal, 91*, 6–28.
Mishel, L., Bernstein, J., & Allegretto, S. (2007). *The state of working America 2006/07* (10th ed.). Ithaca, NY: Cornell University Press.
Mukhopadhyay, S., & Greer, B. (2001). Modeling with purpose: Mathematics as a critical tool. In B. Atweh, H. Forgasz, & B. Nebres (Eds.), *Sociocultural research on mathematics education: An international perspective* (pp. 295–312). Mahwah, NJ: Erlbaum.
Multinational Monitor. (2003). *The wealth divide: The growing gap in the United States between the rich and the rest*. Retrieved July 9, 2007, from http://www.thirdworldtraveler.com/America/Wealth_Divide.html
National Academies. (2006). *Rising above the gathering storm: Energizing and employing America for a brighter economic future* (Executive Summary). Washington, D.C.: Author.
National Association of Manufacturers: Labor Day Report. (2005). The looming workforce crisis: Preparing American workers for the 21st century competition. Retrieved December 2, 2008, from http://www.cmta.net/multimedia/20050902_nam_looming_workforce_crisis.pdf
National Center for Education Statistics. (2003). *Program for international student assessment*. Retrieved October 5, 2007, from http://www.nces.ed.gov/surveys/pisa/pisa2003highlightsfigures.asp?Quest=1&Figure=9
National Center on Education and the Economy. (2007). *Tough times or tough choices: The report of the new commission on the skills of the American workforce*. Washington, D.C.: Author.
National Commission on Excellence in Education. (1983). *A nation at risk: The imperative for educational reform*. Washington, D.C.: U.S. Government Printing Office.
National Council of Teachers of Mathematics. (1989). *Curriculum and evaluation standards for school mathematics*. Reston, VA: Author.

National Science Foundation. (2004). *Science and engineering indicators 2004.* Retrieved November 19, 2007, from http://www.nsf.gov/statistics/seind04/append/c2/at02-34.pdf

Peterson, B. (1995). Teaching math across the curriculum: A 5th grade teacher battles "number numbness." *Rethinking Schools, 10*(1), 1, 4–5.

Project for a New American Century. (2000). *Rebuilding America's defenses: Strategies, forces and resources for a new century.* Washington, D.C.: Author.

Russo, A. (2003, June). Constructing a new school. *Catalyst.* Retrieved March 3, 2004, from http://www.catalyst-chicago.org/06-03/0603littlevillage.htm

Stovall, D. O. (2005). Communities struggle to make small serve all. *Rethinking Schools, 19,* 4. Retrieved September 1st, 2006, from http://www.rethinkingschools.org/archive/19_04/stru194.shtml

Tabb, W. (2007). Wage stagnation, growing insecurity, and the future of the U.S. working class. *Monthly Review, 59*(2), 20–30.

Troppe, M., & Carlson, P. (Eds.). (2006). *An analysis of market and skill changes: The impact of globalization on American jobs in selected industries.* Washington, D.C.: National Center on Education and the Economy.

Turner, E. E., & Font Strawhun, B. T. (2005). "With math, it's like you have more defense." In E. Gutstein & B. Peterson (Eds.), *Rethinking mathematics: Teaching social justice by the numbers* (pp. 81–87). Milwaukee, WI: Rethinking Schools.

Uhalde, R., & Strohl, J. (2006). *America in the global economy.* Washington, D.C.: National Center on Education and the Economy.

U.S. Bureau of Labor Statistics. (2000). *Standard occupational classification system.* Washington, D.C.: U.S. Department of Labor.

U.S. Bureau of Labor Statistics. (2006). *Occupational projections and training data: 2006–07 edition.* Washington, D.C.: U.S. Department of Labor. Retrieved November 22, 2007, from http://www.bls.gov/emp/optd/optd.pdf

U.S. Bureau of Labor Statistics. (2007). *Labor force statistics from the current population survey.* Washington, DC: U.S. Department of Labor. Retrieved November 22, 2007, from http://data.bls.gov/PDQ/servlet/SurveyOutputServlet

U.S. Bureau of Labor Statistics. (2008a). *Employment situation summary.* Washington, D.C.: U.S. Department of Labor. Retrieved June 17, 2008, from http://www.bls.gov/news.release/empsit.nr0.htm

U.S. Bureau of Labor Statistics. (2008b). *Occupational outlook handbook, 2008–09 edition.* Washington, DC: U.S. Department of Labor. Retrieved August 15, 2008, from http://www.bls.gov/emp/optd/optd001.pdf

U.S. Census Bureau. (September 2007). *Historical income tables—households.* Retrieved June 16, 2008, from http://www.census.gov/hhes/www/income/histinc/h04.html

U.S. Department of Education (2005). *Katrina: A teachable moment.* Retrieved December 2, 2008, from http://www.ed.gov/news/speeches/2005/09/09212005.html

U.S. Department of Education. (2006a). *Answering the challenge to a changing world: Strengthening education for the 21st century.* Washington DC: Author.

U.S. Department of Education. (2006b). *Charter: National mathematics advisory panel.* Retrieved November 22, 2007, from http://www.ed.gov/about/bdscomm/list/mathpanel/charter.pdf

U.S. Department of Education. (2006c). *Expanding the Advanced Placement incentive program.* Retrieved November 30, 2007, from http://www.ed.gov/about/inits/ed/competitiveness/expanding-apip.html

U.S. Department of Education (2006d). *Increasing America's competitiveness.* Retrieved December 2, 2008, from http://www.ed.gov/teachers/how/prep/higher/competitiveness.pdf

U.S. Department of Education. (2006e). *Math Now: Advancing math education in elementary and middle school.* Retrieved Nov 1, 2007, from http://www.ed.gov/about/inits/ed/competitiveness/math-now.html

U.S. Department of Education. (2006f). Secretary Spellings' prepared testimony before the House Education and Workforce Committee, press release dated April 6, 2006. Retrieved November 19, 2007, from http://www.ed.gov/news/pressreleases/2006/04/04062006.html

U.S. Department of Education. (2008). *Academic competitiveness and National SMART grants.* Retrieved August 19, 2008, from http://www.ed.gov/about/offices/list/ope/ac-smart.html
Wolff, E. N. (2002). *Top heavy: The increasing inequality of wealth in America and what can be done about it.* New York: New Press.
Woodson, C. G. (1933/1990). *The mis-education of the Negro.* Trenton, NJ: Africa World Press.

7
Conceptions of Assessment of Mathematical Proficiency and their Implications for Cultural Diversity

DALTON MILLER-JONES AND BRIAN GREER

High-stakes testing has become a major driver of the character of classroom experience and of instructional dynamics. Most of this influence is negative, inflicting "collateral damage" on students, teachers, and schools (Nichols & Berliner, 2007).

For the sake of a manageable focus relevant to the concerns of this volume, we concentrate on two conceptions of assessment that have clear implications for culturally responsive mathematics education. First are the effects of the tests designed for purposes of accountability at the national, state, and school district levels that are associated with the No Child Left Behind legislation, which we characterize as an exercise in social engineering. By contrast, we consider assessment in terms of communication in relation to its role as an ongoing part of teaching/learning. What are the practices in mathematics classrooms that can help to determine what it is that students know, understand, and can do (or not), and how can the knowledge so gained inform the ongoing teaching/learning process? In these discussions, we attempt, as far as possible, to deal with concerns specific to mathematics, while recognizing that many are related to assessment in general. Further, our discussions of issue relevant to this volume will inevitably often relate to assessment of mathematical proficiency in general.

As a necessary preliminary, we consider what is implied by the assessment of proficiency in mathematics. We begin with a point that seems obvious to us, but appears not to be generally so recognized, namely that the first step to be taken is to define in some way what mathematical proficiency is to be taken as for the purposes of assessment. If proficiency is intended to include the ability to tackle unfamiliar problems as well as to carry out routine calculations and procedures, and if it is intended to include contextualized as well as decontextualized problems, then the implications for assessment are profound, and the simplistic multiple-choice format that may be adequate for checking decontextualized routine expertise needs to be supplemented, if not totally replaced, by forms of assessment better suited to the purpose. Moreover, if problems posed in a real-world context are to be included, then the need to take into account the diversity of students' lived experience clearly comes into play.

Broadly speaking, the functions of assessment may be categorized as:

- supporting teaching/learning (formative)
- documenting the achievements or potential of individuals (summative)
- evaluating the quality of educational programs or systems (evaluative)

The essence of the difference between formative and summative assessment is captured in the analogy made by Paul Black (Nichols & Berliner, 2007): "When the chef tastes the soup it is formative assessment; when the customer tastes the soup it is a summative assessment" (p. 187). We might add that, if the customer is a health inspector or the Michelin Guide assessor, it is evaluative (and high-stakes) assessment.

Assessment, as embodied in the No Child Left Behind legislation and associated policy, is envisaged as an (extremely blunt) instrument for social engineering of the educational system through the amassing of test scores in the service of accountability. The program is essentially evaluative, with its summative element limited, and its formative element almost nonexistent. Despite rhetorical claims, this form of testing has minimal capability to constructively inform either students or teachers.

Central to the aims stated in NCLB, and responsible for much of its widespread initial, though progressively declining, support is its declared commitment to the education of all children (as implied by the title) and to the "closing of the performance gaps." In the first section of the chapter, we examine the extent to which these aims have been met, and point to rising criticism of the policy. While a full-spectrum critique of NCLB (e.g., Darling-Hammond, 2007; Nichols & Berliner, 2007; Noddings, 2007; Valenzuela, 2005) is beyond the scope of this chapter, assessment is so much at its core that we will inevitably devote attention to it. In particular, we focus on patterns of test score differences between ethnic groups of students and across time, making the point that there is no evidence of NCLB diminishing the "achievement gaps" (we explain below why we prefer not to use that term) and drawing attention to the other gaps in resources and educational opportunities that exist and whose effects have accumulated over time.

A very different conception of assessment is as an integral part of instruction. From this perspective, the key question to ask is: What practices in mathematics classrooms can help to determine how children think mathematically, and what it is that they know and can do?

In particular, in the final section, we consider assessment-within-instruction as a form of communication. At a minimum, an assessment is intended to convey to the student what knowledge and ability is to be manifested, the student is expected to communicate that knowledge and ability back to someone, and some evaluation of the student's performance is communicated to the student and the teacher. We examine various forms of assessment in terms of how effectively this communication operates.

At one end of a spectrum of communicative effectiveness, the typical timed and written test represents a very impoverished form of communication, closed in many ways, and affording many possibilities of noncommunication and miscommunication.

At the other end of the spectrum, the most valuable form of assessment-as-communication comes from conversations among teachers and students extended over time (Wiliam, 2007). One immediate implication of such a standpoint is that cultural and ethnic diversity must be considered, given known cultural differences in linguistic structures and styles and practices of communication.

How Can Mathematical Proficiency Be Assessed?

> You'd think mathematics assessment…would be simple. Would that things were so simple. (Schoenfeld, 2007d, p. 3)

First Decide what Matters

As pointed out by Schoenfeld (2007b, ix–x), many different groups—mathematicians, researchers in mathematical thinking and learning, students, teachers, administrators, policy-makers, test-makers, parents, and others—have interest and stakes in the information that assessments can provide, even if the interests are related to divergent purposes. Quite simply, we take the view that the dominant purpose should be the improvement of teaching/learning mathematics. This purpose has implications for both external and classroom assessment practices—in the former case, because of the ways in which external assessment drives teaching, and, in the latter case, because classroom assessment is an integral part of instruction.

Accordingly, it is essential to begin with the question: What aspects of mathematical proficiency do we want to assess? It seems obvious, but current practice suggests that it is not, that before attempting to assess mathematical proficiency, a value judgment is required about what will count as such. There are, of course, many views on how mathematical proficiency should be characterized (e.g., Burkhardt, 2007; Milgram, 2007; Schoenfeld, 2007a) and indeed, they are at the center of an ongoing debate (Schoenfeld, 2004). The following may represent as close to a consensus as it is possible to get (National Research Council, 2001):

> Recognizing that no term captures completely all aspects of expertise, competence, knowledge, and facility in mathematics, we have chosen mathematical proficiency to capture what we think it means for anyone to learn mathematics successfully. Mathematical proficiency, as we see it, has five strands:
>
> - conceptual understanding—comprehension of mathematical concepts, operations, and relations
> - procedural fluency—skill in carrying out procedures flexibly, accurately, efficiently, and appropriately
> - strategic competence—ability to formulate, represent, and solve mathematical problems
> - adaptive reasoning—capacity for logical thought, reflection, explanation, and justification
> - productive disposition—habitual inclination to see mathematics as sensible, useful, and worthwhile, coupled with a belief in diligence and one's own efficacy
>
> The most important observation we make about these five strands are that they are interwoven and interdependent. (p. 5)

In the context of evaluating the efficacy of a curriculum, Schoenfeld (2005) made the apparently uncontroversial point that part of this evaluation needs to be an analysis of the content and quality of any tests of mathematical proficiency used to generate data for that evaluation. In relation to the ongoing disputes regarding contrasting curricular endeavors, he concluded that "there are no definitive findings regarding the effectiveness of either traditional or reform curricula that take into account the spectrum of mathematical competencies that are now understood to be central to the effective understanding and use of mathematics" (p. 15). To put it simply, if there are two types of curriculum with differing sets of goals, and corresponding assessment instruments aligned with those respective sets, then a fair comparison of the curricula would use both kinds of assessment instruments. Schoenfeld (2007a, p. 63) argues, with illustrative findings from a study by Ridgway et al. (2000) that when the curricula being compared are traditional and reform, students experiencing the latter tend to perform at about the same level on traditional tests of computational and procedural skills, and better on tests of conceptual understanding and problem solving (see also Senk & Thompson, 2003). In short (Schoenfeld, 2007a), "what you assess counts a great deal" (p. 64).

We want to make the same point in another context, namely in relation to ethnic and cultural diversity. What—and how—you assess counts a great deal if your aim is the support of teaching/learning, and not simply a macromanagement tool for the evaluation of schools. To be serious about equity, it is essential to know to what extent assessment instruments truly reveal what students know, understand, and can do. What you assess is intimately related to how you assess it, and to this we now turn.

*When You Know **What** You Want to Assess, Figure out **How***

The advantages of standardized written tests are rather obvious (Miller-Jones, 1989). They provide a cheap way of yielding numbers that have the appearance of objectivity and, as such, are widely accepted by the public and policy-makers as bases for accountability measures at the level of teachers, schools, school districts, and states, and for making selection decisions about students.

Arguments critical of standardized tests of achievement include (Miller-Jones, 1989) many which question whether they can do what is claimed for them. Nichols and Berliner (2007) document "expert opinion from scholars in the assessment and psychometric community, all saying the same thing—namely, that the demands being made of the tests by politicians exceed the capability of the psychometric community to oblige them" (p. 175). The American Educational Research Association (2000) declared, in a position statement, that:

> ...decisions that affect individual students' life chances or educational opportunities should not be made on the basis of test scores alone. Other relevant information should be taken into account to enhance the overall validity of such decisions.... More importantly, when there is credible evidence that a test score may not adequately reflect a student's true proficiency...alternative acceptable means should be provided by which to demonstrate attainment of the tested standards.

Particularly relevant to this volume, testing formats are seldom equivalent or unbiased in either content or procedures—they usually privilege students from the White middle class (and *some* Asians). In particular, there are many aspects to do with language, not only for students for whom English is not their first language. To the extent that assessment goes beyond decontextualized computational and procedural fluency, assessments aimed at determining individual students' understanding should be embedded in culturally meaningful problem contexts that have ecological and cognitive salience for the students being assessed.

Contextualization may be within a more or less realistic frame, or a magical, imaginative, or whimsical setting which acts as a kind of "mental manipulative." Many attempts at contextualization are bizarre. De Lange (2007a, pp. 100–101) cites the following from "a popular U.S. textbook series":

> One day a sales person drove 300 miles in x^2 - 4 hours.
>
> The following day, she drove 325 miles in x + 2 hours.
>
> Write and simplify a ratio comparing the average rate the first day with the average the second day.

We assume the reader has some appreciation of the disconnect herein between context and content (as De Lange puts it). Crucially, in relation to cultural diversity, familiarity or interpretation of the context will vary from student to student. An example discussed by Tate (1995) clearly illustrates the point:

> It costs $1.50 each way to ride the bus between home and work. A weekly pass is $16.00. Which is the better deal, paying the daily fare or buying the weekly pass?

When African-American students were interviewed about how they responded, it was discovered that they "transformed the 'neutral' assumptions of the problem—all people work 5 days a week and have one job—into their own realities and perspectives" (Tate, 1995, p. 440). In their experience, as opposed to White middle-class experience, a job (such as cleaning) might mean making several bus trips every day, not just two, and working more than five days a week. If items of this type are used for assessment, and assumptions are made about the "right" answers, the implications for inequity are clear, given that, as Tate (1995) put it "the underpinnings of school mathematics curriculum, assessment, and pedagogy are often more closely aligned with the idealized experience of the White middle class"(p. 440). To put it bluntly, if success in mathematics requires an African-American student to adopt the worldview of a White, middle-class person, what does that say about the experience of "doing mathematics while Black"?

This example illustrates very clearly how the form of the test matters, and interacts with the content. If the item is presented on a written test and asks for a simple choice between the alternatives, then those students who do not make the "right" assumptions will get the "wrong" answer. If the test allows written explanations, then it would be possible to assess answers appropriately (but note that this would require writing skills for the student and interpretative skills for the assessor). Best would be to assess responses to this item through discussion between the teacher and individual students or with the whole class.

We will argue later in the chapter that the most effective kind of assessment for improving mathematics education is formative (Black & Wiliam, 1998; Wiliam, 2007). While nobody (to our knowledge) disputes that external assessment has a contribution to make, there are much better alternatives to the practices currently dominant in the United States. These alternatives include constructed response items that require verbal explanation, justification, and so on. A relatively simple example from NAEP is the following:

> In 1980, the population of Town A and Town B were 5,000 and 6,000 respectively. The 1990 populations of Town A and Town B were 8,000 and 9,000 respectively.
>
> Brian claims that from 1980 to 1990 the populations of the two towns

> grew by the same amount. Use mathematics to explain how Brian might have justified his claim.
>
> Darlene claims that from 1980 to 1990 the population of Town A had grown more. Use mathematics to explain how Darlene might have justified her claim. (cited in Wearne & Kouba, 2000, p. 186)

There are alternatives used in other countries, such as national exit exams tightly connected to curriculum (De Lange, 2007b, p. 1113). During the 1990s, it seemed that advanced ideas from both Europe (particularly from the Shell Center in England and the Freudenthal Center in the Netherlands) and within the United States might be gaining traction (Lesh & Lamon, 1992; Niss, 1993; Romberg, 1995).

However, limited progress has been observable since the flurry of activity summarized in De Corte, Greer, and Verschaffel (1996, pp. 530–534). A plausible explanation is that the "standards" movement, solidified by NCLB, focused attention on narrow, high-stakes testing, leaving less and less room and resources for more complex, conceptually deep (and expensive), forms of assessment (Darling-Hammond, 2003).

The most important ongoing attempts in the United States that we are aware of are collaborations between U.S. and English mathematics educators that have resulted in the Mathematics Assessment Resource Center (MARS) and the Balanced Assessment Project:

> http://www.balancedassessment.org
> http://www.ctb.com/mktg/balanced_math/overview.jsp

Computer-based tasks from the World Class Arena project from MARS are described in Burkhardt and Pead (2003), and can be sampled under the title of their chapter ("Computer-Based Assessment: A Platform for Better Tests?") at http://www.nottingham.ac.uk/education/MARS/papers/

There are two important closing comments on these enhanced assessments. First, they remain external, in the sense that they have to assume a common experience. Thus, contexts are chosen that are assumed (not always correctly) to be familiar to at least a large majority of students, flattening out the possibilities of relating more directly to the specific lived experiences of specific students.

Second, despite the possibilities opened up by these richer, more complex forms of assessment, the reality, as of the time of writing, is that standardized paper-and-pencil tests, in particular of the multiple-choice variety, dominate the educational landscape of the United States. Indeed, one of the pernicious effects of the unfunded mandate of NCLB is that states are having to cut back on attempts to enrich their assessment (Darling-Hammond, 2007a).

Assessment as Social Engineering

No Child Left Behind

The No Child Left Behind (NCLB) of 2002 had ambitious aims, as expressed thus by Sclafani (2007):

> NCLB is a major step forward for the future of the United States. For the first time in our history, we are taking responsibility for all children; no longer are we just mouthing the slogan "all children can learn," but we are taking responsibility for ensuring all will learn. (p. 24)

How is this immensely worthy aim to be achieved? Sclafani lays out four basic principles: accountability, local control and flexibility, choice, and research-based practice, but the greatest of these is accountability (Sclafani, 2007):

> Accountability for results has taken on a new dimension for educators, one which some are not eager to embrace. Not only are teachers, principals, and superintendents responsible for student performance in the aggregate, but, for the first time, they are responsible for the performance of subpopulations of students. The performance of students of color and of different ethnicities must be examined separately to ensure that all are making progress towards the standards their state has set. (p. 23)

The requirement of progress for identified subgroups was very widely welcomed as a clear commitment to equity. In general, NCLB enjoyed a very strong consensus of bipartisan support at its inception, a consensus that has drastically eroded over the ensuing years.

A particularly thorough diagnosis of what is wrong with NCLB, in practice, has been provided by Nichols and Berliner (2007). In particular, Nichols and Berliner have posited that a constellation of malignant consequences stemming from the imposition of high-stakes testing is readily explicable in terms of a principle expounded by Campbell (1975) to the effect that "the more any quantitative social indicator is used for social decision-making, the more subject it will be to corruption pressures and the more apt it will be to distort and corrupt the social processes it was intended to monitor" (p. 35). The book by Nichols and Berliner details the range of corruptions and distortions of education created by the height of the stakes attached to tests.

Pertinent to this book, a division among scholars appears to exist between advocates of progressive education and members of various cultural communities, notably African Americans and Latino/as. On the one hand community advocates (especially African Americans) appear to support the notion of a standards-based curriculum and the use of common standardized tests to hold school systems accountable for their children's learning (e.g., Education Trust, 2006). The equity argument is that if we are clear about what it is we want our students to learn (i.e., that there are clearly stated content standards) then we can better hold schools and teachers more accountable for ensuring that *all* students learn. It is *assumed* that the current tests are valid and reliable indicators of what students know. But even if they are not, these are the metrics that are used to either permit or deny access to further educational resources and opportunities.

Reflective of this view, Gordon (1995) sees issues of equity in assessment as secondary to the issues of "the effectiveness and sufficiency of teaching and learning" (p. 360). He assumes that if students from any cultural background know the material, the kind and content of assessment will not matter. Gordon seems to accept standardized multiple choice tests as inevitable if not valid metrics. While he acknowledges that there may be problems with existing instruments and practices, he argues that ultimately students from diverse cultural backgrounds must accommodate to these existing measures. Gordon applauds "efforts to be responsive to diverse learner characteristics and pluralistic social standards" (p. 360) but asserts that there are limits to what can be done to make the design and development of assessment technology and procedures culturally appropriate. We challenge this notion for the measurement of individual student's capabilities.

On the other hand, many scholars who otherwise are strong supporters of efforts to increase achievement and real learning for students from culturally diverse and typically poorly served communities are critical of these tests and the culture of testing that has burgeoned with NCLB policies (e.g., Kohn, 2000; Noddings, 2007). It seems to us that the imposition of NCLB and associated policies reflects an aspiration to drive the school system in black-box mode (cf. Black, Harrison, Lee, Marshall, & Wiliam, 2004). Outside the box are the levers, the sticks (mostly) and carrots of evaluation, accountability, and sanctions. Inside the box, hidden from view, are the students, teachers, principals, and administrators. The external levers are intended to control their behavior without needing to consider their circumstances or the details of how they meet the required standards. Under the influence of the levers, the people involved will have to figure out how to achieve the desired results.

Test Score Differences: The Construction and Communication of Success/failure

"Quantitative tests of aptitude and achievement have given U.S. education a way to sort children by race and social class, just like the old days, but without the words "race" and "class" front and center" (McDermott & Hall, 2007, p. 11). Test scores have become the major currency for making claims about comparative performance among groups and across time. For example, in a press release on September 25, 2007, about the 2007 NAEP results, the Secretary for Education, Spellings, issued a press release entitled "Secretary Spellings Highlights Gains Made on the Nation's Report Card under No Child Left Behind" which included the following: "Math scores for 4th- and 8th-graders and the reading scores for

4th-graders are at historic highs and the biggest gains were made by African American and Hispanic students."

Commenting on the same data, the advocacy group Fairtest issued a statement under the title "NAEP Results Show NCLB Is Leaving Children Behind," that begins by declaring that "the evidence from a look at NAEP scale scores shows that the rate of improvement on NAEP has slowed since NCLB was passed." Faced with such conflicting interpretations, a concerned citizen can access and analyze the data for her- or himself. Our interpretation of the data, taking into account the full set of data from 1990 (available at: www.nces.ed.gov/nationsreportcard/neapdata) suggests that the following statements can be made with some confidence:

1. NAEP scores for all subgroups have been steadily rising across the whole period. (So the use of the term *historic highs* is an exaggerated way of saying that this trend has continued.)
2. Overall, the changes since the passing of NCLB do not obviously depart from the trend since 1990. It is probably too soon to say, therefore, *on the basis of NAEP scores analyzed in isolation,* whether there is any effect, either beneficial or detrimental, that could be attributed to its introduction.
3. There is no indication that the differences in mean test scores between White and African- American, Latino/a, and Native American students are decreasing more than minimally or that they have decreased more rapidly since the passing of NCLB.

In general, people have become so accustomed to terms such as *achievement gaps*, which need to be "closed" that they mold and channel thinking in ways to which, without strong effort, we do not have cognitive access. A pervasive aspect of this framing of how we think about education is to focus on the students and their teachers that are doing the failing and the groups that are manifesting the gaps, rather than the system and the culture that produces the phenomena so labeled (McDermott & Varenne, 2006). We acknowledge the existence of the phenomena—gaps in performance are real, with real consequences for flesh-and-blood individuals and groups—but point to the role of social construction in the ways in which society frames discourse about the failing/succeeding, the calculus of achievement, ethnic classifications, problems, and proposed solutions. The creation of a popular discourse, and in particular the labeling of individuals and groups, sets up looping effects (Hacking, 2002) whereby categorizing and associated discourse change the individuals and groups so labeled and described, and those changes in turn modify the categorizations. It is also appropriate to ask to what extent the "achievement gaps" are artifacts of the measuring instruments.

The Other Gaps: Savage Inequalities, the Education Debt, and Opportunities to Learn

The declaration by fiat that all children will achieve proficiency by 2014 will not withstand a reality check, such as this (Darling-Hammond, 2007):

> At Luther Burbank school, students cannot take textbooks home for homework in any core subject because their teachers have enough textbooks for use in class only.... Some math, science, and other core classes do not have even enough textbooks for all the students in a single class to use during the school day...Luther Burbank is infested with vermin and roaches, and students routinely see mice in their classrooms....
>
> Eleven of the thirty-five teachers at Luther Burbank have not yet obtained regular, nonemergency credentials, and seventeen of the thirty-five teachers only began teaching at Luther Burbank this school year. (*Williams v. State of California*, 2001, pp. 247–248)

The notion that ethnic minorities have achieved equity and social justice now, *even if it were true*, needs to be further qualified by taking into account what Ladson-Billings (2006) called "the education debt." Many types of explanation have been offered for the "achievement gaps" (in quotation marks for reasons explained). However, with reference to African Americans in particular, Ladson-Billings poses the challenging question: "Black students in the South did not experience universal secondary schooling until 1968.... Why, then, would we not expect there to be an achievement gap?" (p. 5). Whether talking about Native Americans, Latino/as, African Americans, and others, how do you characterize, let alone quantify, the results of decades or centuries of education as a tool of discrimination?

The test score gaps of African Americans, Latino/as, and Native Americans need to be backgrounded by the educational debt and the other gaps that affect these groups—and also other groups, such as some Asians who are not part of the popular stereotype of "model minority" (CARE, 2008). These gaps include inequitable funding of schools (Kozol, 1991), the opportunity gaps, including lack of access to well prepared teachers (Flores, 2008), the demographic mismatch between teachers and students (Villegas & Lucas, 2002), gaps in opportunity to learn (Moss, Pullin, Gee, Haertel, & Young, 2008), and the association between ethnicity and poverty and its effects on educational achievement (Berliner, 2005).

Test Scores for Political Communication

Writing about international comparative assessment exercises, De Lange (2007b) comments that they "are indeed about politics, about political communication" (p. 1112). In the case of the United States, much of the political communication associated with international comparisons (De Lange, 2007b) takes the form of dire warnings about the implications of poor performance for future economic competitiveness (Gutstein, chapter 6 this volume).

Assessment in the service of politics can:

- be used to establish a positive public profile for the government by being seen to be concerned
- be used to claim value for public money
- be used to impose a particular world view upon society by selective emphasis in the school curriculum…
- be used to legitimize social inequalities in salary and status
- be used to offer a rationale for economic failure. (Ridgway & Passey, 1993, p. 66)

The "selling" of No Child Left Behind has involved massive effort at political communication by the administration and its agencies, and by proponents and opponents among the many stakeholders (see, for example, the starkly contrasted interpretations of trends in NAEP data described above).

Assessment as Communication in the Service of Teaching/Learning Mathematics

As Schoenfeld (2007c) points out "In many ways, tests can have a strong impact on the very system they measure" (p 3), a truth encapsulated in the WYTIWYG principle discussed below, a succinct expression of the fact that the nature of assessment communicates what is valued and what, in a context of ruthless accountability, will pay off (often literally)—at least in the short term. These signals lead to the strong tendency for teachers to distort their teaching accordingly by "teaching to the test," and to (mis)spend much time in test preparation, with deleterious effects that have been documented by Nichols and Berliner (2007).

What You Test Is What You Get (WYTIWYG)

Consider the following example (made up but, we suspect, all too plausible). A state's standards include something like this: "Students understand that when a two-dimensional figure is enlarged by a factor n, the area of the figure is increased by a factor of n^2." Now suppose that understanding of this principle is typically tested either by reference to a square or a circle. "Teaching to the test" could then take the form of drilling the students on these two particular examples, rather than genuinely attempting to help them understand the general principle.

It is important to note that the WYTIWYG effect is not inherently negative. There have been cases where enlightened assessment practices have positively influenced mathematics instruction. This potential relates to a point made earlier—before constructing tests, you should decide what you value and would like to promote by appropriate assessment.

Large-Scale Written Tests: Communicatively Limited

A test is intended to communicate to the student what aspects of that student's knowledge he or she is required to reveal. The student is expected to communicate back through her or his responses. After the student's responses are evaluated, information is given back to the student. How effective is this process as communication?

Typically, the time-scale is such that any information that gets back to the teacher is too late to be of much use. Gross scores convey little information. And there is plenty of evidence that such tests do not accurately determine or communicate what the student does or does not know. A pencil-and-paper test is a very artificial situation, closed in terms of time, access to information, social interaction, and communication. One manifestation of artificiality is that, to a considerable degree, performance on the test can be affected by knowledge of the "rules of the game." Much lore exists about multiple-choice tests in particular; for example, the story of children being taught to chant "Three in a row, no, no, no!" implying that the same choice of answer does not occur three times in succession. Too often the test-taker is trying to construe what the test-constructor wants, not trying to apply reason. Further, many multiple-choice items have the property that the answer can be derived in ways that demonstrate intelligence but not the mathematical knowledge that the item-writer presumably intended.

For example, consider the following item, cited with approval by the National Mathematics Advisory Panel (2008, p. 6–7):

> Mona counted a total of 56 ducks on the pond in Town Park. The ratio of female ducks to male ducks that Mona counted was 5:3. What was the total number of female ducks Mona counted on the pond?
>
> A. 15 B. 19 C. 21 D. 35
>
> Comment: A student has to decide which fractions are relevant.

There are various routes to D, but it is sufficient to realize that there are more female than male ducks and choose the only answer that is greater than half of 56—which hardly amounts to deciding which fractions are relevant. As with many multiple-choice items, this specimen offers many possibilities for false positive responses relative to what it purportedly tests.

An important question is the extent to which purely linguistic factors differentially affect the performance on mathematics tests of ELL students (Moschkovich & Nelson-Barber, chapter 5 this volume). Schoenfeld (2007d) cites this daunting problem from an Arizona test:

If x is always positive and y is always negative, then xy is always negative. Based on the given information, which of the following conjectures is valid?

A. $x^n y^n$, where n is an odd natural number, will always be negative.
B. $x^n y^n$, where n is an even natural number, will always be negative.
C. $x^n y^m$, where n and m are distinct odd natural numbers, will always be positive.
D. $x^n y^m$, where n and m are distinct even natural numbers, will always be negative. (p. 13)

He comments: "Imagine yourself a student for whom English is a second language. Just what is this sentence assessing?" Indeed, the same question could be asked for any student. (And a logician would deem the question nonsensical, since it cannot be answered on the basis of the information given!)

Consider a student in California whose birth language was Spanish but who has been taught mathematics in English (Fillmore, 2007). In attempting to understand an item on a written test in English, this student faces a constellation of linguistic challenges:

1. Understanding the "everyday" English words.
2. Understanding the formal mathematical words.
3. Understanding the logic of the question itself (see item above) which may involve, for example, the notoriously complex word *if.*

All of these sources of miscommunication occur in a context in which there is no possibility of asking for clarification. Fillmore (2007) analyzes examples from probability, an area of mathematics in which it is especially difficult to communicate to the test-taker, in the best of circumstances, what the nature of the task is.

Even if the test is given in a Spanish version, the student may well be at a loss because of a history of mathematical education in English and even, perhaps, because of differences between the formal Spanish of the test and her or his vernacular. The complexities and implications of bilinguality need to be much more deeply understood (Moschkovich & Nelson-Barber, chapter 5 this volume). Brown (2005) concluded that "[literacy-based performance assessments], together with the current assessment-driven accountability system, seriously undermine equal treatment for [English language learners]" (p. 337).

The quality of communication afforded by a written test can be significantly enhanced when constructed answers are allowed. As shown by the example from NAEP cited above, a student may be asked to communicate not just an answer, but the reasoning behind that answer. At the same time, having constructed responses requires fluency of expression and writing from the student and interpretative skills from the person grading the test. Computer-administered tests offer possibilities of tasks that exploit interactivity and other potentials; but trying to automatize processing of natural language remains, and is likely to remain, their major limitation (Burkhardt & Pead, 2003).

An example of an alternative approach based on written tests is the Silicon Valley Mathematics Assessment Collaborative (MAC) (Foster, Noyce, & Spiegel, 2007). MAC uses Balanced Assessment tests (Burkhardt, 2007), with constructed-response tasks developed by MARS (see above) which are scored by teachers, using a rubric. The detailed discussions of the tasks and of the students' responses provide professional development for teachers. Further, they are encouraged to review the tasks with their students. Consider ways in which this set-up enhances communication: the students get to express more of their thinking; teachers working together to evaluate the students' responses think deeply about the nature of the items and students' (mis)conceptions; the evaluation teams can feed useful information back to the test constructors; and teachers and students who review the tasks deepen their understandings together.

Formative Assessment

Stiggins (2004) draws the distinction between assessment *of* learning and assessment *for* learning. Elaborating on this point, Black et al. (2004) assert that:

> Assessment for learning is any assessment for which the first priority in its design and practice is to serve the purpose of promoting pupils' learning. It thus differs from assessment designed primarily to serve the purposes of accountability, or of ranking, or of certifying competence. An assessment activity can help learning if it provides information to be used as feedback, by teachers, and by their pupils in assessing themselves and each other, to modify the teaching and learning activities in which they are engaged. Such assessment becomes "formative assessment" when the evidence is actually used to adapt the teaching work to meet learning needs. (p. 9)

Black and Wiliam (1998) found, from a survey of research, that teachers who engage in formative assessment raise their students' scores on traditional tests typically between 0.4 to 0.7 standard deviations. To give a feel for what this kind of change means, they state that a gain of 0.7 standard deviations in TIMSS would have raised the position of the United States from the middle of the pack to the top five. However, they pointed out that there is ample room for improvement in that "there is a wealth of research evidence that the everyday practice of assessment in classrooms is beset with problems and shortcomings" (p. 141). They made a number of suggestions that were then largely implemented in a research project in six English schools, with two mathematics and two science teachers from each school (Black et al., 2004). For the 19 teachers on whom they had complete data, the average effect size was about +0.3 standard deviations—

enough, if replicated across the board, to raise a school in the bottom quartile to well above average in a performance league table.

Many of the strategies promoted by Black et al. could be categorized as improving the quality of the communication about assessment. For example, they highlight the importance of the quality of feedback on both oral and written work, and point out that comments on written work are much more attended to if *not* accompanied by grades. Even summative tests could be turned to advantage, if the students are involved in discussion of how they might be of use in improving learning. Peer assessment and self-assessment contribute in ways that cannot be achieved in any other way. Many of their recommendations (and see Wiliam, 2007) amount to engaging students in critical reflection on the activity system of teaching/learning mathematics, including assessment, and are aligned with recent emphasis on the quality of talk in mathematics classrooms (Franke, Kazemi, & Battey, 2007).

To change their pedagogy in the directions prompted by Black et al. (2004) "for the teachers, courage is necessary" (p. 19). Accordingly, they need support. Given that teachers in general are not particularly good at designing tests (Black & Wiliam, 1998, p. 141), curricular materials that support assessment are useful. A good example of such material emanated from the QUASAR project (Parke, Lane, Silver, & Magone, 2003). They present 16 mathematical tasks with guidance on how to use them in classroom assessment with specific attention to six types of activity: exploring multiple strategies, representations, and answers; editing responses to improve their quality; using established scoring criteria to evaluate the quality of responses; developing scoring criteria to evaluate the quality of responses; assessing students' existing knowledge; monitoring students' learning during instruction.

Talking With Students

It is worth remembering that, in pursuit of his core interest in how knowledge develops, Piaget became interested in children's thinking through talking to children about their wrong answers to items on intelligence tests. This example makes a point central to this chapter, namely that if you really want to find out what children know and how they think, you need to talk with them.

Barton (2008, pp. 73–77) has constructed a delightful and instructive parable about a teacher who asks students to calculate ¼ + 3/8 and receives four different answers, 4/12, 5/16, 3/32, and 5/8. For a written test, all that would remain would be to mark the first three students wrong and the fourth right. However, this imagined scenario takes place in a classroom in which the teacher can ask the students to explain their answers. The first three students all provide meaningful arguments based on situations that could plausibly be modeled by "adding" fractions, whereas the fourth student is distressed because, although believing that she has followed the correct procedure, she does not see how it makes sense.

The most intensive form of teacher–student interchange is the clinical interview, a way of "entering the child's mind" (Ginsburg, 1997). A long and detailed interview of a 6th grade student, probing his knowledge and understanding of fractions, is a tour de force of its kind (Ball, 2007). It was conducted in front of the participants (including the second author of this chapter) at the first Workshop on Critical Issues in Mathematics Education at the Mathematical Sciences Research Institute in Berkeley in 2004. It can be viewed at: http://www.msri.org/publications/ln/msri/2004/assessment/session5/1/index.html. Schoenfeld (2007b) commented:

> The more that teachers can "get inside their students' heads" in an ongoing way, in the way that Ball interacted with Brandon, the more they will be able to tailor their instruction to students' needs. To the degree that we can foster such inclinations and skills in all teachers, and add the diagnostic interview to their toolkits (in addition to more formally structured assessments) the richer the possibilities for classroom instruction. (p. 277)

Culturally Responsive Formative Assessment

These examples of teacher/student interactions do not specifically address the issue of cultural responsiveness, as with the examples of higher quality external tests discussed above, though it is implicit in all of them that the need and opportunity for cultural responsiveness is present.

Sclafani (2007) commented that classroom assessment is connected to the qualifications of the teachers and the need for them to have a deep understanding of mathematics. It is not reasonable, however, to imply that profound knowledge of mathematics is sufficient as well as necessary. Mathematics educators emphasize not just content knowledge, but pedagogical content knowledge (Hill, Sleep, Lewis, & Ball, 2007). Beyond those two requirements, a third form of knowledge is knowledge about diverse students (Gay, chapter 8 this volume). Given the demographic mismatch between students and teachers discussed earlier, it is vital for teachers to develop cultural responsiveness (Gay, 2000; Villegas & Lucas, 2002). Gay (chapter 8 this volume) pointedly asks: "How can middle-class, monolingual European-American math teachers work better with students who are predominantly of color, attend schools in poor urban communities, and are often multilingual?"

A classic study was carried out by the educational anthropologist George Spindler in the classroom of a teacher who was given the pseudonym Roger Harker, and was considered an excellent teacher by all, including himself. Roger Harker and his classroom of students diverse in class and ethnicity were observed in great detail for six months (Spindler & Spindler, 2000). Spindler observed that: "He ranked highest on all dimensions, including personal and academic factors, those children who were most like himself—Anglo, middle to upper-middle social class, and, like him, ambitious (achievement-oriented)"

(p. 204). Spindler further commented, based on classroom observations: "He most frequently called on, touched, helped, and looked directly at the children culturally like himself. He was never mean or cruel to the other children. *It was almost as though they weren't there*" (p. 205, emphasis added).

Spindler concluded that Harker "was locked into a self-reinforcing, self-maintaining sociocultural system of action, perception, and reward" (p. 208). To break into this system required what Spindler later termed "cultural therapy" whereby Harker was, not without considerable effort, made aware of his behavior. It is a legitimate question to ask: How many teachers like Harker are there in American schools, and what is the effect of their behavior?

Multiple aspects of language, discourse, and styles of communication have a bearing on interpersonal interactions and all are sensitive to the diverse cultures of the teachers and students. Unfortunately, the research that relates to this aspect with specific reference to mathematics is very limited, although there is related work on literacy. For example, in a classic study of language socialization practices among three Southern U.S. communities, Shirley Brice Heath (1982) observed important differences in interrogative practices. In particular, she noted a clear tendency among European-American families, both middle and working class, to ask children lots of questions that she termed "known-answer questions." By contrast, the African-American children were asked questions that sought information.

Other relevant work relates to the complex relationships between academic and everyday language; for example, as studied in general by Gee (2004) and in relation to mathematics by Adler (2001), Fillmore (2007), and Moschkovich (2007).

Final Comments: Humanizing Assessment In Mathematics Education

The main points we would like the reader to take from this chapter are as follows:

- The classroom should not be treated as a black box.
- It is essential to go beyond assessment *of* learning to assessment *for* learning.
- A principled analysis of what students need to learn should drive the design of tests, rather than tests distorting teaching/learning. Design and construction of tests of mathematical proficiency is too important to be left to the psychometricians and the mathematicians (though both groups have important contributions to make).
- Assessment methods should be rigorously tested for how accurately they reveal what the students know and can do. Multiple forms of assessment can contribute to the total picture, but in each case the form of the test should be related to its ability to serve a stated purpose.

- Good assessment is possible, and there is no lack of good models, but it needs the political will, commitment, and investment.
- Assessment, like education, like IQ tests, is not culture-free. In mathematics, this is particularly so when the items involving modeling aspects of the real world.
- Research needs to tackle the deep issues, and be complemented by judgment calls made on the basis of values and experience. One such question is: To what extent are the test score differences among ethnic groups a reflection of other gaps and of the nature of the assessment machinery and what are the looping effects in the attribution of lower achievement to individuals and groups?

The issues dealt with in this chapter are embedded in more general political questions about what the citizens of the United States want from its public education system and are prepared to pay for. For example, taking account of the linguistic aspects of learning mathematics for students whose first language is not English cannot be separated from attitudes and policies toward bilingualism and cultural diversity. Test score differences need to be considered against the background of resource gaps and differences in opportunity to learn; improved assessment and narrowing the opportunity gaps are dependent on the political will to spend dollars and direct resources.

An excellent summary for this chapter is the following, from Kilpatrick (1993):

> The challenge for the 21st century, as far as mathematics educators are concerned, is to produce an assessment practice that does more than measure a person's mind and then assign that mind a treatment. We need to understand how people, not apart from but embedded in their cultures, come to use mathematics in different social settings and how we can create a mathematics education that helps them use it better, more rewardingly, and more responsibly. To do that will require us to transcend the crippling visions of mind as a hierarchy, school as a machine, and assessment as engineering. (p. 44)

References

Adler, J. (2001). *Teaching mathematics in multilingual classrooms*. Dordrecht, The Netherlands: Kluwer.

Ball, D. L., with Peoples, B. (2007). Assessing a student's mathematical knowledge by way of interview. In A. H. Schoenfeld (Ed.), *Assessing mathematical proficiency* (pp. 213–267). Cambridge, UK: Cambridge University Press.

Barton, B. (2008). *The language of mathematics: Telling mathematical tales*. New York: Springer.

Berliner, D. C. (2005, August 2). Our impoverished view of educational reform. *Teachers College Record*. Retrieved November 30, 2008, from, http://www.tcrecord.org/content.asp?contentid=12106

Black, P., Harrison, C., Lee, C., Marshall, B., & Wiliam, D. (2004). Working inside the Black Box: Assessment for learning in the classroom. *Phi Delta Kappan, 86*(1), 9–21.

Black, P., & Wiliam, D. (1998). Inside the Black Box: Raising standards through classroom assessment. *Phi Delta Kappan, 80*(2), 139–148.

Brown, C. L. (2005). Equity of literacy-based math performance assessments for English Language Learners. *Bilingual Research Journal, 29*, 337–363.

Burkhardt, H. (2007). Mathematical proficiency: What is important? How can it be measured? In A. H. Schoenfeld (Ed.), *Assessing mathematical proficiency* (pp. 77–97). Cambridge, UK: Cambridge University Press.

Burkhardt, H., & Pead, D. (2003). Computer-based assessment: A platform for better tests? In C. Richardson (Ed.), *Whither assessment?* (pp. 133–148). London: Qualifications and Curriculum Authority. http://www.nottingham.ac.uk/education/MARS/papers/whither/cba_better.pdf

Campbell, D. T. (1975). Assessing the impact of planned social change. In G. Lyons & D. T. Campbell (Eds.), *Social research and public policies: The Dartmouth/OECD Conference* (pp. 3–45). Hanover, NH: Public Affairs Center, Dartmouth College.

CARE. (2008). *Asian Americans and Pacific Islanders: Facts, not fiction—setting the record straight.* The College Board. Retrieved August 15, 2008, from http://www.nyu.edu/projects/care/reports_pubs.html

Darling-Hammond, L. (2003, February 16). Standards and assessment: Where we are and what we need. *Teachers College Record.*Retrieved November 30, 2008, from http://www.tcrecord.org/content.asp?contentid=11109

Darling-Hammond, L. (2007a, May 21). "Evaluating "No Child Left Behind." *The Nation.* Retrieved November 30, 2008, from http://www.thenation.com/doc/20070521/darling-hammond

Darling-Hammond, L. (2007b). Race, inequality and educational accountability: The irony of "No Child Left Behind." *Race, Ethnicity and Education, 10, 245*–260.

De Corte, E., Greer, B., & Versachaffel, L. (1996). Mathematics teaching and learning. In D. Berliner & R. Calfee (Eds.), Handbook of Educational Psychology (pp. 491–549). New York: Macmillan.

De Lange, J. (2007a). Aspects of the art of assessment design. In A. H. Schoenfeld (Ed.), *Assessing mathematical proficiency* (pp. 99–111). Cambridge, UK: Cambridge University Press.

De Lange, J. (2007b). Large-scale assessment of mathematics education. In F. K. Lester, Jr. (Ed.), *Second handbook of research on mathematics teaching and learning* (pp. 1111–1142). Charlotte, NC: Information Age.

Education Trust. (2006). *Education Watch 2006 State Summary Reports.* Retrieved November 30, 2008, from http://www2.edtrust.org/edtrust/summaries2006/states.html

Fillmore, L. W. (2007). English learners and mathematics learning: Language issues to consider. In A. H. Schoenfeld (Ed.), *Assessing mathematical proficiency* (pp. 333–344). Cambridge, UK: Cambridge University Press.

Flores, A. (2008). The opportunity gap. In R. S. Kitchen & E. Silver (Eds.), Promoting high participation and success in mathematics by Hispanic students: Examining opportunities and probing promising practices. *TODOS Research Monograph, 1*, 1–18.

Foster, D., Noyce, P., & Spiegel, S. (2007). When assessment guides instruction: Silicon Valley's Mathematics Assessment Collaborative. In A. H. Schoenfeld (Ed.), *Assessing mathematical proficiency* (pp. 137–154). Cambridge, UK: Cambridge University Press.

Franke, M. L., Kazemi, E., & Battey, D. (2007). Mathematics teaching and classroom practice. In F. K. Lester, Jr. (Ed.), *Second handbook of research on mathematics teaching and learning* (pp. 225–256). Charlotte, NC: Information Age.

Gay, G. (2000). *Culturally responsive teaching: Theory, research, and practice.* New York: Teachers College Press.

Gee, J. P. (2004). *Situated language and learning: A critique of traditional schooling.* New York: Routledge.

Ginsburg, H. P. (1997). *Entering the child's mind: The clinical interview in psychological research and practice.* Cambridge, UK: Cambridge University Press.

Gordon, E. W. (1995). Toward an equitable system of educational assessment. *Journal of Negro Education, 64*(3), 360–372.

Hacking, I. (2002). Making up people. In I. Hacking, *Historical ontology* (pp. 99–114). Cambridge, MA: Harvard University Press.

Heath, S. B. (1982). What no bedtime story means: Narrative skills at home and school. *Language and Society, 11*, 49–76.

Hill, H. C., Sleep, L., Lewis, J. M., & Ball, D. L. (2007). Assessing teachers' mathematical knowledge: What knowledge matters and what evidence counts. In F. K. Lester, Jr. (Ed.), *Second handbook of research on mathematics teaching and learning* (pp. 111–155). Charlotte, NC: Information Age.

Kilpatrick, J. (1993). The chain and the arrow: From the history of mathematics assessment. In M. Niss (Ed.), *Investigations into assessment in mathematics education: An ICMI study* (pp. 31–46). Dordrecht, The Netherlands: Kluwer.

Kohn, A. (2000). *The case against standardized testing: Raising the scores, ruining the schools.* Portsmouth, NH: Heinemann Press.

Kozol, J. (1991). *Savage inequalities: Children in America's schools.* New York: Crown

Ladson-Billings, G. (2006). From the achievement gap to the education debt: Understanding achievement in U.S. schools. *Educational Researcher, 35*(7), 3–12.

Lesh, R., & Lamon, S. J. (1992). *Assessment of authentic performance in school mathematics.* Washington, D.C.: American Association for the Advancement of Science.

McDermott, R., & Hall, K. D. (2007). Scientifically debased research on learning 1854–2006. *Anthropology & Education Quarterly, 38*(1), 9–15.

McDermott, R., & Varenne, H. (2006). Reconstructing culture in educational research. In G. Spindler & L. Hammond (Eds.), *Innovations in educational ethnography: Theory, methods, and results* (pp. 3–31). Mahwah, NJ: Erlbaum.

Milgram, R. J. (2007). What is mathematical proficiency? In A. H. Schoenfeld (Ed.), *Assessing mathematical proficiency* (pp. 31–58). Cambridge, UK: Cambridge University Press.

Miller-Jones, D. (1989). Culture and testing. *American Psychologist, 44*(2), 360–366.

Moschkovich, J. (2007). Beyond words to mathematical content: Assessing English learners in mathematics classroom. In A. H. Schoenfeld (Ed.), *Assessing mathematical proficiency* (pp. 345–352). Cambridge, UK: Cambridge University Press.

Moss, P. A., Pullin, D. C., Gee, J. P., Haertel, E. H., & Young, L. J. (Eds.). (2008). *Assessment, equity, and opportunity to learn.* Cambridge, UK: Cambridge University Press.

National Mathematic Advisory Panel. (2008). *Report of the task group on assessment.* Washington, D.C.: U.S. Department of Education.

National Research Council. (2001). *Adding it up.* Washington, D.C.: National Academy Press.

Nichols, S. L., & Berliner, D.C. (2007). *Collateral damage: How high-stakes testing corrupts America's schools.* Cambridge, MA: Harvard Education Press.

Niss, M. (1993). *Investigations into assessment in mathematics education: An ICMI study.* Dordrecht, The Netherlands: Kluwer.

Noddings, N. (2007). *When school reform goes wrong.* New York: Teachers College Press.

Parke, C. S., Lane, S., Silver, E. A, & Magone, M. E. (2003). *Using assessment to improve middle-grades mathematics teaching and learning.* Reston, VA: National Council of Teachers of Mathematics.

Ridgway, J., Crust, R., Burkhardt, H., Wilcox, S., Fisher, L., & Foster, D. (2001). *MARS report on the 2000 test.* San Jose, CA: Mathematics Assessment Collaborative.

Ridgway, J., & Passey, D. (1993). An international view of mathematics assessment—Through a glass, darkly. In M. Niss (Ed.), *Investigations into assessment in mathematics education: An ICMI study* (pp. 57–72). Dordrecht, The Netherlands: Kluwer.

Romberg, T. A. (Ed.). (1995). *Reform in school mathematics and authentic assessment.* Albany, NY: SUNY Press.

Schoenfeld, A. H. (2004). The math wars. *Educational Policy, 18*(1), 253–286.

Schoenfeld, A. H. (2006). What doesn't work: The challenge and failure of the What Works Clearinghouse to conduct meaningful reviews of studies of mathematics curricula. *Educational Researcher, 35*(2), 13–21.

Schoenfeld, A. H. (2007a). Issues and tensions in the assessment of mathematical proficiency. In A. H. Schoenfeld (Ed.), *Assessing mathematical proficiency* (pp. 59–73). Cambridge, UK: Cambridge University Press.

Schoenfeld, A. H. (2007b). Preface. In A. H. Schoenfeld (Ed.), *Assessing mathematical proficiency* (pp. ix–xviii). Cambridge, UK: Cambridge University Press.

Schoenfeld, A. H. (2007c). Reflections on an assessment interview: What a close look at student understanding can reveal. In A. H. Schoenfeld (Ed.), *Assessing mathematical proficiency* (pp. 269–281). Cambridge, UK: Cambridge University Press.

Schoenfeld, A. H. (2007d). What is mathematical proficiency and how can it be assessed? In A. H. Schoenfeld (Ed.), *Assessing mathematical proficiency* (pp. 3–15). Cambridge, UK: Cambridge University Press.

Sclafani, S. (2007). The No Child Left Behind Act: Political context and national goals. In A. H. Schoenfeld (Ed.), *Assessing mathematical proficiency* (pp. 23–27). Cambridge, UK: Cambridge University Press.

Senk, S. L., & Thompson, D. R. (2003). *Standards-based school mathematics curricula: What are they? What do students learn?* Mahwah, NJ: Erlbaum

Spindler, G., & Spindler, S. (2000). Roger Harker and Schoenhausen: From familiar to strange and back again. In G. Spindler (Ed.), *Fifty years of anthropology and education 1950–2000* (pp. 201–226). Mahwah, NJ: Erlbaum.

Stiggins, R. (2004). New assessment beliefs for a new school mission. *Phi Delta Kappan, 86*(1), 22–27.

Tate, W. F. (1995). School mathematics and African American students: Thinking seriously about opportunity-to-learn standards. *Educational Administration Quarterly, 31*, 424–448.

Valenzuela, A. (Ed.). (2005). *Leaving children behind: How "Texas-style" accountability fails Latino youth.* Albany, NY: State University of New York Press.

Villegas, A. M., & Lucas, T. (2002). *Educating culturally responsive teachers.* Albany, NY: SUNY Press.

Wiliam, D. (2007). Keeping learning on track: Classroom assessment and the regulation of learning. In F. K. Lester, Jr. (Ed.), *Second handbook of research on mathematics teaching and learning* (pp. 1051–1098). Charlotte, NC: Information Age.

Williams v. State of California (Superior Court of the State of California for the County of San Francisco, 2001), Complaint 58–66.

Wearne, D., & Kouba, V. L. (2000). Rational numbers. In E. A. Silver & P. A. Kenney (Eds.), *Results from the seventh mathematics assessment of the National Assessment of Educational Progress* (pp. 163–191). Reston, VA: National Council of Teachers of Mathematics.

II
Teaching and Learning

8
Preparing Culturally Responsive Mathematics Teachers

GENEVA GAY

This discussion is structured around the question: How can mathematics teaching be more culturally responsive for ethnically diverse students, and by extension, be more effective? Embedded within it are the more specific issues of (1) How can middle-class, monolingual European-American math teachers work better with students who are predominately of color, attend schools in poor urban communities, and are often multilingual; and (2) how can the general principles of culturally responsive teaching be applied in practice in mathematics education?

Preparing math teachers to be culturally responsive to ethnically diverse students includes acquiring new knowledge, attitudes, belief, and skills about self, students, subject matter, teaching, and learning. An explanation of all of these is beyond the scope of this discussion. Only a few of the components are described as a means for starting the process of change. Among them are demystifying math, understanding the ideology of culturally responsive teaching (CRT), and developing culturally responsive pedagogical skills. None of these can be done adequately without a deeper and broader knowledge base about the cultures, contributions, histories, and heritages of different ethnic groups. Some suggestions are made for how this knowledge can be acquired.

The guiding premise underlying all of these discussions is that both teachers in training and those already in service should learn about culturally responsive teaching in ways similar to the ones they should use with students in their own classroom. This principle applies regardless of whether they teach elementary, middle, or high school, or college students, and basic introductory or advanced mathematics subject matter. This approach to the preparation of teachers lends additional credibility to the viability of CRT because in their own learning the teachers experience a close facsimile of what their students will encounter.

Challenges to Confront

These questions and related discussions are based on the assumption that responsiveness to cultural differences is fundamental to effective teaching and learning. Gloria Ladson-Billings (1995) relates this idea specifically to teaching and learning mathematics. She says, "all students can be successful in mathematics when their understanding of it is linked to meaningful cultural referents, and when the instruction assumes that all students are capable of mastering the subject matter" (p. 141). Yet, many teachers are reluctant to embrace this ideology or the reality of cultural differences between themselves and their students; and they are not willing to act aggressively to incorporate these realities into their classroom practices. They continue to hold onto the mistaken notions that good teaching is culturally neutral, that " best practices" exist that are applicable to all learning circumstances and populations, and that some subject matter is "universally true," and therefore beyond the influence of particular cultures. If there really are any "universal teaching best practices" they exist in the most general and abstract terms, to the extent that they have little meaning in actual practice. Even then they are not culturally neutral or value-free since they emerge out of given sociocultural contexts and ideological frameworks. For example, best practices such as "expectations of excellence for all students" and "teaching higher order thinking skills," do not indicate what they mean or look like when actualized in practice. Their embedded meanings convey certain value preferences as well, including performance on measures of cognitive skills in standardized tests in high status subjects such as math and science. The fact that math has been assigned high status among the subjects taught in schools is, in itself, an indication of it not being culture- or value-free. Similar status is not associated with the fine and performing arts, domestic sciences, or physical education. If math were value-free this status differential between it and other school subjects would not exist.

A frequently declared statement among proponents of math as value-free is, "Numbers don't lie, nor are they susceptible to relativistic meanings." As a result, many math teachers feel they are preempted from having to deal with demands for cultural relevance in their curriculum and instruction. These attitudes are based on misconceptions about culture, misunderstandings about culturally responsive education, distorted notions of teaching, and narrow conceptions of mathematics. They exist among more than a few ultra-conservative, traditional, inexperienced, or naive math educators; and they have to be addressed directly in designing reform programs to make high-level mathematics education more accessible to a wider range of students in public schools.

Even if math were culture-free, it still has to be taught to students, many of whom are not middle class, European Americans, and fluent speakers of Standard Academic English like their teachers. These ethnic and cultural divides between students and teachers are widening daily. As Villegas and Lucas (2002) noted: "most [in-service] teachers and prospective teachers have no windows into the lives of increasingly greater numbers of their students" (p. 22). They cannot evoke shared frames of reference to make meaningful connections between classroom instruction and the cultures, lives, and experiences of racially, ethnically, socially, and linguistically different students. Since both teaching and learning are cultural enterprises, it is little wonder why so many nonmainstream students are having difficulty learning in schools, and the achievement gap persists largely unabated year after year. If teachers cannot build learning bridges that cross the cultural divides in their teaching then ethnically diverse, underachieving students will continue to perform far below their potential. This is true regardless of the subject or skill being taught, but especially so for high-stakes, high-status arenas of learning such as mathematics.

For this reason, it is even more imperative for those areas of school curricula to be targeted for culturally responsive reform. All dimensions of their teaching need to be modified, but to examine how and why is beyond the scope of this discussion. A choice of emphasis had to be made; and I have chosen to address teacher preparation for culturally responsive instruction. This initiative alone cannot do all that needs to be done to make learning more effective for ethnically diverse students, but it is a critical component that must be addressed, and a viable place at which to begin the deep level changes required. Without question, the best curricula and instructional materials are only as good as the teachers who implement them, Teachers who are not adequately prepared to understand and do culturally responsive teaching are at a major disadvantage in today's schools with respect to the effectiveness of their teaching, as well as the quality and level of learning for the increasingly diverse student populations in U.S. schools.

Because of their importance in shaping instructional behaviors, teacher beliefs about students, subjects, and teaching should be a central focus of professional development. This need is particularly imperative for teaching high status subjects to underachieving students of color, students living in poverty, and those from linguistically different backgrounds. There is often a collision between the insidious negative prejudices toward those students that are deeply embedded in the fabric of the U.S. educational system, and the positive bias associated with high status subjects, without teachers knowing what to do or why they are unable to pursue instructional decisions and actions that serve the constructive interests of both low-status students and high-status contents. This is the reason for the emphasis placed here on the discussions in this chapter regarding beliefs about mathematics, and teaching it to ethnically, racially, and culturally diverse students.

To resolve these dilemmas, and move forward behaviorally with better learning results for students, teachers need to have a thorough understanding of the subject-associated perceptions and socializations of mathematics, how they are manifested, and how they affect students from various ethnic groups so that they can develop strategies to counteract them (Leonard, 2008). They also need to develop some paradigms about how to teach culturally diverse students that are different from those that have been in place for generations and have not produced acceptable results.

Several proposals are made in this discussion for preparing culturally responsive math teachers. The focus of their attention is more on orientations to teaching as *ways of being in relationship with diverse students and subject matter* than methodologies for teaching specific math content. This emphasis seems reasonable since teachers never teach only subject matter; *they must always teach subject matter content and skills to students.* Contrary to the suggestions of some contemporary education reformers who endorse disciplinary knowledge in teacher preparation to the virtual exclusion of pedagogical skills, teaching is much more than conveying knowledge to students. Too many of us have painful memories of former teachers who were highly intelligent and knowledgeable about their disciplines but did not know how to teach their students in interesting, exciting, engaging, and academically successful ways. Teachers must know students as well as content, in order to determine how best to effectively convey the knowledge and skills to be learned. Ayers (2004) makes a compelling point about teachers needing to know their students as a precondition to providing quality education for them. He says:

> Teachers must know their students, reach out to them with care and understanding in order to create a bridge from the known to the not-yet-known. Teaching that is more than incidental, more than accidental, demands sustained empathic regard. Teaching is initially the art of invitation, and it is virtually impossible to invite people to learn if they are strange or inscrutable to you. Good teachers find ways to know and understand learners. They observe and record students at work and at play. They create dialogue. They inquire. They map social and cultural contexts. Odd or unfamiliar contexts place a straightforward demand upon teachers: Become a student of your own students as a prerequisite to teaching them. (p. 25)

This advice is particularly pertinent to teachers of ethnically, racially, and culturally diverse students.

Demystifying Math

Unquestionably, attitudes, values, and beliefs shape teachers' instructional and learning behaviors. This is a well-established fact in research and classroom observations of teacher attitudes toward students, and student attitudes toward the different subjects taught in school (Good & Brophy, 2003; Oakes, 2005; Oakes & Guiton, 1995; Oakes & Lipton, 2007). Research also indicates that the beliefs of preservice teachers about teaching, subjects, and students influence their knowledge acquisition and subsequent instructional decisions and classroom practices (Downey & Cobbs, 2007). A less known (or readily acknowledged) reality among educators is how the values and beliefs assigned to different subjects (and aspects within them) affect student and teacher attitudes toward them. Yet we know this intuitively, from personally lived experiences, and from cross-generational memories.

These ascriptions go beyond the typical designations of "college prep" and "noncollege prep" (or "regular" classes as they are often called), or required and elective courses. Some subjects have the reputation of being "hard" or intellectually rigorous while others have come to be known as "easy," or "no-brainers." Some are perceived as substantively significant and others as merely tolerable because of their ritualistic and symbolic meaning; some are worthy of respect because of their iconic positions and historical persistence, while others are trailblazers, and "cutting edge" in establishing new terrains of intellectual insights. Some are for students and teachers who cannot and others are for those who can (with respect to intellectual prowess). Some are associated with developing future, stellar leaders, but others are reserved for individuals who will be a part of the common masses. These beliefs toward school subjects, the caste system they generate, and the inequities embedded in them, are transmitted to students, such that those enrolled in high status classes receive better quality learning opportunities than those taking low status subjects.

In these designations mathematics holds a position of status, power, and privilege—its advanced versions are even referred to as "gateways" and "gatekeepers." The discipline is perceived as being of high class and high status especially in secondary schools and colleges. As such, it is presumed to be learnable by only a select group of students. A distinguished African-American mathematician, Abdulalim Shabazz, described his professional community to Gilmer (1991) as "very elitist," and explained further that its members:

> ...view mathematics as pure thought and largely take the position that any mathematics dealing with applications or practicality is not really mathematics. They do not acknowledge contributions to the field made in Africa and South and Central America where there exist monuments to the mathematical and technological genius of our people. This must change since there is nothing anyone can do with abstract or pure thought in and of itself. (p. 2)

This "positive bias" attached to mathematics privileges some students and disadvantages others. It causes large numbers of students of color and those who live in economic poverty to be excluded from access to mathematics learning beyond the most rudimentary basics.

Revisioning the "socially constructed identity of mathematics," accepting the culturally responsive as a requirement of quality education for ethnically different students, and crafting instructional actions that exemplify them are crucial components of teachers' preparation if they are to provide more equitable learning opportunities for diverse students. This is so because educational equity is essential to culturally responsive teaching; and high levels of educational success for diverse students are contingent on culturally responsive teaching (Gay, 2000; Villegas & Lucas, 2002). Leonard (2008) and Moses and Cobbs (2001) add social justice and civic efficacy to these purposes of mathematics education.

While problematic, some of the status designation for school subjects is probably unavoidable in a capitalistic, highly competitive, and class-conscious society (although the latter is frequently denied vehemently!) such as the United States. The consequences are most troubling when the race and ethnicity of students intersect with the status attached to different areas of learning. Too often for comfort, some educators convey attitudes that disproportionate numbers of students from certain ethnic groups will not perform well in high status, high stakes subjects such as math, and they assign them to watered down versions, or exclude them from enrollment entirely. Thus, mathematics becomes a proxy for academic racism, ethnic inequities in educational opportunities, and a means for perpetuating a class system of "haves" and "have nots." Many math educators argue passionately against these descriptions of their discipline, especially noting that "this should not be; high level math knowledge should be for everyone." This may indeed be what should be, but too often it is not. And, it is not very useful as a change strategy to merely deny its existence, or focus only on the ideal. Change should begin with a careful, thorough, and critical analysis of what currently is.

Therefore, a major part of preparing teachers to be culturally responsive math educators is deconstructing the aura of incontestability and status that now surrounds mathematics, and certain notions about what constitutes quality instruction. Teachers-in-training should examine questions such as: What is it about the way math has been socially constructed that is exclusive, rather than inclusive to culturally, racially, ethnically, and socially diverse students? Who are these specific groups of students, and how are they affected differently by conventional perceptions of, and approaches to, math education? What are the underlying beliefs that generate these behaviors? Once these factors have been identified, then the analysis should proceed to determining what new teachers coming into the profession (and others already in classroom), can do to change the image and practices of mathematics to ones that convey accessibility and equity to a wider range of students. These analyses will not be easy undertakings because they involve challenging deeply embedded and institutionalized customs, values, and traditions. Therefore, teacher education students and professors must resist temptations to take a course of least resistance by leaving things as they are, making quiet personal commitments to changing their discipline, or doing ritualized, superficial analyses and cosmetic changes. If the attitudinal profiles are not changed at their deep core, they are likely to surface again and again in the midst of efforts to culturally diversify math programmatic features, and co-opt potential positive effects that could occur.

Another part of the math mystique that needs to be demystified is the assumption that its content is devoid of any human presence. This may be more a matter of the way math is usually taught in K-12 schools than an inherent feature. But, the idea exists in the minds and experiences of many students. They find it difficult to see the relevance of many math concepts, principles, and operations to real life, when they are perpetually presented as decontextualized formulas and abstractions. Teachers need to be taught how to humanize mathematics, and to place these reconstructions into the lived realities of different racial, cultural, social, and ethnic groups. In other words, it is not sufficient in the humanization process to include only middle class, Eurocentric experiences and perspectives. Given that most teachers are European Americans, and are not knowledgeable about different ethnic groups' cultures, they may not be very successful in their efforts to incorporate culturally diverse versions of humanness into math curriculum and instruction. They need to acquire more cultural knowledge about ethnic groups in order to humanize mathematics.

A third myth that interferes with math mastery for some students is its disciplinary language. It is beyond comprehension for many students. It does not make practical sense to them because it is not a language they use in their everyday lives. This does not mean, however, that math is not part of their daily living, or that they may not have a lot of math knowledge, or at least the potential to acquire it. Quite the contrary is true, but this knowledge is codified in a linguistic system very different from the one typically used in academic mathematics. Many students are unable to translate "academic math language" into a discourse of practicality, or to convert their social discourse into the language of school mathematics. They may reason that if the language of math is meaningless and incomprehensible to them, the content itself is worthless, too. Or, because the language is so difficult to understand, the content will be, too. After all, language is the mechanism through which cognitive processes are made manifest in expressive form.

According to Sinclair (2006), the communicative mystery of math extends beyond language to encompass a disciplinary culture, with institutionalized values and aesthetics. She explains that:

> As a culture, mathematics is driven by a distinct set of values…that distinguish it from other human domains of inquiry in terms of the production, perception, and communication of knowledge, as well its organization for posterity. These values are responsible for the way in which the very human practice of doing mathematics gives rise to abstract, dehumanized ideas. (p. 139)

These values include claims of rationalism, objectivism, control, progress, openness, and mystery. Mathematical knowledge is supposed to be beyond subjective interpretation, since "facts speak for themselves." These convey a form of aestheticism grounded in detachment, timelessness, permanence, and universality (Sinclair, 2006).

A counterargument to perceptions of math as dehumanized, abstract, and exclusive is offered by some scholars such as Posamentier (2003) and Sinclair (2006). They suggest that mathematics has inherent beauty and aestheticism. For example, Posamentier believes that more attention should be given to teaching students about the beauty of mathematics instead of always focusing on its practicality. He acknowledges that for many people math is unpopular, induces fear, and is consequently intimidating. They even treat their weakness in it as a "badge of honor." Teachers can do a lot to redirect these attitudes in students. Once they see math differently for themselves, they can become "ambassadors to the beautiful realm of mathematics," entice "youth toward a love for this magnificent and time-tested subject" (p. xii), and teach students to "appreciate it for its beauty and not only for its usefulness" (p. xiii). However, to accomplish these goals, the enthusiasm of teachers, the intended audience, and the manner in which math is taught have to be considered along with the inherent nature of the discipline itself. These perceptions are part of what Leonard (2008) calls the mathematics socialization and identity of students, and Sinclair (2006) refers to as the culture of the discipline. Whether positive, negative, inviting, or intimidating, they need to be targeted for reconstruction and redirection in making mathematics more accessible, relevant, and effective for underachieving ethnically diverse students.

All of these claims about the language, culture, and mystic of mathematics should be subjected to critical analysis in preparing teacher preparation programs. It will not be an easy or popular undertaking. No cultural critique or reform is. But, the need is imperative and should not be avoided or slighted. The task should be approached with a clear understanding of how resilient any culture can be, and especially one anointed with high status, such as that accorded to mathematics. To counter these perceptions, and improve student achievement, teachers need to learn (1) why the language and culture of math are so mystifying for so many, and to whom; (2) how this mystification affects teaching and learning attitudes and behaviors; and (3) techniques for translating the technical language and culture of mathematics into the nontechnical discourse of everyday life.

Contrastive analysis, a technique used by scholars and teachers of language and literacy across cultures, can be applied in teaching these skills. Students are taught explicitly how to recognize similarities, differences, parallels, and interferences among different languages and cultures, and given guided practice in code-switching across the systems under study. Math is definitely a "foreign language and culture" to students who have difficulties learning it. Another approach to teaching teachers how to become math cultural brokers and language translators (Sinclair, 2006) is the one used by Bob Moses and his colleagues in the Algebra Project (Moses & Cobbs, 2001). In teaching algebra to underachieving middle school African Americans they make sure the students understand math concepts, principles, problems, and operations in everyday language and living before abstract ideas and technical language are introduced. The underlying premise of these teaching techniques is that if students do not know the linguistic and cultural codes in which math knowledge is embedded and through which teaching occurs, they will not learn the content of what is taught. This is a common argument made by proponents of bilingualism and biculturalism in other areas of study, such as reading, writing, and literature. It applies to learning mathematics as well.

Culturally Responsive Ideological Guidelines for Practice

A logical next step to follow in the demystification of math teacher education is the study of the major philosophical beliefs and tenets of culturally responsive teaching and their implications for practice. It is not possible to summarize all of them here. Only five are presented here, in order to initiate the learning process and illustrate their instructional implications. These are the importance of culture; the social construction of knowledge; the inclusiveness of cultural responsiveness; academic achievement involves more than intellect; and balancing and blending unity and diversity. As is the case with all good learning, in the process of understanding these few samples of the ideology of culturally responsive teaching, pre- and in-service teachers will discover others to add to their repertoires of beliefs and practice possibilities.

Culture is Important in Teaching and Learning

Central to cultural responsive teaching is the belief that culture influences teaching and learning in fundamental and profound ways (Erickson, 2007; Pai & Adler, 2001). This influence is a reflection of humanity, since all people are social and cultural beings, and all dimensions and expressions of their humanness are shaped by and reflect their cultural socialization to some degree. In reality, this means that culture is an everyday, all-the-time phenomenon, not something reserved for special times and events; it is present in everyone, not just groups who have been marginalized or exoticized; and students and teachers cannot remove themselves from their cultural orientations at will. Therefore, if teaching is to be adequate for diverse students, not to mention equitable and exemplary, it, too, must be culturally diverse.

These beliefs evoke three recurrent concerns of teachers, especially if they are middle class, monolingual European Americans considering the prospect of teaching multilingual, poor, students of color. They are: How can I possibly know enough about all the cultures of my students when there are so many of them? How can I deal with different cultures without stereotyping groups or overgeneralizing their members? Isn't it the individual that counts, not the cultures? This is not the place to answer these questions. Suffice it to say, they are indicative of profound needs in both teacher preparation and classroom practices. Among them are the need of teachers for some basic knowledge about the nature of culture, what the rich body of scholarship in multicultural education and culturally responsive teaching says about dealing with cultural understandings in educational decision making and practice, and teachers analyzing their own deeply held beliefs about culture in human life in general, and different ethnic groups in particular.

Knowledge is Socially Constructed

Another important area of study in examining the philosophical beliefs of culturally responsive math teacher education is the cultural values embedded in the image and status of mathematics in the United States. Mainstream society places high value on objectivity, rationality, and competitiveness (along with an underlying belief in "survival of the fittest"), at least in theory if not in fact. Conventional conceptions of math epitomize these. It is supposed to be the ultimate command for rational thought in learning, and those individuals with this inclination will automatically be the most successful math students. Their ability to demonstrate this skill also will help them matriculate through the hierarchy of courses in math curricula, and into prestigious career options beyond school and college. A problem with these embedded values is that they are not taught explicitly as precursors to the mastery of mathematics content and skills. Instead, they fall into the category of "taken-for-granted cultural assumptions" (Bowers & Flinders, 1991).

Culturally responsive teaching takes the position that all knowledge is socially constructed. As such it can never be a totally objectified or universal truth; it is always influenced by who, when, and why it was create or configured, and for whom and for what purposes. In building their philosophical foundations for culturally responsive mathematics education teachers need to understand how math is a cultural construction, and how this construction, and its related teaching preferences, privilege some students while disadvantaging and marginalizing others.

Inclusivity

Culturally responsive teaching also is an *inclusive* endeavor on multiple levels. It is appropriate for all students and subjects at all grade levels. While its major principles and goals transcend contextual boundaries, how these are translated to instructional practices varies depending on the subject, environmental context, student population, and instructional purposes. For example, a common goal of culturally responsive teaching is to increase students' knowledge of cultural diversity. The actual content to be taught and how it is conveyed to students will be different for mathematics, reading, and social studies. These subjects have different knowledge bases and teaching protocols. Therefore, interjecting information about cultural differences needs to be compatible with these conventions. It would be counterproductive for math teachers to try to teach cultural diversity the same way as it is done in history, home economics, or science. Another factor shaping how culturally responsive teaching is done in practice has to do with the nature of the students in question. Obviously, their ages and grade levels make a difference, but so do their ethnicity and the demographic composition of their classes and schools. Culturally responsive teaching is nuanced somewhat differently in monoracial and multiracial classes, and the particular racial identities of these compositions are important, too. Thus, predominately African-American student populations require some instructional actions that are different from those that are appropriate for Asian or Latino/a Americans. So too, do the particular ethnic mixtures in multiracial classrooms that are majority-minority, and minority-minority students. The combination of these philosophical beliefs might be stated as, *cultural diversity is needed by all students but its actual practice is contextually specific.* They defy notions of teaching and learning being color blind or culture free. By including a wide array of ethnic and cultural values, experiences, perspectives, and contributions in teaching "the dominance of one cultural value system [Eurocentric] is mitigated, [and] a more inclusive educational context is possible and plausible" (Parsons 2003, p. 29).

One other dimension of the inclusivity belief of CRT is worthy of note here; that is, where to place information about cultural diversity in school curricula. The easy answer is "everywhere." But, this does not have much practical or operational meaning. A more informative explanation is that cultural diversity should be placed in the *core* of school subjects taught, not on their periphery; nor restricted to specially designed instructional topics, subjects, events, or programs. This means teaching about cultural diversity on a regular and routine basis, along with what is considered the most fundamental knowledge and skills of different subjects. If teaching young students how to do basic calculations is considered fundamental to their early math understanding, then information about cultural diversity should be woven into learning how to do addition, subtraction, division, multiplication, and fractions. The same idea of combining the mastery of essential subject matter knowledge and skills with cultural diversity applies to more advanced levels of mathematics, such as algebra, geometry, and calculus. Curriculum content is very important, but it cannot accomplish these goals alone. Instructional delivery, student–teacher relationships, classroom climate, policy mandates, and the diagnosis and assessment of student performance are imperative, too. They explain further the meaning of inclusiveness in the philosophy of CRT. Obviously, math teachers need to know a lot about cultural diversity to meet these expectations, and they signify a critical component of their professional preparation.

Academic Achievement Is More than Intellect

Multicultural education and culturally responsive teaching invite educators to rethink analyses of achievement problems among students of color and students living in poverty as being academic only. Even the highly valued and publicized standardized test scores should not be attributed only to students' cognitive skills and intellectual abilities. Like other dimensions of the educational enterprise achievement takes place within particular cultural contexts. If students are not fully engaged in these contexts or know how to navigate them, then their performance will be affected negatively. For example, performing well on standardized tests involves knowing how to take tests and students' intellectual work rhythms being in sync with the rhythm of test administration, as well as knowing the substantive content being tested. Not mastering the former, which might be called the social protocols and cultural capital that govern academic engagement, can cause students to look like they do not know as much as they do. Underachieving students from marginalized or underrepresented groups in particular may be adversely affected by procedural inexperience misdiagnosed as substantive failure because they have not had opportunities to learn the "cultural capital" of test taking. Many of these students do not have individuals in their intimate lives who have legacies of school success to pass on to them, and these procedural skills often are not taught formally in schools.

Other factors that have nothing to do with intellect or cognitive knowledge contribute to, or impinge upon, the academic achievement of culturally and ethnically different students. Much research and scholarship produced over the years make a compelling case about the strong correlation between self-concept, self-esteem, self-efficacy, and teacher expectations on academic achievement. Students who believe they can learn, and have teachers who reinforce this belief with their own, will do incredible things in school. The converse is true as well, and too often this is the situation with learning mathematics. High percentages of students of color have been persuaded that they cannot succeed at math, so they do not. Teachers do not have to be directly biased in conveying these beliefs; they are often so subtle as to be unconscious or unintentional. In other situations, the job is done by agencies and images beyond the schools, and teachers have to counteract it.

Other "environmental" or contextual factors impinging upon students' academic achievement are the quality of the teachers they have, the availability of culturally relevant instructional resources, and the images and reputations of the schools they attend. When the total setting in which teaching and learning occur is negative there is little wonder why students have a difficult time reaching high levels of academic achievement. These possibilities reinforce the importance of the earlier philosophical belief about the impact of comprehensive culturally responsive interventions for improving the performance of ethnically diverse students. Translating them specifically to math education entails curriculum designs that have *significant math-appropriate culturally diverse content*; analyzing frequently used instructional materials and strategies to determine their level of cultural relevance for students from different ethnic groups, and making modifications where necessary; creating learning climates and communities that cultivate math efficacy in diverse students; and using a wide variety of culturally diverse indicators and measures of mathematics achievement. They should comprise the core of the culturally responsive pedagogical knowledge and skills for math teachers. Some of the work on Mexican ancestry students' funds of knowledge that Luis Moll and his colleagues (Gonzales, Moll, & Amanti, 2005) are doing, Jerry Lipka (1998) and his colleagues (Lipka et al., 2005) with the Yup'iks of Alaska, Teresa McCarty (2002) with the Navajos, and Stacey Lee (2005) with Asian Americans, is instructive for teachers in developing these skills.

Balancing and Blending Cultural Unity and Diversity

Many teachers still struggle with creating a workable balance between cultural diversity and cultural unity among the diverse peoples of the United States. Some feel that focusing on differences among these groups and their cultures is divisive and aggravates racial tensions, and that they should be avoided to the extent of denying the existence of differences. At the other end of the spectrum is the belief that cultural diversity is an unavoidable reality among human beings, and within the continuing construction of the United States. Some who ascribe to this ideology will even go so for as to say that differences among groups and cultures is the only thing that counts in educating diverse students. In training culturally responsive teachers these ideological tensions need to be acknowledged and analyzed.

The philosophy of CRT offers a compromise between these two extreme perspectives. It argues that both differences and similarities among diverse groups are real, natural, valuable, and should be promoted. Rather than being inherently contradictory or mutually exclusive, they are reciprocal and complementary to each other. In fact, one can generate the other. Therefore, both cultural differences and similarities should be central themes in teaching and learning.

Even those who are skeptical about accomplishing this possibility may see a glimmer of hope for it when attention is focused on comparing one group with another. It is harder to make sense of how to simultaneously teach ethnically diverse students about their own cultures and mainstream society. These ideological principles and related action possibilities can be better imagined by overlaying another common CRT belief onto them. This is the idea of teaching students knowledge and skills to cross borders, or style shift, among different cultural systems, including the one dominant in schools and the home cultures of various groups. For example, Latino/a American students being taught their own cultures at the same time as they are learning the cultures of the Eurocentric mainstream society, African Americans, Asian Americans, and Native Americans. As they cross these various cultural borders in learning, they take some elements from each and add them to their personal repertoires of being. In a real sense, if cultural teaching and learning proceed as they should, students will become functional multiculturalists. Other scholars have called the results of this learning process *cultural hybridity* (C. D. Lee, 2007).

Translating Beliefs and Principles into Practice

The question now becomes how teachers can be taught to be promoters of cultural hybridity, cultural border-crossing, cultural style shifting, and pan-humanism in mathematics education (Banks & McGee Banks, 2006; Gay, 2000; C. D. Lee, 2007). One technique is to challenge them to recognize and value these phenomena in their personally lived experiences, and to use similar processes applied in their own self-analyses with the students they teach. They can be specified to mathematics by examining how different subject matter concepts, content, and skills are actualized in the cultural practices of different ethnic groups. An example is the presence of geometrical concepts in the folk arts, crafts, and architecture of Native, African, Asian, Latino, and European ancestry groups. The arrangements of notes (i.e., full, half, quarter, etc.) and rhythmic patterns in the musical traditions of different ethnic groups can be used to teach proportions, percentages, and fractions. Similar math skills, as well as more advanced ones, can be taught through other ethnic customs and traditions, such as the design and execution of ethnic festivals, ceremonies, and celebrations; ethnic population, employment, residential, and educational statistics; immigration patterns across different time periods and ethnic groups; and the different types and levels of participation of various ethnic groups in economic activities (such as small business ownerships and consumer retail within and beyond their own ethnic communities). The idea here is for teachers to teach students more information about their own ethnic groups' contributions to mathematics, show how mathematics operates in other dimensions of culture and areas of learning, and reveal parallels among the uses of mathematics in different cultural contexts of various ethnic groups. Thus, cultural similarities and differences, and multiple layers of cultural knowledge are taught at the same time that students are learning math skills. These interconnections between math and other subjects, and between math in school and in life beyond school increases its relevance for all students, and their academic achievement in all kinds and levels of mathematics (Grouws & Cebulla, 2008).

It is imperative for teachers to stay within the conceptual and disciplinary boundaries of multicultural education as they "culturalize" math instruction. Parsons (2001) defines *culturalizing instruction* as the deliberate enactment of culturally diverse values, information, and resources to change the contexts and content of learning to improve academic outcomes. Leonard (2008) calls this approach to teaching *culturally specific pedagogy*. Both are synonyms for culturally responsive teaching. Regardless of the nomenclature used, these ideas for improving student achievement share a focus on issues of ethnic, racial, and cultural diversity within the boundaries of national, not world, settings. The latter may be termed international or global education. While some points of reference beyond the boundaries of the United States are necessary in the study of all ethnic groups, the emphasis and primary units of analysis need to be within the the United States for them to qualify as multicultural education.

This distinction needs to be made in general and especially in discussions about the contributions of different ethnic groups to mathematics. Many teachers respond to the challenge by lifting up the mathematical genius of the ancient

Greeks, Romans, Egyptians, Chinese, Mayans, and Africans. While this historical knowledge is important for students to know it is not analogous to culturally responsive math education for contemporary ethnically diverse students, even for those who share these ancestral origins. Teachers need to learn about the contributions of different ethnic groups and individuals in more contemporary times and within the United States, so that they can pass them on to their students. This knowledge acquisition can begin with conducting research studies on the contributions, careers, and cultural profiles of African, Asian, Latino, and Native Americans to mathematics and related fields, including math in indigenous cultural practices. The results can be shared using different expressive genres and presentation styles, such as conversational dialogues, interviews, expository writing, teleconferencing, video logs, and simulated demonstrations of the mathematical applications these individuals employ in the work they do. For instance, case studies of Native Alaskan fisheries, Native American totem carvers, and Native American casino industries will reveal the application of complex and sophisticated concepts, knowledge, and operations at every conceivable levels of mathematics, from the most pragmatic to the most theoretical, from the most simplistic to the most complex skills.

Other valuable knowledge about cultural diversity in mathematics content and instruction can be accumulated by interacting with mathematicians and mathematics educators at different ethnic heritage institutions, such as historically Black colleges and universities, and Native American Heritage Colleges. Since they are likely to be more actively and routinely engaged in the practice of culturally responsive math teaching than their counterparts at predominately White institutions the suggestions and advice they offer will be rich sources of pedagogical knowledge. A graphic illustration of this potentiality for helping teachers increase their culturally responsive math content and pedagogical knowledge is Dr. Abdulalim Shabazz, an African-American mathematician who taught at Atlanta University in the 1960s and 1970s. During his tenure there he produced more than 50% of all African Americans who went on to receive PhDs in the discipline (Delpit, 2006; Gilmer, 1991). Surely, there are many instructional lessons for teachers to learn about culturally responsive math education from Dr. Shabazz's stellar accomplishments. Furthermore, he can be added to their lists of contemporary mathematicians of color and their contributions to be taught to K-12 students. Distinguished individuals from other ethnic groups also should be identified and highlighted in teacher education programs.

These research studies, interactions, and presentations can be accompanied by strategies for using similar learning activities with K-12 students. Thus, pre- and in-service teachers have opportunities to develop culturally responsive competence on three levels at once. They increase their own knowledge about the contributions of ethnic individuals and groups to the field of mathematics; they confront and deconstruct conventional beliefs about the relationship between cultural diversity and mathematics, and develop new ones; and they participate in guided practice on transferring what they learn into teaching possibilities for their own students. In other words, math cultural content, knowledge, and pedagogical skills are developed simultaneously, and teacher education programs will offer exemplary models for teachers to teach math to their students in culturally responsive ways as they were taught.

In this cycle of learning everybody wins—teachers become more efficacious; students feel personally validated and reach higher levels of academic achievement; students and teachers learn more about each other culturally; and mathematics becomes more accessible, desirable, inviting, and exciting to students from a wider range of ethnic, racial, cultural, social, and ability backgrounds. When this happens we can say, with confidence, that genuine progress is being made toward accomplishing academic equity and social justice in mathematics education for African, Asian, European, Latino, and Native Americans, for poor and middle class students.

References

Ayers, W. (2004). *Teaching the personal and the political: Essays on hope and justice.* New York: Teachers College Press.

Banks, J. A., & McGee Banks, C. A. (Eds.), *Multicultural education: Issues and perspectives* (6th ed.). New York: Wiley.

Bowers, C. A., & Flinders, D. J. (1991). *Culturally responsive teaching and supervision: A handbook for staff development.* New York: Teachers College Press.

Erickson, F. (2007). Culture in society and in educational practices. In J. A. Banks & C. A. McGee Banks (Eds.), *Multicultural education: Issues and perspectives* (6th ed., pp. 33–61). New York: John Wiley

Delpit, L. (2006). Lessons from teachers. *Journal of Teacher Education, 57*(3), 220–231.

Downey, J. A., & Cobbs, G. A. (2007). "I actually learned a lot from this": A field assignment to prepare future math teachers for culturally diverse classrooms. *School Science and Mathematics, 107*(1), 391–403.

Gay, G. (2000). *Culturally responsive teaching: Theory, research, and practice.* New York: Teachers College Press.

Gilmer, G. F. (1991). *An interview with Abdulalim Abdullah Shabazz.* Retrieved August 30, 2008, from http://www.sankofaworldpublishers.com/sankofawponline/sankofawp-Abdulalim%20Shabazz%20Interview.htm

Gonzales, N., Moll, L. C., & Amanti, C. (Eds.). (2005). *Funds of knowledge: Theorizing practice in households, communities, and classrooms.* Mahwah, NJ: Erlbaum.

Good, T. L., & Brophy, J. E. (2003). *Looking in classrooms* (6th ed.). New York: HarperCollins.

Grouws, D. A., & Cebulla, K. J. (2000). Improving student achievement in mathematics, Part 2: Recommendations for the classroom. Retrieved December 2, 2008, from http://findarticles.com/p/articles/mi_pric/is_200012/ai_4154818456.

Ladson-Billings, G. (1995). Making mathematics meaningful in multicultural contexts. In W. G. Secada, E. Fennema, & L. B. Adajian (Eds.), *New directions for equity in mathematics education* (pp. 126–145). New York: Cambridge University Press.

Lee, C. D. (2007). *Culture, literacy, and learning: Taking bloom in the midst of the whirlwind.* New York: Teachers College Press.

Lee, S. J. (1996). *Unraveling the "model minority" stereotype: Listening to Asian American youth.* New York: Teachers College Press.

Lee, S. J. (2006). *Up against Whiteness: Race, school, and immigrant youth.* New York: Teachers College Press.

Leonard, J. (2008). *Culturally specific pedagogy in the mathematics classroom*. New York: Routledge.

Lipka, J., Hiogan, M. P., Webster, J. P., Yanez, E., Adams, B., Clark, S., et al. (2005). Math in a cultural context: Two case studies of a successful culturally-based math project. *Anthropology & Education Quarterly, 36*(1), 367–385.

Lipka, J., with Mohatt, G. V., & the Ciulistet Group. (1998). *Transforming the culture of schools: Yup'ik Eskimo examples*. Mahwah, NJ: Erlbaum.

McCarty, T. L. (2002). *A place to be Navajo: Rough Rock and the struggle for self-determination in indigenous schooling*. Mahwah, NJ: Erlbaum.

Moses. R. P., & Cobb, Jr., C. E. (2001). *Radical equations: Math literacy and civil rights*. Boston: Beacon Press.

Oakes, J. (2005). *Keeping track: How schools structure inequality* (2nd ed.). New Haven, CT: Yale University Press.

Oakes, J., & Guiton, G. (1995). Matchmaking: The dynamics of high school tracking decisions. *American Educational Research Journal, 32*(1), 3–33.

Oakes, J., & Lipton, M. (2007). *Teaching to change the world* (3rd ed.). Boston: McGraw-Hill.

Pai, Y., & Adler, S. A. (2001). *Cultural foundations of education* (3rd ed.). Upper Saddle River, NJ: Merrill.

Parsons, E. C. (2003). Culturalizing instruction: Creating a more inclusive context for learning for African American students. *The High School Journal, 86*(4), 23–30.

Posamentier, A. S. (2003). *Math wonders to inspire teachers and students*. Alexandria, VA: Association for Supervision and Curriculum Development (ASCD).

Sinclair, N. (2006). *Mathematics and beauty: Aesthetic approaches to teaching children*. New York: Teachers College Press.

Villegas, A. M., & Lucas, T. (2002). *Educating culturally responsive teachers: A coherent approach*. Albany, NY: SUNY Press.

Wheeler, R. S., & Swords, R. (2006). *Code-switching: Teaching Standard English in urban classrooms*. Urbana, IL: National Council of Teachers of English.

9
Mathematics Literacy and Liberation
Reframing Mathematics Education for African-American Children

DANNY BERNARD MARTIN AND EBONY O. MCGEE

> African Americans, like other racial-ethnic-cultural groups, determine the functional significance of literacy based on their successful negotiation in educational, economic, family, and social contexts. It is not surprising, then, that although anecdotal accounts of what literacy means in African-American communities yield a range of introspections, the collective tone of these accounts suggests that literacy is not only important, but is requisite for human[e] existence and "successful" survival. (Qualls, 2001, p. 3)

> Culturally relevant teaching involves students in the knowledge-construction process, so that they can ask significant questions about the nature of the curriculum. The ultimate goal is to ensure that they have a sense of ownership of their knowledge—a sense that it is empowering and liberating. (Ladson-Billings, 1994, p. 77)

We raise this question: Why should African-American children learn mathematics? Having raised this question, we give specific attention to the embedded questions that include: Why should *African-American* children learn mathematics? Why should African-American children learn *mathematics*? These latter two questions highlight the necessity of giving particular attention to the needs and realities of African-American children *as* African-American children, on the one hand, and specifically situating mathematics in the lives of these children, on the other.

As we address these questions, we simultaneously offer a reconceptualization and reframing for the "structure, ideology, and content" (Anderson, 1988) of mathematics education for African-American learners. Taking our cue from the two quotes presented above, we advocate for mathematics education and the development of mathematics literacies that are (1) worthy of being experienced as part of African-American children's development as full human beings; and (2) that are liberating in nature by virtue of being responsive to the oppressive forces that African-American children will confront throughout the social contexts that define their lives.

While we recognize that many mathematics educators and policy makers frame mathematics education for African-American children by invoking broad diversity arguments, increased course enrollments, and workforce preparation (e.g., National Council of Teachers of Mathematics, 1989, 2000; National Research Council, 1989; National Science Board, 2003; RAND Mathematics Study Panel, 2003; U.S. Department of Education, 1997), we situate mathematics education and mathematics literacy for African-American children in a much broader context. Ultimately, we argue for mathematics education that allows African-American learners to use mathematics—uninhibited by forces like racism and inaccurate assessments of their skills and abilities—to change the conditions and power relations in their lives (Skovsmose, 1994). This will entail challenging the very education system in which school mathematics is learned and reshaping the opportunity structure in which it is argued that African Americans must participate. Gutstein (2005) calls this "reading and writing the world with mathematics," symbolizing the fact that mathematics learning can be a powerful means to uncover and resist injustice (D'Ambrosio, 2007). In our view, mathematics education that is committed to anything less is irrelevant for African-American children.

We see the task of reframing mathematics education for these students as important because of the implications for teacher selection and development (Martin, 2007), pedagogy and curriculum selection (Leonard, 2008), culturally relevant assessment, school–community partnerships, and mathematics education policy (Martin, 2003, in press). More important, however, we believe this task has nontrivial implications for the development of robust racial, academic, and mathematical identities among African-American learners (Berry, 2003; Martin, 2000, 2006a, 2006b; McGee, 2006, in press; Nasir, 2002, 2006; Stinson, 2004). The shaping of positive identities through the development of meaningful mathematics literacies can contribute to productive agency and empowerment among African-American children. Like Ernest (2002), we conceptualize *empowerment* along several dimensions—social, mathematical, epistemological—so as to implicate mathematics in the personal development of African-American children but also in their ability to create change in society. As defined by Ernest (2002):

> Mathematical empowerment concerns the gaining of power over the language, skills and practices of using and applying mathematics. This is the gaining of power over a relatively narrow domain e.g. that of school mathematics.

> Social empowerment through mathematics concerns the ability to use mathematics to better one's life chances in study and work and to participate more fully in society through critical mathematical citizenship. Thus it involves the gaining of power over a broader social domain, including the worlds of work, life and social affairs.
>
> Epistemological empowerment concerns the individual's growth of confidence not only in using mathematics, but also a personal sense of power over the creation and validation of knowledge. This is a personal form of empowerment: the development of personal identity so as to become a more personally empowered person with growth of confidence and potentially enhanced empowerment in both the mathematical and social senses (and for the mathematics teacher—enhanced professional empowerment). (pp. 1–2)

It will become very apparent that our approach to mathematics education among African-American children is in stark contrast to perspectives that focus on testing outcomes and achievement disparities in ways that, we claim, contribute to the reification of so-called racial differences in mathematical ability and the construction and acceptance of a *racial hierarchy of mathematical ability* (Martin, in press). This hierarchy locates African-American children at the bottom, even amongst people of color. In our view, framings for mathematics education that are driven by the closing of these so-called racial achievement gaps are problematic because they (1) require that one accept the inferiority of African-American children as the starting point in research and policy discussions; (2) conceptualize mathematics education for African-American children in ways that are contingent on the status and well-being of White children; and (3) render African-American children as change worthy according to standards and norms that typically emerge from White cultural frames of reference.

In addition, we see calls for closing racial achievement gaps as being related to models of assimilation that idealize and normalize White middle-class standards (Gilborn, 2006; Hilliard, 2003; Martin, in press; Perry, 2003). Viewed in this light, we argue that widely proliferated rhetoric calling for *Mathematics for All* contradicts mathematics education for the purposes of liberation. Later in this chapter, we support our claims by giving examples from mathematics education policy documents that attempt to frame mathematics education and mathematics literacy for African Americans based on the well-being of White children (National Research Council, 1989).

Our stance on these prior framings and portrayals of African-American children is clear: we do not know any normal African-American children who are incapable of learning mathematics and achieving at the highest levels and we have yet to discover evidence to the contrary. Therefore, we have no interest in following the strategies associated with previous framings that have emphasized "demonstrating" and "explaining" why African Americans "do not achieve up to the level of white and Asian children in mathematics."

In our view, any relevant framing of mathematics education for African Americans must address both the historical oppression that they have faced and the social realities that they continue to face in contemporary times. As noted in the opening quote by Qualls (2001), these social realities continue to be marked by the struggle for humane existence and survival against pernicious assaults on Black identity in the media, research, and public policy (Anderson, 2004; Ladson-Billings, 2006; Martin, 2007; Perry, 2003). We note that these social realities are also marked by resistance—what Watts and Serrano-Garcia (2003) call *emergent liberation behavior*—to marginalization and social devaluation and the continued pursuit of education in spite of these conditions (e.g., Anderson, 1988; Harding, 1981; Ladson-Billings, 2006; Williams, 2005).

Throughout this chapter, our conception of *liberation* considers freedom from subjugation in societal and school contexts as well as continued resistance to miseducation and policies and practices that promote the social devaluation of African-American status, in particular, and *Blackness*, more generally. Although there are numerous definitions and conceptualizations available in the extant literature, we draw on the recent work of Watts, Williams, and Jagers (2003), who engage in a Frereian (1970, 1973) analysis of the relationship between the oppressor and the oppressed, and who define *liberation* as both a process and an outcome:

> …liberation in its fullest sense requires the securing of full human rights and the remaking of a society without roles of oppressor and oppressed…. It involves challenging gross social inequities between social groups and creating new relationships that dispel oppressive social myths, values, and practices. The outcome of this process contributes to the creation of a changed society with ways of being that support the economic, cultural, political, psychological, social, and spiritual needs of individuals and groups. (pp. 187–188)

In addition to drawing on historical context, we consider contemporary forces that shape not only how African Americans develop their orientations toward mathematics literacy but also how mathematics education for African Americans has been framed by others, including teachers, researchers, and policy makers (e.g., National Council of Teachers of Mathematics, 1989, 2000; RAND Mathematics Study Panel, 2003). While color-blind rhetoric in mainstream mathematics education research and reform movements (e.g., *Mathematics for All*) is used to mask racialized constructions of the so-called achievement gap and while many White Americans continue to believe that barriers like racism no longer exist for African Americans in the post-civil rights era, social science research continues to document that many African Americans still cite race-based obstacles to their progress in society (e.g., Bonilla-Silva, 1997, 2003; Forman, 2004; Gilborn, 2006).

Although no longer restrained by overt Jim Crow and racist practices of earlier decades, African Americans of all backgrounds continue to confront barriers to their educational, economic, and political progress. Our conception of liberation also involves the transformation of oppressive social structures and psychological conditions associated with oppression (Watts et al., 2003). Clearly, we do not view liberation as the sole responsibility of African Americans. But there are plenty of historical and contemporary examples where African Americans have engaged in transformative action for the betterment of society. For example, in the current presidential primary elections, Texas republicans have worked overtime to make it harder for key democratic voting groups to vote and be represented fairly. The redistricting games they have played are infamous. For the precinct containing the historically Black university Prairie View A&M University, republicans located the early polling place more than seven miles from the university. So what did the African-American college students at Prairie View do? They shut down the highway as they marched seven miles to cast their votes on the first day of early voting.

In addition to specific incidents like the one just described, a snapshot of life for many African Americans reveals the following challenges to their progress in society (DeNavas-Walt, Proctor, & Lee, 2006; National Urban League, 2004):

- Real median income for Blacks decreased from 2004 ($31,101) to 2005 ($30,858);
- The three-year average Black poverty rate for the 2003–2005 period was 24.7%;
- Fewer than 50% of Black families own their own homes;
- Mean income of Black males is 70% of White males ($16,876 gap); mean income of Black females is 83% of White counterparts ($6,370 difference);
- Teachers with less than three years experience teach in minority schools at twice the rate that they teach in White schools;
- On average Blacks are twice as likely as Whites to die from disease, accident, and homicide at every stage of life.

Many of these barriers exist across class boundaries and research has shown that racism, for example, continues to mitigate the life opportunities of African Americans. This is evidenced by a growing literature on the experiences of well-educated, middle-class and upper middle-class African Americans who identify psychologically taxing microaggressions in their daily lives, particularly within majority-White contexts (e.g., Cose, 1995; Feagin & Sikes, 1994; Pattillo-McCoy, 1999).

Within contemporary mathematics education research, Martin (2000, 2006a, 2006b, in press) has documented—across African Americans of varied socio-economic, educational, and family backgrounds—how mathematics learning and participation can be characterized as *racialized forms of experience*; that is, as experiences structured by the relations of race and power that exist in the larger society. We argue that this conceptualization of mathematics learning and participation may be more relevant to the mathematical experiences of African-American learners than the dominant perspectives which typically characterize mathematics learning and participation as cultural, situated, or cognitive because this conceptualization situates the realities of racism and racialization (Miles, 1988) at the center of these experiences, not only for African-American children but also for children in other socially defined racial groups. This perspective also necessitates that mathematics education for African-American children should be framed in ways that counter negative, racialized mathematical experiences in school contexts. Finally, considering racialized forms of experience helps to account for why curriculum selection, teacher dispositions, assessment of student ability, and pedagogy are all influenced by the forces of racism and racialization.

In no way are we suggesting that the diversity of African-American experience can be essentialized in terms of struggle and oppression. That is, we do not begin and end our analysis with African-American oppression, thereby offering up our own form of subjugation and degradation. Although we acknowledge the instrumental and function value of mathematics literacy, we are not suggesting that mathematics literacy is sufficient for African-American liberation from oppression and social devaluing. This would require an end to White supremacy and other forms of material and symbolic violence (Bourdieu & Passeron, 1977), a comprehensive strategy of laws and enforcement, unfettered opportunity, grass-roots mobilization, and more.

While our reframing of the purposes, structure, and goals of mathematics education and mathematics literacy for African-American children will also highlight aspects of our own pedagogical practices and research, we admittedly stop short of offering up a prescriptive, comprehensive liberatory pedagogy that satisfies the demands of scholars like Baker (1997):

> Further, it is impossible from a perspective in critical pedagogy to conceive of a genuinely "black education" that does not articulate specific, carefully detailed syllabi, classroom exercises, filmographies, behavioral objectives, parent-teacher organizing strategies, and ideological mappings of school-board/black-student-body relationships. Only such specificity will result, I think, in a critical black pedagogy geared to a specific, local urban context of black struggle. (p. 127)

We offer no prescription because there is no prescription. To suggest otherwise would undermine our own understanding of the complex nature of African-American learning experiences in mathematics. We do, however, point to the work of African-American scholars whose work serves as exemplars of African-centered and critical race approaches that begin to chip away at the oppression of African-American children in school contexts (e.g., Hale, 2001; Ladson-Billings, 1994; Leonard, 2008; Lynn, 1999, 2004; Madhubuti & Madhubuti, 1994; Murrell, 2002; Potts, 2003; Shujaa, 1994; Tate, 1997; Watts et al., 2003). According to Shujaa (1994), African-centered analyses:

> Put the interests of African people first. [These analyses] are concerned with the extent to which the education afforded Africans (or what has passed for education) has benefited others more than we. Consequently, [these analyses are] not constrained by attempts to define what is best for African people in ways that are linked to the best interest of European-centered hegemonic nation states. There are no "trickle-down" approaches taken here. (p. 9)

Lee (1994) stated that an African-centered pedagogy is needed to "support a line of resistance to the imposition of Eurocentric bias" and highlighted the following characteristics of an African-centered pedagogy:

- Legitimizes African stores of knowledge
- Positively exploits and scaffolds productive community and cultural practices
- Reinforces community ties and idealizes service to one's family, community, nation, race, and world
- Imparts a world view that idealizes a positive, self-sufficient future for one's people without denying the self-worth and right to self-determination of others
- Supports cultural continuity while promoting critical consciousness (p. 297)

Arguing that African-centered analyses also have an emancipatory component, Potts (2003) characterized this kind of education as follows:

> ...one that (1) explicitly addresses social oppression, situating community problems (and targets of primary prevention) within historical context, (2) acknowledges students as agents for social change, and (3) affirms African cultural resources for healing and social transformation. Emancipatory education seeks to invoke the liberatory potential of education for children and society. African-centered emancipatory education affirms identity and agency, helps restore a sense of history, and provides opportunities for social action. (p. 175)

We believe that by drawing on African-centered and critical race pedagogies, mathematics education researchers, policy makers, and practitioners can begin to fashion a liberatory and emancipatory role for mathematics education and mathematics literacy in the lives of African-American learners. Within these approaches, for example, the concept of pedagogy is differentiated from mere teaching and instruction in the following way:

> A pedagogy is more than just a set of strategies and approaches—it entails a philosophy of education. A pedagogy engenders answers to the implicit question: What should be the function and purpose of public education in this contemporary society? A pedagogy works well when it addresses

> this question appropriately for the children, family, and communities being served. (Murrell, 2002, p. 55)

Murrell (2002), in his theoretical framework for African-centered pedagogy, offered seven premises that can serve as a guide for mathematics teachers who work with African-American children. These premises stress the complexities of learning and development in African-American contexts, insuring that the abilities and competencies of African-American children are not simply framed in terms of how they differ from White children. The premises in Murrell's (2002) African-centered framework include:

> Premise one: human cognition and intellectual development are socially and culturally situated in human activity.
> Premise two: the core of learning is meaningful and purposeful activity, which is embodied in practices and represented by a system of signs to communicate understanding and create a common system of meaning making.
> Premise three: meaning making is the principal motive for learning, and not merely reinforcement for the acquisition of information or new knowledge.
> Premise four: the most important form of learning is the appropriation of signs and practices of worthwhile adult activity.
> Premise five: community and symbolic culture are significant to the learning of individuals—children grow into the cognitive life of those around them.
> Premise six: the development of children's capacity to think, reason, communicate, and perform academically is a matter of practice—a matter of knowledge-in-use that is enacted in socially situated and culturally contextualized settings.
> Premise seven: black achievement is linked to conditions of schooling that reduce racial vulnerability. (p. 46)

Just as some African-American scholars have argued that African-American children experience "too much schooling and too little education" (e.g., Shujaa, 1994), we argue for mathematics education and mathematical experiences that are deeper in their philosophy and purpose than workforce needs and increasing African-American presence and participation in selected mathematics courses like algebra. We reject the mere commodification of African-American students and we point out that once courses like algebra are removed as gatekeepers, it is likely that other kinds of gatekeepers will be enacted (e.g., high school exit exams).

In the remainder of this chapter, we structure our discussion around four themes. First, we seek to link historical and contemporary social realities of African Americans in order to demonstrate that discussions of the structure, ideology, and content of mathematics education for African Americans cannot ignore these realities. Second, we applaud the necessary conversation but offer some pushback on the emerging perspective of *culturally responsive mathematics education*. We raise questions about how such a perspective deals with the issues of race and racism, particularly as they relate to students' mathematical experiences and mathematical identities. With the realities of racism and racialized experience acknowledged, we then raise the following question with respect to culturally responsive mathematics education: *to what end*? What is being argued for in this perspective and what are the goals for African-American learners? Third, we argue for a *moral* and *ethical* framing of mathematics education and mathematics literacy for African Americans (e.g., D'Ambrosio, 2007); one that appeals to the humane existence referenced by Qualls (2001) at the beginning of this paper.

In prioritizing racism, struggle, oppression, and empowerment in our discussion of the structure, ideology, and content of mathematics for African Americans, we realize that this strategy has the potential to stifle conversations or create unease among those who prefer a color-blind or content-focused approach to mathematics learning and participation or those who subscribe to meritocratic ideals and rhetoric. Yet, our direct experiences with African-American learners, coupled with our critical analysis of extant research and policy, demands that we raise these issues.

Positionality and Power With Respect to African-American Children

In formulating our perspectives in this chapter, we juxtapose our scholarly backgrounds and our experiences as African-American teachers of mathematics. Although it is common among many scholars and policy makers who attempt to discuss what is best for African-American learners, we do not ignore or fail to discuss our own positionality and subjectivity. Both of us self-identify as African American and, although we define and give meaning to this identity in different ways, between us we share many similarities and shared experiences as we do with the African Americans we research and teach. Although we derive a certain amount of privilege from our roles as professor and instructor, we are not disconnected from the struggles that encompass large parts of African-American experience. We are staunch advocates for African-American children—the second author is the mother of an African-American child—and we believe that our shared cultural frame of reference allows us to generate relevant and useful knowledge about these children.

In terms of our own trajectories into mathematics, we both have academic backgrounds and high-level training in mathematics and engineering. We share a combined, 25-year program of teaching and research involving African-American adults and adolescents in various contexts. The focus of this work has been on understanding the salience of race and identity in African Americans' struggle for mathematics literacy and in their self-constructions as doers of mathematics in school and nonschool contexts. For example, in a series of papers (Martin, 2000, 2003, 2006a, 2006b, in press), the first author has attempted to characterize mathematics learning and participation among African Americans as experiences that draw on sociohistorical and community knowledge not only about mathematics but also about issues of race, African-American identity, and struggle. Studies conducted by both authors have documented how this knowledge construction process involves ongoing negotiations of: (1) what it means to be African American, and (2) what it means to be literate in mathematics. For the participants in our research, mathematics literacy is linked not only to its classical uses in school and the larger opportunity structure but, given the history of African Americans in the United States, it is linked to a philosophy of education that has been passed down in the African-American narrative tradition: *literacy for freedom and freedom for literacy* (Perry, 2003).

Mathematics Education and Mathematics Literacy in Global Perspective

We are very cognizant of the fact that African-American experiences are broad and diverse and that the same is true for African-American contexts. We cannot possibly capture their full complexity in a single chapter. Furthermore, we acknowledge that meaningful mathematics education for African-American children should not only help them function in their local contexts in U.S. society but should also help them to function as citizens of the globe, to function across boundaries of difference, and to recognize similarities in human conditions among people who wage the struggle against oppression. We also believe that African Americans, as members of an African Diaspora, should develop knowledge and mathematics literacies that reveal to them the condition of other Blacks on the planet (e.g., *Negritos* in the Philippines, *Aboriginals* in Australia, *Sidis* in India, Blacks in South Africa) and how mathematics education and mathematics literacies are implicated in their liberation as well (e.g., Julie, 2006).

Math Literacy and Liberation to Combat White Privilege: Linking Historical and Contemporary Social Realities

Our conception of mathematics literacy is rooted in perspectives that highlight empowerment and robust mathematics identities (e.g., Ernest, 2002; Gutstein, 2005; Julie, 2006; Skovsmose, 1994) and uses of mathematics that extend beyond those that are merely functional. Although we stress empowerment for, and through, the narrow lens of mathematics education, we raise questions about the opportunities associated with the acquisition of math literacy by African Americans, where it is often assumed that math literacy translates easily into expanded opportunity in society. In a highly racialized society, we are mindful of the fact that opportunities and privileges are not always conferred on the basis of skills and documented literacy levels.

We also draw from the perspectives of Gutstein (2003, 2005) and Frankenstein (1990) who stress the need for learners to develop both classical (functional) mathematical literacy and *critical* mathematical literacy, the former emphasizing the use of school-based math skills to carry out school-related and basic life tasks, the latter emphasizing the use of mathematics to critically analyze, and subsequently change, the social conditions impinging upon one's life.

Given this critical orientation, we recognize that addressing the question, *Why should African children learn mathematics*? requires great care so as not to take a paternalistic stance toward these children. As scholars, we can only provide partial answers to this question, especially if we take seriously issues of individual and collective agency and self-efficacy. Very rarely can we unilaterally decide what is best for our fellow human beings. However, our direct experiences with those whom we wish to support in making appropriate and meaningful decisions for their lives can often shape, or reshape, our own perspectives in important ways.

For example, several years ago, the first author began a program of research and teaching that has focused on mathematics education among African-American adults, adolescents, and their teachers. In one research study involving mathematics success and failure among African-American middle school students (Martin, 2000), he observed students in classroom and extracurricular activities and subsequently interviewed them regarding their beliefs about mathematics and their motivations to develop mathematics knowledge. In comparing and contrasting the mathematics identities of "successful" and "less successful" students, he found that many of the students in the latter group responded that they believed it was important to learn mathematics to "be able to count my money and not be cheated" (Martin, 2000). The early conclusion was that this reasoning was somehow less sophisticated than the responses of students who had been identified as successful—responses that included references to college admissions, careers, and sheer enjoyment of mathematics. In the years following that early study, and based on findings in additional studies (Martin, 1998, 2002), the first author gained a greater appreciation for the seemingly simply response of "not being cheated."

In contextualizing mathematics education for African Americans, we argue that the idea of developing mathematics literacy for the purpose of not being cheated is grounded in the history and reality of African-American experience. In other words, contemporary conceptualizations of, and dispositions toward, mathematics literacy among African Americans have a historical basis. For example, scholars have noted that newly freed people sought to develop reading and numeracy skills so as not to be cheated in contracts and transactions with former slave owners and other Whites (Anderson, 1988; Cornelius, 1991; Williams, 2005). Educational historian James Anderson (1988) highlighted this point:

> Many postslavery developments provided ex-slaves with compelling reasons to become literate. The uses and abuses of written labor contracts made it worthwhile to be able to read, write, and cipher. Frequently, planters designed labor contracts in ways that would confuse and entrap ex-slaves. As the Freedman's Bureau superintendent observed, "I saw one

> [labor contract] in which it was stipulated that one-third of seven-twelfths of all corn, potatoes, fodder, etc., shall go to the laborers." Hence when a middle-aged black woman was asked why she was so determined to learn to read and write, she replied, "so the Rebs can't cheat me."...More fundamentally, the ex-slaves' struggle for education was an expression of freedom. (p. 18)

Similarly, Qualls (2001) pointed out that "Early Blacks attempting to vote were required to pass illegal and grossly unfair literacy tests while local registrars, who themselves had questionable literacy in many cases, waived the literacy requirements for Whites" (p. 18). Modern-day literacy challenges continue to exist for African Americans. Recent research (Fellowes, 2006) has provided evidence that residents in poor African-American communities are often forced to pay a "ghetto tax" marked by increased prices for basic goods and services. For example, predatory lending institutions that utilize usurious financing schemes and practices—issuing payday loans and car title loans at exorbitant interest rates; offering rent-to-own merchandise with prolonged payment plans and confusing contractual language—often set up shop in these communities. These financing plans and contracts often bear a strong family resemblance to the contracts used by former slave owners. We would also argue that university admissions procedures that rely heavily on ACT or SAT scores and advanced placement (AP) courses also represent a challenge to African-American literacy. Given that many African-American students attend schools where there is limited access to high-quality advanced coursework (Oakes, 1985, 1990; Oakes, Joseph, & Muir, 2004), admissions decisions based on these criteria amount to a modern-day literacy test much in the same way these tests were used to prevent African Americans from exercising their right to vote.

Although the middle school students whose concerns about being cheated were probably unaware of the larger history of African-American literacy struggles, we believe it is no accident that so many of them shared this particular conceptualization of why mathematics literacy is important. As African Americans develop their motivations and identities relative to mathematics literacy, these identities and motivations take into account not just the importance of mathematics in school settings but also are developed in the context of beliefs and experiences reflecting what it means to be African American in U.S. society (Martin, 2000, 2006a, 2006b; McGee, in press). In this way, the contemporary efforts by African Americans to develop and utilize mathematics literacy are linked to their historical struggles. Research, policy, practice, and reform in mathematics education must take this into account. In fact, we argue that the *ahistorical* nature of recent math education reforms, and the concomitant framings of the purposes and aims of mathematics education for African-American students, help explain the limited success of research, reform, and policy efforts designed to raise achievement and persistence levels among African-American learners. Particularly problematic has been the inability of mainstream math education research and policy efforts to conceptualize so-called "achievement gaps" and their supposed causes in historical context.

Qualls (2001) notes: "When considering the current state of literacy in African Americans, one must acknowledge the impact of historical and social events that uniquely shape the literacy profile of this population" (p. 17). Anderson (2004), writing about the historical development of African-American education and literacy also noted:

> It is due to the closing of the other achievement gaps [literacy, school attendance, school completion] that we can now focus so exclusively on the test score gap. It made no sense, for example, to focus on the test score gaps during the periods when African American students were denied basic access to elementary and secondary schools. Now that African Americans, through centuries of struggle for full equality, have finally gained more educational opportunities than before, a host of scholars and pundits seem puzzled and dismayed that Black students did not eliminate the test score gap.... The history of past victories over the other critical achievement gaps provides the only record of the strengths and possibilities for engaging what may be the last frontier in a series of achievement gaps. (p. 14)

Moreover, the tendency to rely on Black–White comparisons has the potential to generate suggestions for what is best for African-American children based on perceptions of what is best, or better, for White children. As pointed out by McLoyd (1991), such analyses tend to:

> ... study African Americans in terms of how they differ from European Americans.... (a) point to the ways in which African American children do not behave rather than how they do behave, yielding data that are limited in their informative value, virtually useless in generating theory and ultimately, capable of supporting only superficial analyses of individual differences and their determinants among African Americans...and (b) foster indirectly the views that African American children are abnormal, incompetent, and changeworthy since differences between African Americans and European American children are typically interpreted, if not by the author, by a significant portion of the readers, as deficiencies or pathologies in the former rather than in cultural relativistic or systemic terms. (pp. 422–424)

Building on this point, we argue that so-called achievement gaps—much like the concept of race—are socially constructed phenomena (Martin, in press).[1] Rather than gaps, discriminatory forces and inequitable access to resources have produced *lags* in achievement. As African-American students continue to gain access to needed resources and reach levels of achievement that were once deemed acceptable for White children—many of whom go on to enjoy additional educational and economic opportunities—history shows that these same standards are often deemed unacceptable when attained by African Americans. In this sense, low achievement among African Americans is historically contingent and politically expedient.

Culturally Responsive Mathematics Education? To What End?

Our continued rethinking of the ways that mathematics education and literacy has been framed for African Americans has caused us to pay close attention to reform-oriented approaches that claim to have the interests of African-American learners in mind. The theme of this book—part of a growing movement in mathematics education—is *culturally responsive mathematics education*. The editors have chosen this theme against the backdrop of "a growing awareness of the historical, cultural, social, and political contexts of mathematics and mathematics education." They also state that, because of its orientation, this book helps to develop a debate "about how the teaching of mathematics should acknowledge and valorize cultural diversity."

As scholars committed to meaningful mathematics education for African Americans, we raise a number of issues and questions about *culturally responsive mathematics education* as we work toward our particular charge in this chapter—to situate mathematics literacy among African Americans within the context of their ongoing, collective struggle against oppression and social devaluation in U.S. society. The issues and questions that we raise are intended to push not just the larger conversations in this book, but also the conversations in the field of mathematics education more broadly, particularly as they concern African-American children.

In raising questions about movements in the field toward culturally relevant approaches to teaching and learning, we ask critical questions not just about the end goals but also about the assumptions and theoretical underpinnings of these shifts. For example: to what extent does a *cultural* framing of mathematics education (for African-American children) obscure the way that race (racialization) operates in the mathematical experiences of learners and the ways that those experiences are conceptualized and orchestrated? Moreover, is culture conceived of in such a way that it applies only to "students of color," allowing our discussions to circumvent students who are socially constructed as White and the privilege that often accompanies their social realities and mathematical experiences? Does the inadequate theorizing of race in mainstream mathematics education research (Martin, in press) contribute to the normalization of Whiteness in discussions of mathematics learning and participation?

Closer scrutiny shows that studies of mathematics learning among White students, when they are identified as such, rarely, if ever, introduce the concepts of race or culture into the analyses, perhaps highlighting the belief that race does not apply to these students and that the cultural backgrounds of White students have no bearing on their mathematical development. On the other hand, in comparative studies of mathematics achievement (e.g., Lubienski, 2002; Secada, 1992; Strutchens & Silver, 2000; Tate, 1997), *race* is commonly introduced as a way to disaggregate data and as a variable to explain *low* achievement among African-American, Latino/a, and Native American students, a strategy that is flawed both theoretically and methodologically (Helms, Jernigan, & Mascher, 2005; Martin, in press; O'Connor, Lewis, & Mueller, 2007; Zuberi, 2001). The underlying logic of these race-comparative studies also fosters the belief, and supporting intellectual framework, that African-American students must become race*less*—that is, more like White students—in order to achieve at higher levels (Fordham & Ogbu, 1986).

Also implicit in studies employing Black–White comparisons are negative conceptualizations of *Blackness*[2] while *Whiteness* is typically left unexamined and allowed to function in its privileging role. As a result, the framing of goals and outcomes of mathematics education and mathematics literacy for African-American children often proceeds based on deficit perspectives of African-American children and normalized views of White children (e.g., Clements & Sarama, 2007).

Our strategy for understanding how *Blackness* has been used to inform conceptualizations of mathematics education and mathematics literacy for African-American children has been to draw from rich sociological and critical race literatures as well as from African Americans themselves (e.g., Bell, 1992; Bonilla-Silva, 1997, 2001, 2002, 2003; Delgado & Stefancic, 2001; Forman, 2004; Gunaratnam, 2003; Lewis, 2003a,b, 2004; Marable, 1983; Parker & Lynn, 2002; Royster, 2003). These literatures have been underutilized by mathematics educators. Sociologists have noted that Blackness has, in many contexts, come to serve as a metaphorical and symbolic marker that is used to distinguish those whose behaviors are deficient in relation to those who are considered normal, those who are deserving from those who are not, and those who are considered intelligent from those who are not. It is these uses of Blackness that we believe are highly relevant to the present discussion and that must be countered in reframing mathematics education for African-American children. We are argue that negative social constructions and representations of African-American children are likely to engender problematic framings for mathematics education in their lives (Martin, 2007).

Empirically, Martin (2007, in press) collected and analyzed examples from mathematics education policy documents to explore social constructions of African-American children within mathematics education research and policy documents. He provided several examples to show how *being* African American is often framed in discussions of mathematics literacy and points out how these characterizations contribute to the construction of a racial hierarchy of mathematical ability—one that locates, in a way that is represented as natural, African-American children at the bottom of this hierarchy. One of the examples he cited was the following, taken from *Everybody Counts* (National Research Council, 1989):

> Apart from economics, the social and political consequences of *mathematical illiteracy* provide alarming signals for the survival of democracy in America. Because mathematics holds the key to leadership in our information-based society, the widening gap between *those who are mathematically literate* and *those who are not* coincides, to a frightening degree, with *racial* and economic categories. We are at-risk of becoming a divided nation in which knowledge of mathematics supports a *productive, technological powerful elite* while a *dependent, semiliterate majority, disproportionately Hispanic and Black*, find economic and political power beyond reach. Unless corrected, *innumeracy* and *illiteracy* will drive America apart. (p. 14, emphasis added)

This example and others—through their simultaneous portrayal of African Americans as mathematically illiterate and unnamed White students as mathematically powerful—helps demonstrate how mathematics learning and participation and the development of mathematics literacy are rendered as *racialized forms of experience* (Martin, 2006a, 2006b, in press). It is these kinds of constructions against which African-American learners must often contend. It is also clear that part of the motivation for math reform, as called for in this document, is to preserve the status of Whites, whose abilities to thrive are threatened by the mathematical illiteracy of African-American, Latino/a, and Native-American learners.

Despite these attempts to maintain a racial hierarchy of mathematical ability, we have found that as African Americans assert their *own* meanings for *Blackness*, particularly in relation to mathematics literacy, some resist the kind of social devaluing that is present in statements like the one presented above and that they exercise agency to assert their individual and collective identities as doers of mathematics (Martin, 2000, 2006a, 2006b, in press). In fact, we profess to knowing few African Americans who identify themselves as "mathematically illiterate" or as threats to the "survival of democracy in America." Participants in our research and teaching also argue for *meaningful* participation in mathematical practices in recognition of the fact that the development of mathematics literacy, absent of the opportunity to utilize it in contexts free of oppression, calls for continued struggle. The following quote, taken from an interview with a 37-year-old African-American male (Martin, 2006a) brings together many of the issues that we raise in this regard:

> If African Americans got together down in Silicon Valley, an African-American group of engineers got together, and [said] "We're not going to stand for this anymore. We want you to now start interviewing African American supervisors that can work in [an] engineering capacity for this firm. We know that they're out there. But unless you do this, we're not coming to work."… It would change things…. [In the past,] you had Afri-

> can Americans get together, fought, struggled for voting rights. You had African Americans sit down in the restaurant and say, "We're not going to the back anymore." When there's a struggle that we're all knowing about, that we can associate with, we get together as a group and say "We're not going to stand for it anymore." (p. 217)

What is particularly interesting about this statement is that it frames mathematics literacy in the larger context of African-American struggle and links to a history of resisting oppression. This kind of knowledge construction process among African Americans often challenges shortsighted thinking among scholars who argue for greater participation and persistence in math and science coursework but who fail to acknowledge the barriers—like social networks that exclude potential African-American employees (Royster, 2003) or state policies that redirect university-eligible high school graduates to community colleges (Martin, 2003)—which mitigate African-American gains in mathematics learning and participation. It has also been well-documented that schools all across America, both deliberately and inadvertently, utilize mechanisms like academic tracking as a means of shutting out many African-American students from college preparatory mathematics classes at the critical transition between middle and high school (e.g., Oakes, 1985, 1990; Oakes, Joseph, & Muir, 2004; Solórzano & Ornelas, 2002, 2004). The lack of opportunity for African Americans to develop mathematics literacy via participation in meaningful practices impacts their ability to experience equity in various sectors of life. Against the backdrop of such realities, increased test scores and the closing of so-called achievement gaps, though highly desirable, will not reduce or alleviate deeply held, pathological perceptions of African-American children.

While research and policy discussions of African Americans and mathematics often contribute to the negative socially constructed meanings for *Blackness*—as inferior, lacking in intelligence, and pathological—we believe it is important to bring to light the socially constructed meanings, power, and privilege that accompany *Whiteness*. As pointed out by Frankenberg (1993):

> Naming "whiteness" displaces it from the unmarked, unnamed status that is itself an effect of dominance. Among the effects on white people both of race privilege and of the dominance of whiteness are their seeming normativity, their structured invisibility.... To look at the social construction of whiteness, then, is to look head-on at a site of dominance. (And it may be more difficult for white people to say "whiteness has nothing to do with me—I'm not white" than to say "Race has nothing to do with me—I'm not racist."). To speak of whiteness is, I think, to assign *everyone* a place in the relations of racism. It is to emphasize that dealing with racism is not merely an option for white people—that is, rather, racism shapes white people's lives and identities in a way that is inseparable from other facets of daily life. (p. 6)

The movement toward more inclusive mathematics education would seem to require a specification not only of those who should be included for high quality mathematical experiences but also of those who currently enjoy these benefits. So, while poor, limited English proficient and minority students are explicitly mentioned, we typically hear little about White middle-class and upper-class students as beneficiaries of not only prior advantages but also of those created under the umbrella of reform.

We believe that many of the mathematics education goals for African Americans that are espoused in progressive rhetoric and reforms are conceived of in such as way that they must also serve the interests of White students, representing what some critical race scholars have called *interest convergence* (Delgado & Stefancic, 2001). There have yet to be mainstream reform or policy efforts in mathematics education that privilege the needs of African-American students—or other students of color—without also according benefits to White students. As indicated by Ratteray (1994):

> The education of African-Americans has been profoundly shaped throughout history by two major problems. One is access to educational opportunities and the other is the quality of accessible schooling. Unfortunately, the struggle for access diverted the energies of African-Americans from the task of designing and providing quality schooling. In addition, the content of the schooling that African-Americans did receive was designed to meet the needs of politically empowered European-Americans and not the particular needs of African-Americans. (p. 123)

One clear example of how White privilege emerges in the school context is teacher demographics. Nearly 90% of teachers are White (National Center for Education Information, 2005) while African Americans continue to face a number of barriers to entering the teaching profession (King, 1993a, 1993b). Despite a growing literature on mathematics teacher knowledge, much of this research focuses on teachers' *content knowledge* and *pedagogical content knowledge* (Hill & Ball, 2004; Hill, Rowan, & Ball, 2005). Typically absent are discussions of the personal qualities and cultural knowledge needed be effective teachers of African-American children. Instead, a color-blind approach to mathematics teacher development prevails; one in which it is thought by many that good teaching is simply good teaching (Martin, 2007). There also appears to be an assumption in much of this research that White teachers' content knowledge and pedagogical content knowledge will trump any negative beliefs and dispositions that teachers have developed—due, in many cases, to a lack of exposure—about African-American students (Martin, 2007).

A second example of how White privilege structures the mathematical experiences of African-American students is found in the push for all students to enroll in algebra in 8th or 9th grade, part of the *Mathematics for All* and *Algebra for All* movements that have proliferated in the last 15 years or so (Martin, 2003). While touted as a way to insure that more students of color enroll in this gatekeeper course, many schools have resorted to watered-down versions that continue to maintain separate tracks for students—White and Asian students dominating the normal algebra courses and African-American and Latino/a students populating the lower-quality courses (Oakes et al., 2004). In some instances, these include two-year algebra courses that split the traditional course material over two years. In other instances, low-quality courses are simply renamed. In both scenarios, students of color find themselves disproportionately enrolled in these courses and those who maintained their advantage continue to do so. Therefore, we argue that framing mathematics for education for African-American children simply in terms of access is shortsighted if these framings do not consider the roles of bias and White privilege in mitigating access.

So, beyond "valorizing cultural diversity," how might mathematics educators and policy-makers frame goals for mathematics education with respect to social realities that are marked by struggles against oppression, historically and in contemporary times? We offer some pushback on the call for culturally responsive mathematics education by asking: culturally responsive mathematics education *to what end*? Given the social realities of students, why do we want them to learn mathematics? Just as important, given their own framings of their social realities, how do learners situate mathematics literacy within their lives? We argue for attention to the dissonance between "emic" (insider) conceptualizations among African Americans and the "etic" (outsider) conceptualizations that are typically found in mainstream mathematics education research and policy contexts.

We believe that the answers scholars and policy makers formulate to the "to what end?" question should not only reflect their views and goals but should align with the realities that characterize, and sometimes constrict, the opportunities of students from marginalized and socially devalued communities. Appeals to increased workforce participation are necessary but not sufficient against the backdrop of workplace discrimination that limits entry and mobility of African Americans. Arguing for increased minority participation in mathematics to justify workforce needs is an example of what has been called "socially enlightened self-interest" (Secada, 1989). While the rhetoric of increased workforce participation appears to benefit African Americans, increased participation often comes on the condition that benefits also extend to others—international competitiveness for the *country*, for example. As pointed out by Arthur Powell:

> The argument for increased participation of African Americans in technological areas of the workforce assumes that the structure of the US economy and the priorities of capital align with the needs and interests of African Americans. It assumes that African Americans should and want to participate in the politics and policies of U.S. capitalism and globalization. (personal communication, August 12, 2005)

Martin (2003) has used the term *opportunity mathematics* to describe the kind of mathematics that will help African-American students improve their conditions in life and overcome the barriers that they will likely encounter as a result of their minority status. In our view, not all mathematics meets this criterion and the kind of mathematics that does meet this criterion is seldom the kind to which African Americans have access. For example, while algebra has been identified as a gatekeeper to higher-level math courses, many states require only one or two additional courses beyond algebra for high school graduation. Given that entrance requirements for many universities exceed these additional courses, the two or three courses taken by many students are rendered useless for university admissions, particularly at selective and elite schools.

In the state of California, for example, students who have not completed high school calculus stand very little chance for admission to the University of California system. Moreover, math remediation rates as high as 50% among freshman at many universities speak to the quality of the high school math coursework completed by these students. For example, Fall 2005 system-wide data from the 23-school California State University (CSU) system showed that 37.3% of regularly admitted first-time African Americans were judged to be proficient in mathematics as measured by the Entry Level Math (ELM) assessment. These students are further limited in their choice of major and they often experience delayed progress in their studies. We are not claiming that math assessments like the ELM accurately depict the mathematical knowledge of African-American students. However, given that these exams are used to determine access to universities, it is important to know how African Americans fare and whether the quality of the courses they are given access to will help them accomplish their goals. Moreover, we see these assessments as revealing more about the racialized conditions in which students are often forced to learn rather than as reflecting student deficiencies.

Despite our critical questions, we do believe that the notion of *culturally responsive mathematics education* can be mined to address many of the issues we raise in this chapter. We note that in her conceptualization of *culturally responsive teaching*, Gay (2000) also emphasizes its empowering and emancipatory nature. As mathematics educators continue to appropriate research on culturally responsive teaching and work towards clarity on what this means in the context of mathematics education, this focus on empowerment and emancipation should be kept in mind, particularly in response to the "to what end?" question.

African-American Cultural Knowledge and Pedagogies of Liberation

Because we are keenly aware of the negative ways that African Americans have been socially constructed in research and policy contexts, we have taken great strides to resist these constructions not only by articulating alternative scholarly views of African-American learners but also engaging in liberatory acts of teaching and research that address the social realities of our African-American students and that help them to utilize mathematics in ways to transform their lives. For example, the first author was able to build on his in-school teaching efforts with African-American parents in the community college context to develop math programs for African-American (and Latina) mothers in community contexts. The first author was also able to help contribute to an institutional response to African American underrepresentation in mathematics and science by helping to secure scholarship funding and mentoring support for students as components of an alternative socialization model that helped students transfer from the community college to four-year institutions. Within this alternative socialization model, he was able to serve not only as instructor for African-American students but also as a mentor in relationships that continue to this day. These relationships often included explicit discussions of African American social realities and the relationships between mathematics literacy and these social realities.

In her mathematics content courses for prospective teachers—taught at a majority Black university in the city of Chicago—the second author has asked the students to rewrite curriculum to, in their view, better reflect the cultural assets of African-American and Latino/a populations—communities where many of these prospective teachers would decide to teach. In addition, assignments and discussions were designed to include group and classroom discussions of how stereotypes and societal influences factor into mathematical achievement. Following these discussions, students wrote essays on strategies that could be incorporated into teaching and learning processes that could resist impoverished perspectives of African-American and Latino/a students' mathematical abilities and that challenge the taken-for-granted assumptions about the abilities of White and Asian students.

The second author also designed a series of the mathematical activities and practices with the intent of increasing knowledge of African, Latino/a and African-American contributions to mathematics. These aspiring teachers were also encouraged to think of ways to make mathematics more relevant to the largely African-American student population that they would be eventually teaching. One assignment required that each student give a brief presentation on two historical or contemporary Black or Latino/a mathematicians who work in a career that they might encourage their students to pursue. Presentations included historical figures such as Imhotep and references to the Dogon people of Mali and to Latino/as and African Americans in fields such as urban planning, cryptography, and Java development. Reflecting on this assignment afterward, students expressed the view that the lack of exposure in their earlier years to the proud legacy of mathematics achievement for African Americans hindered their ability to relate to mathematics, and in many cases contributed to their disinterest or disdain for mathematics. These students also stated the belief that early exposure to African-American role models and mentors who are in mathematics-based fields can help to foster and sustain interest in mathematics careers for young students. There are clear implications for curriculum design and teacher selection and development. Participants in Martin's research (2006a) extended the implications to the role of African-American communities themselves:

> In the community where so many people just don't know, and don't understand the point of higher math or higher education, you're going to have to have places where people [who] look like those students come back to their community [and] teach these kids to be excited about math.—Larry, African-American father and community college student

> So when you don't have a lot role models, you figure you can get away with that. It's something you don't need. So maybe it's something in the back of their heads that's saying "Why is it so important? I've heard people say so [but] what's that got to do with me?" I think we're going to have to have more Black role models, more Black people like you to go into the communities and maybe go to different community centers and get together a math group. If you're having trouble with math, this group meets at this time. Parents would have to be involved. Taking them there so they could get these skills. And I think that would, like a snowball, you know, gradually build up over years where we would have a race of Black people that aren't scared of math.—Chantal, African-American mother and community college student

In addition to the activities mentioned above, students from one of the second author's classes spoke candidly about forces that they believed impeded their own progress in mathematics. These students identified stereotypes, racism, and other forms of discrimination through their essays and classroom discussions. Below are some excerpts of students who identified the social barriers that they believed limited their participation in mathematics:

> Stereotyping has greatly impacted the level of success that Blacks can attain in mathematics. If messages have been internalized that you just can't do mathematics and its okay because there's always basketball or manager at Wal-Mart or being a secretary, then you are more likely to accept that as truth.—Ella, a junior nursing student

> Stereotyping students—such as Black, Hispanics, and the socioeconomic disadvantaged—while teaching can lead to unsuccessful results. If the teacher is teaching based on stereotypical assumptions, the child could suffer.… Now children [are] failing because the teacher is failing the child as a result of discrediting the child's own natural abilities.—*Dance, a* senior elementary education student

> I don't buy into the myth that being good in math means acting White. My grandma told us of stories where our ancestors had their fingers cut off for reading. What they endured to learn and to be educated is part of the Black experience of being in America. Instead of acting White I would suggest it be called "fighting for academic success while Black."—Tim, a sophomore physical education student

Most students in the second author's classes realized that differences in mathematics underachievement are, in part, a reflection of the unequal resources and opportunities in schools and communities. These students articulated that mathematics classrooms are not immune to the stress, prejudices, inequalities, and inequities that exist in the larger society. Some students expressed the belief that schools and mathematics classrooms participate in maintaining and extending differential economic, political, and cultural power (Apple, 1992, 1995) through the differentiation of mathematics literacy based on beliefs about a racial hierarchy (Martin, in press). Quotes from students included the following:

> My struggle to learn mathematics is embedded in my struggle to survive as a Black man. Mathematics and Black men, as a combined school of thought, means flunking out. [This is] because success and Black males are polarized as opposites. Anything that breaks the mold is an anomaly. —Anthony, a junior economics student

> I am not better in mathematics because the educational system has failed Latino and Black people. They have failed to properly educate us and they don't understand or accept our culture. Try placing a 13-year-old White male, who grew up in the U.S.—the land of White opportunity—in [particular Latin country], where they don't even like White people, and just see if he achieves academically in that anti-White culture.—Charlie, a junior accounting student

The cultural knowledge—about African-American struggle, racism, and liberation—that we often share and coconstruct with our students can be used in service to their own efforts to utilize mathematics literacy for liberatory purposes. Our efforts to do so build on a documented legacy within African-American scholarship and community agency. For example, Gordon (1993), writing about liberatory education for African Americans, stated:

> African-American cultural knowledge—as expressed through the beliefs, values, perspectives, and worldview—can be found in the autochthonous cultural artifacts generated within the African-American cultural, social, economic, historical, and political experience.... Becoming knowledgeable about one's culture is part of the manner in which cultures perpetuate themselves—knowledge about culture and history is passed on to the next generation.... Such knowledge can assist African Americans to place themselves and their history in the global history of humankind. Moreover, this knowledge demonstrates definitively that people can engage in action to change societal structures in ways that result in the improvement of their lives. These, I believe, are at least some components of an education that is liberatory. Students do not learn to read and write; they read and write to learn. Liberatory education provides them with the heuristic tools and skills to critique ideas. (pp. 456–457)

bell hooks (1994), feminist and African-American scholar, refers to education as an act of liberation that frees teachers and learners from the powers of domination. Reflecting on hooks's thoughts, we ask: How can mathematics educators conceive of curriculum and classroom practices that can aid African-American students in transforming their lives? How do these same mathematics educators transform themselves in devoting themselves to the liberation of African-American students?

Toward Critical Mathematics Literacy in African-American Contexts

While linking literacy and liberation—educational, economic, and political—for African Americans is not a new idea and continues to receive attention among African-American education scholars (e.g., Anderson, 1988; Gadsden, 1993; Perry, 2003; Shujaa, 1994; Woodson, 1933/1990), extant research and policy in mainstream mathematics education has largely ignored this approach.

We argue that a critical and liberatory mathematics education is one tool that African Americans can use to understand and challenge the world around them. Mathematics education of this type must encourage critical thinking, social involvement, positive identity, and a sense of personal agency. Liberatory practices in mathematics literacy can inspire African-American children to know more about and appreciate their culture, to believe in themselves as learners, to become more efficacious, to believe they can and must make a difference in their community, country, and world. Liberatory mathematics education for African Americans also includes improvement of social conditions such as diminishing poverty and violence and increased health and education benefits. As researchers moved by the voices of African-American mathematics learners, we strive to conduct research grounded in social reality and liberatory change.

For example, the first author's multiyear studies revealed that some African-American parents embraced the development of mathematics literacy as a way to understand and fight against racism and, at the same time, worked to help their children engage in school mathematics (see Martin, 2000, 2006a, 2006b, in press).

Another notable example is the work taking place in the Algebra Project (e.g., Moses & Cobb, 2001; Moses, Kamii, Swap, & Howard, 1989). Founder Robert Moses, veteran civil rights activist and mathematics teacher, equates the struggle for mathematics literacy in contemporary times with the fight for citizenship during the 1960s. Moses and Cobb (2001) remind us, through historical reference to grass-roots civil rights struggle, how youth can be empowered to fight for their liberation on their own terms:

> It wasn't until those at the bottom made the demand that the system capitulated. You needed the force coming up from the bottom to get the people who control the levers of power to say we're going to overthrow

> those who stand in opposition to this happening. The same issue confronts us today. The young kids have got to make the demand first on themselves that, yes, this is our education and this is what we want, and then translate that demand into various institutions in the society. (p. 3)

Moses argues for mathematics literacy via curriculum organized around, and anchored in, familiar, culturally relevant experiences. He notes that African-American children are drawn into learning mathematics when they can find an image of their own future in the visibly present. He argues that this more culturally affirming orientation toward mathematics literacy can aid in learning.

One of Moses's core arguments is that students must master algebra—a gatekeeper to advanced mathematics—to succeed in the workplace of the future. Therefore, a major goal of his work is to address the lack of economic access plaguing many African-American communities through the development of mathematics literacy. A criticism of Moses's rationale is that gaining mathematical competency in order to develop the technology literacy required for today's job market does not promote the kind of critical consciousness needed for individual and community awareness of social, political, and economic struggle. The workforce which Moses targets for greater participation by African Americans is also a place where African-American status is often devalued and where inequities in society are reproduced. Moreover, the rise of service-sector jobs, the computerization of many others, and the outsourcing of others often requires learning some very basic procedures but not mastering substantially more demanding skills which require high-order mathematics abilities. We question the idea of advocating for African Americans to simply fit into these oppressive structures rather than transforming them.

A Moral Imperative

As we continue to reflect on the question: Why should African-American children learn mathematics? And offer yet another answer to the subquestion: Why should *African-American* children learn mathematics? We argue for a moral imperative that answers this question as follows: *If not African-American children, then who*? This response reflects our belief in mathematics education for African-American children that resonates with their cultural and racial identities and that is not based on what is best for other children with the hope that African-American children *may* benefit as a trickle down effect. Although there is diversity in African-American experience, many African Americans face common sets of experiences related to society's tendency to devalue African-American status. A mathematics education that implicates mathematics literacy in African-Americans' ability to challenge this social devaluation and not simply strive to participate in structures of domination is what we would argue for and support.

Moving Forward

In looking to mainstream research and policy arenas for answers to the question, Why should African Americans learn mathematics? we have argued that the vast majority of responses are limited in scope and fail to contextualize mathematics learning and participation among African Americans in their historical context and in the context of contemporary social realities. These limiting views ignore, for example, the reality of how racism and racialization processes often play themselves out in the very contexts for which African Americans are expected to utilize mathematics literacy. Moreover, in conceptualizing an agenda for mathematics education that addresses these social realities, many prominent research and policy documents fall short. For example, in *Mathematical Proficiency for All Students: Toward a Strategic Research and Development Program in Mathematics Education* (RAND, 2003), the authors claim:

> This report proposes a long-term, strategic program of research and development in mathematics education. The program would develop knowledge, materials, and programs to help educators achieve two goals: to raise the level of mathematical proficiency and to eliminate differences in levels of mathematical proficiency among students in different social, cultural, and ethnic groups. In the short term, the program is designed to produce knowledge that would support efforts to improve the quality of mathematics teaching and learning with the teachers and materials that are now in place or that will become available over the next several years. More important, over 10 to 15 years, the program would build a solid base of knowledge for the design and development of effective instructional practice. That instructional practice, in turn, would enable the dual goals of increased levels of proficiency and equity in attaining proficiency to be achieved. (pp. xi-xii)

Although laudable in many respects, this "long-term, strategic program of research and development" is somewhat problematic and limited in its vision because it continues to echo a belief that equity in mathematics education is a natural and residual product of good teaching and good curriculum. Moreover, it frames equity efforts in mathematics education outside of the larger social realities that often mitigate these efforts. Equally problematic is a lack of urgency for such research and development efforts. We are reminded of the all-deliberate-speed conditions of larger societal reforms. In response, we call for a culturally responsive mathematics education research and policy agenda in which African Americans are no longer cheated. We offer the following as necessary steps in these directions:

- Reframe the purposes of mathematics education for African-American children beyond course completion and workforce participation. Orient mathematics education to helping African-American children develop critical,

not just classical, mathematical knowledge. Focus on mathematical, social, and epistemological empowerment for African-American children.
- Learn from proven pedagogical models that benefit African-American children: African-centered pedagogy as one example.
- Do not construct mathematics education for African-American children based on simple framings and conceptions of how they differ from White children.
- Realize the fallacy of constructing differential schooling experiences and outcomes as a *racial* achievement gap.
- Develop adequate theories of racism, and interventions, in relationship to students' mathematical experiences in school and nonschool contexts.

Synthesizing the needs and realities of African-American children and mathematics literacy is a monumental but necessary task to ensure full citizenship. The issues in the bulleted list above are just a beginning. We challenge mathematics reform efforts of all shapes and sizes to understand, appreciate, and include the racialized experiences of all students, inside and outside the mathematics classroom, in ways that break away from the White middle-class culture as the mold. We argue that framings of mathematics education for African-American children that take the above considerations into account will help disrupt the standards that serve to judge and convict African-American children in mathematics. Our claims are supported by emergent research in mathematics education that links mathematics learning and participation among African-American children to their historical and contemporary oppression.

We also believe that the development of robust mathematics identities can enhance the agency of African-American children and empower them to stand in resistance against the socially constructed racial hierarchy that encourages and reifies their underachievement. To gain mathematical knowledge free from school and societal subjugation is not a privilege but a right—a human right for all children and adults. A liberatory framing of mathematics education allows us to not only challenge the gross inequities that exist for African-American children but also encourages a fundamental change in how African-American children are treated. Practical approaches for incorporating a liberatory framework such as African-centered pedagogy serve as excellent starting points to empower African-American learners because such an approach values the complexities of learning in African-American contexts along with the affirmation of African culture and cultural resources.

As African-American children strive for full and meaningful participation, a liberatory mathematics education emphasizes equitable learning and participation experiences inside the classroom, which can lead help foster equity outside the classroom. Critically addressing the question, Why should African Americans learn mathematics? requires empowering African-American children to develop their mathematics literacy, not only to increase and expand educational opportunities, but to change the conditions of their lives, and impact the lives of others.

Acknowledgments

Portions of the research described here were funded by a Spencer Postdoctoral Fellowship awarded to Martin in 1998 and a National Science Foundation grant (ID: 0204138) awarded in 2002, both while the author was a faculty member in the Department of Mathematics at Contra Costa College. The views expressed here are those of the author and do not reflect those of the Spencer Foundation or the National Science Foundation.

Notes

1. Some critics have pointed out that the persistence of such gaps is also an artifact of the test construction process itself when one considers the inclusion and exclusion of test items based on Differential Item Functioning (DIF) and Item Response Theory (IRT).
2. Our choice to focus on *Blackness* is very deliberate. Other notions like "non-Whiteness" continue to privilege Whiteness and do not shift it from the center of the analysis. In addition, we acknowledge the very specific assaults on African-American identity and humanity that are linked to societal meanings for Blackness. It is African Americans who are used to create *Black* as the lowest level of the social hierarchy.

References

Anderson, J. D. (1988). *The education of Blacks in the South, 1860–1935*. Chapel Hill: University of North Carolina Press.

Anderson, J. D. (2004, Summer). The historical context for understanding the test score gap. *The National Journal of Urban Education & Practice, 1*(1), 1–21.

Apple, M. (1992). Do the standards go far enough? Power, policy, and practice in mathematics education. *Journal for Research in Mathematics Education, 23*(5), 412–431.

Apple, M. (1995). Taking power seriously: New directions in equity in mathematics education and beyond. In W. Secada, E. Fennema, & L. B, Adajian (Eds.), *New directions for equity in mathematics education* (pp. 329–348). Cambridge, UK: Cambridge University Press.

Baker, H. (1997). Review of the book *Race, culture, and the city: A pedagogy for black urban struggle. African-American Review, 31*(1), 125–128.

Banks, J. (1993). The canon debate, knowledge construction, and multicultural education. *Educational Researcher, 22*(5), 4–14.

Bell, D. (1992). *Race, racism and American law*. Boston: Little, Brown.

Berry, R. Q. (2003). *Voices of African American male students: A portrait of successful middle school mathematics students*. Unpublished doctoral dissertation, University of North Carolina at Chapel Hill.

Bonilla-Silva, E. (1997). Rethinking racism: Toward a structural interpretation. *American Sociological Review, 62*, 465–480.

Bonilla-Silva, E. (2001). *White supremacy and racism in the post-civil rights era*. Boulder, CO: Reinner.

Bonilla-Silva, E. (2002). The linguistics of color blind racism: How to talk about blacks without sounding "racist." *Critical Sociology, 28*(1–2), 41–64.

Bonilla-Silva, E. (2003). *Racism without racists: Color-blind racism and the persistence of racial inequality in the United States*. Lanham, MD: Rowman & Littlefield.

Bonilla-Silva, E., & Glover, K. (2004). "We are all Americans": The Latin Americanization of race relations in the United States. In M. Krysan & A. Lewis (Eds.), *The changing terrain of race and ethnicity* (pp. 149–183). New York: Russell Sage.

Bourdieu, P., & Passeron, J. (1977). *Reproduction in education, society and culture*. London: Sage.

Clements, D. & Sarama, J. (2007). Early childhood mathematics learning. In F. Lester (Ed.), *Second handbook of research on mathematics teaching and learning* (pp. 461–556). Charlotte, NC: Information Age.

Cornelius, J. (1991). *When I can read my title clear: Literacy, slavery, and religion in the Antebellum South.* Columbus, SC: University of South Carolina Press.

Cose, E. (1995). *The rage of a privileged class: Why do prosperous blacks still have the blues?* New York: Harper Perennial.

D'Ambrosio, U. (2007). Peace, social justice and ethnomathematics. *The Montana Mathematics Enthusiast* (Monograph *1*, 25–34).

DeNavas-Walt, C., Proctor, B., & Lee, C. (2006). *Income, poverty, and health insurance in the United States: 2005* [Electronic version]. Current Population Reports P60-231. U.S. Census Bureau. Washington, DC: U.S. Government Printing Office. Retrieved November 18, 2008, from: http://www.census.gov/prod/2006pubs/p60-231.pdf

Delgado, R., & Stefancic, J. (2001). *Critical race theory: An introduction.* New York: New York University Press.

Ernest, P. (2002). Empowerment in mathematics education. *Philosophy of Mathematics Journal, 15.* Retrieved April 18, 2003, from http://www.ex.ac.uk/~PErnest/pome15/contents.htm

Feagin, J., & Sikes, M. (1994). *Living with racism: The black middle-class experience.* Boston: Beacon Press.

Fellowes, M. (2006). *From poverty, opportunity: Putting the market to work for lower income families.* New York: Brookings Institution.

Fordham, S., & Ogbu, J. U. (1986). Black students' school success: Coping with the burden of 'acting White.' *The Urban Review, 18*(3), 176–206.

Forman, T. (2004). Color-blind racism and racial indifference: The role of racial apathy in facilitating enduring inequalities. In M. Krysan & A. Lewis (Eds.), *The changing terrain of race and ethnicity* (pp. 43–66). New York: Russell Sage.

Frankenberg, R. (1993). *White women, race matters: The social construction of whiteness.* Minneapolis, MN: University of Minnesota Press.

Frankenstein, M. (1990). Incorporating race, gender, and class issues into a critical mathematical literacy curriculum. *Journal of Negro Education, 59*(3), 336–347.

Freire, P. (1970). *Pedagogy of the oppressed.* New York: Seabird Press.

Freire, P. (1973). *Education for critical consciousness.* London: Sheed & Ward.

Gadsen, V. (1993). Literacy, identity, and education among African-Americans. *Urban Education, 27*(4), 325–369.

Gay, G. (2000). *Culturally responsive teaching: Theory, practice, and research.* New York: Teachers College Press.

Gilborn, D. (2006). Public interest and the interest of white people are not the same: Assessment, education policy, and racism. In G. Ladson-Billings, & W. F. Tate (Eds.), *Education research in the public interest* (pp. 173–195). New York: Teachers College Press.

Gordon, B. (1993). African American cultural knowledge and liberatory education. *Urban Education, 27*(4), 448–470.

Gunaratnam, Y. (2003). *Researching 'race' and ethnicity: Methods, knowledge and power.* London: Sage Publications.

Gutstein, E. (2003). Teaching and learning mathematics for social justice in an urban, Latino school. *Journal for Research in Mathematics Education, 34*(1), 37–73.

Gutstein, E. (2005). *Reading and writing the world with mathematics: Toward a pedagogy for social justice.* London: Routledge.

Hale, J. (2001). *Learning while Black: Creating educational excellence for African American children.* Baltimore, MD: Johns Hopkins University Press.

Harding, V. 1981. *There is a river: The Black struggle for freedom in America.* New York: Harcourt, Brace, Jovanovich.

Helms, J., Jernigan, M., & Mascher, J. (2005). The meaning of race in psychology and how to change it: A methodological perspective. *American Psychologist, 60*(1), 27–36.

Hill, H., & Ball, D. (2004). Learning mathematics for teaching: Results from California's mathematics professional development institutes. *Journal for Research in Mathematics Education, 35*(5), 330–351.

Hill, H., Rowan, B., & Ball, D. (2005). Effects of teachers' mathematical knowledge for teaching on student achievement. *American Educational Research Journal, 42*(2), 371–406.

Hilliard, A. (2003). No mystery: Closing the achievement gap between Africans and excellence. In T. Perry, C. Steele, & A. Hilliard (Eds.), *Young, gifted, and black* (pp. 131–165). Boston: Beacon Press.

hooks, b. (1994). *Teaching to transgress: Education as the practice of freedom*. New York: Routledge.

Julie, C. (2006). Mathematical literacy: Myths, further inclusions and exclusions. *Pythagoras, 64*, 62–69.

King, S. H. (1993a). Why did we choose teaching careers and what will enable us to stay? Insights from one cohort of the African American teaching tool. *Journal of Negro Education, 62*(4), 475–492.

King, S. H. (1993b). The limited presence of African-American teachers. *Review of Educational Research, 63*(2), 115–149.

Ladson-Billings, G. (1994). *The Dreamkeepers: Successful teachers of African-American children*. San Francisco, CA: Jossey-Bass.

Ladson-Billings, G. (2006). From the achievement gap to the education debt: Understanding achievement in U.S. schools. *Educational Researcher, 35*(7), 3–12.

Lee, C. D. (1994). African-centered pedagogy: Complexities and possibilities. In Mwalimu Shujaa (Ed.), *Too much schooling, too little education: A paradox in African-American life* (pp. 295–318). Trenton, NJ: Africa World Press.

Leonard, J. (2008). *Culturally specific pedagogy in the mathematics classroom*. New York: Routledge.

Lewis, A. E. (2003a). Everyday race-making. *American Behavioral Scientist, 47*(3), 283–305.

Lewis, A. E. (2003b). *Race in the schoolyard: Negotiating the color line in classrooms and communities*. New Brunswick, NJ: Rutgers University Press.

Lewis, A. E. (2004). "What Group?" Studying whites and whiteness in the era of "Color-Blindness," *Sociological Theory, 22*(4), 623–646.

Lubienski, S. (2002). A closer look at Black-White mathematics gaps: Intersections of race and SES in NAEP achievement and instructional practices data. *Journal of Negro Education, 71*(4), 269–287.

Lynn, M. (1999). Toward a critical race pedagogy. *Urban Education, 33*(5), 606–626.

Lynn, M. (2004). Inserting the "race" into critical pedagogy: An analysis of "race-based epistemologies." *Educational Philosophy and Theory, 36*(2), 153–165.

Madhubuti, H., & Madhubuti, S. (1994). *African-centered education*. Chicago: Third World Press.

Marable, M. (1983). *How capitalism underdeveloped Black America*. Boston: South End Press.

Martin, D. (1998). *Mathematics socialization and identity among African Americans: A multilevel analysis of community forces, school forces, and individual agency*. Proposal submitted to National Academy of Education/Spencer Postdoctoral Fellowship competition.

Martin, D. (2000). *Mathematics success and failure among African American youth: The roles of sociohistorical context, community forces, school influence, and individual agency*. Mahwah, NJ: Erlbaum.

Martin, D. (2002). *Mathematics socialization and identity: A sociocultural analysis of African American information technology workforce participation*. Project proposal funded by National Science Foundation.

Martin, D. (2003). Hidden assumptions and unaddressed questions in mathematics for all rhetoric. *The Mathematics Educator, 13*(2), 7–21.

Martin, D. (2006a). Mathematics learning and participation as racialized forms of experience: African American parents speak on the struggle for mathematics literacy. *Mathematical Thinking and Learning, 8*(3), 197–229.

Martin, D. (2006b). Mathematics learning and participation in African American context: The co-construction of identity in two intersecting realms of experience. In N. Nasir & P. Cobb (Eds.), *Diversity, equity, and access to mathematical ideas* (pp. 146–158). New York: Teachers College Press.

Martin, D. (2007). Beyond missionaries or cannibals: Who should teach mathematics to African American children? *The High School Journal, 91*(1), 6–28.

Martin, D. (in press). Researching race in mathematics education. *Teachers College Record.*

McGee, E. (2006). *Chronicles of success: Black students achieving in mathematics, science and engineering.* Paper presented at the Success Summit of the African American Success Foundation, Fort Lauderdale, FL. Published online: http://www.blacksuccessfoundation.org/

McGee, E. (in press). When it comes to the mathematical experiences of African Americans…Race Matters. *Negro Educational Review.*

McLoyd, V. C. (1991). What is the study of African American children the study of? In R. L. Jones (Ed.), *Black psychology* (pp. 419–440). Berkeley, CA: Cobb & Henry.

Miles, R. (1988). Racialization. In E. Cashmore (Ed.), *Dictionary of race and ethnic relations* (2nd ed., pp. 246–247). London: Routledge.

Moses, R. P., & Cobb, C. E. (2001). *Radical equations: Math literacy and civil rights.* Boston: Beacon Press.

Moses, R. P., Kamii, M., Swap, S. M., & Howard, J. (1989, November). The Algebra Project: Organizing in the spirit of Ella. *Harvard Educational Review, 59*(4), 423–443.

Murrell, P. (2002). *African-centered pedagogy.* Albany, NY: State University of New York Press.

Nasir, N. (2002). Identity, goals, and learning: Mathematics in cultural practice. *Mathematical Thinking and Learning, 2–3,* 213–248.

Nasir, N. (2006). Identity, goals, and learning: The case of basketball mathematics. In N. Nasir & P. Cobb (Eds.), *Improving access to mathematics: Diversity and equity in the classroom* (pp. 132–145). New York: Teachers College Press.

National Center for Education Information. (2005, August 18). *Profile of teachers in the U.S. 2005.* Retrieved December 1, 2005, from http://www.ncei.com/POT05PRESSREL3.htm

National Council of Teachers of Mathematics. (1989). *Curriculum and evaluation standards for school mathematics.* Reston, VA: Author.

National Council of Teachers of Mathematics. (2000). *Principles and standards for school mathematics.* Reston, VA: Author.

National Research Council. (1989). *Everybody counts: A report to the nation on the future of mathematics education.* Washington, D.C.: National Academy Press.

National Science Board (2003, August). *The science and engineering workforce: Realizing America's potential.* Arlington, VA: National Science Foundation.

National Urban League (2004). *The state of black America 2004: The complexity of black progress.* New York: National Urban League.

Oakes, J. (1985). *Keeping track: How schools structure inequality.* New Haven, CT: Yale University Press.

Oakes, J. (1990). Opportunities, achievement and choice: Women and minority students in science and mathematics. In C. B. Cazden (Ed.), *Review of research in education* (Vol.16, 153–222). Washington, D.C.: AERA.

Oakes, J., Joseph, R., & Muir, K. (2004). Access to achievement in mathematics and science: Inequalities that endure and chance. In J. A. Banks & C. A. M. Banks (Eds.), *Handbook of research on multicultural education* (2nd ed., pp. 69–90). San Francisco: Jossey-Bass.

O'Connor, L. A., & Mueller, J. (2007). Researching "Black" educational experiences and outcomes: Theoretical and methodological considerations. *Educational Researcher, 36*(9), 541–552.

Parker, L., & Lynn, M. (2002). What's race got to do with it? Critical race theory's conflicts with and connections to qualitative research methodology and epistemology. *Qualitative Inquiry, 8*(1), 7–22.

Pattillo-McCoy, M. (1999). *Black picket fences: Privilege and peril among the black middle class.* Chicago: University of Chicago Press.

Perry, T. (2003). Up from the parched earth: Toward a theory of African-American achievement. In T. Perry, C. Steele, & A. G. Hilliard III (Eds.), *Young, gifted, and Black: Promoting high achievement among African American students* (pp. 1–10). Boston: Beacon Press.

Potts, R. (2003). Emancipatory education versus school-based prevention in African-American communities. *American Journal of Community Psychology, 31*(1–2), 173–183.

Qualls, C. (2001). Public and personal meanings of literacy. In J. Harris, A. Kamhi, & K. Pollock (Eds.), *Literacy in African-American communities* (pp. 1–19). Mahwah, NJ: Erlbaum.

RAND Mathematics Study Panel. (2003). *Mathematics proficiency for all students: Toward a strategic research and development program in mathematics education.* Santa Monica, CA: RAND.

Ratteray, J. (1994). The search for access and content in the education of African-Americans. In M. J. Shujaa (Ed.), *Too much schooling, too little education* (pp. 123–141). Trenton, NJ: African Free World Press.

Royster, D. (2003). *Race and the invisible hand: How white networks exclude black men from blue-collar jobs.* Berkeley: University of California Press.

Secada, W. (1989). Agenda setting, enlightened self-interest, and equity in mathematics education. *Peabody Journal of Education, 66*(2), 22–56.

Secada, W. (1992). Race, ethnicity, social class, language, and achievement in mathematics. In D. Grouws (Ed.), *Handbook of research in mathematics teaching and learning* (pp. 623–660). New York: Macmillan.

Shujaa, M. J. (1994). Education and schooling: Can you have one without the other? In M. J. Shujaa (Ed.), *Too much schooling, too little education: A paradox in Black life in white societies* (pp. 13–36). Trenton, NJ: African World Press.

Skovsmose, O. (1994). *Toward a critical philosophy of mathematics education.* Dordrecht, The Netherlands: Kluwer.

Solorzano, D., & Ornelas, A. (2002). A critical race analysis of advance placement classes: A case of educational inequalities. *Journal of Latinos and Education, 1*, 215–229.

Solorzano, D., & Ornelas, A. (2004). A critical race analysis of advance placement classes and selective admissions. *High School Journal, 87*, 15–26.

Stinson, D. (2004). *African-American male students and achievement in school mathematics: A critical postmodern analysis of agency.* Unpublished doctoral dissertation, University of Georgia, Athens, GA.

Strutchens, M. E., & Silver, E. A. (2000). NAEP findings regarding race/ethnicity: Students' performance, school experiences, and attitudes and beliefs. In E. A. Silver & P. A. Kenney (Eds.), *Results from the 7th mathematics assessment of the National Assessment of Educational Progress* (pp. 45–72). Reston, VA: NCTM.

Tate, W. F. (1997). Race, ethnicity, SES, gender, and language proficiency trends in mathematics achievement: An update. *Journal for Research in Mathematics Education, 28*(6), 652–680.

U.S. Department of Education. (1997). *Mathematics equals opportunity.* Washington, D.C.: U.S. Government Printing Office.

Watts, R., & Serrano-Garcia, I. (2003). The quest for a liberating community psychology: An overview. *American Journal of Community Psychology, 31*(1–2), 73–78.

Watts, R., Williams, N., & Jagers, R. (2003). Sociopolitical development. *American Journal of Community Psychology, 31*(1–2), 185–194.

Williams, H. (2005). *Self-taught: African American education in slavery and freedom.* Chapel Hill: University of North Carolina Press.

Woodson, C. G. (1990). *The mis-education of the Negro.* Trenton, NJ: African World Press. (Original work published 1933)

Zuberi, T. (2001) *Thicker than blood: How racial statistics lie.* Minneapolis, MN: University of Minnesota Press.

10
Culturally Responsive Mathematics Education in the Algebra Project

ROBERT MOSES, MARY MAXWELL WEST, AND FRANK E. DAVIS

Why does $a - b = a + (-b)$? For 20 years, the Algebra Project has been posing perplexing mathematics problems like this one in various groups, such as parents at a high school in New Orleans, teachers at Algebra Project institutes, researchers at the Spencer Foundation, and mathematicians at the Mathematical Sciences Research Institute.

The question produces a range of responses. Some people note the symbols that they recognize as the language of mathematics, but lack ways to attach meanings to them. Mathematicians may dispute among themselves about the meanings, contrary to the public image of the certainty of mathematics. To parents, or students, the difficulty of answering this question may point to a failure of our current system of education and the complexity of achieving reform in mathematics education.

Posing such a question helps project members learn how people actually think about some of the mathematics that our children must learn, and is simultaneously a way to engage stakeholders in the subject. In other words, it is a kind of organizing work. It is work that requires a type of dynamic cultural responsiveness where classrooms, community meetings, and other forums are seen as occasions for developing shared meanings about mathematics and mathematics education.

Foundations in the Civil Rights Movement

The Algebra Project actually began when founder Bob Moses sensed that his son Omo would not fall easily into that line of students who marched two by two into the first grade at the M. L. King School in Cambridge, MA, and that Omo would be better off in the "alternative" and "open" classrooms next door. It also appeared to him that his daughter Maisha, as well as Omo and a number of other Black students, might benefit from an approach to learning mathematics that would provide deeper understanding of the concepts in Algebra I. But Moses looked back to lessons learned by him and others in the civil rights movement, in thinking about the problem that his children and others were facing.

> As the Algebra Project took shape, my civil rights movement experience was guiding my thinking as much as my training in mathematics. Part of understanding the movement is understanding change. Part of what happened in Mississippi was the creation of a culture of change—a change in the climate of the consciousness of Black people in that state. Part of what was involved was tapping into a consensus. People agreed that if they could get the vote it would be a good thing, and they would be better off. I felt, as I worked in the Open Program [his children's school], that the same dynamics were at work around the issues of mathematics literacy. I think everyone agrees that if it is possible to open the door to real mathematical understanding, it would be good thing. If we can do it, then we should. (Moses & Cobb, 2001, p. 111)

Tapping into this consensus, in turn, relied on organizing and working from the ground up:

> The community organizing approach to bringing innovation into the education process differs profoundly from the traditional educational intervention. At universities, scholars design interventions they theorize will result in outcomes they can predict.... In sharp contrast, working in the tradition of Ella Baker, the community organizer seeking an innovative breakthrough in education will use the principle of "cast down your bucket where you are." The organizer becomes part of the community, learning from it, becoming aware of its strengths, resources, concerns, and ways of doing business. The organizer does not have the complete answer in advance—the researcher's detailed comprehensive plans for remedying a perceived problem. The organizer wants to construct a solution with the community.... I did not know that my concern for Maisha's math education would lead to the Algebra Project's raising questions about ability grouping, effective teaching for children of color, experiential learning, and community participation in educational decision making. I pulled these issues up when I cast down my bucket. (Moses & Cobb, 2001, p. 112)

Following in this tradition, the Algebra Project attempts to gather groups together to examine their experiences, and decide on their own action plans. The project continues to convene groups of the various stakeholders, ranging from the students, to teacher groups, community groups, and national groups of mathematicians or educators. In the case of students, the crucial setting is the classroom.

In the beginning, there was concern for the proportions of African-American students in particular who were not being prepared for the college track. As the project grew, others invited the project into their sites, including sites with high percentages of Latino/a students or a mixture of ethnicities.

During the 1980s and 1990s, the Algebra Project worked in the southern United States, as well as in cities such as Chicago and San Francisco. The project developed a prealgebra "curricular intervention" called the *Transition Curriculum,* and professional development for teachers, as well as community development and youth leadership development initiatives. The *Transition Curriculum* assisted students and teachers to transition from the arithmetic thinking of the elementary grades to the algebraic thinking needed for higher mathematics. In the late 90s the project involved teachers in grades 4 through 8 in 18 urban and rural sites in 12 different states. Most teachers implemented Algebra Project materials along with other instructional materials, and participated in Algebra Project professional development. Community members developed various local initiatives around their schools, and youth initiatives emerged.

In middle schools where a majority of students had participated in the project, graduates enrolled in (and passed) high school college preparatory mathematics courses at about twice the rate of their peers from non-Algebra Project schools in the same districts: in Jackson, MS, San Francisco, and Cambridge, MA (Davis & West, 2000; West & Davis, 2005).

Under a National Science Foundation (NSF) grant for teacher professional development, the project formed teams of teachers and university math and science specialists that facilitated professional development for over 700 teachers in southern states, the New York City area, and district wide in Cambridge, MA. The facilitators in Cambridge gained district-wide respect, and were hired by the district to lead professional development in any of several optional math programs, not only the Algebra Project. The project's potential to engage teachers was indicated in that, across the NSF funded sites, 31% of teachers committed more than the minimum hours recommended by NSF and 17% participated voluntarily for two to four times the minimum.

After Moses worked for several years with students at Brinkley Middle School in Jackson, MS, in 1995, he gained permission to follow a cohort of successful eighth graders (who had participated in the Algebra Project and passed Algebra I) into their high school, to instruct them in geometry. This school was Lanier High School, which was historically the lowest performing of the nine high schools in Jackson, MS. The students are all African American as are most teachers and administrators, and about 85% of students qualify for free or reduced-cost lunch. Soon, he was asked to teach Algebra there, and learned of the struggles of the typical ninth grader who has not yet taken Algebra, and enters below grade level in several subjects. Thus began the current initiative to establish a "floor" of mathematics literacy for the many students around the country who are not succeeding in high school mathematics.

Judging from the research on high schools with low graduation rates, this population now includes not only African-American and Latino/a students, but also American-Indian students, and White students who are experiencing difficulty with math concepts. Most states require mastery of beginning algebra in order for any student to obtain a high school diploma, but African-American, Latino/a, and American-Indian students graduate at a rate from 20 to 30% lower than White and Asian students. In high poverty areas, more than 40% of the student loss occurs at the ninth grade, compared with 27% in low-poverty settings (EPE Research Center, 2006, cited in Olson, 2006). More than one third of the students who are lost from the high school pipeline are lost between 9th and 10th grade. Students who do not pass Algebra I in grade 9 are more likely to be retained in grade, which in turn is a strong predictor of failing to graduate (Campbell, Jolly, Hoey, & Perlman, 2002).

The NSF found in 2004 that finishing a course beyond Algebra II in high school more than doubled the odds that a student who entered postsecondary education completed a bachelor's degree. Among students who successfully completed rigorous mathematics courses, race/ethnicity and socioeconomic status had little or no impact on their likelihood of completing college (National Science Board, 2004).

The Algebra Project seeks to develop a demand for math literacy in those most affected by its absence—the young people themselves. This approach, which places a high value on the importance of peer culture, is an outgrowth of experience in the civil rights movement of the 1960s, as well as the emergence of Algebra Project graduates into a group with their own perspectives and initiatives. As Moses notes, it was not radical in the 60s to do voter registration, but it was radical to do it in the Mississippi Delta among people who were said to be apathetic. Similarly, it is not radical today to teach math using games and enjoyable experiences. What is radical is to teach math to students at the bottom in a way that allows them to rise to the middle and top.

The Algebra Project is developing instructional materials for schools where students are performing in the bottom quartile on state and national achievement tests. The materials are designed for students not only to pass typical state tests in high school but also to provide a sturdy enough understanding of key concepts that students will not need remedial courses in college. This approach seeks to "raise the floor" of mathematics literacy, providing a quality mathematics education to those who have not been reached by existing curricula.

In 2000, Moses began collaborating with university mathematicians to develop high school instruction that would enable students to meet these goals. The first cohort entered ninth grade in 2001 to 2002. Students were assigned in the ninth grade to the Algebra Project (or to non-Algebra Project teachers) on the basis of scheduling—neither students nor parents were volunteers. At the end of ninth grade, 56% of the Algebra Project students (n = 108) passed the state Algebra I exam on first attempt, compared to 38% (n = 85) of their peers in the same school. By Grade 12, while only 41% of the original Grade 9 Algebra I students in the whole school were still at Lanier taking math, 85% of these were Algebra Project students who chose to remain in the project for all four years. The project has now piloted several modules for an Algebra I course in Proviso, IL, near Chicago, Petersburg, VA, and rural Summerton, SC, and is preparing for additional piloting in San Francisco. These modules have been developed by Moses in collaboration with a team of university mathematicians/scientists that now includes: Greg Budzban, Southern Illinois University; Ed Dubinsky, Florida International University; David Henderson, Cornell University; Staffas Broussard, United Nations; and Gary Benenson, City College of New York. Moses has collaborated with several mathematicians to produce two modules for Grade 9 Algebra I that have been piloted in Proviso IL, Petersburg, VA, and rural Summerton, SC.

Based on its experience with the first student cohort supported throughout high school, and two others in progress in Jackson, MS and Miami, the project makes certain recommendations to schools, students, and parents. The project recommends that students be enabled to form a cohort that stays together throughout high school, take math every day in 90-minute periods, and receive supplemental support in math and other subjects in summer institutes or after-school sessions. Summer institutes should assist students academically, and also enable them to form a cohesive peer group with a positive culture for learning. Ideally, classes should be small (fewer than 20 students) and teachers should have common planning periods (if there is more than one teacher). Teachers should be prepared and supported to use Algebra Project materials in summer and winter institutes and follow-up support.

Although many schools now mandate a "double dose" of math (*Education Week*, 2006), this is done by enrolling students in remedial courses alongside of regular math courses. In contrast, the project materials build basic concepts and introduce topics not usually covered in high school, but seen by project affiliated mathematicians as crucial for college mathematics.

Instructional Design

Like other projects reported in this volume (e.g., Lipka and colleagues in Alaska, chapter 11; Brenner and colleagues in Hawaii (see Barta & Brenner, chapter 4, this volume), the design of instruction in the Algebra Project begins by looking closely at the local knowledge and sociocultural experiences that could create a bridge toward mathematics concepts. Moses's story of how he began to develop instructional materials illustrates the history of a module on the number line that uses a class trip as an experiential basis for learning addition and subtraction of integers:

> In the fall of 1985, an eighth grader in the Open Program at the Martin Luther King School in Cambridge, Massachusetts, who didn't know his multiplication tables, wanted to do Algebra. His 6th grade math teacher,

> Lynne Godfrey, told me he would "hide" behind anything or anybody when math time came around. But Ari was Danny's best friend, Danny was Omo's best friend, Ari wanted to do their math, and, last but not least, Omo is my son.
>
> That entire school year I sat Ari down next to me and we worked our way through an Algebra text, one problem at a time. When we got to numbers on the number line, Ari always produced internally consistent, wrong answers. After a while, I saw that Ari had a question he was answering—it just wasn't the question the text had in mind. He had "How many?" questions, as in "How many fingers? How many toes?" After another while I saw that he needed a second question in his mind. But what?
>
> I finally decided he needed "Which way?" questions. Ari obviously already had some of those. What he needed was to link them to his "How many?" questions [and to] those pesky number line concepts. (Moses, 2006a)

So the Algebra Project's version of "culturally responsive" instruction began by examining what students bring to their encounters with the mathematical symbols and signs contained in textbooks and purveyed by teachers in mathematics classrooms. The project asked, how can we make meaningful what is encoded in the textbooks, the school mathematics programs that require them, and the assessments that students must inevitably negotiate? How can we link students' worlds to what initially appear as inscrutable products of some other social or cultural experience? How can we enable students to construct meaning for the expression: $a - b = a + (-b)$?

Giving Students Evidence for Mathematics

Moses has proposed that developing instructional materials for students like Ari means providing students with "evidence" for the mathematics under discussion:

> I first wrestled with questions about evidence at Harvard, where Willard Van Orman Quine was disposed, in the 1950s, to wonder about mathematics and its affinities to Theoretical Physics. Quine belittled the difference, but he did not deny it. He thought the two were like non-identical twins: however close the call, you could tell them apart; but, he insisted, the evidence that sustained them both could not serve such a purpose.
>
> Nor, in Quine's view, did [there appear to be a need for] evidence [that] distinguish[ed] scientists from local people. There is no scientific privileged access to evidence; what is distinctive, and serves to distinguish scientists, is the care they take and the systems they construct with the same kind of evidence local people encounter.
>
> The kind of evidence also available to Ari and the effort to link "Which

way?" to "How many?" The Algebra Project wondered aloud about the types of evidence students offer for their mathematical statements and the diagrams about which we ask them to ponder and reflect.

We used school math to examine Quine's thoughts that evidence comes in types. Quine was inclined to "see a major discontinuity not between mathematical theory and physical theory, but between terms that can be taught strictly by ostension and terms that cannot." (cited in Schilpp & Herman, 1982)

In school math, this discontinuity occurs between students' "observation sentences"—representations that can be labeled "True" or "False" based on directly observable evidence; versus their "theoretical statements"—representations to marshal arguments for, listen to arguments about. The latter is evidence as a chain of reasonings or a proof.

Many of us in the Algebra Project thought long and hard about the deceptively simple equation that appears early on in school algebra texts: $a - b = a + (-b)$. Is it "theoretical"? We decided "yes" and constructed suitable metaphors and observation sentences for numerical interpretations of its separate sides. (Moses, 2006a)

Quine worked this problem about evidence through an analysis of language:

He insisted that elementary arithmetic, elementary logic, and elementary set theory get started by what he called the "regimentation of ordinary discourse, mathematization in situ." Scientists, Quine said, put a straitjacket on natural languages. (Moses & Cobb, 2001, p. 198)

Quine's ideas represent a research tradition focused on untangling the contents of mathematics from a philosophical point of view. The Algebra Project has defined a "five-step curricular process" which is its analysis of how to lead students from their social–cultural world and language to a mathematization of this experience, from which they acquire the needed conventional mathematics concepts. Students (or any participants) (1) engage in a physical experience, which they then (2) represent in their own words and pictures, including (3) everyday language ("people talk") which are then (4) structured into a more regimented language called "feature talk" that is more amenable to mathematical expressions; and into (5) the abstract symbolic representations and procedures used in today's conventional mathematics (Moses & Cobb, 2001). This process underlies all of the project's middle school materials, as well as activities carried out in teacher professional development workshops and other events. The five-step process was found to be an effective heuristic for triggering changes in teachers' beliefs and practices (West, Conner, McGee, & Bland, 1995).

A second research tradition, involving psychological theories about experiential learning as conceptualized in the work of John Dewey, Kurt Lewin, and Jean

Piaget, has proved equally important. Experiential learning theory is grounded in the countless cyclical experiences in which people try something (experience), then think about what they did (reflection), then make improvements (abstract conceptualization), then practice their improvements (application). Moses has summarized the link between these two traditions as follows:

> You can think of it is as a circle or clock: at twelve noon they [the students] have an experience; quarter past they are thinking about it; half past they are doing some conceptual work around their reflections, and at quarter to, they are doing applications based on their conceptual work. In the Algebra Project, this movement from experience to abstraction takes the form of a five-step process that introduces students to the idea that many important concepts of elementary algebra may be accessed through ordinary experiences. Each step is designed to help students bridge the transition from real life to mathematical language and operations. Because of this connection with real life, the Transition Curriculum [project's middle school material is] not only experiential, but culturally based. The experiences must be meaningful in terms of the daily life and culture of the students. (Moses & Cobb, 2001, pp. 119–120, emphasis added)

Algebra Project modules begin with experiences that are eventually "mathematized." In the Trip Line, for example, students are led from the experience of a class trip to a way of proving that $b - a = b + {}^{-}a$. First, students take a trip and represent it in their own language and drawings. They identify key features of the trip, and create a "trip line" that shows, with photos, the various stops on the trip. They write sentences about the relationships of stops on the trip, and identify important people/objects, actions, and relationships. These "observation sentences" are gradually transformed into mathematical expressions, which enable students to consider the argument in Figure 10.1 (Algebra Project, 2008b):

Another unit called the Road Coloring Problem is based on an actual problem in research mathematics. Students experience the problem by laying out on the floor, "cities" made of three or more "buildings," connected by "roads" that can be traveled in only one direction (indicated by color Blue or Red). One student stands in each "building." The task for other students is to figure out what series of instructions (walk Blue or Red roads) will produce the outcome where all students end up in the same building at the same time. This activity becomes the ground for learning about functions and their representations, including matrices. The worksheet in Figure 10.2 illustrates how students represent the Red and Blue instructions as functions in what are called arrow diagrams. Students also represent the functions using matrix notation, and compute the products of these matrices using the composition of functions. In this example, if students follow the Blue instruction, then the Red instruction they will all finish in "Building 3." The sequence "Blue-Red" is called a "synchronizing instruction" (Algebra Project 2008a).

We will prove that $b - a = b + {}^-a$ by showing that the movement $b + {}^-a$ takes you from a *to* b.

Mathematician: Let's do it. How do we express **starting** at a and making the **movement** $b + {}^-a$?

Student 3: $\boldsymbol{a + (b + {}^-a)}$.

Student 1: Why did you use **parentheses**?

Student 3: Because $b + {}^-a$ is the **movement** I want to make so this is what I must **add** to a.

Student 2: Are you saying that putting it in parentheses makes it a separate *thing*.

Student 3: Right. Then I can think of it as $a + c$ which means: start at $\boldsymbol{a}$ and make the movement $\boldsymbol{c}$.

Student 1: What is c?

Student 3: c is $\boldsymbol{b + {}^-a}$.

Mathematician: Very good. Now we will make the proof. We will do it in two columns: one column for the steps of the calculation and one column for the justification for each step.

STEP	JUSTIFICATION
$a + (b + {}^-a)$	**Start at a and make the movement $(b + {}^-a)$**
$a + ({}^-a + b)$	**Commutative property**
$(a + {}^-a) + b$	**Associative property**
$0 + b$	**Opposite or inverse property**
b	**Zero property**

Mathematician: So what have we done?

Student 1: We **started** at a…

Student 2: Made the **movement** $b + {}^-a$…

Student 3: And **ended** at b.

Mathematician: So what does that mean?

Student 1: That $\mathbf{b + {}^-a}$ is the movement that takes you from $\boldsymbol{a}$ to $\boldsymbol{b}$.

Student 2: And that movement is $\boldsymbol{b - a}$.

Student 3: So $\boldsymbol{b - a = b + {}^-a}$!

Mathematician: That's it! You have completed the proof.

Figure 10.1 Lesson from the Algebra Project Trip Line Module.

As for the learning trajectory that will enable students to gain knowledge of that mathematics, the beginning points are students' experiences and ordinary language. The project sees the language of mathematics as a conceptual language that no one speaks, that taps into something universal in human experience. This conceptual language can be accessed through ordinary language—*any* ordinary language. The five-step process can be adopted into any language, as did teachers from Mali who attended an Algebra Project teacher institute. During the

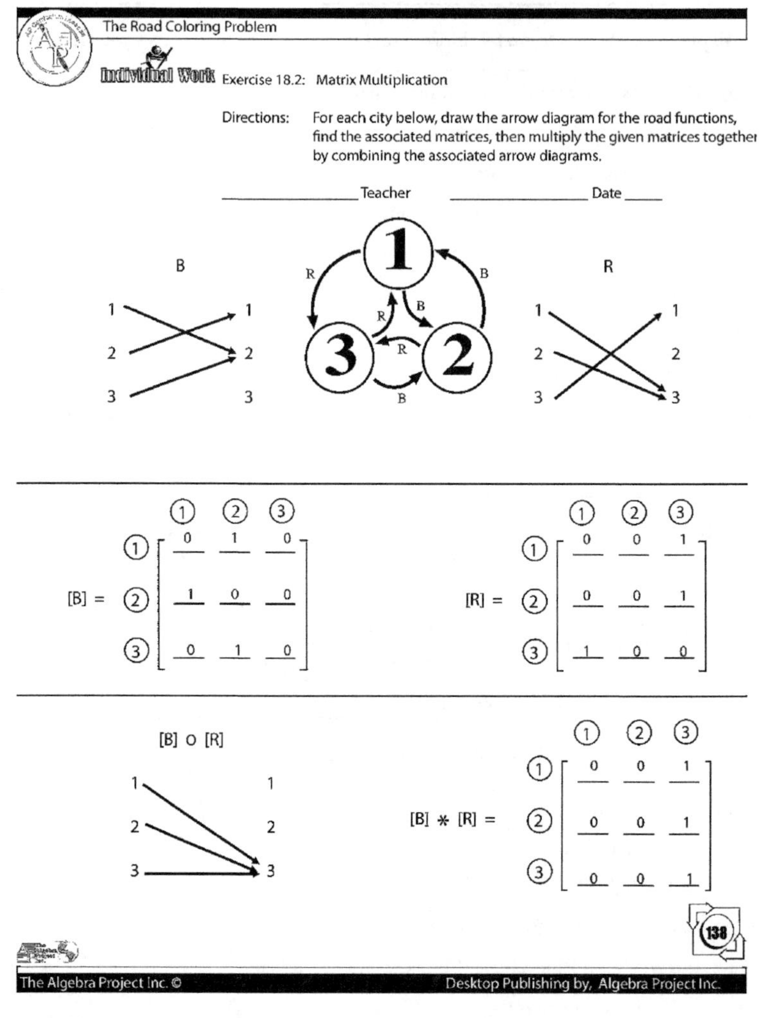

Figure 10.2 The road coloring problem.

institute, these teachers spontaneously began to adapt the process from English, into French, and into their native Bamana. They returned to Mali, and were excited to be using the process through their own language. When they found no available term in Bamana, they turned to Kiswahili. This example suggests that different languages may afford different paths to the mathematics in the current curriculum, but the important point is that ordinary discourse can be a route toward those concepts.

While many will agree that mathematics is derived through experience, just what is experienced or postulated to be a mathematical object leads to very different conceptions of evidence. The often-cited conflict between a Platonist view (mathematical objects have an independent existence and are absorbed) and a constructivist view (mathematical objects are constructed by individuals in both physical and social interactions) is an example (see Ernest, chapter 2 this volume). While it may not be possible to actually say which arguments about knowledge are correct, they uniformly assume that a process of examining and reflecting on evidence is an essential and perhaps universal aspect of learning mathematics, and of learning in general.

When Is "Cultural" also Universal?

Scholars of African-American education have identified cultural features that can serve as classroom resources (e.g., Delpit, 2002; Gay, 2000; Ladson-Billings, 1994, 2002; Lee, 2001; Lee, Spencer, & Harpalani, 2003; Murrell, 2002; Perry, 2003). Some studies have also linked use of culturally familiar activities or problem features to increased student achievement (see Barta & Brenner, chapter 4, this volume; Hilliard, 2003; Lipka & Adams, 2004; Lipka et al., chapter 11 this volume; Tate, 2002). The Algebra Project materials also contain references to some experiences that may have meanings for students and teachers. For example, the middle school materials contain lessons with stories about Making Do, which is a familiar experience for many students. There is a module on ratios using African drumming rhythms (Moynihan & Belcher, 1993–2007). The trip taken by classes to begin the module Trip Line is designed by teachers and students to take in locally important sites.

How do such references function in learning? In the case of the African Drums module, there is a reference to one's cultural heritage (African drums) that also involves an experience (listening to and doing drumming) that scaffolds specific mathematics (ratios). These various references, some of which are in the materials, and some of which are added in local adaptations, are not essential in themselves to the scaffolding of mathematics concepts but may create important affirmations of one's cultural identity. Incorporated into mathematics lessons, they convey that "we can do math." As others have pointed out, such affirmation can be critical for groups disenfranchised from access, or stereotyped as not interested, or not competent in mathematics, or resisting this educational path. To project members, it is a further sign of success when students create their own culturally based math products, as did students in Jackson. Algebra Project students there created and performed a "rap" about prime numbers.

The Algebra Project high school materials also use scripted dialogues in nearly every module, in which students converse with a "mathematician." These dialogues, which are read aloud in class, with students taking turns being the "mathematician" as well as the "students," model mathematical discourse, how students may raise questions, and how mathematicians think about the discipline of mathematics and how mathematical knowledge is constructed.

Culturally based pedagogy is also present in the social interactions modeled in teaching. An example in the Algebra Project is its modeling of the social facilitation methods that draw out the full participation of all members of a group.

This work may be analogous to Lipka and colleagues' use of elders' knowledge and ways of communicating, which included "expert-apprentice modeling, joint productive activity, and cognitive apprenticeship." Similarly, the Algebra Project draws on the elders of the South, and their strategies for organizing. Later the Algebra Project codified some of these strategies into the program for professional development of teachers.

One simple routine that values joint participation is not unique to the Algebra Project—cooperative small-group work and "reporting out." In Algebra Project classrooms and teacher workshops, participants work in small groups and then "report out" their results to the whole group. This method is well suited to the project's goals, but reporting out has special importance. Davis, West, and their colleagues observed routines that may draw from culturally based traditions of "performance" in the classrooms of Moses, Marian Currell in San Francisco, and other African-American teachers, as well as in large community meetings and public presentations conducted by Moses. In the classroom, and in public meetings, students were often placed front and center, and enabled to demonstrate their mathematical competence. They were given "leading roles." Davis and West have noted that giving students leading roles, in which they display mathematical competence, makes mathematics a "worthy" subject, and also assists students to see themselves as competent (Davis, West, Greeno, Gresalfi, & Martin, 2007). Through such demonstrations, participants and audiences also see that "we can do it," which helps to create the "minimum common conceptual cohesion" needed for organizing (Moses & Cobb, 2001, p. 92). The importance of these public demonstrations is also consistent with Theresa Perry's finding that schools that produce high-achieving African-American students engage in *public* demonstrations that communicate and celebrate high achievement (Perry, 2003).

In Currell's classroom in San Francisco, Davis and West observed that these methods were effective in a group that was ethnically and linguistically diverse. Similarly, Lipka and colleagues found that modules based on local knowledge of Alaskan Indian/Alaskan Native (AI/AN) communities in Alaska benefited other students as well as the AI/AN students (chapter 11 this volume). The use of modeling and imitation in Algebra Project classrooms, enhanced through performances, may be an example of the "coordinated functioning of multifaceted cultural practices in human development" as described by Rogoff and Angelillo (2002). We may not be able to trace the exact origins of some of the routines that we observed in Moses's and Currell's classrooms, over centuries of blending of cultures. Moreover practices that may be identifiable with particular cultures may be effective with others without such deep or particular cultural knowledge, and may draw on universals in human functioning.

An example of possibly *universally effective* methods for teaching and learning are the use of physical movement in space and of games. These are used in classroom modules as well as activities for out-of-school settings. Many activities involve walking out mathematics structures on the floor. Activities may also be structured as competitive games that are timed. Observations clearly show that these experiences engage students, and Moses notes that getting students' attention is the first step. However, to learn the abstract symbolic representations and procedures of conventional Western mathematics, much more work will be needed on the part of students and teachers. This is the point at which the "evidence" for mathematics again becomes crucial to learning.

Fostering Active Growth of Participants

As formulated by the Algebra Project, fostering the active growth of participants is not a simple task. As Moses noted in a presentation to the Mathematical Sciences Research Institute:

> A passage from John Dewey resonates with what the SNCC [Student Nonviolent Coordinating Committee] learned from Ella: "To pursue a common good for others in ways which leaves them passive prevents the results from being either good or common: not good, because it is at the expense of the active growth of those to be helped, and not common because these have no share in bringing about the result." These insights from Ella and Dewey support earned insurgency as an essential practice for the peaceful evolution of our democracy and a "workable government." (Moses, 2006a)

The purpose of the project is actually to produce "mathematics *insurgents*"—who are the young people, as well as teachers, parents, and mathematicians. This goal entails additional elements that problematize notions of "cultural responsiveness." The task requires that meetings enable those various groups of stakeholders to move beyond the constraints that their roles place on them, as well as to take on views that may not be popular in their current cultural milieu and activities that place additional demands on their time and energy.

As Moses explains:

> What was at the heart of Ella's strategy vis-à-vis the sit-in movement was to help it give birth to its OWN organizational form—a formalizing of it—that should come about by the participants themselves straight-jacketing their movement. It shouldn't happen by absorbing the movement into any of the traditional organizations. So that way, I think, she helped the movement actually realize the active growth of its participants. So you didn't get what Dewey talks about here, where you have an effort to further the common good at the expense of the active growth. Then the other piece of that is, it was "common" because the people in the movement sit-ins were to be directly involved in bringing about the end result. (Moses interview, 2006b)

Student Development

The project has evidence of successful outcomes both in students' mathematics literacy (according to traditional measures as well as project-designed tests), and in students' development as active citizens and mathematics "insurgents." The project's best outcomes for mathematics achievement appear where a critical mass or group has been created. In middle schools, where more than half of the students participated in the project (which had classroom as well as parent and community development initiatives), Algebra Project students enrolled in (and passed) high school mathematics courses in the college track at about twice the rate of their peers who were not in the project. Similarly, the first high school cohort at Lanier High School in Jackson outperformed their non-Algebra Project peers in the same school in Grade 9 on the state test, and in Grade 12, in their continuing enrollment in college preparatory mathematics.

Examples of Algebra Project graduates' choices for social action include those of the Young People's Project, the Baltimore Algebra Project, and the Finding Our Folk organization formed by project graduates to address the aftermath of Hurricane Katrina. In the mid-90s, Algebra Project graduates from Cambridge, MA, and Jackson, MS, formed the Young People's Project (YPP) whose stated mission is "to use mathematics literacy as a tool to develop young leaders and organizers who radically change the quality of education and quality of life in their communities so that all children have the opportunity to reach their full human potential." The group has extended its work into Chicago, Miami, New Orleans, Petersburg, VA, and other sites. It was awarded an NSF grant for informal education and works collaboratively with many local community based organizations, providing services to after-school and summer programs. The Baltimore Algebra Project began in a school but continues now as an after-school program. It has produced articulate and politically active young people who were featured in a PBS documentary (Brancaccio, 2007).

In the aftermath of Hurricane Katrina, Algebra Project graduates joined with numerous other organizations in a project designed to document the stories of survivors, and to consider the current and past causes of the tragedy: the Finding Our Folk tour. This group's mission is:

> ...to raise the voices of Katrina's survivors and connect them with the voices of America's survivors, the brothers and sisters in all corners of the country who remain on the margins of citizenship. We seek to use the tools of education, documentation, healing, and organizing to explore and discuss the conditions that led to the devastating impact of Katrina; to join the voices of resistance, the veterans of past and continuing movements, with the voices of hiphop, blues and jazz; to celebrate African and indigenous cultures as they have been expressed in New Orleans and throughout the world; to find our folk, to reconnect the individuals, families and com-

munities that are scattered across the country, living in exile. In finding our folk, we hope to find ourselves. (Finding Our Folk, 2006)

Social Facilitation, Teacher Development, and Youth Leadership Development

If we are to enable people who come to group events to *change*—to adopt new ideas and roles—it is necessary for group facilitators and project leaders to have expert social and communication skills. The Algebra Project developed a professional development program that codified those skills as they pertain to teacher development. Consistent with the project's organizing approach, the facilitators developed in this program also led meetings of other groups such as community meetings, project meetings, meetings with funders, and so on.

The need for teacher "trainers" (as they were called at the time) became clear in the late 1980s as more and more sites wanted to participate in the Algebra Project. Moses called upon James Burruss, a Harvard-trained clinical psychologist, to help develop a program to produce individuals who could train Algebra Project teachers. Concerning the importance of expert social facilitation skills, Moses notes:

> From my point of view, that idea should permeate the *whole* project. We have been trying to put it into place from every turn. One place was in the classroom and the teaching, where the idea is that, at a certain point in the movement, the meeting was our main tool. In education, the classroom was our meeting, for students to be empowered. And the issue for the training of teachers was the empowerment for teachers to become trainers, and to move into higher levels in their profession, not necessarily even within the project. The same process gave rise to the Young People's Project. The Young People's Project is the formalization of this process as it became encapsulated among the young students and graduates of Algebra Project classrooms, and has been a success so far. (Moses, 2006b)

Burruss began by observing Moses working with teachers, and added those observations into his body of research on the competencies of people in the "helping professions." The result was a scheme including three major competencies and scales on which individuals could be rated from observations of their practice. The competences were called Cultural Sensitivity, Accurate Empathy, and Cognitive Flexibility. They are described at length in the training manual. For example, Cultural Sensitivity, which could be assessed by trained observers on a 10 point scale, was described as follows in the Overview:

> Cultural Sensitivity is the ability to appreciate and respect the norms of another person or culture even though you do not agree with them. This competency is especially necessary in the teaching and helping professions because the very nature of your task is to challenge conventional ways of

thinking and behaving. Effective teachers challenge a person to change their behavior or to explore new ways of looking at their world. They are effective at doing this because they continue to respect the value of the current norms for that person. (10-point scale for behavioral assessment)

Etiology: Where does it come from?

Cultural Sensitivity seems to develop from a combination of (1) exposure to people of different cultures and (2) social education that encourages you to respect and appreciate the basis for those differences. This is particularly true when the individual is going through a stage of establishing their own identity. This tends to begin around ages 3 to 5, but is repeated at various levels of intensity throughout our adult lives.

Obstacles: One of the biggest obstacles to cultural sensitivity is social education that places a positive or negative value on differences between people. Such instruction early in life leaves us inclined to be evaluative of differences rather than appreciating them.

Development Implications: Cultural sensitivity can be developed be exposure to others in a non-evaluative environment. Candid discussion of your mutual perceptions can help to develop greater appreciation for the value of differences. (Algebra Project, 1994)

To become an Algebra Project teacher trainer, the candidate was observed and assessed while doing training. With additional experience and if they passed further observational assessments, a candidate could advance to become "associate" or "full" trainer. This process can be seen as a kind of apprenticeship which provides very specific feedback for improvement. By 2000, more than 50 Algebra Project "trainers" were produced in this program. While serving or after serving in the Algebra Project, many went on to earn PhDs and entered into high levels of professional responsibility outside of the project.

In the late 1990s, with support from the Open Society Institute, this model was expanded based on another round of empirical work by Burruss and researchers at McBer Inc./Hay Group in Boston, Massachusetts. As a result, in 2000, the original three competencies were elaborated into a larger set, organized into four major categories (the Algebra Project Model of Excellence for Training and Teaching): How I See Myself and Others (3 competencies): Creating the "We" (3 competencies); Helping Others (3 competencies); and Communicating the Math (3 competencies).

Reflections

The Algebra Project's version of "culturally responsive mathematics education" uses manifestations of culture that are both broad and narrow. Some are perhaps based in experiences that are universally part of human cultural experience, and some are clearly specific to local cultural identities. The project attends to the experiences and notions of students and teachers where they begin, which is always cultural. Some materials refer to specific cultural artifacts, such as the Making Do lesson on equivalence, or the African Drums lesson on ratios; but others draw on experiential elements that may be more universal in our human experience.

On the one hand, the positive references to artifacts related to a particular culture denotes to teachers, students and the community a valuing of the culture that, in the case of a group with decades or centuries of a policy of assimilation or eradication, could be a critically important affirmation. Second, using experiences that are culturally familiar to students could benefit them by providing a stronger conceptual foundation from which to build the mathematics in the curriculum. These two resemble Brenner's levels (see Barta & Brenner, chapter 4, this volume).

The Algebra Project aims to improve mathematics education for those who are currently performing in the lowest quartile nationally. This group includes many African-American and Latino/a students, as well as Native-Americans and White students from various backgrounds who have difficulty learning mathematics. It has taken hold in sites with various demographics, including the original Cambridge site in which African Americans were a small minority, sites in the South which are almost entirely African American, sites in other states that include large percentages of Latino/a students (Chicago; Yuma, AZ), and sites that include a diverse array of ethnicities (San Francisco). While education has a particular urgency as the path to freedom for African Americans who were systemically denied education for so long, it is today still the primary vehicle by which all people in the United States seek economic opportunity and freedom from poverty.

References

Algebra Project. (1994, September 11). *Training of trainers institute manual.* Cambridge, MA: Author. Unpublished document.

Algebra Project. (2008a, Summer). *Algebra Project high school curriculum : Road coloring.* Field test version). Cambridge, MA: Author. (Original work published 2007)

Algebra Project. (2008b, Summer). *Algebra Project high school curriculum: Trip line.* Field test version). Cambridge, MA: Author.

Brancaccio, D. (Producer). (2007, July 15). *Robert Moses and the Algebra Project.* New York: Public Broadcasting System.

Budzban, G. The Road Coloring Problem, the Algebra Project, and the writing of K-12 curricula based on "mathematically rich experiences." Unpublished paper.

Campbell, P. B., Jolly, E., Hoey, L., & Perlman, L. K. (2002). *Upping the numbers: Using research-based decision-making to increase diversity in the quantitative disciplines.* (Report commissioned by the GE Foundation). Newton, MA: Education Development Center.

Cavanagh, S. (2006, June 14). Students double-dosing on reading and math. *Education Week, 25*(20), 1, 12–13.

Davis, F. E., & West, M. M. (2000). *The impact of the Algebra Project on mathematics achievement.* Cambridge, MA: Program Evaluation & Research Group, Lesley University.

Davis, F. E., West, M. M., Greeno, J. G., Gresalfi, M., & Martin, T. (2007). Transactions of mathematical knowledge in the Algebra Project. In N. S. Nasir & P. Cobb (Eds.), *Improving access to mathematics: Diversity and equity in the classroom* (pp. 69–88). New York: Teachers College Press.

Delpit, L. (2002). No kinda sense. In L. Delpit & J. K. Dowdy (Eds.), *The skin that we speak* (pp. 31–48). New York: New Press.

Education Week. (2006, June 14).

Finding Our Folk. (2006, Jan. 14–Feb. 5). http://www.findingourfolk.org/index.php?s=14.

Gay, G. (2000). *Culturally responsive teaching: Theory, research, and practice*. New York: Teachers College Press.

Hilliard, A. (2003). No mystery: Closing the achievement gap between Africans and excellence. In T. Perry & C. Steele & A. Hilliard (Eds.), *Young, gifted and Black: Promoting high achievement among African-American students* (pp. 131–165). Boston: Beacon Press.

Ladson-Billings, G. (1994). *The dreamkeepers: Successful teachers of African American children*. San Francisco: Jossey-Bass.

Ladson-Billings, G. (2002). But that's just good teaching: The case for culturally relevant pedagogy. In S. J. Denbo & L. M. Beaulieu (Eds.), *Improving schools for African American students* (pp. 95–123). Springfield, IL: Thomas.

Lee, C. D. (2001). Is October Brown Chinese? A cultural modeling activity system for underachieving students. *American Educational Research Journal, 38*(1), 97–142.

Lee, C., Spencer, M. B., & Harpalani, V. (2003). "Every shut eye ain't sleep": Studying how people live culturally. *Educational Researcher, 32*(5), 6–13.

Lipka, J. & Adams, E. (2004). *Culturally based math education as a way to improve Alaska Native students' math performance*. The Appalachian Collaborative Center for Learning, Assessment and Instruction in Mathematics. Retrieved November 5, 2008, from http://www.acclaim-math.org/

Moses, R. P. (2006a, May 7). *We, the People*. Keynote address to the Mathematical Sciences Research Institute Conference, Raising the Floor: Progress and Setbacks in the Struggle for Quality Mathematics Education for All, Berkeley, CA.

Moses, R. P. (2006b, June 27). Phone interview by M. M. West and F. E. Davis.

Moses, R. P., & Cobb, C. E. (2001). *Radical equations: Math literacy and civil rights*. Boston, MA: Beacon Press.

Murrell, P. C. (2002). *African-centered pedagogy*. Albany, NY: SUNY.

National Science Board. (2004). *Science and engineering indicators, 2004*. Arlington, VA: Author.

Perry, T. (2003). Up from the parched earth: Toward a theory of African-American achievement. In T. Perry & C. Steele & A. Hilliard (Eds.), *Young, gifted and Black: Promoting high achievement among African-American students* (pp.1–108) . Boston: Beacon Press.

Quine, W. V. O. (1981). *Theories and things*. Cambridge, MA: Harvard University Press.

Rogoff, B., & Angelillo, C. (2002). Investigating the coordinated functioning of multifaceted cultural practices in human development. *Human Development, 45*, 211–225.

Tate, W. (2002). African American children and Algebra for all. In S. J. Denbo & L. M. Beaulieu (Eds.), *Improving schools for African American students* (pp. 147–157). Springfield, IL: Thomas.

West, M. M., & Davis, F. E. (2005). *Research related to the Algebra project's intervention to improve student learning in mathematics* (Report to State of Virginia Department of Education). Cambridge, MA: Program Evaluation & Research Group.

West, M. M., Conner, S., McGee, T., & Bland, C. (1995). *Changing middle school teaching: The development of Algebra Project teachers in the Mississippi Delta*. Paper presented at the American Educational Research Association, San Francisco, CA.

11
A Two-Way Process for Developing Effective Culturally Based Math
Examples from Math in a Cultural Context

JERRY LIPKA, EVELYN YANEZ, DORA ANDREW-IHRKE, AND SHEHENAZ ADAM

Math in a Cultural Context (MCC) is an unqualified success on any number of criteria. It distinguishes itself from many other projects in the field of culturally based mathematics, ethnomathematics, or reform-oriented math. These are bold statements. However, this chapter provides a description of this long-term project's processes and products that substantiate this claim.

Adam, Alangui, and Barton (2003) have identified five different ways of conceptualizing ethnomathematics curriculum:

- Mathematics as meaningful, affecting the way learners think about math;
- Mathematics content such as decorative patterns found throughout different cultures;
- Mathematics as a stage in the progression of mathematical thinking—from the child's or cultural perspective to global mathematics;
- Classrooms are situated within a cultural context;
- An integration of mathematical concepts and practices from the target culture to formal mathematics.

Adam et al. suggest that it is an empirical question to determine how ethnomathematics impacts students' math learning. Since Meriam's report (1928) to the federal government to include indigenous culture in schooling to Demmert and Towner's (2003) review of thousands of studies on culturally based curriculum and pedagogy—they stated there is little to no empirical evidence that culturally based curriculum or ethnomathematics impacts student learning. Naively, we believed like so many in the commonsense proposition that using local knowledge, local ways of relating and communicating in a familiar context would result in improved academic performance. Yet, despite the face validity, culturally based curriculum and pedagogy makes sense, the lack of empirical studies with supporting evidences continues to make the efficacy of culturally based curriculum and pedagogy an open question. MCC distinguishes itself from other ethnomathematical and culturally based approaches by bringing both qualitative and quantitative evidence to the debate on the potential efficacy of culturally based curriculum and pedagogy.

In today's climate of high stakes testing, evidenced-based results have become the currency by which educational programs are judged. These issues are becoming increasingly more critical as No Child Left Behind (NCLB; 2002) and school districts not making adequate yearly progress (AYP) undermine efforts at reform-oriented math education, in particular culturally based and ethnomathematics programs can no longer rest on a priori commonsense "data" to get these programs into schools under the present climate. Because schools districts and schools not making AYP are under direct pressure for their students to "pass" standardized test benchmarks, making it more expedient for these districts to "choose" programs that can deliver short-term "gains" at the expense of local knowledge, local culture, and local control. NCLB pressures school districts to meet "standards" at the potential cost of their students' cultural identity, their ancestral language, and culture. At the time of this writing, one school district that most of the authors have long-term ties with is under pressure to end its Yup'ik immersion program because it is seen as increasingly marginal and directly in the way of students' making adequate yearly progress (Rebecca Adams, personal communication, 2008).

These ongoing and increasing pressures place a heavier responsibility on academic researchers to make the case to policy makers, school district decision makers, and the local communities that culturally based curriculum[1] can improve the academic performance of American Indian/Alaskan Native (AI/AN) as well as other indigenous and minority students' academic performance as well as support local knowledge, values, and ways.

MCC has taken on this challenge directly—to show that a culturally based or ethnomathematics curriculum can improve students' mathematical understanding through rigorous controlled experiments while also conducting qualitative and more ethnographic case studies. In this way, MCC increases the possibilities that culturally based and ethnomathematical programs can meet the requirements of school districts. Further, this rather conservative approach is adaptive to meet current political exigencies and the long- standing challenge urged by Merriam almost a century ago to include local knowledge in the processes and products of schooling. The inclusion of Yup'ik elders' knowledge is a direct response to colonial and neocolonial policies of excluding indigenous peoples' knowledge in schooling. "Bringing local knowledge into AI/AN education requires reversing historic power relations that continue to separate school knowledge from community knowledge" (Lipka, 1994, p. 2). Also, as we show, lessons from Yup'ik elders permeate MCC's curriculum from math content to pedagogical strategies and these lessons have been applied effectively to teachers through our professional development component; it is interesting to note that all students from a wide array of backgrounds have benefited from MCC curriculum.

MCC also distinguishes itself from many other efforts in culturally based curriculum and pedagogy and ethnomathematics because of the nature of its long-term collaboration between Yup'ik Eskimo elders and Yup'ik teachers, mathematicians and math educators, educators, and Alaskan school districts. This 20-year-old project at its core represents an unlikely cast of characters (from Yup'ik elders to mathematicians) involved in an enterprise of working together to understand the mathematics of everyday activity and language and apply it to schooling. Some approaches to ethnomathematics have been about identifying "math" through an indigenous or African groups artifacts (see Ascher, 1991; Zaslavsky, 1973) while MCC's approach is to work with indigenous elders and teachers for the purpose of improving the math performance of their children and other Alaskan children's math performance. We work with an existing vibrant and evolving cultural group not for the purpose of identifying "exotica" (Powell & Frankenstein, 1997) but to use Yup'ik cultural knowledge and integrate it with Western, particularly, reform-oriented mathematics for the dual purposes of improving students' math performance and including AN cultural knowledge in the products and processes of schooling.

Further, Yup'ik cultural knowledge was not limited to "mathematical content" but also included contextual knowledge to make the setting of the "math" more familiar, and to pedagogical knowledge which includes communication patterns and social relations that at least resemble ways of relating and valuing that occur in Yup'ik communities outside of the classroom (Lipka, with Mohatt & the *Ciulistet* group, 1998). Thus, the project became a living and evolving process of working with elders to understand their knowledge and to find ways of bringing that knowledge into the heart of schooling. Beyond the long-term collaborative relationship with MCC and its ramifications for academics doing research within indigenous communities, we were determined to find out if this supplemental math curriculum for elementary school students, the project's major goal, was effective. Effectiveness, of course, is not limited to experimental designs and statistical significance. However, we decided to find out if MCC's math curriculum met Gregory Bateson's notion of a difference that makes a difference (Bateson, 1972).

This chapter provides a broad view of MCC's processes (ways of working with Yup'ik elders), translating that knowledge into school math, and the impacts that MCC has had on students' mathematical performance. More specifically, the chapter begins with a summary of MCC's findings from its quantitative and qualitative studies. Next, we describe MCC's local collaborative process of working with elders' local knowledge and the mathematics involved in that knowledge. We conclude the chapter with the next steps that MCC needs to take to more systematically impacts schools in Alaska.

Math in a Cultural Context's Key Studies: Quantitative Findings

At the time of Demmert and Towner's (2003) study there were only a handful of culturally based studies that met their criteria of rigorous design and statistically significant results. From 2001 to 2005 MCC has conducted more than 15 quasi-experimental and experimental trials on seven different MCC modules, testing more than 3,000 children and more than 200 teachers, in, at least 10 different Alaskan school districts, both urban and rural. The results consistently and repeatedly show that MCC's curriculum and professional development makes a statistically significant difference when compared to comparable control group students using their district's adopted math curriculum. See Table 11.1 below for summary statistics.[2]

Because of the strong evidence presented in Table 11.1, the U. S. Department of Education's Institute of Educational Science encouraged MCC to conduct a rigorous experimental design on two of MCC's second grade modules. Therefore, we established a rigorous experimental design, randomly assigning schools (teachers and students assigned accordingly to either the treatment [MCC] or the control condition [the standard curriculum in place]). The purpose of this study was quite simply to test the efficacy of two MCC modules and more specifically with rural and urban students (see Kisker, Lipka, Adams, and Rickard, under review). Table 11.2 below outlines the basic demographics of the random assignment.

This study took place in rural communities that include distinct cultural groups—(Athabaskan, Inupiaq, Tlingit, and Yup'ik) —and in two urban communities (Anchorage and Juneau) with mixed ethnicities. Figure 11.1[3] shows Alaska's unique and diverse cultural groups and Alaska's immense geographical regions.

The two MCC modules studies in the randomized control study were "Picking Berries: Connections Between Data Collection," "Graphing, and Measuring and Going to Egg Island: Adventures in Grouping and Place Values." Each of these modules had previously been studied on four separate occasions (see Table 11.2). Schools were randomly assigned to either treatment or control conditions. If schools had multiple teachers at the second grade, all teachers were assigned to the same condition; this is what accounts for the different number of teachers and students in the treatment and control conditions in this study. In summary, the following tables show that these MCC modules outperformed the control group, the condition as is, by statistically significant margins and with moderate to high effect sizes. Table 11.3 below summarizes the study.

Table 11.1 Summary Statistics[1]

Title of Curricula and Trial Date	Treatment			Control			Statistic		
	N	M	SD	N	M	SD	D	t, F	Effect Size
Fish Racks Spring 2001	160	13.40	15.79	98	2.37	15.44	11.03	t= 5.522*	0.715
Egg Island Spring 2002	128	19.66	17.02	87	13.95	16.37	5.71	t= 2.471**	0.349
Fish Racks Spring 2002	141	14.70	17.49	142	17.18	18.95	−2.48	t=-1.146***	
Egg Island Fall 2002	203	20.69	18.30	139	12.12	17.99	8.57	t= 4.298*	0.477
Fish Racks Fall 2002	204	15.63	16.11	118	6.28	16.08	9.35	t= 5.023*	0.581
Berry Picking Spring 2003	89	21.80	21.38	32	4.27	14.45	17.53	t= 5.129*	1.213
Berry Picking Fall 2003	93	69.35	21.31	152	57.38	18.36	11.98	F=20.006*	0.652
Drying Salmon Fall 2003	84	40.49	15.11	107	32.75	15.97	7.73	F=11.949*	0.484
Parka Patterns Spring 2004	122	53.33	13.11	80	46.78	13.23	6.55	F=11.868*	0.495
Fish Racks Spring 2004	99	55.10	15.99	47	40.69	16.60	14.42	F=24.588*	0.868
Egg Island Fall 2004	88	56.51	16.00	94	50.04	16.05	6.47	F= 7.313**	0.403
Star Navigation Fall 2004	131	68.49	17.91	70	46.05	22.89	22.44	F=51.085*	0.980
Berry Picking Spring 2005	45	44.92	12.15	85	43.31	12.06	1.61	F=27.772*	0.134
Smokehouse Spring 2005	70	47.74	15.92	101	34.77	15.94	12.98	F=25.676*	0.814

1. Table 1 lists the summary statistics for 14 trials conducted between the spring of 2001 and the spring of 2005. In each case the sample size, average, and standard deviation is shown for both the treatment and control groups. Further results presented include the difference in group means (D), the statistic of interest (t or F), and the effect size calculated by dividing D by the standard deviation of the control group. Prior to fall 2003 to test differences among means of the groups we used the gain score (pre-test subtracted from post-test) and performed analyses using a standard t-test at the student level. Starting in fall 2003 we used a modified post-test score adjusted using pre-test covariates and carried out analyses of covariance at the student level using fixed factors of urban and rural. In all but one trial, we found statistically significant results with a variety of effect sizes, most at a medium to strong level.

Notes: M and SD are calculated for the gain score (post-pre) as represented by *italics (scores above the dotted line).* Otherwise, M and SD are calculated for the post-test scores adjusted by pre-test covariate. D is the difference in means ($M_{Treatment} - M_{Control}$)

*$p \leq 0.001$, **$p \leq 0.01$.

***Rural treatment vs. rural control was statistically significant with p-value of 0.0008 (*means: 19% vs. 8% gain*)

Table 11.2 Demographic Data of Experimental Design

	Schools	Teachers	Students
Treatment	25	27	236
Control	25	40	467

Table 11.3 clearly shows that MCC modules outperformed the control group by statistically significant margins for both modules and on the retention items. This trend held for both urban and rural settings, although rural students did slightly better than their urban counterparts. Further, not shown in these tables, the students of novice treatment teachers' students outperformed those of novice control group teachers' students and experienced treatment teachers' students outperformed control group students.

In this series of 17 studies each one showed that rural treatment students outperformed their rural counterparts; and in all but one study urban treatment students outperformed their urban control group students. This result adds considerable evidence to the potential efficacy of culturally based and ethnomathematics curriculum and pedagogy. In no small part, the success of this program is based on Yup'ik elders' knowledge, both content and pedagogical. The following sections of this chapter outline how we worked with the elders to identify and bring out the math content that was embedded in their everyday activities, and their way of teaching and communicating, which leads to the pedagogy of MCC.

The Development of Math in a Cultural Context

This collaborative effort arose from the dedication of a core group of Yup'ik elders and teachers at the 2003 Summer Math Institute in Fairbanks, Alaska led by George Moses, who recognized the threats to their cultural and linguistic

Table 11.3 Student Level Outcomes

Outcome	Student-Level Unadjusted Means: Control Group	Student-Level Unadjusted Means: Treatment Group	Impact Adjusted for Clustering (From HLM)	Effect Size
Gain in Fall Test Scores	M 9.62% pts SD 12.96 N 461	M 21.92% pts SD 13.02 N 233	10.35% pts (p=.000)	0.82 ***
Gain in Spring Test Scores	M 6.80% pts SD 19.52 N 467	M 15.54% pts SD 20.44 N 236	9.74% pts (p=.001)	0.39 ***
Gain in Retention Item Scores	M 18.76% pts SD 22.57 N 454	M 27.76% pts SD 24.42 N 223	7.77% pts (p=.014)	0.53 *

***$p \leq 0.001$, **$p \leq 0.01$, *$p<0.05$.

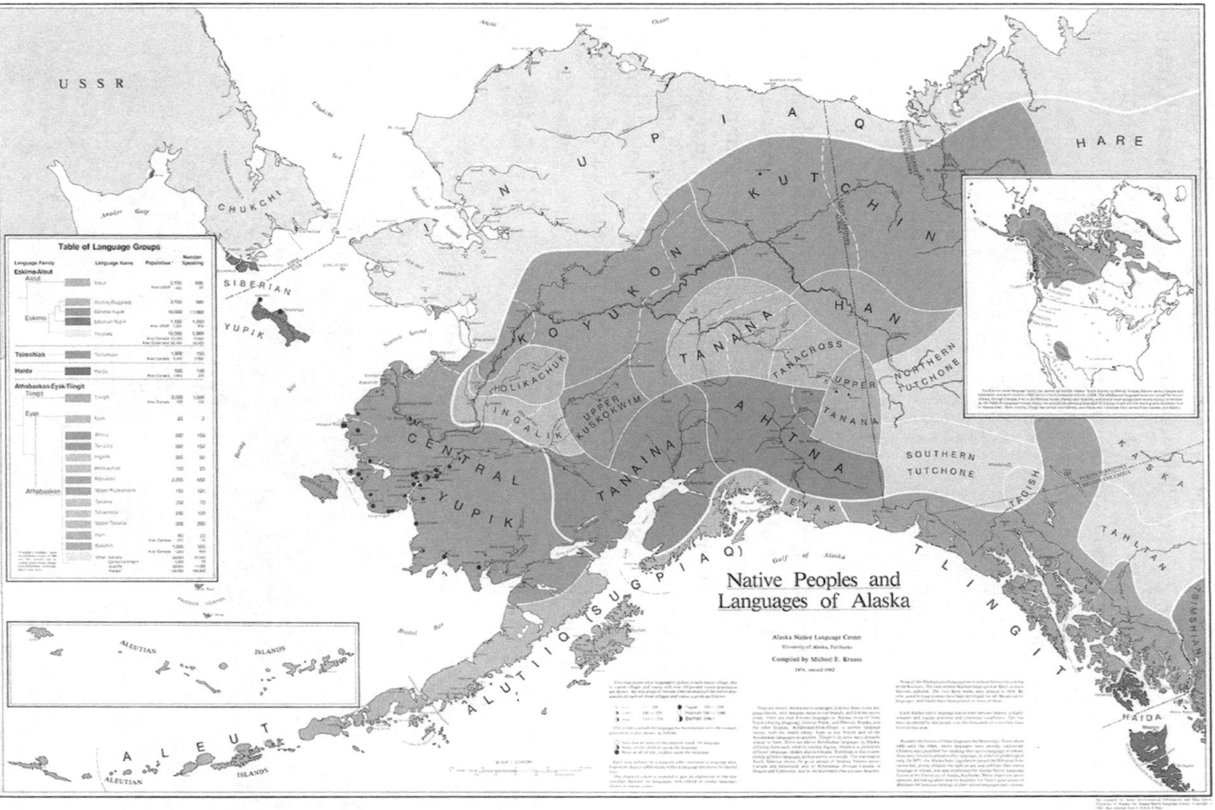

Figure 11.1 Alaska's diverse linguistic and cultural regions.

continuity and viewed MCC as a healthy alternative to cultural loss and resulting social ills. Through demonstrations and explanations, this group of elders conveyed cultural knowledge around topics as diverse as how to build a kayak, how to design and sew a border pattern, and how to navigate using the stars. From approximately 1995 to 2002, we held two to three meetings a year with Yup'ik teachers and elders; as our grants changed we have held fewer meetings with elders from 2003 to the present. We joined the elders and teachers in building fish racks and making model smokehouses. We also participated in star navigation and collected traditional stories and games. Over the years we worked together to develop an integrated supplemental math curriculum.

Framing the Collaborative Work

In the summer of 2002 we held our first Summer Math Institute as a prelude to teachers implementing MCC modules. At that time, we emphasized a module that connected summer salmon harvesting with mathematics embedded in building fish rack. Henry Alakayak, an elder from Manokotak and a leader in this project, initiated an activity that frames this work. Henry used the metaphor of a fish rack as a way in which insiders and outsiders were not in opposition but were mutually interdependent. He poetically explained the metaphor. The four individuals shown in Figure 11.2 below each stood as the "posts" that will hold the fish rack firm and steady; these posts form the foundation to support the rest of the structure.

Figure 11.2 Working together.

He deliberately chose four different individuals to represent the four corners. He placed Lipka first (project PI) because of his leadership role in the project with other academics and as a bridge to the Yup'ik teachers and their communities. The first post is the main post with which the other posts are aligned. Next he placed Jonah Lomack, a community member, for the important role of connecting to the community. He placed Peter Wiles, math educator, perpendicular to the community member, thus forming a second dimension. He placed the teacher Mark Biberg last for the pivotal role of bringing these pieces together to complete the whole. He spoke elegantly about the need for the group to be with one mind. When we speak and work with one mind then we can accomplish our goals. Interestingly, Henry Alakayak's remarks resemble those of the eminent scholar Smith (1999) on the need for some indigenous minorities that are small in number and power to find ways to effectively work together with the larger majority that surrounds them (Smith, 1999). Henry understood this.

This philosophical and operational principle guided our work. Working together with "one mind" was also meant to get us to think beyond simplistic dualism, such as insider and outsider. Therefore, we viewed elders' knowledge as knowledge that exists within a cultural and historical context. This knowledge is no less valuable than the privileged knowledge of Western schooling, but it was dismissed and thought of as useless for schooling—useless knowledge—until most recently. As trust deepened, elders slowly began to "reveal what was once hidden." Through this process of revealing, elders taught those of us in the project, and we began to appreciate the mathematics embedded in everyday activities that included: ways of measuring, numerating, estimating, designing, patterning, locating, and navigating (Bishop, 1988), as well as ways of communicating and instructing.

The systematic exclusion of local knowledge has been a hallmark of colonialism. However, to reverse this process we set out to include local knowledge in the processes and products of schooling. We worked together and sought ways in which knowledge in one context (Yup'ik) could be included and thus transform knowledge in another context (schooling) somewhat analogous to Freire's (1972) work in Brazil. Our work has not been anthropological in the sense of "studying elders" or the culture. It is a partnership to find ways to change schooling to include this knowledge (content and processes) for the purpose of making learning more meaningful to students, thereby improving their ability to think, solve problems, and identify with their local culture.

Culturally Based Curriculum

Culturally based curriculum is too often misunderstood as being "exotic" and not necessarily relevant to "the rest of us." Culturally based curriculum is, in fact, a misnomer, since all curricula are culturally based. The key question is: Whose culture is it based on? In AI/AN and in many other indigenous, postcolonial, and minority contexts, curriculum is typically based on the norms, values, and wisdom of the mainstream society and too often skewed toward large-scale publishers who dominate the marketplace—market-based curriculum. Likewise, in small countries, the curriculum is based on a "Western" curriculum from a more technologically developed country that is believed to be more prestigious.

MCC begins at two radically different points from mainstream curriculum: (1) with local knowledge, in this case, Yup'ik Eskimo elders' knowledge and (2) connecting that knowledge to the knowledge of math educators. We view MCC and its highly collaborative framework for developing math curriculum as recontextualizing the knowledge of elders and math educators to fit modern schooling. We do not attempt to teach elders' knowledge; elders are best equipped to teach their knowledge. However, what we try to accomplish is an authentic representation of both local and Western knowledge, bringing them together in a new way, which we call a "third way" (Gutierrez, Baquedano-Lopez, & Tejeda, 1999). This is not necessarily the elders' knowledge nor necessarily typical Western pedagogy. It is an integration of Yup'ik everyday knowledge (which embeds pedagogical and mathematical knowledge) with Western math and forms of pedagogy (particularly reform-oriented problem-solving math). We do this through situating math knowledge in a context familiar to Alaska students yet novel enough and different enough from national math curriculum to most likely increase students' motivation and access to the material. Thus, issues of culture, power, and creativity are weaved together to form a third space—the newly recontextualized content and an environment that surrounds learning that content—without losing sight of the critical importance of improving student math learning.

We believe that the theoretical assumptions underlying this approach make MCC curriculum and pedagogy more effective. The assumptions include that students will gain increased access to the math curriculum because they can identify with the curriculum and pedagogy on multiple levels, from familiar contexts to familiar knowledge, and that they will have multiple ways of engaging with the material. These theoretical assumptions are supported by empirical research (Sternberg, 2006; Sternberg, Lipka, Newman, Wildfeuer, & Grigorenko, 2006; Sternberg, Nokes et al., 1998) which has shown that including local knowledge makes a difference in students' academic achievement. Further, it is assumed that the inclusion of local knowledge, language, and culture may well have a positive effect on students' identity that will be different from the typically reported process of schooling that marginalizes the identity of so many AI/AN students (LaFromboise, Coleman, & Gerton, 1997); or as Garrett (1996) noted, the very act of learning required a student to deny his or her personal, cultural, and linguistic heritage. Thus, MCC has been intentionally designed to create a classroom atmosphere that embraces AN students' identity, thereby increasing motivation and access to learning.

The next part of the chapter begins to deconstruct some of the processes we used in codeveloping MCC. As mentioned before, during almost two decades we have slowly accumulated a body of material relating to how Yup'ik elders navigate by the stars, build and use kayaks, and make fancy parka patterns, among other topics. As we work with the elders and learn how they perform everyday tasks, we also pay attention to the social and cultural norms associated with how they teach and organize learning. Often, elders tell stories as a way of conveying critical lessons. Sometimes we later associate these stories with specific modules, which is the case for the modules discussed in this paper.

The Process of Developing MCC's Curriculum and Professional Development

Here we describe the development of two modules in the MCC series: "Designing Patterns: Exploring Shapes and Area," a third to fifth grade module having to do with the geometry of shapes that emphasizes the rhombus, and "Patterns and Parkas: Investigating Geometric Principles, Shapes, Patterns, and Measurement" (Pendergrast, Lipka, Watt, Gilliland, & Sharp, 2007), a second-grade module about geometric relationships that emphasizes the square. Both modules include the mathematics of how Yup'ik people make patterns and apply them to clothing. Boundary work (education across cultures) requires bridges between elders and schooling. Three of the authors (Yanez, Andrew-Ihrke, and Lipka) have played that role and have worked together for approximately 25 years. During this time we have slowly learned how to work with elders and how to bring outsiders such as mathematicians and math educators and school district personnel into the project.

One way we tapped into the culture of the community and connected it to the development of the "Patterns and Parkas" module was through Evelyn Yanez's reminiscences about her childhood. As a child she would hear stories and then redraw scenes through storyknifing (drawing symbols) and tell about the plot. One of the stories that she heard was about Iluvaktuq, an almost mythical hero who lived during the 1800s. Today descents of Iluvaktuq wear symbols on their parkas that identify them as related to him. At a recent meeting with Annie Blue, a well respected storyteller from Togiak, she told us the Iluvaktuq story and it became part of the "Patterns and Parka" module and thus connected both to the math of the module making patterns and to literacy (see Figure 11.3 below).

Due to the symbolism of parkas and because of the elaborate parka border patterns, we connected the story of Iluvaktuq to these two modules, "Designing Patterns" (Watt, Lipka et al., 2006) and "Patterns and Parkas" (Pendergrast et al., 2007) These inclusions of traditional, contextual, and embedded math stories is an approach that MCC is developing to connect the teaching of math through story, vocabulary development, and the importance of key words.

Making Patterns—Developing the Math of the Module

Lipka was aware of the connection between parkas, patterns, and traditional stories and their ways of making pattern pieces and was excited by the prospect

Figure 11.3 Parka showing parka designs.

of working with elders from St. Mary's, Alaska. A few years ago, while conducting a school in-service, he invited elders from the community to share their ways of making patterns. Years before that, while working with the late Mary George of Akiachak, Alaska, and Marie Napoka of Tuluksak, common Yup'ik border patterns used to adorn women's clothing and other objects were identified.

Another Yup'ik elder, Winifred Beans of St. Mary's, Alaska, is known as a designer of fancy border patterns. One of the pattern pieces that she cuts out from a rectangular piece of material is rhombus-shaped. It was obvious that when she made a rhombus from a rectangle, there was considerable mathematics involved. She makes her pattern pieces [*tumaqcat*], by carefully folding the rectangle into quarters (a smaller rectangle), then just as carefully cuts the quarter rectangle from one corner to another, making sure to cut across the center of the original rectangle so that it remains intact. When the result is unfolded, Mrs. Beans has made a rhombus and four congruent right triangles (Figure 11.5).

She taught us her way of making a rhombus by having us observe her and then try to make these pieces when we were ready. Working with Mary Beans (Winifred Beans daughter who also resides in St. Mary's), helped to clarify Winifred Beans's method. On the plane ride home, Lipka outlined some of the mathematics involved in what Mrs. Beans demonstrated. Using Winifred Beans's knowledge, he visualized what a module about making rhombus pieces from a rectangle could consist of:

- Properties of a rhombus—it is a quadrilateral with four equal sides and opposite angles equal. Like a rectangle, a rhombus has two lines of symmetry.

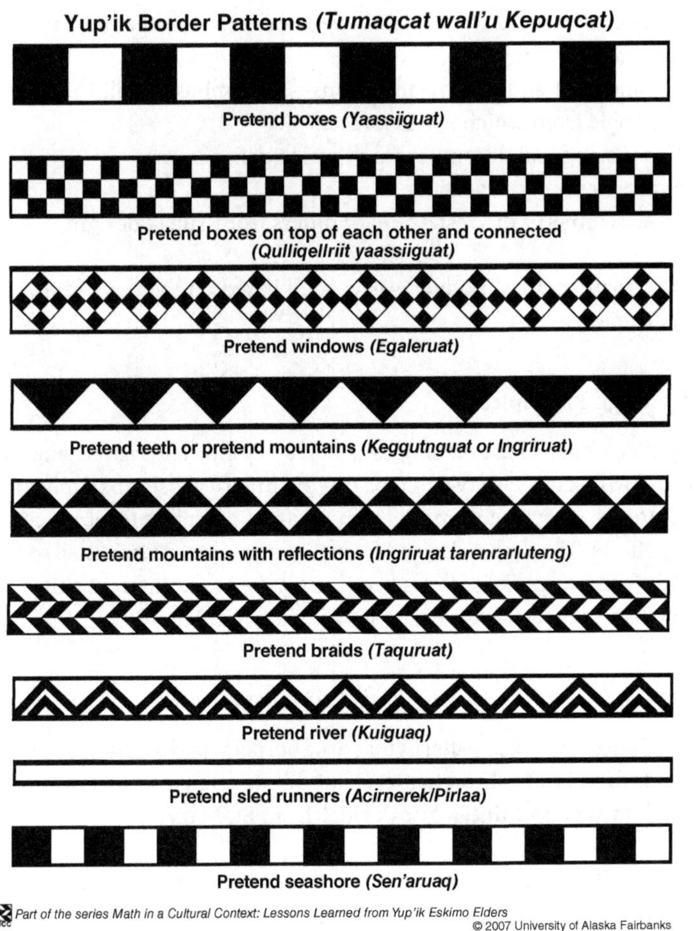

Figure 11.4 Yup'ik border patterns.

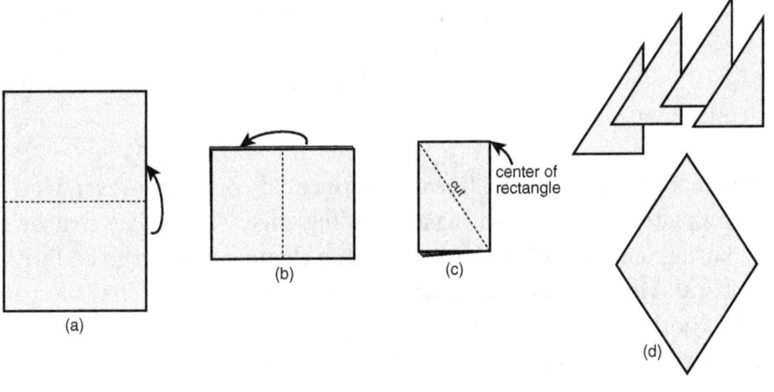

Figure 11.5 Winifred Beans' method of making a rhombus from a rectangle.

Unlike a rectangle, these go from vertex to vertex, rather than through the midpoints of the sides.
- Geometrical and area relationships—a rhombus is half the area of the rectangle from which it was formed
- Composing and decomposing geometric shapes
- Symmetry and congruence
- How symmetry in Western math differs from Yup'ik design[4]

Thus, a mathematics module was written based on the way Winifred made her pattern pieces.

Yup'ik Design Principles

Yup'ik pattern-makers use rectangles, squares, rhombi, and right triangles in different sizes to create a variety of interesting symmetrical patterns similar to linear frieze patterns. They use shapes of two contrasting colors to produce visually pleasing effects. The shapes derived from rectangles or squares fitted together in several different ways. This allows people to make many different patterns using the same basic shapes. A few examples are shown in Figure 11.6.

Symmetrical Linear Patterns and Basic Repeating Elements

Yup'ik designers use linear patterns for parka borders (parka bottoms and sleeves), headbands, and boots. These patterns all follow a few rules (these rules were explained by Theresa Mike, a Yup'ik elder from St. Mary's):

- Start with a basic combination of shapes in contrasting colors. This becomes the basic repeating element; these shape combinations are usually arranged so that shapes line up edge to edge.
- The basic repeating elements are repeated over and over in a linear sequence to complete the pattern.
- Each pattern has a "balance point" at the center, with an equal number of design elements on either side of the balance point.
- Usually (but not always) the balance point is a line of symmetry for the entire shape.[5]

Mathematically, a repeating linear pattern could continue forever. However, a practical pattern has a beginning and ending edge. These edges may be constructed using only part of the basic repeating element in order to end with the edge vertical. Headband patterns usually end in such a way that the pattern would be continuous if one edge could wrap around to meet the other. Making linear patterns is part of the *Designing Patterns* module, and the practical problems of how you make your starting piece and ending piece match up become a component of this module.

Figure 11.6 Repeating linear patterns.

To more fully understand how Yup'ik linear patterns and balance differ from Western concepts of symmetry, we worked with Yanez and Andrew-Irhke. Yanez stated:

> We don't make patterns like this [Figure 11.7 below] because they do not have meaning. Patterns are named after things that they resemble. For example, the pretend mountains resemble mountains, and the braid resembles braids, etc. Traditionally we didn't use the trapezoid shape. Also,

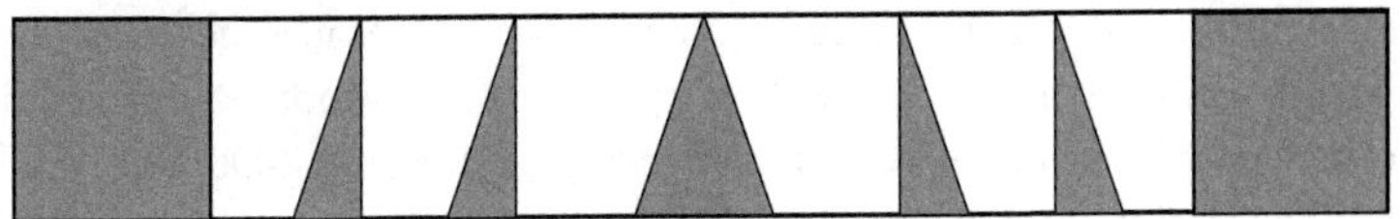

Figure 11.7 A linear pattern that lacks balance and meaning.

this pattern lacks balance between white and dark. The small dark shapes are out of balance with the white larger trapezoids. Aesthetically, this is not pleasing to a Yup'ik eye.

Although the purpose for creating parka pattern pieces has to do with aesthetics, culture, and ceremonies, the above described processes embed a substantial amount of mathematics. The math educators and educators associated with the project then connect this knowledge to school based math. While accomplishing this, the key components of MCC's pedagogy such as expert–apprentice modeling, joint productive activity, and cognitive apprenticeship were embedded into the activities of the module. Thus, students' math learning is embedded in activities that relate to the community and incorporate, in part, elders' knowledge and ways of doing and communicating. Further, as noted earlier, we further connect elders' knowledge of traditional stories to the teaching of math. This process builds on local knowledge and engages students in challenging mathematics.

Summer Math Institute and Professional Development—A Two-Way Process

Each summer for the last four years, we have conducted a Summer Math Institute (SMI) in Fairbanks, Alaska, to provide mathematical, pedagogical, and cultural support for teachers who use MCC modules. Two summers ago, we choose to organize the SMI around the *Designing Patterns* module; the module at that time was complete and we were using it to prepare the teachers to use it. To strengthen the cultural component of SMI, we invited the cultural experts Theresa Mike, Elias Polty, and Lilly Afcan from St. Mary's to join Yanez, Ihrke, and Sharp. In planning meetings led by Melissa Kagle, an MCC curriculum writer and faculty member, we decided that the major project of the SMI would be making a headband. The Yup'ik consultants, particularly those from St. Mary's, suggested interweaving traditional Yup'ik song and dance and ending the SMI with a ceremony resembling traditional ceremonies, where each teacher would wear their headdress, dance, sing, and celebrate the SMI. All headdresses would be made following the design principles mentioned earlier. Thus, we began to integrate and recontextualize the module based on these ideas. At the meeting, we gained more insights into some of the design principles that Theresa Mike explained and demonstrated to us.

Further, Ihrke extended the math module as she showed us how she make additional pattern pieces—a circle from a square. She talked about the symbolic importance of circles in Yup'ik cosmology and the circle motif can be included in the headdress. This is explained below. However, because of this acquired knowledge major revisions in the development of the module were required. With these revisions, during the fall and spring of 2005 and 2006, SMI teachers piloted the "Designing Patterns module."

Figure 11.8 Dora Andrew-Ihrke wearing a traditional Bristol Bay headdress.

Deepening the Cultural and Mathematical Connections of the Module

Yanez and Ihrke, aware of regional cultural and linguistic differences between St. Mary's and Bristol Bay (where they grew up), decided that the module needed to include a traditional headdress from the Bristol Bay region as well. Irkhe had traveled to Germany a number of years ago and had the opportunity to visit the Museum Fur Volkerkunde in Berlin to see Yup'ik artifacts in their collection. Among them was a traditional Yup'ik headdress from the Bristol Bay region of Alaska. These cultural artifacts are no longer common. Above in Figure 11.8 is a picture of Ihrke wearing a headdress she recently made.

Figure 11.9 Importance of circular strips in a headdress.

Ihrke's describes how to make a beaded headdress (*nacarrluk* in Yup'ik); see Figures 11.8 and 11.9 above. She learned this from her mother and other Yup'ik elders. Irhke began by making a square from uneven materials without instrumentation such as rulers, and the square would be turned into a circle. This circle represents the earth (*nuna*), which is connected by strips from the circle to the universe. These strips represent rings that encompass the stars, constellations, and planets of the universe.

She begins the process of making a square by measuring the space between the first and the second knuckle, using the index finger as a way to measure; measure two of these for the length and two for the width to create a square. Cut out a square that is this size (see Figure 11.10 below).

Next, she establishes a process of "proofing" that she has a square by locating the center point of the square by folding it into quarters to form smaller squares.

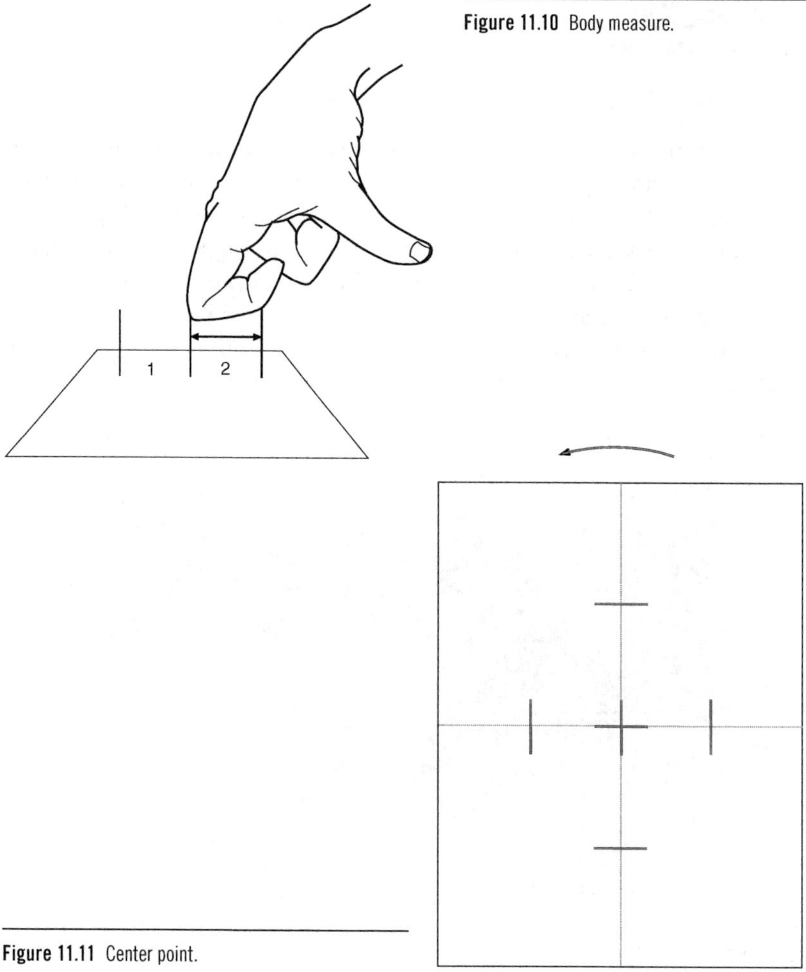

Figure 11.10 Body measure.

Figure 11.11 Center point.

She used a process of folding half one way and then another way to ensure that the sides matched and she folded along one diagonal and then along the diagonal again to ensure that each half-square matched in each direction. Interestingly, Dr. Susan Addington, who worked with us during a December 2007 meeting, further elaborated the math involved in what Ihrke was demonstrating. She commented on Irhke's approach to creating and checking and proofing to see if you had a square. Addington stated that if this was a Euclidean proof it would require "something is a square when all four sides are equal and all angles are right angles." She said, "Dora checked differently. Dora is using transformational geometry…it is about what you do to the shape that stays the same… that is a reflection…the two sides of the mirror—the image and the original match…. Dora's folding along the diagonal…is another reflection. This goes beyond the Euclidean proof by checking in all possible ways that each reflection matches" (Addington, personal communication, December 7, 2007).

Using a similar process, Ihrke then took this square and began to make it into a circle. She stated, cutting a strip of paper the length of this smaller square as Dr. Addington described, "Dora creates a unit of measure from the North wind [see Figure 11.12 below] to the center." This becomes the template for the radius of the circle.

Fold the square along its diagonals and open it up. Each diagonal represents the four directions of the earth and they also become part of the system of transformational geometry that Ihrke uses along the diagonals and then in between the diagonals as she continues to fold. See Figures 11.12 to 11.14 below. Use the template to mark the distance from the center along each diagonal fold.

Figure 11.12 Dora Ihrke creating an instrument to turn a square into a circle.

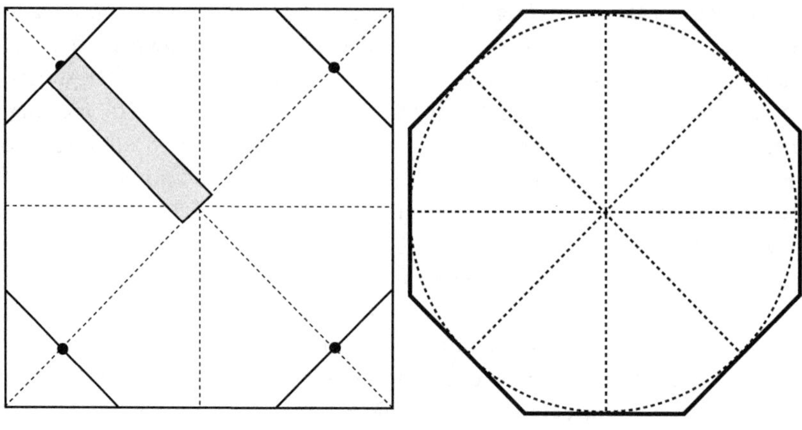

Figure 11.13 Template to make a circle.

Figure 11.14 Octagon.

Draw a straight line at each mark, perpendicular to the fold. Cut along each line to form an octagon (Figure 11.13). Use scissors to round the edges (Figure 11.14).

After Ihrke completed this process Dr. Addington explained that "this method is extremely accurate and complementary to the compass [as a way to make] a circle. You have a regular octagon—8 sides and 8 angles are equal. This is checked through symmetry not by measuring those angles of the octagon or the lengths of the sides…it is done through folding. Dora checked 16 lines of symmetry which is sufficient to ensure that the square is transforming into a circle" (Addington, personal communication, December 7, 2007).

The number of the strips depends on the size of the beads. For example, if you have small beads you might have three strips. And if you have larger beads you might have two strips. The space between the strips is measured by the index and the middle fingers. The bottom strip is measured right over the eyebrow, over the top of the ear around the back of the head. When Elena Pat (the elder Ihrke worked with) measured her headdress with the string, she started the measurement at the center of the forehead, positioned right over the eyebrow and top of the ear. She then proceeded measuring with the string in a right-to-left direction around the head, until the string met again at the center. This formed the bottom strip. The second strip was measured the same way, but three fingers apart from the bottom.

This last addition to the module both increased and deepened the potential mathematical and cultural content.

Putting all the Pieces Together in the Making of a Module

The centerpiece of the *Designing Patterns* module is making a rhombus from a rectangle. We unpacked the mathematics of this process to make the geometric relationship between the rhombus and the rectangle from which it was derived. The elders' use of lines of symmetry, congruence, midpoints, and diagonals lay the foundation for the math of the module. Further, the ways in which elders teach others to make such patterns became a key component of the pedagogy of the module—expert–apprentice modeling, joint productive activity, and cognitive apprenticeship. We realized the connection between literacy and parka patterns when we were told the story of Iluvaktuq and how modern parka patterns include a symbol to show a familiar relationship. Therefore, the module contained both math and literacy. Ihrke deepened both the cultural and mathematical connections by showing us, telling us, and demonstrating how to make a traditional Bristol Bay headdress. This revealed deeper cultural knowledge about Yup'ik cosmology as well as how to make a circle out of a square and the use of transformational geometry that was involved in that process. We included the making of a headdress as a key project in the module, based on the guidance of elders and community members who worked with us in that SMI. In addition, a community group that we worked with in St. Mary's created songs and dances having to do with this module and other stories collected by the project. In honoring MCC, the community of St. Mary's presented songs and dances originally told by Annie Blue. The development of this module as noted from what is described above includes local knowledge and community initiative as they partially designed and influenced the modules' final product. Such two-way processes for developing curriculum and evolving pedagogical forms are quite rare. Although these modules have not been rigorously tested, they follow MCC's curricular and pedagogical principles and from past experiences with other modules in this series, we also expect these modules to perform as well.

Where Do We Go From Here?

Despite the major accomplishments of MCC, as noted throughout this chapter, major challenges remain for this supplemental math curriculum to impact schools in Alaska. Briefly (because this section could be a chapter in its own light), NCLB and schools not making AYP under this federal mandate affects a number of the schools that MCC is working with under its current grants. As alluded to earlier, pressures to meet "standards" and pass AYP have begun to marginalize programs like MCC. Although MCC has met the "gold standard" for evidenced based curriculum, a number of rural school districts have been classified "level 5" under NCLB meaning that they are in need of urgent intervention and thus some of these school districts have come under the Alaska Department of Education's control. Efforts at restructuring require the energy and time of district administrators and teachers. At the present time, MCC is seeking a path so that it can be included in the district's improvement plans. The outcome of this process remains uncertain.

Conclusion

This chapter begins to outline the complex relationship between insiders and outsiders and how we have worked together over many years to create school math that is contextualized in culturally familiar ways. Further, the project works collaboratively with community members, elders, Yup'ik teachers and consultants, and math educators and mathematicians until we are able to create a math module that represents both the standards of the people we work with and state and national math standards. The project has compared treatment students' math knowledge to control groups and these studies consistently show that MCC students outperform students using their regular math curriculum. The approach that we have taken underrepresents the strength of the modules and what students learn because we have not measured differences in math attitudes, cultural knowledge learned, or other affective factors. However, what this chapter emphasizes is the importance of a two-way collaborative process between groups of unlikely partners, the university and communities, resulting in a creative, culturally responsive, and rigorous math curriculum for elementary school students. This partnership has also resulted in closing the perennial academic gap. MCC's processes in developing CBE, in rigorously testing many of the modules in the series, resulting in favorable outcomes for AN students and all other students who use MCC contributes to the slowly evolving literature on the efficacy of CBE. One major implication of MCC is that culturally based curriculum and pedagogy has favorably impacted students across geographical and cultural regions in Alaska.

Thus, MCC's approach does appear to reverse sociohistoric power relations and assimilative processes and replace them with more collaborative and inclusive ways of producing curriculum and pedagogy. Lastly, we hope that our model of CBE clearly shows how issues of power and culture are highly interrelated. Although the site of this work may be exotic to some, what is actually taking place is the bringing together of diverse people and communities for the common purpose of improving schooling for the next generation which is central and critical to many.

Notes

1. By culturally based curriculum we mean curriculum that is, at least in part, developed from the perspective of the indigenous group. All curriculum is culturally based where the key question is: Whose cultural is it based on?
2. Table 1 lists the summary statistics for 14 trials conducted between the spring of 2001 and the spring of 2005. In each case the sample size, average, and standard deviation is shown for both the treatment and control groups. Further results presented include the difference in group means (D), the statistic of interest (t or F), and the effect size calculated by dividing D by the standard deviation of the control group. Prior to fall 2003 to test differences among means of the groups we used the gain score (pre-test subtracted from post-test) and performed analyses using a standard t-test at the student level. Starting in fall 2003 we used a modified post-test score adjusted using pre-test covariates and carried out analyses of covariance at the student

level using fixed factors of urban and rural. In all but one trial, we found statistically significant results with a variety of effect sizes, most at a medium to strong level.

3. Courtesy: Benny Boyd, Alaska Native Language Network, http://www.ankn.uaf.edu/IKS/subsistence/languagemap.html
4. Dan Watt, a consultant to the project, explained this difference after observing Theresa Mike, an elder from St. Mary's, Alaska demonstrate her way of putting pattern pieces together to make a pleasing design. Dan Watt, Evelyn Yanez, Dora Andrew-Ihrke, and Lilly Afcan all worked together to come to this understanding.
5. Dan Watt helped to clarify Theresa Mikes illustrations and discussions.

References

Adam, S., Alangui, W., & Barton, B. (2003). A comment on: Rowlands & Carson "Where would formal, academic mathematics stand in a curriculum informed by ethnomathematics?" A critical review. *Educational Studies in Mathematics, 52*, 327–335.

Ascher, M. (1991). *Ethnomathematics: A multicultural view of mathematical ideas.* Boca Raton, FL: Chapman & Hall/CRC.

Bateson, G. (1972). *Steps to an ecology of mind: Collected essays in anthropology, psychiatry, evolution, and epistemology.* Chicago: University of Chicago Press.

Bishop, A. J. (1988). *Mathematical enculturation: A cultural perspective on mathematics education.* Dordrecht, The Netherlands: Kluwer.

Demmert, W. G., Jr., & Towner, J. C. (2003). *A review of the research literature on the influences of culturally based education on the academic performance of Native American students.* Portland, OR: Northwest Regional Educational Laboratory. Retrieved August 26, 2008, from http://www.nwrel.org/indianed/cbe/

Freire, P. (1972). *Pedagogy of the oppressed.* New York: Herder & Herder.

Garrett, M. (1996). Two people: An American Indian narrative of bicultural identity. *Journal of American Indian Education, 36*(1), 1–21.

Gutierrez, K. D., Baquedano-Lopez, P., & Tejeda. C. (1999). Rethinking diversity: Hybridity and hybrid language practices in the Third space. *Mind, Culture, and Activity: An International Journal, 6*, 286–303.

Kisker, E. E., Lipka, J., Adams, B., & Rickard, A. (under review). The potential of a culturally-based supplemental math curriculum to reduce the math performance gap between Alaska Native and non-native students. *Journal of Research in Math Education.*

LaFromboise, T., Coleman, H., & Gerton, J. (1997). Psychological impact of biculturalism: Evidence and theory. In L. A. Peplau & S. E. Taylor (Eds.), *Sociocultural perspectives in social psychology: Current readings* (pp. 241–276). Upper Saddle River, NJ: Prentice-Hall.

Lipka, J. (1994). Culturally negotiated schooling: Toward a Yup'ik mathematics. *Journal of American Indian Education, 33*(3), 14–30.

Lipka, J., with Mohatt, G. V., & the *Ciulistet* Group. (1998). *Transforming the culture of schools: Yup'ik Eskimo examples.* Mahwah, NJ: Erlbaum.

Meriam, L. (1928). *The problem of Indian administration.* Baltimore: Johns Hopkins Press.

Pendergrast, S., Lipka, J., Watt, D. L., Gilliland, K., & Sharp, N. (2007). *Patterns and parkas: Investigating geometric principles, shapes, patterns, and measurement.* Calgary, Alberta: Detselig Enterprises Ltd.

Powell, A. B., & Frankenstein, M. (Eds.). (1997). *Ethnomathematics: Challenging Eurocentrism in mathematics education.* Albany, NY: SUNY Press.

Smith, L. T. (1999). *Decolonizing methodologies: Research and indigenous peoples.* London: Zed.

Sternberg, R. J. (2006). Recognizing neglected strengths. *Educational Leadership, 64*, 30–35.

Sternberg, R. J., Lipka, J., Newman, T., Wildfeuer, S., & Grigorenko, E. L. (2006). Triarchically-based instruction and assessment of sixth-grade mathematics in a Yup'ik cultural setting in Alaska. *Gifted and Talented International, 21*, 6–19.

Sternberg, R. J., Nokes, K., Geissler, P. W., Prince, R., Okatcha, F., Bundy, D. A., et al. (1998). The relationship between academic and practical intelligence: A case study in Kenya. *Intelligence, 29*, 401–418.

Watt, D. L., Lipka, J., Webster, J. P., Yanez, E., Andrew-Ihrke, D., & Adam, A. S. (2006). *Designing patterns: Exploring shapes and area.* Calgary, Alberta: Detselig.

Zaslavsky, C. (1973). *Africa counts; Number and pattern in African culture.* Boston: Prindle, Weber, & Schmidt.

12
Native-American Analogues to the Cartesian Coordinate System

RON EGLASH

Every society exhibits one or more "design themes"—geometric abstractions that are manifested in myriad concrete forms. Fourfold symmetry is a deep design theme in many Native-American cultures. This essay will describe how fourfold (and related bifold) symmetry is used as an organizing principle for religion, society, and technology in many Native-American cultures. It will explore the ways in which this design theme has emerged through native structures analogous to the Cartesian coordinate system, and describe some software applications that help teachers make use of this ethnomathematics in the classroom.

Avoiding Essentialism

The term *essentialism* is used in cultural anthropology to describe the misleading way that complex social categories like "female" or "Asian" can be reduced to simple stereotypes—the delusion, for example, that it is the essence of women to be intuitive, or that it is the essence of Asian people to be unemotional. Essentialism is misleading for two reasons: first that it is often used to support the myth of biological determinism (as if there is an intuition gene in women), second that it makes the diversity in these social categories invisible (lots of women pride themselves on being analytic rather than intuitive). Thus, if we are to avoid essentialism when we characterize a geometric design theme for some particular culture we need to keep two things in mind. First, that the use of this theme does not automatically imply some psychological or social trait: just because Africans tend to use fractals in their designs (Eglash, 1999) doesn't mean they are mentally chaotic, any more than Pythagoras' interest in triangles implies he was having an affair. Second, that the use of this theme does not mean that everyone in the culture is using it at every opportunity; there may be a great deal of geometric diversity as well as cultural diversity.

Native-American Analogues of the Cartesian Grid

Having made that caveat, we can now examine the pervasive use of fourfold symmetry in Native-American culture. This is mainly evident in design geometry, but appears in other ways as well. Many Native-American languages, for example, use four as a counting base or subbase. Base 20 systems were common, the Mayan being the best known example, but there are many other examples. In California for instance, there was the mixed base-8/base-16 system employed by the Yuki, the mixed base-4/base-16 system of the Chumash, and the 5-10-40 base system of the Pomo (Closs, 1986). Among the Yana of Northern California, the word for four is *daumi*, which is derived from the word *dau*, "to count" (Sapir & Swadesh, 1960, cited in Closs, 1986). Eells (1913) analyzed the use of multiplication in Native-American number words and found that the most common multiple was 4 (70% of 122 languages).

Other examples outside of design geometry include the prayers offered to "the four winds," the Navajo belief in four sacred mountains, and the patterning of drum beats in groups of four during ceremonies. Neihardt (2004) recounts a 1931 oral history from Black Elk, a medicine man of the Oglala Sioux Indians: the account of his visions makes resounding use of the number four (he begins at age 4, horses in his vision come in four colors, "marching four by four," and then flee to the "four quarters of the world," he is told he will see four generations, he sees a tribe with four chieftains, a sacred herb with four blossoms, and so on).

However it is in the geometry of design that we find the link to Cartesian graphs. One key aspect here is the link to cardinal directions. For instance, many of the plains Indians created teepees with four base poles, each placed in relation to one of the four directions. The nations of the Iroquois—Seneca, Oneida, Onondaga, Cayuga and Mohawk—all used a "longhouse" building that was oriented along the east–west axis. When they came together as a confederacy, they collectively called themselves Haudenosaunee—"people of the long house"—and assigned each nation to a household position along the east–west axis: the Seneca as Keepers of the Western Door; the Mohawks as Keepers of the Eastern Door, and the centrally located Onondaga as Keepers of the Central Fire. In Ojibway birchbark scrolls the east–west axis of the long house symbolically represents the good direction of spiritual progress, and the north–south axis the bad direction in which progress is derailed (Dewney, 1975). Much of the architecture of the Southwest, such as Hopi kivas, the roads of Chaco canyon, and the rectangular buildings of the Pueblo, show alignment with the cardinal directions.

The best examples of Cartesian analogs are found in smaller artifacts and construction processes. Eglash (2002) describes the ways in which certain Native-American stories contrast the ordered fourfold patterns with the randomness of the trickster (which has implications for native concepts of probability and

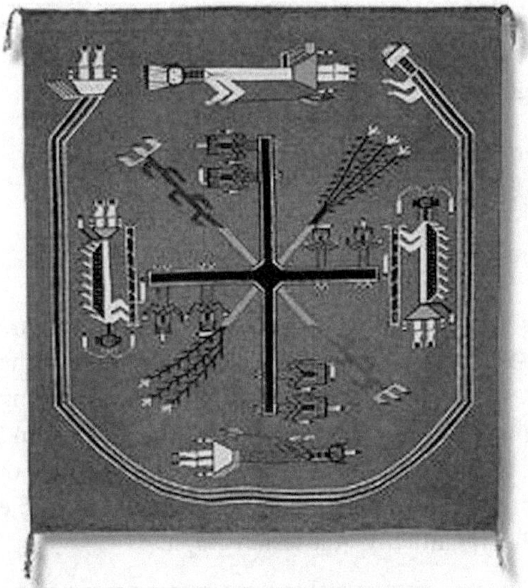

Figure 12.1 Rug based on Navajo sand painting.

biodiversity). In some cases these fourfold patterns clearly show two axes. Navajo sand painting offers a particularly good example. These sand paintings are used in healing ceremonies. A medicine man (*hataalii*) completes the drawing in one day, using colored powder such as crushed stone. The painting is brushed away later that night, along with the illness. In the Navajo religion, the *hataalii* heals through the balance of forces. Sand paintings often use reflection symmetry to show these paired forces. Some of these structures are similar to a Cartesian graph. Navajo tradition does not permit photos of sand paintings, so Figure 12.1 was derived from a Navajo rug based on a sand painting (the weaver has deliberately introduced errors to prevent this from being a copy, which would

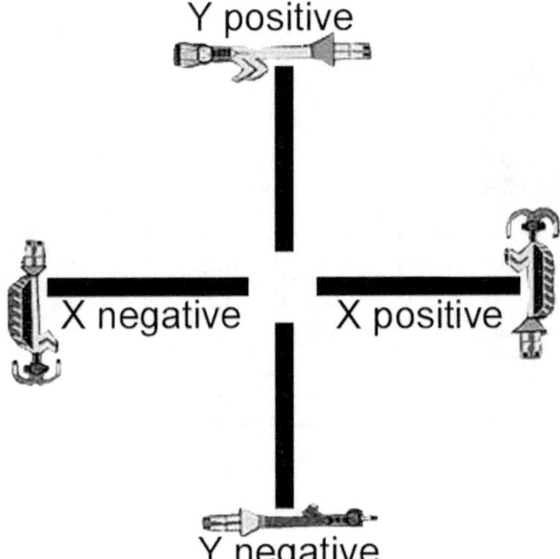

Figure 12.2 Rug as Cartesian graph.

not be permitted).[1] Here we see four human figures. Figures on the horizontal axis are hunched over with back packs. Those on the vertical axis have straight backs. As a Cartesian graph (Figure 12.2):

+X = Right-side up figure with backpack
–X = Upside-down figure with backpack
+Y = White straight figure
–Y = Dark straight figure

In Alaska, Yup'ik story parkas are created with symmetric decorations (Figure 12.3). According to Engbloom-Bradley (2008), professor of education at the University of Alaska, the Yup'ik say it is important to have both sides looking exactly the same, so they developed a coordinate system, measuring vertical and horizontal distance on the parka using the width of two fingers as the unit of length (Figure 12.4). These decorations are positioned by using the navel as the origin point. In other words, it is a quantitative Cartesian graph.

Figure 12.3 Yup'ik story parka.

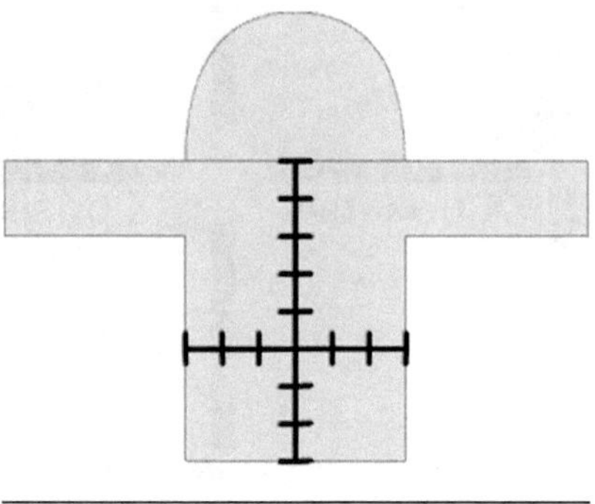

Figure 12.4 Yup'ik parka construction.

The process by which many native designs are created—warp and weft in rug looms, the rows and columns of bead looms, and the grids of rectangular baskets—also reflect a Cartesian-like structure. Klein (1982) provides evidence for the ways in which Mesoamerican cosmology may have been expressed through a weaving analogy. Similarly there is a Cartesian grid in the streets of cities such as Teotihuacan in Mexico, where a strong north/south[2] axis ends in the temple of the moon, and a weaker east/west axis aligns the temple of the sun and other buildings, suggesting that architecture also expressed this cosmological significance of the two-axis system.

The Cartesian Coordinate System in Contemporary Native-American Design

Contemporary Native-American use of the two-axis system has not only continued these traditions, but applied them to abstract schemata. The flags of the Oglala Sioux, Northern Cheyenne, Salt River Pima and Maricopa, and Pueblo of Zia all feature symbols with fourfold symmetry, and each has its own symbolic interpretation. Many instances of two-axis schemata are used in educational contexts. Hampton (1995) for example, drawing on the directional symbolism of the Chickasaw pipe ceremony he experienced as a youth, makes use of the four cardinal directions, and then maps various concepts to these axes: North includes winter, struggle, and conflict; South includes summer, freedom, and respect. He calls this the "six directions" organizing principle—six because in addition to the four cardinal directions there is also below (earth) and above (spirit). Structurally it is analogous to a Cartesian grid in three dimensions (so it is actually a three-axis schema). Hampton cautions that this is not a model (which would denote an imperfect replica) but rather a system of organization.

Hampton derives his three-axis structure from the many others (e.g., Calliou, 1995; Klug & Whitfield, 2003) that similarly use the figure of a medicine wheel to map out a two-axis system of organizing principles. *Medicine wheels*—a term now often replaced by *sacred hoop*—are large circles of stone, typically with lines of stone radiating from the center like spokes. One classic example is the Bighorn Medicine Wheel: this 75 foot diameter wheel has 28 spokes, and dates back about 800 years. Evidence indicates that the original use included astronomical observations: the 28 spokes represent the 28 days in the lunar month, and additional stone cairns align the viewer with points on the horizon where the sun rises or sets on summer solstice. This also corresponds to the structure of ceremonial buildings such as the Lakota Sundance lodge, with 28 rafters in the roof, and an entrance to the east, facing the rising Sun.

Thus, while it is not clear that the original medicine wheels were meant to embody a two-axis system, there is strong evidence for a meaningful geometry in the orientation of their spokes. For this reason the contemporary Native-American use of medicine wheel structures for two-axis organizational schemata is not merely a fabrication. In many ways it is simply extending the traditional use—a geometric structure that symbolically relates concepts across the diverse domains of the astronomical, architectural, spiritual, and others—into new contexts.

The Origins of the Cartesian Coordinate System in Europe

It is often said that Descartes came up with the idea for the Cartesian coordinate system when he was lying in bed watching a fly on the ceiling, and wanted to numerically describe the fly's position. There is, however, no evidence for this origin story in any historical source: like Newton's apple, it is apocryphal. The actual origins for Descartes's idea are unknown. However, the concept of using horizontal and vertical reference lines have arisen several times in intellectual history. Around 250 BC the philosopher Eratosthenes, from North Africa, used a rectangular grid for a map. Various others improved on this idea over the centuries. Nicole Oresme, born in 1323 in France, applied this to the mathematical analysis of lines, using something like our bar graph to show differences in slope. Oresme had translated some of the Greek sources, so he may have run across the idea there. René Descartes, born in 1596, was the first to apply such "reference lines" to curves. His graphs also had the potential for negative numbers, although he tried to avoid these as much as possible since he felt they clashed with the idea that math corresponded to physical quantities.

Did Descartes simply take the idea from Oresme, who took it from the Greeks? Another intriguing possibility is that Descartes got the idea from Elizabethan mathematician and occult philosopher John Dee (born 1527), who published a "crosse of graduation"—very similar to the Cartesian system— in his introduction to a volume of Euclid. Dee's text was widely available, and would have been of interest to Descartes, who—despite his foundational role in rationalist philosophy—had clearly read works by occult philosophers, especially those such as Dee who worked with mathematics (Aczel, 2005; Shea, 1960/1988). John Dee had very broad interests, which included the reports coming from the New World; he even had an Aztec obsidian disk in his collection.[3] A map of Teotihuacan (probably copied from an indigenous original, since details appear on the map that are not in the description by Cortez; see Mundy, 1988 for discussion) was published in 1524, and clearly showed the two-axis grid of the city layout. Could Dee have been inspired to develop his "crosse of graduation" from this map, or other New World designs showing fourfold symmetry? The idea is sheer speculation, but it's possible that the heritage of the Cartesian cross runs not from Descartes to Oresme to the ancient Greeks, but from Descartes to Dee to the natives of Mesoamerica.

The Virtual Bead Loom

Computer simulation of these Cartesian systems has been developed under the National Science Foundation Culturally Situated Design Tools project (see http://www.rpi.edu/~eglash/csdt.html). These computer simulations enable students to

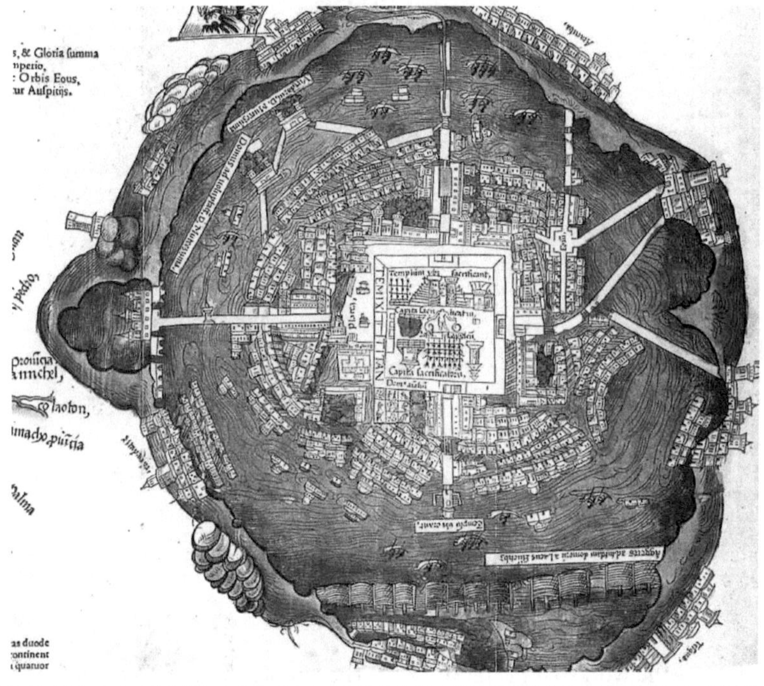

Figure 12.5 Map of Tenochtitlán (154) showing two-axis layout.

learn mathematics through experimentation with these knowledge systems. In our initial evaluation the use of these design tools showed statistically significant improvement of minority student math achievement (Eglash, Bennett, O'Donnell, Jennings, & Cintorino, 2006). At the same time, they offer new ways to explore cultural connections to mathematics.

The opening web page for the Virtual Bead Loom (VBL) allows users to select from four categories: Cultural Background, Tutorial, Software, and Teaching Materials. The cultural background section opens with several examples of fourfold symmetry in Native-American design. Before reading the text, teachers can ask students to look at the designs and describe them; such discussions offer opportunities to introduce symmetry as a term and concept. The text describes, as I have done here, how fourfold symmetry is a deep design theme in many Native-American cultures, and is evident not only in a wide variety of native arts, but also indigenous knowledge systems such as base-4 counting, four-quadrant architecture, and the "four directions" healing practice. A second web page shows how such structures are analogous to the Cartesian coordinate system. Finally, the web page introduces the Native-American bead loom as another example in which we find an analogue to the Cartesian grid.

The tutorial begins by showing how the VBL simulates a traditional Native-American bead loom, and reviews the various tools. The VBL applet features a Cartesian workspace in which designs are created, and tools which appear to

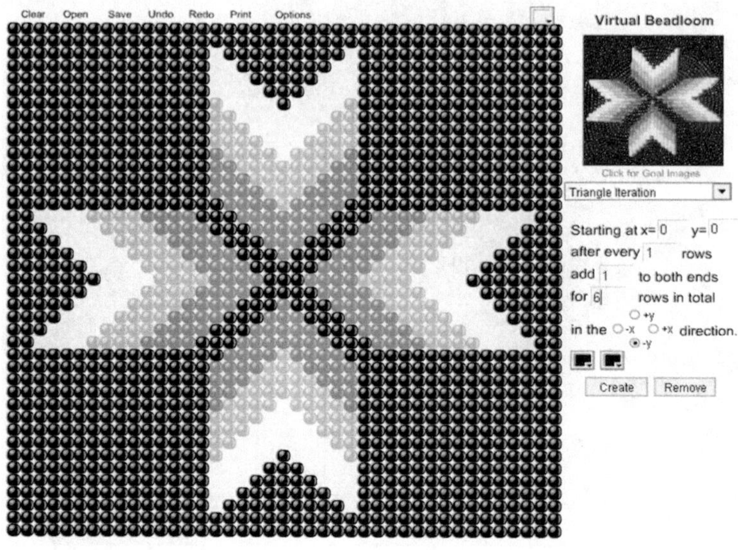

Figure 12.6 The Virtual Bead Loom.

the right of the workspace (Figure 12.6). The simplest tool, for creating or deleting single beads, is at the top. Students enter the X,Y coordinate pairs, select a bead color (or compose a custom color if none of the standard buttons suits their taste), and press the "point" button. Other tools include lines, rectangles, triangles, and iterative patterns. The tools can be used in combinations to simulate traditional beadwork patterns, to allow students to create their own designs, and to engage in a variety of specific standards-based math learning exercises. The VBL was created in collaboration with teachers and students at schools serving the Shoshone-Bannock reservation in Idaho, the Northern Ute reservation in Utah, and the Onondaga Nation reservation in New York, and has been a great success. It has also been used with a wide variety of other ethnic groups, including White students and teachers, with great enthusiasm. Teachers have found a wide variety of concepts and skills, primarily from analytic geometry, which can be taught using the VBL. Another exciting aspect is the ability of students to develop physical bead work based on their virtual designs (Figure 12.6), often by linking an art class with the math class. Additional samples of student work, evaluation tools, teachers' lesson plans, and other materials are in the "Teaching Materials" section of the web page.

Learning Strategies with the VBL

There are three pedagogical frameworks that can be used with VBL. In *application/reinforcement* we start students with the task of simulating one of the original beadwork designs. Teachers have reported success in using this software for teaching Cartesian coordinates, reflection symmetry, and its relation to Cartesian values, numeric aspects of translation, and other subjects. In *structured inquiry* specific math challenges can be proposed by teachers, developing rules for the reflection of polygons about the axis, and numeric descriptions for color sequences. For example, teacher Kristine Hansen at the Shoshone-Bannock reservation school had students create a rectangle in quadrant I (the positive–positive quadrant), and then apply the following:

1. Reflect your rectangle into quadrant II with the following transformation: (x,y) → (-x, y)

   Students then created transformation rules to place the rectangle in other quadrants. Doing this with asymmetric triangles might be even more effective since it would help visualize the reflections. Another exercise carried out by Hansen.
2. Program a green isosceles triangle at the bottom of the screen. Use the transformation (x,y) → (x,y+5) to translate your triangle up 5 units. Continue to iterate this translation by translating your last triangle up 5 units until you reach the top of the grid.

This was assigned in early December; she reports that she had intended that the students create a Christmas tree, but to her surprise the students modified the assignment and closely overlaid the triangles using a multitude of colors, creating what she describes as "the feathered bead pattern we see in a lot of the beadwork here on the reservation." This indicates that one advantage to this more open-ended approach to ethnomath is that it lends itself better to "appropriation" (Eglash, Croissant, Di Chiro, & Fouché, 2004), thus offering a more constructivist-based learning environment in which students' cultural sensibilities can be used as a bridge to math education.

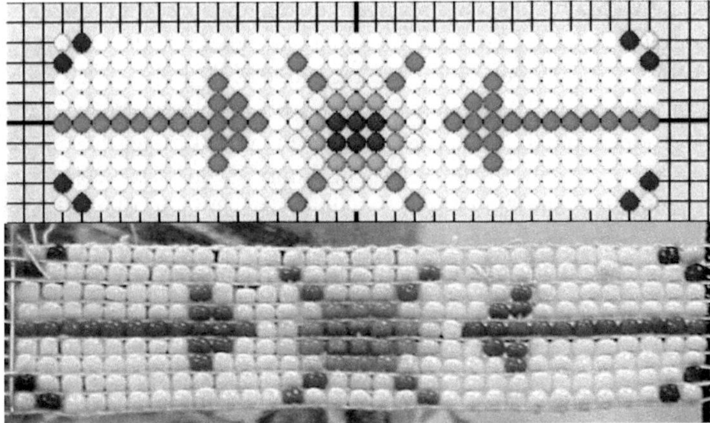

Figure 12.7 Physical bead work based on virtual bead work.

Finally there is *guided inquiry*, in which students chose their own challenges. For example, one student of Puerto Rican heritage decided to create a beadwork image of the Puerto Rican flag, which includes an equilateral triangle. At first he tried to create an equilateral triangle by having the same number of beads on each side, but that did not work because the beads along the diagonal are spaced farther apart than the beads along the vertical or horizontal. He finally arrived at a solution by using the ratios of a 30-60-90 triangle to provide a discrete approximation (Figure 12.7); a challenge that he might have balked at had it simply been assigned to him.

In addition to general exposure to simulations and computer-aided design, information technology education with the VBL can occur though student use of digital cameras and scanners for sampling the original cultural patterns to be simulated, and student use of multimedia presentations (ranging from image manipulation in Photoshop to website authoring) to show their work.

Exploring Indigenous Algorithms

Recently our team has used the term *ethnocomputing* to describe the attributes of these knowledge systems that better fit analogues to computing than to mathematics (Eglash et al., 2006). The use of iterative patterns in the VBL bears a direct relationship to iteration in computer programming. The initial prototype of the VBL only allowed creation of a pattern with single beads; this was clearly too tedious, and after discussion with potential users we introduced shape tools—you enter two coordinate pairs for a line, three coordinates pairs to get a triangle, and so on. But these virtual bead triangles often had uneven edges—the original Shoshone-Bannock beadwork always had perfectly regular edges (Figure 12.8).

It turned out that our programmer, STS graduate student Lane DeNicola, had looked up a standard "scanning algorithm" for the triangle generation; somehow the traditional beadworkers had algorithms in their heads that produced a different result. After a few conversations with them, it became clear that they were using iterative rules; for example, "subtract three beads from the left each time you move up one row." We developed a second tool for creating triangles, this one using iteration (Figure 12.5)—but kept the first in the VBL as well for comparison. This has provided a powerful learning opportunity: if you tell someone that there is such a thing as a "Shoshone algorithm" they may balk at the suggestion; but let them compare the standard scanning algorithm with that used by the Shoshone beadworkers, and the implications are difficult to ignore.

Future Work

Our current funding from the NSF's "Broadening Participation in Computing" initiative will be used to develop a version of the VBL in which students can write their own algorithms rather than just fill in the numeric parameters for

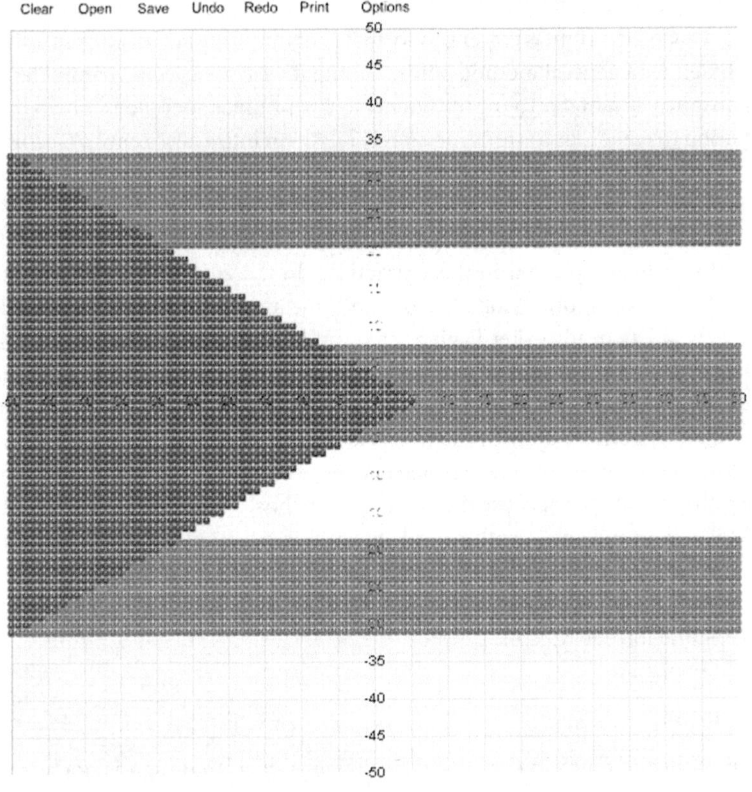

Figure 12.8 A Puerto Rican flag (minus its star) on the VBL.

the algorithms already built in. This brings up a number of research issues. For example, what language or interface design would best facilitate students creating algorithms? Consider the following two examples for a beadwork right triangle 9 rows high, incremented every 3 rows:

Start beading at x = 0, y = 0
After every three rows
Add one bead to the +X end
For 9 rows in total
	add RightTriangleIteration (x1,y1,stepHeight,triangleHeight)
	For t = 1 to triangleHeight
	For s = 1 to stepHeight
	For r=0 to s-1
	add bead(x1+r, y1)
	y1 = y1 + 1 /***increment until filled each row**
	end
	s=s+1 /***increment until filled each step**
	end
	t=t+1 /***increment until filled the entire triangle**
	end;
	RightTriangleIteration(0,0,3,9)

The algorithm on the left is written in "pseudocode," similar to ordinary language. That on the right is closer to a formal programming language such as java, which defines a general method before calling it with the specific parameters of this instance. Is it better to train students to use pseudocode? Does it help them transition to real programming, or merely lull them into a false sense of security? Is it possible to express the general case in pseudocode? Should the pseudocode allow "loose" phrasing, or should it have formal rules?

Another branch of research questions arise in examining the indigenous algorithms already present in these practices. In the 2003 video *Honoring Ute Ways*, James Barta, professor of Distance Education at Utah State University, interviewed Ute beadworker Fabian Jenks, and found that different algorithms corresponding to different slopes were fundamental to Jenks's thoughts when asked about mathematical connections. At the same time, it seemed that Jenks had difficulty coming up with the words to describe this mathematically. In the video he says "you can go one two, one two; or two three, two three; but you don't generally go past four because the beads get too loose." One problem here is that Jenks is describing an algorithm, and algorithms are more a part of computing curricula than math curricula. The inclusion of ethnocomputing will hopefully diminish such obstacles, and allow better translations from indigenous knowledge to academic formal systems.

Conclusion

The presence of fourfold symmetry in Native-American design is not a trivial geometric feature; rather it provides deep cultural connections spanning many facets of life, from religion to astronomy. Moreover its mathematical implications go far beyond that of reflection symmetry, allowing exploration of processes ranging from transformational geometry to iterative computation. This is just one example of the more general need in ethnomathematics to expand from a focus on static images to include process-oriented frameworks that illuminate design in the making, and that offer students a creative medium they can appropriate, for the purpose of expressing their own mathematical and cultural ideas.

Our "Culturally Situated Design Tools" website offers two other Native American tools using this same Cartesian principle, a Navajo Rug Weaver and an Alaskan Basket Weaver. All three tools help to show that the Native-American analogues to the Cartesian coordinate system are not merely hollow conceits, but mathematical ideas and practices that were profoundly present in the traditional native civilizations, and are still an ongoing subject of innovation and exploration by their contemporary descendents.

Acknowledgment

This material is based on work supported by the National Science Foundation under Grant No. 0634329.

Notes

1. In my conversations with Navajo artists and educators (June 13–17, 2005) I found a great deal of variation on this issue: one said showing a photo of a sand painting was a problem but a rug based on a painting was permissible; another said the rug based on the painting was problematic but not a sketch of the rug of the painting. It was striking that the objections were not as much phrased in terms of offending Navajos as they were concern for my spiritual safety; another example of the strong ethical stance associated with these practices.
2. The actual orientation of the grid is about 15 degrees to the east of true north. Malmstrom (1981) suggests that this alignment is with sunset on August 13, which is the beginning of the Mayan long count calendar.
3. Dee's obsidian mirror can be viewed at the British Museum website: http://www.britishmuseum.org/explore/highlights/highlight_objects/pe_mla/d/dr_dees_mirror.aspx

References

Aczel, A. (2005). *Descartes' secret notebook: A true tale of mathematics, mysticism, and the quest to understand the universe.* New York: Broadway.

Barta, J. (2003). *Honoring Ute Ways.* Videorecording, Department of Elementary Education, Utah State University.

Calliou, S. (1995). Peacekeeping actions at home: a medicine wheel model for a peace-keeping pedagogy. In M. Battiste & J. Barman (Eds.), *First Nations education in Canada: The circle unfolds* (pp. 47–72). Vancouver: University of British Columbia Press.

Closs, M. (Ed.). (1986). *Native American mathematics.* Austin, TX: University of Texas Press.

Culturally Situated Design Tools. Available at: http://www.rpi.edu/~eglash/csdt.html

Dewney, S. (1975). *The sacred scrolls of the southern Ojibway.* Toronto: University of Toronto Press.

Eells, W.C. (1913). Number systems of the North American Indians. *American Mathematical Monthly, 20*, 263–299.

Eglash, R. (1999). *African fractals.* New Brunswick, NJ: Rutgers University Press.

Eglash, R. (2002). Computation, complexity and coding in Native American knowledge systems. In J. Hanks & G. Fast (Eds.), *Changing the faces of mathematics: Perspectives on indigenous people of North America* (pp. 251–262). Reston, VA: National Council of Teachers of Mathematics.

Eglash, R., Bennett, A., O'Donnell, C., Jennings, S., & Cintorino, M. (2006). Culturally situated design tools: Ethnocomputing from field site to classroom. *American Anthropologist, 108*, 347–362.

Eglash, R., Croissant, J., Di Chiro, G., & Fouché, R. (Eds.). (2004). *Appropriating technology: Vernacular science and social power.* Minneapolis, MN: University of Minnesota Press.

Hampton, E. (1995). Towards a redefinition of Indian education. In M. Battiste & J. Barman (Eds.), *First Nations education in Canada: The circle unfolds* (pp. 5–46). Vancouver: University of British Columbia Press.

Klein, C. (1982). Woven heaven, tangled Earth: A weaver's paradigm of the Mesoamerican cosmos. In A. Aveni & G. Urton (Eds.), "Ethnoastronomy and archaeoastronomy in the American tropics" [Special issue] *Annals of the New York Academy of Sciences, 385*, 1–36.

Klug, B. J., & Whitfield, P. T. (2003). *Widening the circle: Culturally relevant pedagogy for American Indian children.* New York: Routledge.

Malmström, V. H. (1981). Architecture, astronomy, and calendrics in Pre-Columbian Mesoamerica. In R. A. Williamson (Ed.), *Archaeoastronomy in the Americas* (pp. 249–261). Los Altos, CA: Ballena Press.

Mundy, B. E. (1998). Mapping the Aztec capital: The 1524 Nuremberg map of Tenochtitlan, its sources and meanings. *Imago Mundi, 50*, 1–22.

Neihardt, J. G. (2004). *Black Elk speaks.* Lincoln, NE: University of Nebraska Press.

Sapir, E., & Swadesh, M. (1960). *University of California publications in linguistics: Vol. 22. Yana dictionary.* Berkeley, CA: University of California Press.

Shea, W. R. (1988). Descartes and the Rosicrucian enlightenment. In R. S. Woolhouse (Ed.), *Metaphysics and philosophy of science in the seventeenth and eighteenth centuries* (pp. 73–99). Dordrecht, The Netherlands: Kluwer. (Original work published 1960)

13

Privileging Mathematics and Equity in Teacher Education

Framework, Counter-Resistance Strategies, and Reflections from a Latina Mathematics Educator[1]

JULIA M. AGUIRRE

The low-level production of Latino/a mathematics educators with PhDs is sobering. According to the National Science Foundation (NSF), between 1994 and 2004, 39 out of 1,086 (3.5%) mathematics education doctorates were awarded to Latinos/as (NSF, 2006). I am one of these 39. On average over this decade, the number of Latino/a math education doctorates produced annually can be counted on one hand. This statistic is important because it reflects a confluence of factors that influence my work as a Latina[2] mathematics educator with a deep commitment to transforming mathematics teaching and learning to improve and advance the mathematics education of children traditionally underrepresented in mathematics and science-based careers. I pursued a doctorate to examine issues related to why Latino/a, African American, and American Indian youth struggle in mathematics education, why so few are prepared for college, and even fewer pursue careers in mathematics and science. I felt, as a biracial Chicana[3] with Spanish as my second language coming from a mixed working-class and middle-class upbringing with a strong commitment to equity and social justice, that I had something to contribute to the dialogue in mathematics education to make a difference for my own communities of color. My focus turned to the adults most responsible for the mathematics education of children: teachers.

In this paper, I describe my continuing efforts to privilege equity and mathematics in my teacher education work with preservice and in-service elementary and secondary mathematics teachers. For me, defining equity is an evolving process. My current definition in the context of mathematics teacher education is informed by the work of Freire (1970/1993), Gutierrez (2006), Gutstein (2006), the National Council of Teachers of Mathematics (NCTM; 2000), and Nieto (2000). To me equity means that all students in light of their humanity—personal experiences, backgrounds, histories, languages, physical and emotional well-being—must have the opportunity and support to learn rich mathematics that fosters meaning making, empowers decision making, and critiques, challenges, and transforms inequities/injustices. Equity does not mean that every student should receive identical instruction. Instead, equity demands that responsible and appropriate accommodations be made as needed to promote equitable access, attainment, and advancement for all students.

My definition encompasses a social justice component that goes beyond equal access and opportunity to include transformation and change. Equity and mathematics comprise a powerful dialectic that is continually being constructed. It is important to acknowledge that this work is always evolving because the work for equity and social justice is never a finished product.

To understand how I privilege mathematics and equity in mathematics teacher education, I present a theoretical mapping that elaborates the multiple frames that shape this work. Next, I provide a brief historical overview of my work with pre-service and in-service teachers followed by an examination of counter-resistance strategies that I am developing through this work to help equip teachers with an integrated knowledge base and vision that values both mathematics and equity (Rodriguez, 2005). I offer two new strategies that were developed through "in the moment" responses toward ideological and pedagogical forms of teacher resistance (Rodriguez, 2005). Furthermore, interwoven through this discussion, are the roles my own sociocultural identities play in this work (Hurtado & Gurin, 2004). Finally, implications for teacher preparation, professional development, and doctoral programs in mathematics education are discussed.

Theoretical Underpinnings

I utilize multiple theoretical frameworks to inform this work which is about impacting teacher cognition (e.g., beliefs, knowledge, goals) that, in turn, impact instructional practice. I draw on the literature about teacher beliefs and knowledge, including the work of Ernest (1991), Ma (1999), Pajares (1992), Schoenfeld (1998; 2003), Shulman (1987), and Thompson (1992). Teachers' views on the nature of the discipline, how one learns the discipline, and how one teaches the content shape their practice in complex and important ways. What is often less apparent in the teacher cognition literature are the roles that race, class, culture, and language play in the teaching and learning of mathematics and how those contexts interface with the development of teacher knowledge and beliefs related to teaching mathematics (Aguirre, Kitchen, & Horak, 2005). My work with teachers focuses on these intersections. I make an explicit effort to understand, push, and challenge beliefs and knowledge that may perpetuate deficit views of students that connect with race, class, culture, ethnicity, language, and gender in relation to teaching and learning mathematics. At the same time, my goal is to inform the conceptions and, in many cases, (re)conceptions about the nature of mathematics. The idea is to critically examine equity and mathematics and their interrelationships in order to promote changes in practice that transform persistent inequities we see in mathematics classrooms at all levels.

A second theoretical body of work focuses on teacher learning from a sociocultural perspective. First, acknowledging that learning is a social activity, the multiple communities of practice become central in how teachers negotiate shared meanings, utilize language, shape their identities, and engage in meaningful practices (Lave & Wenger, 1991; Wenger 1998). The role of power in these communities of practice remains an important yet underresearched attribute. Preservice and in-service teachers navigate multiple communities of practice as they develop their instruction (e.g., university, school, department, professional organizations, and family). As a teacher educator I must be sensitive to these issues and recognize the nexus of power and relationships that inform my own interactions with teachers.

A third theoretical perspective that influences my work is liberatory pedagogy and the work of Paolo Freire (1970/1993). Freire defines liberation as "a praxis: the action and reflection of men and women upon their world in order to transform it" (p.60). My obligation as a mathematics educator is to help create situations with the teachers I work with such that they and their students can engage in praxis to generate knowledge. From a liberatory perspective, knowledge is constantly being invented and reinvented through struggle, dialogue, and transformation. And it is to engage in this struggle, this inquiry into our world and with each other, that leads to being more fully human. One of the more powerful lessons I've taken from Freire's work is that to prevent another person from engaging in such inquiry is a form of violence—a dehumanizing action.

> Any situation in which some individuals prevent others from engaging in the process of inquiry is one of violence. The means used are not important; to alienate human beings from their own decision-making is to change them into objects. (p. 66)

Such relationships between thought, learning, power, and transformation are central to why I do this work. Mathematics plays a central role in its politicized position and status in relation to knowledge and intelligence (Ernest, 1991; Gutstein, 2006; Skovsmo, 1994). Thus, to deny others the opportunity to engage in the process of mathematizing the world—to utilize mathematics to make meaning, connect to other forms and knowledge, and inform decisions—is an act of dehumanization. My commitment is to engage with others in the work of liberatory pedagogy and thereby challenge and transform the mindsets and actions (individual, collective, and institutional) that seek to dehumanize with mathematics. From a standpoint of teacher education, tensions exist in the dialectic of this work as I, inevitably, experience forms of conflict with teachers in doing this work. How I negotiate those conflicts or forms of resistance and keep my commitments to liberatory pedagogy is an ongoing struggle and a central focus of this chapter.

Working Conceptual Frame

Figure 13.1, depicts my working conceptual frame for mathematics teacher education that simultaneously values equity and mathematics. It is strongly influenced by Eric Gutstein's characterization of the three important knowledge bases critical for teaching mathematics for social justice: classical mathematical knowledge, community knowledge, and critical knowledge (Gutstein, 2006). The idea is to facilitate the students' development of all three knowledge bases and their interrelationships. In addition, I've added two spectrums designed to highlight important dimensions critical to teaching mathematics for social justice. Teaching across these spectrums respects the dual emphasis on both equity and mathematics. Recently, I have shared this framework with the preservice and in-service teachers with whom I work.

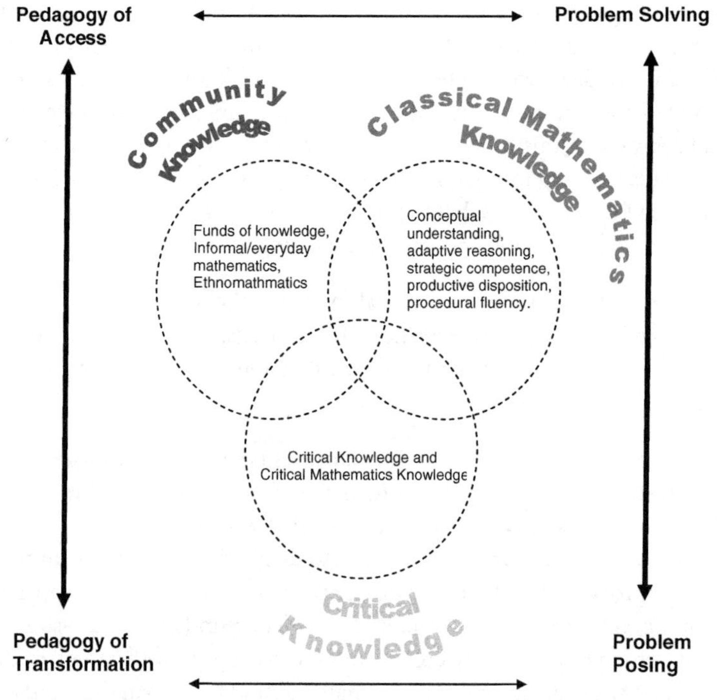

Figure 13.1 Teaching mathematics for equity and social justice: Theoretical framework for mathematics teacher education.

Classical Mathematical Knowledge

Classical mathematical knowledge refers to the mathematical power and competencies needed to make meaning in the world, pass gate-keeping educational and vocational tests, and pursue advanced mathematics and mathematics-related careers. My framework references the "strands of mathematical proficiency" articulated by the National Research Council (2001) as a characterization of important classical mathematical knowledge and associated dispositions. Other documents that could be cited for such characterizations might include the "Principles and Standards for School Mathematics" (National Council for Teachers of Mathematics, 2000) and the various National Science Foundation sponsored mathematics curricula used by schools. It is important for teachers to develop a strong sense of what mathematics (specific content topics, practices, and language) is expected to advance students in our schools.

However, an important critique of this classical mathematical knowledge base is that it is grounded in Western mathematics. Mathematical contributions from indigenous groups, non-Western societies, and previously colonized countries are often unacknowledged or deemed "primitive" and "nonintellectual" (Anderson, 1990; D'Ambrosio, 1985; Gutierrez, 2000; Gutstein, 2006). I agree with Gutierrez (2000) and Gutstein (2006) that what gets valorized as classical mathematics must be problematized. My effort to do some of this work involves focused attention on community knowledge.

Community Knowledge

Community knowledge refers to the universal capacity of "ordinary" people to have and produce knowledge about their lives, experiences, and contexts (Gutstein, 2006). It includes the funds of knowledge (FoK) that underlie household exchanges, traditions, and activities (Moll & Gonzalez, 2004). It also can include the production of mathematical knowledge that undergirds everyday activities such as gardening and sewing (Civil, 2006; Civil & Andrade, 2002), informal (out of school) activities such as candy selling (Saxe, 1988), and basketball (Nasir, 2006); and formal (in school) activities grounded in country-of-origin educational experiences (Perkins & Flores, 2002). Community knowledge encompasses multiple forms of cultural and linguistic knowledge. The work of Gutierrez (2002b), Khisty (1995, 1997), and Moschkovich (2000, 2002, 2006) on Spanish/English bilingual and Latino/a learners demonstrates the complexities of multiple meanings in the use of mathematical language practices in both Spanish and English. Furthermore, Perkins and Flores (2002) describe how mathematical procedures and symbols taught in Latin American countries differ from those in the United States of America and may, depending on how teachers' view these differences, promote opportunities for learning or points of confusion in mathematics classrooms.

By focusing attention on community knowledge and the mathematical knowledge produced from the community, my hope is that teachers develop a sense that there are mathematical resources (rather than barriers) to be mined from the community that can promote productive dispositions, rich mathematical discussions, and learning for their students.

Critical Knowledge

The term *critical knowledge* refers to the mathematical knowledge required to analyze the power relations, social injustices, and inequities that affect our individual, community, and global lives. It is the knowledge needed beyond mathematics to understand various sociopolitical contexts, including multiple histories, policies, institutional structures, and practices that create equity and inequity in our world (Gutstein, 2006). Examples in the mathematics education literature include the work of Frankenstein (1990), Gutstein (2003, 2006), Gutstein and Peterson (2005), Kitchen and Lear (2000), Skovsmose (1994), Tate (1994, 1995), and Turner and Strawhun (2005).

For many of the teachers I work with, it is a new idea to acknowledge that mathematics has an important role to play in analyzing issues that impact our world. Few have been introduced to examples of how this can be done in classrooms. By introducing critical knowledge as part of a knowledge triumvirate that connects to classical mathematics, I believe I can open up a door that transcends mathematics beyond the textbook and content standards. However, this knowledge also requires teachers to engage with, and reflect on, their own views about mathematics and the sociopolitical contexts we are asking them to help students understand, analyze, critique, and ultimately transform. The active politicizing of mathematics creates tensions I often negotiate with teachers in doing this work.

Access-Transformation Pedagogy Spectrum

The left side of the theoretical framework focuses on a pedagogical spectrum that highlights access at one end and transformation at the other. Citing the work of Morrell (2005), Gutstein (2006) argues that learning classical mathematical knowledge is important to obtain access to advanced studies in mathematics. I would add that a focus on access is to create learning opportunities for all students to engage in rich mathematical discourse and practices. The focus on access, parallel to community and classical mathematical knowledge bases, is to acknowledge that many mathematics education researchers focusing on community knowledge have argued for and demonstrated how marginalized students of color can engage in powerful mathematics when instruction utilizes community cultural and linguistic resources. Yet, I often felt that access and opportunity to participate in a system that continues to reproduce inequity is problematic. For example, the attempt to increase the numbers of African-American, Latino/a, and American-Indian students in honors mathematics classes still perpetuates a curricular tracking system that relegates other students from the same cultural, ethnic/racial, and linguistic groups to general mathematics courses replete with low-level mathematics curriculum and instruction (Oakes, Joseph, & Muir, 2004).

Can we move toward a pedagogy that actively works to critique and transform the social injustices and inequities that impact our multiple communities of practice? Can we teach children how to question, critique, and find mathematically based solutions to problems/issues that negatively impact their lives? Pedagogy of transformation parallels critical knowledge for that reason, namely to empower students to use mathematical knowledge to analyze and change their world. According to Gutstein (2006), Morrell (2005) describes this as pedagogy of dissent—harnessing critical knowledge to disrupt the status quo. For me, disruption is part of the struggle for change. Transformation of the status quo is the ultimate goal.

An important point to take away from this spectrum is that emphasizing equity and mathematics requires both pedagogy of access and pedagogy of transformation. Yet, it must also be acknowledged that there are inherent tensions in doing so.

Problem Solving/Problem Posing Pedagogy Spectrum

The right-side of the schematic representation of the knowledge bases (Figure 13.1) also refers to a spectrum of pedagogy. Problem solving has been a key component of reconceptualizing mathematics beyond procedural fluency. More recent documents include adaptive reasoning and strategic competence as elements of problem solving crucial to mathematics proficiency (National Research Council, 2001). In my framework, problem solving parallels classical mathematics knowledge to acknowledge that relationship. Schoenfeld (1992) argues that problem solving "is learning to grapple with new and unfamiliar tasks when relevant solution methods (even if only partially mastered) are not known" (p. 354). Moreover, teaching problem solving is both a challenging and rewarding task for teachers because it pushes teachers to anticipate the implications of various student approaches to problems and determine if those approaches are potentially fruitful and if not how to help make them so. The teacher must also decide when to intervene without usurping active thinking about the problem from the students. Lastly, problem solving may challenge the traditional role of teachers "knowing all the answers." Being able to be flexible with uncertainty requires "experience, confidence, and self awareness" (p. 354). This kind of pedagogy is key to helping students develop the knowledge and analytical tools to tackle "messy" problems. However, few examples exist in the problem-solving literature that tackle problems of inequity and injustice—

politicized mathematical problems. For that, one must include a problem-posing approach to mathematics teaching.

Drawing on the work of Paolo Freire (1970/1993) in problem-posing education, the traditional teacher role as sole source and final arbiter of knowledge is reconfigured to a shared, co-constructed source of knowledge developed through dialogue in which the teacher becomes a learner and the learners become teachers.

> The teacher is no longer merely the-one-who-teaches, but one who is himself taught in dialogue with the students, who in turn while being taught also teach. They become jointly responsible for a process in which all grow.... The problem-posing educator constantly re-forms his reflections in the reflection of the students who—no longer docile listeners—are now critical co-investigators in dialogue with the teacher. The teacher presents the material to the students for their consideration, and re-considers her earlier considerations as the students express their own. (pp. 61–62)

In some ways the description above captures the spirit of teaching from a problem-solving approach characterized by Schoenfeld (1992). However, problem-posing asserts "critical intervention in reality" of the world of the student/learner that is not readily apparent in mathematical problem-solving pedagogy. Freire (1970/1993) argues that:

> Students, as they are increasingly posed with problems relating to themselves in the world and with the world, will feel increasingly challenged and obliged to respond to that challenge. Because they apprehend the challenge as interrelated to other problems within a total context, not as a theoretical question, the resulting comprehension tends to be increasingly critical and thus constantly less alienated. Their response to the challenge evokes new challenges, followed by new understandings; and gradually the students come to regard themselves as committed. (p. 62)

A problem-posing approach embraces the critical knowledge necessary to analyze the world within multiple contexts and relate that knowledge to other phenomena. Thus, the placement of problem posing parallels critical knowledge in the theoretical framework to illustrate that important point. Again, it must be reiterated that both problem solving and problem posing are important pedagogical approaches that highlight flexibility and uncertainty related to privileging mathematics and equity.

The theoretical framework outlined above informs my efforts to promote equity and mathematics in teacher preparation and professional development work. Next, I give a brief overview of that work. I include references to how my own sociocultural identities as a Latina mathematics educator shape this work. This overview sets the stage for examining specific strategies and tensions I encounter in my efforts to promote equity and mathematics.

Teacher Preparation and Professional Development Overview

As with most of my own education experience (high school honors program, undergraduate, and graduate school), the demographics of the teacher preparation programs I have worked with are White and middle-class. Furthermore, as with most teacher preparation programs focusing on elementary education, most of the preservice students were women. The demographics are important given the context and curriculum I teach. I recognized my role as a mathematics education faculty of color to provide an alternative voice and view to preservice students who most likely had not lived experiences similar to those of the students they would be teaching in California. I also recognize that such a commitment requires faculty of color to walk a fine and vulnerable line. On the one hand, I see my role as leading/modeling for my White and privileged students how equity can and should be integrated into their teaching vision and practice to advance all students. This responsibility has made me vulnerable to the critique that I am advocating a perspective that is "too strong" or "prominority." On the other hand, by taking such an explicit stance, I may inadvertently alleviate the responsibility of explicit thinking about equity issues in mathematics teaching and learning from White students. I feel that as a biracial Chicana mathematics education professor teaching a mathematics methods course privileging both mathematics and equity invites conflict on many levels. As a faculty of color, this path of conflict is familiar, and at times painful. My commitment to thinking about race, class, language, culture in relation to mathematics teaching and learning highlights multiple levels of potential conflict that must be negotiated within the classroom and myself.

Preservice Mathematics Methods Course

When I first put the mathematics methods course together my primary focus was community knowledge and classical mathematical knowledge. In terms of classical mathematical knowledge, I wanted the teachers to think of mathematics from an inquiry and relational perspective rather than as discrete topics that they and their students must master (Borasi, 1996; Carpenter, Franke, & Levi, 2003; Skemp, 1987). I emphasized the importance of mathematical proficiency as defined by the National Research Council (2001) consisting of interlaced strands of procedural fluency, conceptual understanding, adaptive reasoning, strategic competence, and productive disposition. The course reader included articles about learning specific topics/domains of mathematics (e.g., subtraction, multiplication, algebra, geometry) and debated topics such as the wisdom of teaching algorithms and using manipulatives.

I also focused on community knowledge. I wanted the teachers to read articles that directly pertained to issues of language and culture in the teaching and learning of mathematics. I wanted to help them nurture the ideas of language and culture being resources to draw upon rather than barriers (Civil, 2002; Khisty,

1995, 1997; Moschkovich, 2000; Perkins & Flores, 2002). I provided readings and videotape examples asking the preservice students to reflect individually and in groups about how teachers made mathematics accessible and meaningful to English learners. I also included specific readings that focused on bridging school and home. The choices in articles and videos were "exemplars" of strong teaching that "challenged conventional wisdom" (Khisty & Viego, 1999) by emphasizing how Latino/a children and English learners can participate in high level mathematical discourse, perform well on standardized tests, and how their parents can be sources for their students' success.

In this case, my course helped teachers think about issues of access to high level mathematics that included problem solving, conceptual understanding, and procedural fluency. An emphasis was placed on utilizing funds of knowledge (Civil, 2002; Gonzalez, Moll, & Amanti, 2005; Moll & González, 2004) and students' primary language to facilitate student learning. These important pedagogical choices exposed and modeled for teachers examples of students, from different ethnic backgrounds and using multiple languages, engaged in mathematical practices to make sense of the mathematics.

I also introduced a few articles that I would characterize as moving more toward a critical mathematical perspective in teaching and learning mathematics. Tate (1994, 1995) provided two readings that were pivotal in the first iterations of the course. His readings racialized curriculum and instruction and provided three different examples in which race and class impacted the learning and teaching of elementary mathematics. The first example focused on African-American student responses to a multiple-choice problem about purchasing a bus pass, a problem that confused their teachers and raised questions about mathematical assumptions used to solve such problems. The second example characterized an African-American male student's disconnection from the mathematics problem context (related to Thanksgiving) that remained unseen by his teacher. The third example detailed how a teacher mined the mathematics in a problem posed by her students about why there were so many liquor stores near the school. I used Tate's work to provoke conversations about the way mathematics can marginalize some youth mathematically and culturally, and how mathematics can be a tool to address issues of inequity.

The main assignments for the course focused on the self (mathematics learning autobiography and interview), learning (case study of English learner or struggling math learner); teaching (detailed lesson plan and analysis of two to three math lessons) and content (inquiry on a specific mathematics topic of interest or one the student was going to be responsible for teaching). All assignments explicitly asked students to make connections to readings. In addition, all assignments asked students to write and reflect about mathematics and issues of equity (e.g., race, class, language, and culture/ethnicity). For example, the mathematics learning autobiography asked students to recall the demographics of their courses and to interview someone from a different ethnic/cultural or linguistic background and compare and contrast their experiences. In addition, the mathematics inquiry assignment asked teachers a series of questions about their topic including, "What kind of cultural/linguistic challenges and resources affect the learning of your topic?" A main goal for these assignments was to help teachers attune to both content and equity.

However, I would argue that my emphases in the first two iterations of the course focused on the interaction between classical mathematical knowledge and community knowledge with emphasis on access and problem solving. While I briefly discussed teaching mathematics as a political act and linked mathematics learning to a civil rights issue (Moses & Cobb, 2001), analysis of my assignments and lecture notes lacked a consistently explicit critical knowledge perspective—the view that mathematics is an analytical tool to challenge and transform social inequities (Gutierrez, 2000; Gutstein, 2006; Skovsmose, 1994). Moreover, moving teachers to a pedagogy of transformation with a focus on problem posing remained implicit (Freire, 1970/1993).

The third iteration of the course included a specific focus on teaching mathematics for social justice in which I provided my preservice students with a theoretical framework that focused their attention on what Gutstein (2006) describes as the three Cs (classical mathematical knowledge, community knowledge, and critical knowledge). I added a required text called, *Rethinking Mathematics: Teaching Social Justice by the Numbers* (Gutstein & Peterson, 2005). And class activities included deconstruction of mathematics lessons that explicitly connected mathematics to social action. What is important to understand is that the readings in the *Rethinking Mathematics* text were required each week along with other readings that focused on the classical mathematical knowledge and community knowledge link. I was so grateful to find a text that had many examples of lessons, descriptions of lessons being implemented in classrooms, and "foundational" pieces (including one of the Tate articles) that provided theoretical underpinnings of this approach. I could have made this text optional or only provide a few readings. Doing that would have been a symbolic approach. However, to me, if social justice was going to be an overarching theme of the course, a substantive strand, then it must be infused from the beginning and made an explicit resource to draw upon throughout the course in terms of readings and activities to support preservice teachers' developing pedagogical vision and instructional practice.

In-service Teacher Professional Development

My in-service work with teachers has a trajectory similar to the development of my methods course. The emphasis was on access and problem solving with strong connections to community knowledge. However, given the traditional professional development formats (one-shot workshops or week-long summer institutes with some follow-up), I felt that explicitly engaging in-service teachers on issues of race, culture, language, and class in mathematics teaching was seriously limited. Time was the main issue. I wanted to be able to explore these issues with teachers over time to support their work in meeting the mathematical needs of their kids.

In 2004, as part of the Center for Mathematics Education of Latinos/as (CEMELA), an NSF-supported center for learning and teaching), I joined a university–school district sponsored teacher professional development initiative that focused on mathematics lesson study. The three-year professional development initiative was spearheaded by one school district working closely with two local universities to support over 100 elementary and secondary mathematics teachers from several school districts in central California. Part of the initiative was to address the "needs of English Language learners." I became part of the planning team that included mathematicians, mathematics educators, district administrators, mathematics coaches, and teacher leaders. It was an opportunity to make explicit an "equity" strand in a three-year project. The district wanted this focus on equity and came to us (i.e., CEMELA) for assistance.

The professional development included ample time to plan mathematics lessons that were videotaped and critiqued, along with special content and equity sessions designed to enhance teacher knowledge of the content as well as issues of language and culture in mathematics teaching and learning. I have been engaged with teachers both as a session leader and as an "equity math consultant" during their planning time. As part of this work, we've provided teachers with a resource binder that includes articles on learning, teaching, assessment, and parent/community involvement in mathematics education. Many of these articles are used in my mathematics methods reader. In addition, as part of a special session on teaching mathematics for social justice, which I lead, each participating school was given a copy of *Rethinking Mathematics* (Gutstein & Peterson, 2005) to add to their curriculum library. Lastly, the special sessions that I designed and led included deconstructing mathematics lessons and analyzing videotapes, activities that again challenged conventional wisdom about what Latino/a students and English learners can do mathematically. My intention with this work is to engage teachers in dialogue about the roles language, culture, race, and class play in mathematics learning and teaching so they are more attuned to these issues as they plan their mathematics lessons.

One key difference between my work with in-service teachers and my work with preservice student teachers is that my power relations with the two groups are different. With preservice students, they are taking my course to set foundations for mathematics teaching. They are assessed on their knowledge of the readings and how they connect to their classroom practicum experiences and the course assignments. In addition, in general, I am the person in the course with the most teaching experience. That is not the case when working with in-service teachers: I cannot hold them accountable to read and utilize materials. While they may see me as an "expert" of some kind, experience has also shown me that veteran teachers hold a healthy bit of skepticism about researchers/teacher educators that must be negotiated when working together. Furthermore, there are wiser, more experienced classroom teachers than myself in most professional development settings. Thus, it is important to respect that professional experience is both critical and complex when discussing issues of equity and social justice in relation to mathematics teaching and learning.

Given the general overview of my work with preservice and in-service teachers, it is clear that my intention is to be more explicit with teachers about the roles that race, culture, language, and class play in mathematics teaching and learning. With the more explicit emphasis on social justice that utilizes mathematics as a tool to challenge and change social inequities, one can imagine how new and veteran teachers may react to such an explicit agenda. The next section highlights particular ways in which some teachers resisted this work and the "counter-resistance" strategies I am developing to respond to teacher resistance in an effort to privilege both equity and mathematics.

Examining Counter-Resistance Strategies

Rodriguez (2005) argues that teacher resistance to multicultural education and teaching for diversity (teaching in culturally and gender-inclusive ways) remains an underexamined research area in teacher education. To move the field forward, Rodriguez identified two types of teacher resistance to teaching for diversity: resistance to ideological change (RIC) and resistance to pedagogical change (RPC). RIC is defined as, "the resistance to changing one's beliefs and value system" (p. 5). For example, teachers may believe that a student's work ethic is what is most important in student learning, not the status of the student's culture, race, language, and gender. ("If you are lazy, you won't learn the math, no matter what color you are or what language you speak.") RPC focuses on teachers' perceptions of what it means to be an effective teacher. He defines RPC as "resistance to learning to teach for understanding due to avoiding, refusing, or feeling unable to change one's perceptions of what constitutes being an effective teacher" (p. 7). For Rodriguez and his colleagues, teaching for understanding means utilizing constructivist, inquiry-based, and intellectually challenging pedagogical approaches (Rodriguez & Kitchen, 2005). An example of RPC is a teacher believing that students learn best when specifically shown how to do a problem through a well-constructed lecture followed by lots of practice solving similar problems. This view may come from hesitancy on the part of many preservice teachers to move away from the transmission model of learning they traditionally experienced as students (Borasi, 1996; Tyack & Cuban, 1995).

The studies reported in the edited volume of Rodriguez and Kitchen (2005) describe different "counterresistance strategies" utilized by mathematics and science educators to "positively address prospective teachers' difficulties, concerns, and/or direct opposition to the notion that all educators can (and should) create multicultural and gender-inclusive learning environments where all students feel supported to learn" (p. 7). These counter-resistance strategies are pedagogical approaches that may address one or both of these forms of teacher resistance. These forms were examined in the preservice context, but I have found similar examples in my work with in-service teachers in professional development settings. Upon examination of my course assignments, video analysis activities, and reading reflections, I feel I include several of the counter-resistance strategies identified, all of which address both RIC and RPC, including (1) observing diverse students succeed in mathematics; (2) making connections between students' home language and mathematics instruction; (3) writing autobiographies based on own experiences and those of others in mathematics courses; (4) modeling lessons that are socially and politically relevant.

Next I highlight some counterstrategies I am developing to negotiate and positively address teacher ideological and pedagogical resistance in teacher preparation and professional development settings.

RIC—Recycling the Cultural Deficit Position in Mathematics Learning

In my first year of teaching the mathematics methods course, I encountered some teacher education students who held a cultural deficit view of Latino/a children and their parents. Many of these students worked in classrooms with high populations of Latino/a and English learners.

For many of these preservice teachers, the pedagogical strategies they observed with their co-operating teachers were inconsistent with what they were learning in my course. For example, while different method course activities modeled problem solving and inquiry approaches, the preservice teachers frequently observed mathematics being taught using rote worksheets and an emphasis on direct instruction. In addition, many felt their co-operating teachers were afraid of mathematics (often asking the student teacher to teach that segment of the day) or were working in classrooms constrained by accountability policies requiring highly scripted skill-based curriculum and test preparation. Some of these preservice teachers reported that students' "lack of language" (English) was a barrier to students learning math. And some echoed sentiments of their co-operating teachers about unsupportive Latino/a parents. Reasons given included that the parents did not help with homework, they spoke only Spanish, or they or their communities did not value education.

Preservice student criticism of language, culture, Latino/a families and communities did not sit well with me as their instructor. I found myself challenging these students explicitly about the assumptions underlying their comments by asking them what their evidence was for their assertions, how those assertions were connected to our readings, and if any attempt had been made to build mathematical bridges or links to students' homes. I admit, and some of my course evaluations bear out, that while many agreed with perspectives shared in the class, my questioning often put students on the defensive. Upon reflection, the preservice students who worked in classes with large populations of Latino/a children were the students that I questioned most intensively. I partly attribute my strong response to my sociocultural and professional identities as a biracial Chicana mathematics educator who struggles with her bilingualism. Deficit views of Latino/a children, culture, language, and community violated me. These teacher education students were talking about the children of La Raza—children with whom I share similar cultural, linguistic, and historical roots. They were not "other people's children" they were my children (Delpit, 1995). I felt my community was being disrespected and I reacted accordingly.

Counterresistance Strategy: Push for Elaboration and Offer Counterexamples

I have since developed some pedagogical techniques both for "in the moment" comments and ways to address similar issues on class assignments. I have learned to request elaboration, listen carefully, problematize respectfully, and offer counterexamples in order to further dialogue. Two salient examples come from recent in-service teacher professional development sessions. In June 2005, I worked with middle school and high school mathematics teachers during a week-long summer mathematics institute. I led one session focused on mathematics teaching and learning with English learners and Latino/a students. We were discussing teachers' perspectives on why English learners and, specifically Latino/a youths struggle in mathematics. One high school teacher, a 30-year veteran and chair of a math department, indicated that in his experience, it was not the recent immigrant students who were "the problem." They worked hard and had parents who sacrificed a lot to come to this country. He indicated that it was the second and third generation Hispanics, "those Chicanos," that did not care about education, did not come to school, and had parents who did not care. Furthermore, he feared that the recent immigrants would be "contaminated" by the second and third generation students and would in time also perform poorly in school. While provocative, this statement reveals something very important. This teacher does not hold a monolithic view of the Latino/a community. He has observed generational differences and links them to school performance (Valenzuela, 1999). Nobody spoke at first, and then I responded that I was interested in his perspective and wanted him to elaborate further because he was talking about my father and myself as second and third-generation Chicanos/as. While I admit that his comment stung and that I had to take a deep breath before I responded, I found it important to encourage him to elaborate on his view, seeking to uncover complexities hidden under such a provocative statement. I also wanted him to see that I offered him a "counterexample" to his generalization. My father and I represented second and third- generation Chicanos/as that valued and supported education and, in my case, have pursued it to the highest levels. I wanted to problematize his statement in a way that did not shut him down, but challenged his perceptions to further dialogue.

In another example from a recent in-service session, I was asked to review some "key ideas" for making mathematics comprehensible, rigorous, and relevant to English learners and Latino/a youth. One of the points was to infuse mathematically rich and complex problems that may have a variety of solutions, solution strategies, and real-life "messy" applications. A middle school teacher shared with the group that she had recently watched a documentary on the prison population. The documentary noted that many prisoners are high school dropouts and working on their general education equivalency degree (GED) while in prison. She reported that an example of a math problem these inmate students worked on was calculating their time spent in jail. She lamented that almost every student in her class knew someone in jail. Her point focused on depleted educational resources at home and in their communities. She stated that they lacked positive community role models. She questioned whether it was possible to find mathematics linkages within their communities. I agreed with her statement that many of her students do know someone in jail, but I also stated that for every one person they know in jail, they also know more people who are not in jail. And it is those people in their family and the community that teachers/schools must connect with as "mathematics education allies." Furthermore, it was important for teachers to then "mine" the mathematics in those contexts (Freire, 1970/1993). Connections with the business owners, community leaders, church leaders, parents, and grandparents are crucial because they care deeply about the education of their children. I acknowledged that it would take some work, but these resources exist and are waiting to be tapped. Again, the idea is to help teachers shift their mindset from communities and parents as barriers to resources in children's mathematics education. I've learned to listen patiently, ask teachers to elaborate their views, and try to offer counterexamples in the moment to acknowledge, problematize, and respectfully challenge deficit thinking about Latino/a children and their communities.

It is important to recognize that both examples above are limited in scope if taken in isolation. However, if the counterexamples are consistent in both "in the moment" situations and followed up in a variety of contexts either through an assignment or through continued discussions in professional development settings, it helps to continue to dismantle deficit thinking in relation to mathematics learning one piece at a time. The key is to further the dialogue.

RIC/RPC: Calling into Question the Appropriateness of All Students Mathematizing Issues of Equity and Social Justice

My most recent iteration explicitly focused on teaching mathematics for social justice, as I previously described in the course overview. With the inclusion of a required text, journal reflections, and other counterstrategies, including models of mathematics lessons that were socially and politically relevant, I hoped to provide both content and context that would enable preservice teachers to see these principles and the goals of this perspective as critical to their instructional vision and doable in their developing instructional practice. During one class (near the end of the quarter) following a videotape analysis debrief of a measurement lesson in which one of the reflection questions asked how the activity reflected classical, community, and critical knowledge, one of my preservice teachers publicly questioned whether teaching mathematics for equity and social justice was doable or even appropriate for young children. While she indicated that she "bought into" the ideas of teaching mathematics for social justice, she correctly noted that all of our readings and video or material lesson examples were aimed at upper elementary and middle school students. Was this even possible, for example, with first graders?

The question and observation is an important one from an ideological and pedagogical standpoint. When might you engage young people in critical thinking about issues of race, class, discrimination, social inequity while learning mathematics? Can young children engage in meaningful conversations about those issues using mathematics as an analytical tool? The course had not provided evidence that this was possible. It was clear from the student's comments that she was convinced that teaching mathematics for social justice as a pedagogical approach had its merits. The resistance manifested in envisioning such interactions with young children.

Prior to the start of this class, I had also thought about this issue. Unclear of an answer I approached my colleague Eric Gutstein, one of the coeditors of the text we were using and the author of the theoretical framework for teaching mathematics for social justice I had introduced to the class (Gutstein, 2006; Gutstein & Peterson, 2005). I posed a similar question. While he acknowledged that he did not know of any lessons or existing articles himself, he referred me to the Rethinking Schools website as a possible resource (http://www.rethinkingschools.org). He indicated that there were examples of classroom lessons that focused on issues of race and racism at the primary level. His suggestion led me to the idea that my goal with the preservice teachers would be to mathematize a lesson that focused on race and racism and to find the mathematics that would help young children engage in such important critical dialogues.

Counter-Resistance Strategy: Prioritize Problem Posing

While I had anticipated this question and planned to pose it as an issue to consider, as an educator it is a wonderful experience to have students raise the issue themselves in the class. It came from them. Thus, I used this moment to engage in another counter-resistance strategy, which was to prioritize problem posing.

While other instructors adhering to different principles might have cursorily answered the question or dismissed it altogether because of time constraints or comfort level with discussions about equity issues such as racism. Prioritizing problem posing enabled us to use this question to further our learning together as a class and eventually take it to a wider audience. I asked the preservice teachers if they would like the opportunity to be at the "cutting edge" of research and practice. I indicated that this would be new territory for me as well and that we could do this together. They agreed to jointly embark on this opportunity.

The following week I presented the preservice teachers with a group task centered around an article I found on the Rethinking School website entitled, "Brown Kids Can't Be in Our Club" (Tenorio, 2004). Written by a first-grade teacher, the article discusses how this teacher and her students explored issues of race and racism through literature, writing, science, art, and history. The article offers several examples of activities and affirms the possibility that young children can engage in critical discussions about race and racism and how it affects themselves, peers, families, and communities. In small groups, I asked my preservice teachers to read the article and to "mathematize" one of the activities discussed in the article or develop another inspired by the article (see Figure 13.2). I also asked them to "think about the classical mathematical knowledge, the community knowledge, and the critical knowledge you want kids to develop."

Their task was to create a poster describing their lesson idea. The teachers were given 1.5 hours of in-class time for this activity. I served more as a consultant during this activity. I listened carefully to different groups brainstorming ideas for possible mathematics lessons. While I did not know what their end products might be, I found many of the groups grappling with the setting or context of their lesson and not being as explicit about the mathematics concepts or skills they wanted to develop. The tension for me was to make sure the mathematics was central to the lesson. We debriefed their posters during the next class session.[4]

With the exception of one group, most chose to mathematize an activity described in the article. One of the activities was called "Me Pockets" which was used as an introductory activity in which each child was given a clear plastic sleeve and asked to put anything inside it that would tell the class more about them and what was important to them. In mathematizing the "me pocket" activity, the preservice math lessons focused on statistics and data analysis (i.e., content

Teaching Mathematics for Social Justice

The question has been raised, what does this look like in the primary grades?

YOUR TASK

- Look at the "Rethinking Schools" lesson/unit for first/second graders on issues of race.
- Mathematize one of the activities and/or develop your own inspired by the article.

- Think about the classical mathematics knowledge, the community knowledge, and the critical knowledge you want kids to develop.
- Use the racial profiling lesson, the teen boom lesson, and ladybug video and the questioning data video for possible ideas.

Figure 13.2 Teaching mathematics for social justice in the primary grades – class assignment.

from classical mathematics). The contents of the "me pockets" were organized and categorized. Students were to develop "frequency tables" and "bar graphs" to display the data such as number of languages spoken, number of siblings, and kinds of pets. The class would engage in a whole group discussion about the findings. The community knowledge component of the lesson was the contents of the "me pockets," as one poster described, "the information and experiences, from their personal lives." And the critical knowledge component of the lessons focused on engaging students in critically analyzing and reflecting on the data they collected. One poster connected their "me pockets" discussion to facilitating a "skin color" discussion described in the article emphasizing the importance of "similarities within differences." While they (children) may have different skin colors, they also share similar interests and experiences. For the final debrief, this group's poster summarized their goal with students as, "raising social and racial consciousness by challenging stereotypes and opinions."

Another group combined several activities highlighted in the article to develop a mathematics lesson focused on statistics and data analysis. This lesson included building on a science activity to investigate skin color and another activity in which partners discussed questions such as, "What is a put-down?" and "How do they (put-downs) make you feel?" In this case, the preservice teachers envisioned those activities as lead-in activities for students to make a picture graph using their skin color painted handprints in response to questions such as, "Have you ever been put down because of your skin color?" "Do you know anyone who has been put down because of their skin color?" and "Have you ever put anyone else down because of their skin color?" The teachers expected students to "analyze the graph, discuss the trends, and role-play ways to deal with/stop put-downs."

What is important to note is the effort made by these preservice teachers to grapple with classical mathematical, community, and critical knowledge bases to develop mathematics lessons that connect with their developing vision for teaching mathematics for social justice. These preservice teachers focused on the mathematics. In fact, the predominant classical mathematics of the lessons developed focused on statistics and data analysis. This included some mention of concepts like addition and counting that are foundational in statistics and key concepts at the primary level. While a few groups included measurement and proportional reasoning when asking students to mix paint to "match" their skin color, the mathematics that enabled these teachers to envision themselves engaging with young children in dialogues about race and racism utilized statistical concepts like measures of central tendency (i.e., mode) and data representation (bar graphs, frequency tables).

These teachers focused on the community as an asset or resource for learning by including opportunities in the lesson for students to tap their funds of knowledge such as personal/family experiences and cultural traditions (Civil, 2002; Gonzalez, Moll, & Amanti, 2005). And they mined critical knowledge by engaging students in dialogues using the mathematics to support discussions about issues of race and racism. Thus, they envisaged mathematics as an analytical tool, in the words of one group's poster, "to raise social and racial consciousness by challenging stereotype and opinion."

By prioritizing problem posing, these preservice teachers and I pushed our own thinking about what is possible mathematically to engage young children in critical discussions about inequity and injustice. While I hope these teachers choose to integrate the goals of teaching mathematics for social justice in their vision for teaching, I am confident that the course gave them an opportunity to develop proof that these goals can be realized at all educational levels.

Discussion and Implications

The counter-resistance strategies discussed above highlight the importance of furthering dialogue as part of the teacher learning process. Offering counterexamples and prioritizing problem posing are strategies designed to simultaneously challenge, empower, and liberate teachers/learners from perpetuating inequity and injustice. A central tenet of this work is to privilege the mathematics and equity in those professional development and teaching preparation contexts.

My approach to teacher preparation and professional development shifted from a pedagogy of access to one that emphasized transformation. In the first iterations of the course there was a strong emphasis on the community knowledge and classical mathematical knowledge link. While the focus on access is fundamental to working toward achieving equity and social justice in mathematics education, I have always found myself wondering is access enough? Is access all that we want for our children? Or, do we want the dismantling of systems that perpetuate inequities? Do we want more children taking advanced placement courses, including mathematics, or do we want all children to fulfill the mathematics education requirements for a college education if they choose that path? The latter requires a fundamental rethinking and pedagogy of transformation at both the individual classroom level and the collective level (school/department).

It is the critical knowledge component that I have more recently explicitly integrated into my course and professional development work. Moving toward a pedagogy that emphasizes transformation—challenging and changing the status quo—demands counter-resistance strategies such as elaboration with counterexamples and problem posing to engage teachers in respectful critical dialogue about mathematics and equity with a goal of replication in their own mathematics classrooms. Activities that engage teachers in mathematizing issues of equity promote critical reflection among teachers and provide them with tangible examples they can use in their own classrooms.

Mathematics and Equity: An Issue of Foregrounding

A common viewpoint of this work still questions the mathematics legitimacy and rigor of the approach. It is as if talking about issues of equity and social justice precludes discussions of "real mathematics." I would argue that real mathematics must occur in these contexts in order to fully engage in discussions about equity and social justice. The issue is what gets *foregrounded* and when. In the case of the elaboration and counterexample, my "in the moment" responses focused less on mathematics and more on equity contexts: the roles that culture, language, and race may play in how these teachers depicted Latino/a youth and communities. I needed to provide counterexamples that addressed context before engaging with the mathematics discussion. From my perspective, letting deficit views remain unchallenged perpetuates apathy and the lack of motivation to rethink mathematics teaching and learning, particularly for students of color. In the problem posing example, mathematics and equity were foregrounded in different ways and at different times. However, both were present in the final products of the preservice teachers' mathematics lessons.

Implications for Mathematics Educators

For mathematics educators, in general, I understand that privileging equity with mathematics may push some out of their comfort zone. In other words, the comfort and safety is within the mathematics—and to a certain extent the belief that mathematics is apolitical. It is just mathematics. However, with the growing acknowledgment that knowledge in general and mathematics in particular are highly political, teacher preparation and professional development (sources of teacher knowledge) necessitate infusing them with equity and social justice (Gutierrez, 2002a, 2006; Gutstein, 2006; Rodriguez & Kitchen, 2005).

As this paper demonstrates, it is not always easy. And for mathematics educators of color, the inherent tensions and complexities are greater, particularly in the face of teaching populations that are predominantly White, middle-class, monolingual English, and female. It is clear that aspects of my sociocultural identities impacted course design, implementation, and responses to participants. I elected to integrate issues of culture, language, race, and class into my mathematics methods course and professional development work because of who I am and my commitments to youth of color and our communities. This opens me up to harsh critiques and racialized comments that I must respond to from a mathematics, sociocultural, and political perspective. I cannot dissociate myself, who I am, from this work. It is not an option for me. What is an option for me is to critically reflect on how my sociocultural identities play out in my teacher preparation and professional development contexts. That is an ongoing activity that continually informs this work.

Furthermore, I often feel that there is higher scrutiny of my work in this arena, particularly from a mathematical perspective. Is the work mathematical enough? While this may be an aspect of my own self-critique, I still feel the messages are mixed in the greater mathematics education community about whether privileging both mathematics and equity is even possible. Because, as one person recently said to me, "Your focus on language and culture while they are important, in the end, your job is to make sure that teachers leave knowing how to teach math." What I glean from such a statement is that equity issues are fine, *but* if they (teachers) do not know how to teach math, then students will not learn mathematics. It is that implicit dismissal about the importance of equity within the context of mathematics teaching and learning that is at the heart of resistance, both ideological and pedagogical, that pervades the greater mathematics education community. I explicitly choose to combat this resistance with counterresistance strategies that privilege both mathematics and equity, are informed by my sociocultural identities, commitment to communities of color, and to an explicit equity and social justice agenda.

In addition, I have been asked if my work in this area is a function of my individual "talents." Do we or can we produce more "Julia Aguirres" to teach like this. The answer is yes and no. No, you cannot replicate me. The totality of my experiences and what I bring to my scholarship and teaching are uniquely mine and continue to be developed in dialectic with new experiences. However, you can substantively infuse mathematics education doctoral programs with requirements that address issues of equity such as language, culture, race, class, and gender. It cannot be an option nor can it be a "mini" unit. It must be infused in all aspects of the program both as single-focus courses and pervasive in more "core" courses. Doctoral students must learn to be critical of how their own and others' sociocultural identities inform their work. This necessitates acceptance of change from all who participate in the mathematics education professoriate. If we produce mathematics educators without this integrated knowledge base that privileges both the mathematics and equity, then producing teachers with such a knowledge base will be unattainable.

An important beginning of this transformative work for teacher preparation and professional development in mathematics education comes from examining counter-resistance strategies to ideological and pedagogical forms of resistance (Rodriguez & Kitchen, 2005). I have shared a comprehensive theoretical framework that shapes this work and offered two additional strategies to consider: elaboration with counterexamples and prioritizing problem posing. These strategies are tightly coupled to my sociocultural identities, professional identities, and commitments to children and communities of color. Privileging both mathematics and equity demands that these links be acknowledged, valued, and nurtured to promote real change in mathematics teaching and learning.

Notes

1. This research was supported by the National Science Foundation, under grant ESI-0424983, awarded to CEMELA (The Center for the Mathematics Education of Latino/as). The views expressed here are those of the author and do not necessarily reflect the views of the funding agency.
2. I often use the term Latina/o as a pan-ethnic label to express my cultural and political solidarity with people who are descendents of or natives of a Western hemisphere country south of the United States including Mexico, Central and South America, and the Caribbean (Hurtado & Gurin, 2004). I prefer to use this term rather than Hispanic because it is more progressive

and acknowledges Indigenous, African and European ancestries that the term Hispanic does not.

3. My father is Chicano and my mother is White (English, French, Irish). I consider myself biracial. I strongly identify as a Chicana. The term emphasizes pride in Mexican American culture, history and indigenous roots, as well as an emphasis in activism that seeks to fight against discrimination. Hurtado and Gurin (2004, p. 51) state the following, "Calling oneself a Chicano/a by definition implies consciousness—that is, awareness that members of this group (Mexican-descent) are unfairly treated in a discriminatory manner and furthermore that the discrimination is group-based, rather than stemming from personality or individual characteristics."
4. Students were also free to work on this activity outside of class.

References

Aguirre, J., Kitchen, R., & Horak, J. (2005). *Mathematics teachers' conceptions and instructional practices to address student diversity.* Paper presented at the National Council of Teachers of Mathematics Research Pre-Session, Anaheim, CA.

Anderson, S. E. (1990). World math curriculum: Fighting Eurocentrism in mathematics. *Journal for Negro Education, 59,* 348–359.

Borasi, R. (1996). *Reconceiving mathematics instruction: A focus on errors.* Norwood, NJ: Ablex.

Carpenter, T., Franke, M., & Levi, L. (2003), *Thinking mathematically: Integrating arithmetic and algebra in elementary school.* Portsmouth, NH: Heinemann.

Civil, M. (2002). Culture and mathematics: A community approach. *Journal of Intercultural Studies, 23,* 133–148.

Civil, M. (2006). Building on community knowledge: An avenue to equity in mathematics education. In N. S. Nasir & P. Cobb (Eds.), *Improving access to mathematics: Diversity, equity and access to mathematical ideas* (pp. 105–117). New York: Teachers College Press.

Civil, M., & Andrade, R. (2002). Transitions between home and school mathematics: Rays of hope amidst the passing clouds. In A. J. Bishop, G. de Abreu, & N. C. Presmeg (Eds.), *Transitions between contexts of mathematical practices* (pp.149–169). Dordrecht: Kluwer.

D'Ambrosio, U. (1985). Ethnomathematics and its place in the history and pedagogy of mathematics. *For the Learning of Mathematics, 5,* 41–48.

Delpit, L. (1995). *Other people's children: Cultural conflict in the classroom.* New York: Norton.

Ernest, P. (1991). *The philosophy of mathematics education.* London: Falmer Press.

Frankenstein, M. (1990). Incorporating race, gender, and class issues into a critical mathematical literacy curriculum. *Journal of Negro Education, 59,* 336–359.

Freire, P. (1993). *Pedagogy of the oppressed.* New York: Continuum. (Original work published 1970)

González, N., Moll, L., & Amanti, C. (2005). *Funds of knowledge: Theorizing practices in households and communities.* Mahwah, NJ: Erlbaum.

Gutierrez, R. (2000). Is the multiculturalization of mathematics doing us more harm than good? In R. Mahalingam & C. McCarthy (Eds.), *Multicultural curriculum: New directions for social theory, practice, and policy* (pp. 199–200). New York: Routledge.

Gutierrez, R. (2002a). Enabling the practice of teachers in context: Toward a new equity research agenda. *Mathematical Thinking and Learning, 4,* 145–187.

Gutierrez, R. (2002b). Beyond essentialism: The complexity of language in teaching Latina/o students in mathematics. *American Educational Research Journal, 39,* 1047–1088.

Gutierrez, R. (2006). (Re)defining equity: The importance of a critical perspective. In N. S. Nasir & P. Cobb (Eds.), *Improving access to mathematics: Diversity and equity in the classroom* (pp. 37–50). New York: Teachers College Press.

Gutstein, E. (2003). Teaching and learning mathematics for social justice in an urban Latino school. *Journal for Research in Mathematical Education, 34,* 37–73.

Gutstein, E. (2006). *Reading and writing the world with mathematics: Toward a pedagogy for social justice.* New York: Routledge.

Gutstein, E., & Peterson, B. (Eds.). (2005). *Rethinking mathematics: Teaching social justice by the numbers*. Milwaukee, WI: Rethinking Schools.

Hurtado, A., & Gurin, P. (2004). *Chicana/o identity in a changing U.S. society: Quién Soy? Quiénes Somos?* Tucson: University of Arizona Press.

Khisty, L. L. (1995). Making inequality: Issues of language and meanings in mathematics teaching with Hispanic students. In E. Fennema, W. G. Secada, & L. B. Adajian (Eds.), *New directions for equity in mathematics education* (pp. 279–298). Cambridge: Cambridge University Press.

Khisty, L. L. (1997). Making mathematics accessible to Latino students: Rethinking instructional practice. In *Multicultural and gender equity in mathematics classroom: The gift of diversity—NCTM yearbook* (pp. 92–101). Reston, VA: National Council of Teachers of Mathematics.

Khisty, L. L., & Viego, G. (1999). Challenging conventional wisdom: A case study. In W. Secada (Ed.), *Changing the faces of mathematics: Perspectives on Latinos and Latinas* (pp. 71–80). Reston, VA: National Council of Teachers of Mathematics.

Kitchen, R. S., & Lear, J. M. (2000). Mathematizing Barbie: Using measurement as a means for girls to analyze their sense of body image. In W. G. Secada (Ed.), *Changing the faces of mathematics* (pp. 67–74). Reston, VA: National Council of Teachers of Mathematics.

Lave, J., & Wenger, E. (1991). *Situated learning: Legitimate peripheral participation*. Cambridge: Cambridge University Press.

Ma, L. P. (1999). *Knowing and teaching elementary mathematics: Teachers' understanding of fundamental mathematics in China and the United States*. Mahwah, NJ: Erlbaum.

Moll, L. C., & González, N. (2004). A funds-of-knowledge approach to multicultural education. In J. A. Banks & C. A. McGee Banks (Eds.), *Handbook of research on multicultural education* (2nd ed., pp. 699–715). San Francisco: Jossey-Bass.

Morrell, E. (2005, February 3). *Doing critical social research with youth*. Talk given at DePaul University, Chicago.

Moschkovich, J. N. (2000). Learning mathematics in two languages: Moving from obstacles to resources. In W. G. Secada (Ed.), *Changing faces of mathematics: Perspectives on multiculturalism and gender equity* (pp. 85–93). Reston, VA: National Council of Teachers of Mathematics.

Moschkovich, J. N. (2002). A situated and sociocultural perspective on bilingual mathematics learners. *Mathematical Thinking and Learning, 4*, 189–212.

Moschkovich, J. N. (2006). Bilingual mathematics learners: How views of language, bilingual learners, and mathematical communication affect instruction. In N. S. Nasir & P. Cobb (Eds.), *Improving access to mathematics: Diversity and equity in the classroom* (pp. 89–104). New York: Teachers College Press.

Moses, R., & Cobb, C. E. (2001). *Radical equations: Math literacy and civil rights*. Boston: Beacon Press.

Nasir, N. (2006). Identity, goals and learning: The case of basketball mathematics. In N. S. Nasir & P. Cobb (Eds.), *Improving access to mathematics: Diversity and equity in the classroom* (pp. 132–145). New York: Teachers College Press.

National Council of Teachers of Mathematics. (2000). *Principles and standards for school mathematics*. Reston, VA: Author.

National Research Council. (2001). *Adding it up: Helping children learn mathematics*. Washington D.C.: National Academy Press.

National Science Foundation. (2006, November). Statistics report on mathematics and science education doctorates 1990–2004. Available at: http://www.norc.org

Nieto, S. (2000). *Affirming diversity: The sociopolitical context of multicultural education* (3rd ed.). New York: Longman.

Oakes, J., Joseph, R., & Muir, K. (2004) Access and achievement in mathematics and science: Inequities that endure and change. In J. A. Banks & C. A. McGee Banks (Eds.), *Handbook of research on multicultural education* (2nd ed., pp. 69–90). San Francisco: Jossey-Bass.

Pajares, M. F. (1992). Teacher's beliefs and educational research: Cleaning up a messy construct. *Review of Educational Research, 62*(3), 307–332.

Perkins, I., & Flores, A. (2002). Mathematical notations and procedures of recent immigrant students. *Mathematics Teaching in Middle School, 7*(6), 346–351.

National Council of Teachers of Mathematics. (2000). *Principles and standards for school mathematics*. Reston, VA: Author.

Rodriguez, A. J. (2005). Teachers' resistance to ideological and pedagogical change: Definitions, theoretical framework, and significance. In A. J. Rodriguez & R. S. Kitchen (Eds.), *Preparing mathematics and science teachers for diverse classrooms: Promising strategies for transformative pedagogy* (pp. 1–15). Mahwah, NJ: Erlbaum.

Rodriguez, A. J., & Kitchen, R. S. (2005). *Preparing mathematics and science teachers for diverse classrooms: Promising strategies for transformative pedagogy*. Mahwah, NJ: Erlbaum.

Saxe, G. B. (1988). Candy selling and math learning. *Educational Researcher, 17*, 14–21.

Schoenfeld, A. H. (1992). Learning to think mathematically: Problem-solving, metacognition, and sense making in mathematics. In D. A. Grouws (Ed.), *Handbook of research on mathematics teaching and learning* (pp. 334–370). New York: Macmillan.

Schoenfeld, A. H. (1998). Toward a theory of teaching in context. *Issues in Education, 4*, 1–94.

Schoenfeld, A. H. (2003). How can we examine the connections between teacher's world views and their educational practices? *Issues in Education, 8*, 217–227.

Shulman, L. S. (1987). Knowledge and teaching: Foundations of the new reform. *Harvard Educational Review, 57*, 1–22.

Skemp, R. R. (1987). *The psychology of learning mathematics*. Hillsdale, NJ: Erlbaum.

Skovsmose, O. (1994). *Toward a philosophy of critical mathematics education*. Dordrecht, The Netherlands: Kluwer.

Tate, W. F. (1994). Race, retrenchment and reform of school mathematics. *Phi Delta Kappan, 75*, 447–485.

Tate, W. F. (1995). Mathematics communication: Creating opportunities to learn. *Teaching Children Mathematics, 1*, 344–349.

Tenorio, R. (2004). Brown kids can't be in our club. *Rethinking Schools*. Retrieved August 31, 2008, from http://www.rethinkingschools.org/archive/18_03/club183.shtml

Thompson, A. (1992). Teachers' beliefs and conceptions: A synthesis of the research. In D. Grouws (Ed.), *Handbook of research on mathematics teaching and learning* (pp. 127–146). New York: Macmillan.

Turner, E., & Strawhun, B. (2005). With math it's like you have more defense: Students use math to investigate overcrowding at their school. In E. Gutstein & B. Peterson (Eds.), *Rethinking mathematics: Teaching social justice by the numbers* (pp. 81–87). Milwaukee, WI: Rethinking Schools, Ltd.

Tyack, D., & Cuban, L. (1995). *Tinkering toward utopia: A century of public school reform*. Cambridge, MA: Harvard University Press.

Valenzuela, A. (1999). *Subtractive schooling: U.S.–Mexican youth and the politics of caring*. Albany, NY: SUNY Press.

Wenger, E. (1998). *Communities of practice: Learning, meaning, and identity*. Cambridge, UK: Cambridge University Press.

14

Latina Mothers' Perceptions about the Teaching and Learning of Mathematics

Implications for Parental Participation

MARTA CIVIL AND BEATRIZ QUINTOS

In this chapter we argue that a fundamental component for establishing a culturally responsive education is a dialogue that breaks down the hierarchical and hegemonic practices that often characterize parental involvement in U.S. schools, particularly in low income, minoritized communities. Our position is that all learning is embedded within a specific community and is therefore socially mediated (Darder, 1991; Vygotsky, 1978). Mathematics learning is no exception. Thus the teaching of mathematics should include elements of the learners' culture such as language, values, beliefs, practices, traditions, and history. One way to access these community resources is through conversations with students' parents or caretakers. In this chapter we present our analysis from conversations regarding mathematics education with a group of mothers of school-age children and discuss the implications of our findings. We first give a brief description of the parental engagement project in which our research took place. We then give an overview of the literature on parental involvement that informs our work. In particular, we draw on the research in this area that critically examines issues of power and perceptions of parents (especially minoritized and working-class parents; Delgado-Gaitan, 2001; Henry, 1996; Horvat, Weininger, & Lareau, 2003; Pérez, Drake, & Calabrese Barton, 2005; Reay, 1998). The rest of the chapter focuses primarily on three mothers' perceptions of, and expectations for, the teaching and learning of mathematics. Although our focus is on these three mothers, we also introduce comments from other mothers to further support the complex processes at play, since some of the issues expressed were common to many parents.[1]

Our work centers on the voices of parents who are seldom heard in conversations about mathematics education—working-class parents, particularly those belonging to minoritized ethnic/language groups. Through our dialogue with the mothers in this project we have developed a better understanding of their views and beliefs about the teaching and learning of mathematics, with a specific focus on issues related to mathematics education reform. We believe that these conversations are critical for researchers, school staff, and parents to communicate in an egalitarian and informed way. Listening—rather than merely informing or "talking to" parents—and conducting classroom observations with the parents, supported our effort of a dialogue in the academic realm, which has the potential to contribute to everyone's role in children's education.

Context

This research took place in the context of a large outreach project (Math and Parent Partnerships in the Southwest [MAPPS])[2] that focused on parental involvement in mathematics education in a working—class, Latino/a community. The partnering school district was largely Latino/a (85%) (primarily of Mexican origin) with 77% of the children on free or reduced lunch at the time of the study. The goal of MAPPS was to promote the leadership of parents in mathematics activities in home and school through three components:

1. Leadership development sessions in which parents, teachers, and administrators came together to explore issues around different learning styles, to learn how to facilitate workshops for the larger parent community, and to work on parent recruitment issues.
2. Mathematics Awareness Workshops (MAWS) which were open to parents in the district and ranged over key topics in K-12 mathematics (e.g., multiplication and its different representations, "discovering π"). These workshops were self-contained and lasted about two hours. Children and parents attended together but the children were usually dismissed at some point in the workshop (and went to a different room where childcare was provided). This allowed for the parents and other family members to engage as adult learners or to discuss and analyze their children's thinking. In the first year members of the project staff facilitated the MAWS. However, in subsequent years members of the leadership teams became the facilitators. Also, each team of facilitators had a mentor, a parent or a teacher who had previously been a workshop facilitator.
3. Math for Parents (MFP) courses in which parents on the leadership teams had an opportunity to explore mathematical topics in more depth. These courses met for eight weeks in two-hour-long sessions. We developed five MFPs—in algebra, geometry, fractions, decimals and percents, numbers, and data. These courses were taught by experienced instructors (e.g.,

teachers or university professors), some of whom were the authors of the MFP materials.

The research reported on in this chapter took place during the third year of the project. At the time of the study, there were 33 parents (mothers or grandmothers), 25 teachers, and seven administrators in the Leadership Teams. Each semester consisted of one MFP course, approximately 36 MAWS, and several sessions focusing on leadership development. In this chapter we focus on the experiences of three mothers, two of whom joined MAPPS the first year and the third in the second year. Thus, they were familiar with all the components of the project and at the time of the study two of them were facilitators of MAWS, while the third one had been a facilitator and was now a mentor.

Researchers (Lehrer & Shumow, 1997; Peressini, 1998) have documented the frequent mismatches between the aspirations of reformers in mathematics education and those of parents and other community members in the communities where reforms are being implemented. In this chapter we address these possible mismatches by engaging in conversations with, and listening to, the voices of these three mothers as they reflect on what they value in the teaching and learning of mathematics. These conversations serve not only in lessening mismatches regarding mathematics reform but also to encourage the regular inclusion of parents' voices in matters of academic content and teaching.

We focus on these mothers from three different angles: (1) as adult learners in the Math for Parents minicourses; (2) as parents conducting classroom visits in the participating schools; and (3) as facilitators of the Math Awareness Workshops (MAWS), open to all parents in participating schools. These three angles combined offer an approach to parental participation, one that focuses on parents engaging with academic content at different levels. These three angles are based on our proposed model for parental participation in mathematics education, a model that emerged from our interactions with the parents as we learned about their expectations, desires, and interests (for more on this model see, Civil, Bratton, & Quintos, 2005). The model has four components: Parents as Parents (i.e., parents originally joined MAPPS because they wanted to help their children with their mathematics education); Parents as Learners (parents became learners for themselves; some even pursued further education); Parents as Teachers/Facilitators (parents became facilitators of mathematics workshops for other parents in the community); Parents as Leaders (e.g., parents became advocates for the education not only of their children but for all the children in the district).

Theoretical Framework

Our work draws on several bodies of research, including the literature on adult education and parental involvement from a sociocultural and critical perspective.

We conceptualize schools and community relationships as mediated by the historical and sociopolitical context of schools (Calabrese Barton, Drake, Perez, St. Louis, & George, 2004). Therefore, particular interactions have to be analyzed as part of a historical but dynamic process mediated by participants' understood roles, goals or objects, resources or tools, as well as the asymmetrical power relations and norms that permeate society. Our work is based on research that has critically examined issues of power and perceptions of parents (especially minoritized and working-class parents) (Henry, 1996; Lareau, 2000; Reay, 1998; Vincent, 1996). This work rejects a deficit model that situates the problem within families (see Valencia & Black, 2002 for a discussion regarding debunking the myth that Mexican Americans do not care about education) and instead we argue for a sociocultural perspective that seeks to learn from the families and children and accounts for the institutional biases inherent in schools that have contributed to the mismatch between home and school. As Valenzuela (1999) argues, schooling is a process that often subtracts social and cultural resources from Mexican-American and Mexican-immigrant students. Her research highlights how the structural composition of the school, curricular biases, limitations on bilingual education (e.g., Proposition 203 in Arizona,[3] Proposition 227 in California), and the lack of caring relationships between the schools' staff and the community serve as contributors to the perpetuation of inequalities. In this context our work aims to open *spaces* within the educational sites in which the object of *dialogue* with the families generates transformations in relationships among schools and families. We think of these spaces as a collective zone of proximal development, to borrow from Vygotsky's (1978) theories of sociocultural development, which create new possibilities through praxis, the sharing of knowledge, and a constant reflection. The object of dialogue becomes a means for participatory democracy (Dewey, 1916). It supports the examination of the larger social systems and the collective action to review commonly held views of parents' roles in the particular institution of the school.

Most people accept without question the concept that parental involvement plays a positive role in children's education; in fact it is a mandate in contemporary educational settings. Yet, what is meant by involvement is often unclear and this can be problematic (Lankshear, Gee, Knobel, & Searle, 1997; Vincent, 1996). As Olivos (2006) writes, "For me the term 'parental involvement' has far too often been diluted in the professional literature and in practice to a laundry list of activities that the 'experts' feel good parents 'do' to blindly support the schools' agendas" (p. 13).

Political agendas push for concerted efforts of parental involvement and "choice" to solve problems in the education of underserved students or a publicized educational crisis. Critical to our focus is the counter reality, that is, the increasing control over content through policy and standardized testing. For instance, in some states, such as ours, Arizona, Spanish-speaking parents are marginalized from their children's learning by the curtailment of bilingual education (Combs, Evans, Fletcher, Parra, & Jiménez, 2005). Furthermore standardized testing and the push for accountability are the forces "guiding" instruction, to the detriment of content and approaches encouraged by reform-based mathematics. In opposition to these policies, we assert that the particular communities of the schools need to be part of the dialogue to make the decisions about what their children are going to learn. This dialogue must to be embraced and supported by educational policies, and school and district structures, in order to enable a systematic connection of the school and the community. As Olivos (2006) writes,

> I contend that the U.S. education system is part of a complex system of domination which creates and recreates asymmetrical power relations based on race, class, and gender and that the most effective way to "combat" this system is to become cognizant of the contradictions found within it…I argue that bicultural parents must begin to understand their roles within the socioeconomic and historic context from which their subordination and their children's academic failure arises if they are to effectively contribute to the transformation of the school system. (pp. 16–17)

Reay (1998), in her research on mothers' involvement in their children's schooling in Britain, points out the different roles and approaches among middle-class and working-class mothers:

> [For the middle-class mothers] educational problems, when they did arise, were due to deficits in schooling, rather than located in either themselves or their child…. In contrast many of the working-class women had learnt from their own experience of schooling that educational difficulties were due to failings in the individual, rather than the system. (p. 64)

Furthermore, Reay's interviews with immigrant women underscored the difficulties that many of them encountered as they tried to build on their cultural capital for their children's benefit. Their experiences with schooling were so different from what their children were experiencing in their new country that their cultural capital was of little use in their current situation. Therefore it would seem that families from the dominant culture with a higher economic status tend to have more power in the school in advocating for their own children's needs than working-class, immigrant families. Where are the voices of the "other" parents? Our work is specifically concerned with the voices of these "other" parents. As Ramirez (2002) notes, teachers and schools need to be explicitly open to and strive for communication between the school and students' families. Through her longitudinal research study, Delgado-Gaitan (2004) suggests that it is critical to encourage feedback and comments from parents and not just give them information about the content.

Our work centers on engaging with parents in talk about the teaching and learning of mathematics. Along these lines, we have found Flecha's (2000) concept of dialogic learning particularly helpful. His work is grounded on the experiences of a group of adults in a working-class neighborhood who participate in a literary circle. A key concept in dialogic learning is the notion of an egalitarian dialogue, which refers to a dialogue in which the validity of a contribution is not determined on the basis of who is giving the contribution; that is, his or her position of power. The validity is determined through discussion in the group. What may this look like in a mathematics setting? Could we envision a "mathematical circle" in which adults and facilitator(s) engage in dialogic learning about mathematics? As Flecha (2000) points out, dialogic learning involves a sociocultural component: "The meaning formation process does not depend solely on the intervention of education professionals, but also on all the people and contexts related to the student's learning" (p. 23).

Although educational rhetoric often talks about the importance of parental involvement, the form that this parental involvement may take often goes unexamined and seems to be based on a limited array of possibilities, such as presence of parents in the schools. Those parents who are visible in the school are seen as "involved parents." What they actually do while they are in the schools, or what the parents who cannot spend time at school may be doing to be "involved" is not so often addressed (see Calabrese Barton et al., 2004, for a critique of views on parental involvement grounded on a deficit model). Yet parents are involved in their children's schooling in diverse forms. Social and school factors as well as parents' beliefs and prior experiences influence their chosen form of involvement. These issues are critical to consider in order to establish respectful and egalitarian relationships, as Mapp (2003) underscores in her research.

Listening to and Learning from Parents

Our research is grounded on a phenomenological methodology (Van Manen, 1990) that relies heavily on participants' contributions to the experience. Through this orientation, the lived experience of each parent is considered significant and our goal is to try to capture it in our analysis and writing. The main sources of data for this article include: (1) feedback forms for MAPPS activities (MAWS, MFP); (2) field notes of classroom observations; (3) debriefings of classroom observations; (4) debriefings with MAWs facilitators; and (5) group interviews. All the debriefings and interviews were audiotaped and videotaped. The classroom observations were not only part of our research methodology, but our effort to engage in a conversation about mathematics teaching and learning where the parents would take the lead in the dialogue. The classroom was a concrete learning context that opened the space for us to learn about their experiences as parents, and as learners (in their childhood and now as adults).

As previously mentioned, learning about these mothers' perceptions relating to the teaching and learning of mathematics is essential to the development of authentic dialogues between schools, families, and researchers. Additionally, these voices serve to inform our efforts toward parental participation in mathematics education. Although our focus is on these three mothers, at some points we include comments from other parents to further illustrate the shared views about teaching and learning mathematics.

The Mothers

Esperanza Ballesteros[4] joined MAPPS the first year of the project. Esperanza is Spanish dominant. At the time of the study she had a fair understanding of English and spoke it a little. She had facilitated Math Awareness Workshops (MAWS) for almost a year. She had one daughter in second grade, another daughter in seventh grade, and a son who had graduated from high school two years prior. Esperanza was working at her younger daughter's elementary school.

Marisol López had also been with the program since the beginning and is Spanish dominant as well. At the time of the study, she understood and spoke English, though she was not fully fluent yet. She was a mentor for Esperanza's MAWS team (Marisol and Esperanza are close friends). The year before, Marisol had been a facilitator in a team in which she was the only parent (the other team members were all teachers). She had one child in second grade and one in preschool. Marisol was a volunteer at her older son's school.

Jillian Velmont joined MAPPS in year two. She is English dominant with minimal understanding of Spanish. At the time of the study she was in her first year as a facilitator for MAWS workshops. She had one daughter in second grade, one son in fifth grade, one son in eighth grade, and one son in ninth grade. Jillian was a volunteer at the middle school her son attended. Esperanza and Marisol were born and raised in Mexico; Jillian was born and raised in the United States (her mother was Mexican American) and she described herself as "human, Mexican, Italian."

Parents as Adult Learners: What they Value

The general approach to the teaching and learning of mathematics in the MAPPS activities can be characterized as reform-oriented (National Council of Teachers of Mathematics [NCTM], 1989, 2000). The materials developed built on several standards-based K-12 curriculum resources and textbooks. The pedagogical approach emphasized group work, discussions about mathematics, solving problems in several different ways, and using manipulative materials and calculators. Conceptual understanding and connections among various topics in mathematics were emphasized.

The Voices of Esperanza, Jillian, and Marisol

What do these three mothers value as adult learners of mathematics? We asked them to reflect on this question and we encouraged them to feel free to talk about what they valued and how they felt as adult learners in general, not just about mathematics (e.g., Esperanza had been learning English for some time as well as preparing for the General Education Development [GED] tests, which when passed would certify her as having high school-level academic skills. This is what they wrote (we have these remarks in writing because they were getting ready to present at American Educational Research Association [AERA] and this is what they were planning to say):

Esperanza

As a student, the best experience that I have had is to be able to share with other adults in the classroom; to see how we can go back to other times and compare how we learned when we were children; and how for the majority of people, it is difficult to learn English as a second language, how there are words that no matter how much one practices them, still cannot give them the same sound or pronunciation; to look back and see how much I have been able to move forward and everything that one can do with willpower and desire.

Jillian

Groups, groups, very important. Math for Parents has taught me it's great to have individual help, like kids need one-on-one with the teacher or other children. Being in MFP has been a learning tool for then teaching other parents, as we become leaders. So encouraging for myself. My children look at me differently. It's exciting to learn, I *can* do it. I needed to have these classes to realize I can do it and it's exciting to show other parents and have them go "I get it." Must feel like when teachers know kids get it.

Marisol

As the saying goes, "to remember is to live again...." To use manipulatives that were not available when I was a child; to be with other parents who are in the same situation as myself and to share different ways of learning; to learn about the interest among other parents as to how to help their children; to share experiences.

These three mothers' comments capture some of the themes that were shared by most parents in MAPPS. Overall, parents agree that their current learning experience in MAPPS is very different from what they went through as school-age students (whether in Mexico or in the United States). The most striking differences that parents consistently pointed out that were: (1) they could work in groups and talk with their peers about the problems; (2) they used manipulatives; and (3) they learned about different ways to do one problem.

Parents in the MFP courses particularly valued the notion of friendship, of coming together with friends to discuss mathematics ("You meet other people and you get to learn with other grown-ups"; "The gathering of many friends in a learning environment"). These parents would probably agree with what FitzSimons (1994) points out as being crucial in working with adult learners, namely, "the need to establish an atmosphere of mutual respect and a feeling of community in which adult learners are encouraged to be independent learners and to share their expertise" (pp. 24–25). Working in groups is the positive feature that appears most often in the evaluation forms and in their interviews ("It's surprising how enjoyable it is to work together on a problem with adults. I wonder if it is the same with children"). The participants were also very appreciative of instructors that made them feel comfortable, that made an effort to establish rapport with them, and that "spoke at their level": "The teacher, [was] easygoing, not intimidating, always had something new that was interesting, I thought he was fantastic. I wished he could have been one my teachers in high school. You never felt you were going to be put down. We weren't afraid to ask questions."

Discussion

These mothers' reflections as adult learners point at a possibility to build bridges between parents, teachers, and the school community. Even if many parents might not have learned in the ways described in reform mathematics, parents and educators have a space to engage in conversations about reform mathematics and to create a common ground. In the following section we describe some mothers' different teaching and learning expectations for themselves and for their children. These mothers' learning experiences served as the grounds for reflection.

It is hard to separate parents as learners from parents as parents; even in their comments about themselves as learners, their children are very much present in their minds, either explicitly such as in Jillian's case, "my children look at me differently", or implicitly, as when Esperanza says, "everything that one can do with willpower and desire." This idea of willpower and desire is a recurrent theme among MAPPS parents not only for themselves (e.g., several of them have gone on to pursue further education), but also they often talk about wanting to show their children that they can also succeed through willpower and desire. The next section illustrates this aspect and then turns to an in-depth look at what these three mothers focus on when observing a mathematics class.

Parents as Parents: What They Value for Their Children's Schooling

A key reason why parents joined project MAPPS was because they wanted to be able to help their children with homework. At the time we started the project, the school district in which our research took place was using reform-based curricula that looked very different from what the parents had ever experienced. As we developed rapport with many of the parents in the project, we realized that we needed to have some kind of joint experience with the parents that related directly to their children's mathematics instruction. For example, parents often mentioned that their children were working in groups and using manipulatives just like they did as parent participants in MAPPS. We were intrigued by these comments and wanted to gain a better understanding of parents' perceptions of how these approaches (e.g., group work, use of manipulatives) were being implemented in K-12 classrooms. This is how the idea of classroom visits with a small group of parents was developed. For example, group work is one of the most often mentioned features of "reform-based" mathematics teaching, but what does it mean to work in groups? Having students sitting in groups does not necessarily mean that students are working together as a group, sharing and building on each other's ideas towards the solution of a given mathematics problem. After a visit to an eighth grade class, our debriefing with Jillian and Esperanza centered on this idea of working in groups. Jillian commented, "I did like her way of teaching, the way she acted with the kids. I like that she let them work together but asked them to make their own thing."

Jillian points to an intriguing feature of working in groups: She liked that they could work together but that they were asked to "make their own thing." Group work can be controversial because some parents (and others) are concerned that by working in groups we may not have an idea of what students can do as individuals. Our (the authors') observations of this class were that even though the students were sitting in groups, most of the work was done individually. Although the teacher did allow them to work together, it seemed clear that there was a classroom management concern lingering, "You can work together, as long as you stay at your table." Or later on, "You can work in groups as long as each of you comes up with your problem. If you are having individual conversations and not working, it will be individual work." Thus, we actually wondered about the group work element and decided to probe more into the mothers' perception of what that meant:

Jillian: I saw a lot of them that were by themselves; others were helping each other. Most of them were doing it on their own. It seemed they chose to, they were more comfortable doing it that way.

Esperanza: What I noticed is that they work on their own but once they are done, they ask each other for opinions and they talk about it.

Jillian suggested a reason for why students at this age may be more comfortable working on their own:

> She [the teacher] was doing a lot of the teaching part. Once everyone understands it's easier to come up…when nobody is sure what the problems were, everyone is quiet. Nobody wants to give the wrong answer, especially in middle school because you'd feel like a big idiot.

The theme of working in groups is a recurrent one in our data on parents as learners. It is one of the aspects they value most about their current experience in the MAPPS program and probably the one that is in stark contrast with what these parents experienced as children when they were in school—when they were not allowed to talk to their classmates during class. But, as these parents' comments show, there are still issues around having students work in groups.

Visiting classrooms with parents has proved to be a powerful way to enter into a dialogue about teaching and learning mathematics (see Civil & Quintos, 2006, for more on classroom visits with parents). With one exception, all the debriefings included only the researchers and the parents. We think that another approach would be to include in the debriefings the teachers observed, so that parents familiar with reform mathematics can dialogue with practitioners about what they observed and how they make sense of it. The idea is that in a nonthreatening environment educators can discuss matters of pedagogy with informed parents, not necessarily as a critique of the lesson observed but more as a way to examine in-depth concepts of reform mathematics.

These classroom visits allow us to address questions such as: What do parents pay attention to when they observe a mathematics classroom? What can we learn about these parents' beliefs and values about the teaching and learning of mathematics based on their reflections on the classroom visits? How do parents understand reform mathematics at work in the classroom? How complete is their understanding of reform mathematics? Does it go beyond the use of group work and manipulates to understanding the larger conceptual pedagogical differences? To illustrate how we explored these questions, we next present a summary of a case of two visits to first grade classrooms.

Visiting Classrooms with Marisol López

Marisol López and the authors visited her son's first grade classroom (teacher, Ms. Montero) and the first grade classroom of one of the MAPPS teachers (Ms. Hall). In Ms. Montero's classroom, the lesson centered on learning about "expanded notation"—that is, writing numbers such as 247 as 200 + 40 + 7. In Ms. Hall's classroom, the lesson centered on one of the modules developed for a MAPPS Math Awareness Workshop. This module deals with children's interpretations of the equal sign.

While in Ms. Montero's classroom, we were able to see her regularly scheduled lesson for that day. Ms. Hall decided to do a lesson based on a MAPPS activity. We want to point this out because, although the lesson turned out to be very interesting from a mathematics education point of view, we did not see a "regular" lesson that day. Our aim is not to compare these two lessons but rather to highlight those aspects of the lessons on which Marisol seemed to focus and to raise some questions about what we can learn from her observations of the class. Marisol really liked Ms. Montero's teaching style and was full of admiration for her: "She is a good teacher, a very good teacher, highly recommended, even those [teachers] who have children here send their children to her.... She is strict and good,... clear and concise."

That Marisol would like teachers who are clear and concise was no surprise to us. This is what she enjoyed as a learner herself. She was a quick learner who often could not see the point of spending too much time looking at the same problem from different angles. Marisol liked the discipline in Ms. Montero's classroom. She valued the organization and the fact that the children were well behaved:

> And the classroom is very organized, the children raise their hands, because she knows how to command respect.... The children are really well behaved and they are on task, because she knows how to command respect. The children don't get up or get distracted when someone comes into the classroom, they are on task.

Marisol also valued the use of different approaches and techniques to teach and the fact that the teacher explained things over and over until the children understood:

> There are other teachers who teach a class and do not make sure that children participate.... They only teach the class and consider it done. But she doesn't, she explains and explains until they understand, and then she does exercises with them on the board and then reaffirms it with individual work.... And she did it in three ways, she explained, [by] participation, and individual work.... And I like the expressions she uses, the "abracadabra, stick it with a zero," children find it catchy and they get the clue about what they have to do.

Marisol had a harder time with Ms. Hall's classroom. Let's keep in mind that this was her first visit and thus she was not familiar with the routine. On the other hand, she often volunteered in Ms. Montero's classroom and felt very comfortable in her classroom. Also, Ms. Hall and Ms. Montero teach in different schools. Marisol seemed particularly concerned with what she perceived as lack of organization in Ms. Hall's approach:

> Look, I thought that in the beginning it was organized. As the class went on and the teacher kept on talking, I think that the group was becoming more disorganized. She didn't have control of 100% of the children, because there were moments in which the children were doing whatever they wanted at their desks, talking.

To the question, "What do you think was missing in this class?", Marisol replied, "Organization in the class, prepare the class, make it more dynamic." In describing Ms. Hall's teaching approach, here is what Marisol said:

> She only posed questions and questions, the children answered but she never told them why they were right or why they were wrong, or why it had to be done a certain way. She only listened. To me, to be honest, it was very

> monotonous. I didn't like it.... She never explained, "We are going to do this and it works like this," she just began talking and asking questions.... But she never explained one to one to the children.... What I did notice is that among the children they were explaining it to each other, for the 10 = 6 + 4, one little boy was explaining it to another boy, instead of the teacher explaining, a classmate was explaining it.

To the questions, "Do you think the teacher met her objective for the lesson? What do you think was the objective for this lesson?" she replied:

> If it was equal or not. But she didn't meet the objective, she asked and asked but never said "this is equal to this." When the children were working on whether 8 + 2 + 4 is equal to 5 + 7, I was the one who explained it to the children with the coins, she never gave them a detailed explanation. I think that we need to explain to them the "why" behind things. And no, all she did was ask questions. She never told them if something was right or wrong.... To meet an objective is to do an activity and that the results are 100% positive, not 85%.

We think that Marisol captured quite well Ms. Hall's teaching approach: she was asking questions, she was listening to the children explain their thinking. She did not go around saying "this is right, this is wrong." The children formulated reasons for their thinking and Ms. Hall helped them out as she saw necessary. For example, when working on whether 20 – 5 = 17 – 2 is true or false, some of the children were struggling with the subtraction. Ms. Hall scaffolded their thinking with the use of cubes and her questioning techniques. We cannot tell for sure if every child left the room with a 100% understanding of the equal sign as dealt with in the lesson. But we cannot tell for sure either if every child in Ms. Montero's class left with a 100% understanding of the expanded notation concept.

These two experiences raise several questions for us. What does it mean for a classroom to be organized? Are children talking and moving around signs of disorganization? How important is this concept of organization in a parent's view of a classroom? For example, we have had several parents commenting on the difference in children's behavior in classrooms in Mexico vs. classrooms in the United States. Their comments often reflect that classrooms in the United States seem noisier than those in Mexico. What does it mean, from the parents' point of view, to teach for understanding? Of course, we know that this answer will vary depending on the parents. We are curious, however, to see if, as parents engage themselves as learners of mathematics, their view of teaching for understanding changes. Marisol seemed to like Ms. Montero's use of expressions such as "Abracadabra, stick it with a zero" because children would find them catchy (which they did, as far as we could tell), and would help them remember what to do. On the other hand, Marisol seemed uncomfortable with Ms. Hall's continuous questioning and her not telling the children whether they were right or not. Ms. Hall was modeling an inquiry-based approach to the teaching of mathematics—asking questions and putting the ball back in the students' court to let them figure it out on their own. But, how far can one push this method? What if it is left too open-ended (of course, this will depend on our differing levels of tolerance for open-ended situations)? Was Marisol looking for some kind of closure to this lesson, in which the teacher would explain the key ideas? What are the implications of having or not having such closure? We pose these questions to underscore some of the aspects that Marisol seemed to value in a mathematics classroom. We do not claim that her views are representative of all the parents in MAPPS. We argue that we need to learn about different parents' perceptions on teaching and learning mathematics in order to capture the diversity and complexity of the situation.

The Voices of Esperanza, Jillian, and Marisol

These three mothers seemed very supportive of and pleased with the teachers in their schools. As we asked them to write about what they would like to see happening in the classrooms (not only for their children but for all children), this is what they wrote:

Esperanza

She reflected on her experience observing in classrooms that were not her children's classrooms:

> When I became involved in this program I began observing classes at different schools. I had different experiences in all of them. Some teachers teach only to fulfill their job requirement, only the time allotted, without explaining or answering questions. Other teachers do it the way I think it has to be done, teaching by asking questions to different children to see if they understand and then giving them a handout based on what was covered to reaffirm that the class understood the content.

Marisol

> Based on my experience and observations from when I started visiting my children's school, I prefer the Traditional Teaching Method. What is the traditional method for me? It is based on the following points:
>
> 1. Discipline in the classroom.
> 2. Clear definition of who is who in the classroom: Student–Teacher
> 3. An atmosphere of respect that has to begin in the family setting.
> 4. Keep in mind that the school is a center of instruction, not a childcare facility.
> 5. Use of conventional methods of teaching without relying too much on

> technology; that is, they have to know the different concepts and once the reasoning is there, then they can use technology.

> Now I would like that the educational system be a mixture of traditional and current, but without forgetting that the atmosphere in the family and its cooperation are crucial toward the success of a student in school. I think that it should be a cycle of reciprocity. (She drew a diagram showing this cycle of reciprocity between parents, student, and school.)

Jillian

> Like Marisol, I would like to see tradition, strict, more discipline, who is the teacher and who is the student. [Teacher's] home phone number is commendable. Lots of parents cannot call at school until after work. Too late. Make tutoring exciting, rewarding. Teachers need a little more authority. Let teachers teach the way they see the kids can learn. Of course, keep guidelines, you have to. But give them more freedom. Too much paper work, need more freedom.

As we see from these written excerpts, Marisol was the most explicit in what she would like to see happening in the classroom. She wants a traditional approach, which she describes. Respect and discipline are key elements in her description. She also makes a reference to the use of technology as coming in after the concept and reasoning are already in place. Jillian and Esperanza seem to focus more on the relationships with the teachers. Jillian does indicate that she also prefers the traditional approach and seems to advocate for a better teacher–parent communication. Esperanza focuses on the diversity among teachers and how some seem to be there just to fulfill a requirement, while others really take the time to reach all children.

The comments of these three mothers point to the diversity in parents' views and expectations about their children's mathematics education. A question we raise is how can their comments be tied in with teachers' comments to begin addressing critical issues in education, in particular in the education of low-income, minoritized children?

Parents as Teachers: What They Value in Teaching Other Parents

After the first year in the program, teams of teachers, administrators, and parents started facilitating workshops for other parents (and teachers and administrators). We think that this model of parents teaching mathematics to other parents is quite powerful toward developing leadership among the parents and potentially changing parent–school relationships. We have seen much growth in parents' confidence when presenting mathematics workshops to other parents. We have also seen how they adapt materials and pedagogical strategies from the Math for

Parents courses and from the Leadership Development sessions, and how they develop their own materials for their presentations. As parents are viewed as resources for the school and for each other, one could extend this idea to other academic content areas. Parents have expertise in other areas and the parents in our groups appreciated listening to and sharing with other parents.

Another aspect that we think is particularly powerful is to have teachers and parents working together in a teaching collaboration, particularly in communities such as this one with low-income and ethnic/language minoritized families. We certainly do not want to imply that this approach is unproblematic. The power structures in place, and the fact that parents are expected to teach a content area that is often considered challenging (even by teachers) made some of the teams work in ways that often conformed more to a pattern of "teachers teach; parents help." Particularly in the beginning of the project, the teachers tended to carry the teaching weight in the presentation of the workshops and the parents took more the role of assistants. As time went by, however, we saw quite a diverse range of leadership roles among the parents, with several of them becoming key facilitators of the mathematical aspects in the workshops. Two of the three mothers featured in this chapter, Marisol and Jillian, became mentors of one leadership team each (see Civil & Bernier, 2006, for more on this mentoring component).

An important component of each Math Awareness Workshop was the debriefing that followed each session. The team mentor was in charge of facilitating the session in which the team members reflected on aspects of the workshop. The possibility of having these exchanges in which we talk about teaching (and learning) while coming from different experiences and backgrounds and of listening to each other's point of view has been extremely rewarding, at least for us (the authors). We present below an excerpt of one such debriefing with Jillian and other members of her team. This debriefing took place after their presentation of the module "Equal or Not" (the one used by Ms. Hall in her first grade class described earlier in this chapter). The first author had a concern that the "Equal or Not" module looked deceptively simple. She liked the message of the module, as she saw its implications for the learning of algebra, but was concerned whether this message was being conveyed in the module. Her concerns were grounded on her teaching experience and on the frequent misuse of the equal sign by students, combined with her observations of how the module was being presented at several workshops (and it did not necessarily matter whether the presenters were teachers or parents). She saw the module presented in a procedural way, as if the presenters were not aware of the subtleties surrounding the use of the equal sign.

During the debriefing, the first author inquired about how this module compared to Garage Patterns, a middle school module that had to do with looking for patterns, making tables, and graphing (the patterns were all linear). This team had also recently presented Garage Patterns at one of the middle schools. This module was more demanding in terms of mathematical content than the Equal or Not module. She openly told them that she was concerned that the message of the Equal or Not module might get lost and thus might be a turn-off for parents because they would find it boring and unrelated to mathematics, while the Garage Patterns module seemed more recognizable as mathematics:

Jillian: If I come to this one [Equal or Not], if I were a parent and didn't have anything to do with MAPPS, this would bring me to go to others, I would come back.

Candida: (another mother in the team): You don't think it was too boring?

Jillian: No, not at all. If I had gone to this one, I'd stay. If I had gone to the Garage Patterns or Step by Step [a module on alternative algorithms], I would have gone, Ah! Ah! This is too much thinking after school.

Marta (first author): I agree with the Garage Patterns, because the graphing and all that, the mathematical complexity, but on the other hand…

Candida: It was exciting though…

Jillian: It was, once you get it but meanwhile it was scary, intimidating, and I would have gone, "I don't want to do anything to do with math." That's how I look at it, I don't have a math background, if I was just a parent that helps her kids after school…well not anymore because I went to the MFP and that really helped me, it made me feel good.

Marta: This module [Equal or Not] was very well presented, that's very clear, you all did a great job, the message was very important. But I am familiar with that, I'm a math educator and I'm going Yes! Yes! But now I am thinking I am a parent who knows nothing about MAPPS, not particularly interested in mathematics, most of the times they were sitting and listening to you, and you were discussing this thing of equal sign, big deal!

Jillian: No offense Marta, you are very educated, you have a doctorate you are a smart girl, a lot of these parents, me included, went to high school, a couple of years of college and that was it, and certainly it wasn't in math. In that aspect, you just because you have so much education…intimidation is a big…especially with teachers and the parents, and the parents are intimidated by the teachers.

James (a teacher on the team): It's an elementary workshop that we're giving and I think that for the parents it's very important that they have something that they can understand and that they can help their child. And I disagree in the fact that I think that the parents who came tonight were interested, even though you know, to you [Marta] it may seem like very simple, and that a lot of people where not doing much and just listening, I still think that it was easy enough to where they could really grasp onto something. I disagree, I think they will come back.

Beatriz (second author): And we may think it's basic but if we connect to algebra and the questioning techniques that you [James] used…

Marta: No, no, I wasnít saying it's basic. Actually it's very difficult; the concept of equal sign is difficult.

The first author (Marta) is not convinced that she got her message across. She feels that this team of parents and teacher thought that she was saying that the concept in "Equal or Not" was so simple that it may have been lost (as being "trivial"), while in fact, what she was trying to say is that the concept was so subtle that it may have been lost. These mothers (and the teacher) seemed to think that the module Equal or Not was a success exactly because it was simple and dealt with concepts that the parents could relate to. The point we want to make here, however, is about the nature of these exchanges. The mothers in the team expressed their opinion, the teacher expressed his, and the researchers expressed theirs. We think that the excerpt presented may qualify as an example of egalitarian dialogue. Let us recall what Flecha (2000) writes: "A dialogue is egalitarian when it takes different contributions into consideration according to the validity of their reasoning, instead of according to the positions of power held by those who make the contributions" (p. 2).

The Parents as Teachers/Facilitators component of our proposed model for parental participation is intended to promote this type of dialogue. By having teams of teachers and parents cofacilitating reform-based mathematics workshops, we seek to break the traditional barriers of who is the teacher, who is the parent (and as in the excerpt above, who is the researcher). In so doing our goal is to engage in dialogues about the teaching and learning of mathematics in which every voice is heard.

The Voices of Esperanza, Jillian, and Marisol

In the previous section we have hinted at some of the issues in having teams of parents and teachers teaching mathematics to other parents (see Civil & Bernier, 2006, for more on this). To a certain extent, there may be some parallels between the work of these parents and that of beginning teachers. One question worth researching further is, what role do parents' beliefs about and understanding of mathematics play in their teaching of these workshops? One difference between the experiences of these parents and those of beginning teachers is that these parents are teaching other parents. They are teaching people like them, with children in their children's schools, with similar concerns about their children's education. Several of the MAPPS parents have mentioned that parents often feel intimidated by teachers (or "university people") teaching them. Parents may be in a better position to establish a link with other parents by directly connecting with their experiences. We asked the three mothers to share with us what draws their attention when they are facilitating a Math Awareness Workshop.

Esperanza: My experience with MAPPS as a teacher is to explain to the parents what their children do in the classroom and familiarize them with the material (manipulatives) that we use and tell them that it is the same material that their children are using; to explain how their children learn; to give them confidence by telling them that I am also a mother like they are and that I may also have doubts and that we are ready to explain something again when they do not understand it. In conclusion, the important thing is to make them feel confident so that they will be encouraged to join this program.

Jillian: First that I understand it and that I can ask for help; that there is a comfortable setting; and that parents know that I am teaching but they are teaching me too, not to make them feel like dummies. Let them contribute as much as I am contributing.

Marisol: To read and review carefully the module to simplify and extract the most interesting and easy-to-show parts without taking away its essence; to adopt a clear language appropriate to the level of understanding of the audience without leaving out the importance of the mathematical terms; the preparation of support materials for the overhead transparencies, so that the teaching can be both visual (overhead projector) and exploration of the materials to be able to connect both methods.

It is important to notice that of the three comments, Marisol's is the one that focuses the most on the pedagogical approach. Consistent with what we saw in her comments on the classroom observation and the follow-up written reflection, Marisol seems to value a direct teaching approach in which she would capture the main points of the module and present those to the parents; she talks about simplifying yet without taking away the substance. Jillian and Esperanza focus more on the personal and affective dimension. They both imply the importance of establishing rapport and that they are not "above" the parents in the workshop. This focus is also consistent with what they value as parents for their children's teachers—relationships. Esperanza refers to the fact that, "I am also a mother like they are and that I may also have doubts," while Jillian says, "I am teaching but they are teaching me too.… Let them contribute as much as I am contributing."

Parents as Learners, as Parents, and as Teachers

As we reflect on the different components presented, namely parents as learners, parents as parents, and parents as teachers/facilitators, and as we pay particular attention to the voices of the three mothers featured in this article, Esperanza, Jillian, and Marisol, we see how these three components provide us with a model that leads toward the participation of parents as intellectual resources in children's schooling. Participating in the Math for Parents courses and in other opportunities as adult learners gave these mothers the confidence to become teachers of other parents and also presented them with an array of possibilities as to what school mathematics could be like. This, in turn, and combined with classroom observations, made them particularly aware of issues surrounding the teaching of mathematics, which could lead to their becoming advocates for a good mathematics education for all children. By doing what Esperanza did when facilitating a workshop—sharing with other parents what teaching mathematics in the schools looks like and familiarizing them with the manipulative materials and the kinds of activities that their children are (or could be) using—these parents were enabling other parents to establish bridges with their children's schooling experience.

Engaging parents as learners of mathematics created a space in which we could dialogue about reform mathematics and the parents' previous learning experiences. Even when the parents had not learned mathematics in the manner described in reform mathematics curricula, we were able to engage in conversations that mediated our understanding to create a common ground. The mothers as adult learners valued being part of a learning community where they learned through group work, discussions about mathematics, solving problems in several different ways, and using manipulative materials and technology. It was also crucial that the topics in mathematics were based on a conceptual understanding and connections among various topics in mathematics and to their everyday life.

Parents' experiences as learners were a mediating factor for their expectations, views, and beliefs about their children's education. In this way, their role as learners mediated their role as parents. Research indicates that working-class parents, and parents from certain cultural groups, historically have had an uphill battle in advocating for their children's best interests in schools. As Esperanza says, "Cuentas pero no cuentas, estás pero no estás, simbólicamente vas pero..." (You count but you don't count, you are there but you are not, you attend symbolically but...).

Coleman (1988), Henry (1996), and Lareau (2000), among others, have discussed the influences of culture, race, and socioeconomic factors on the nature of home–school relationships. In our study, the mothers' views were diverse and at times differed from our views or those characteristic of a reform-mathematics emphasis. As we have seen, for example, one of the mothers seemed to lean more toward an inquiry approach to teaching, while another mother was clearly in favor of a more traditional approach to teaching. Still, the three mothers underscored the ultimate importance of the relationship between student and teacher (and this is recurrent theme with other parents beside the three featured in this chapter). These conversations demonstrate the complexity of bringing parents' voices to the dialogue. Nonetheless, these conversations, based on the principles of an egalitarian dialogue (Flecha, 2000), should stem from a deep respect for children's family and communities.

Parents as teachers for other parents became a source of pride for the mothers themselves, their children, and a powerful source of connection for other parents to the school curricula. Parents had multiple and diverse expertise and the parents in our groups appreciated listening to and sharing with other parents. This concept of parents as resources for academic aspects of school life is consistent with a key concept in our approach to research, that of parents as intellectual resources (Civil & Andrade, 2003).

Extending learning opportunities for parents in academic areas and capitalizing on their intellectual resources is a way to enhance relationships with schools. Working in tandem with teachers can also be a valuable tool to inform other parents. As parents listen to other parents, schools develop two-way communication with parents, not just about logistical issues of schooling such as fundraising, but also in matters of content. Parents then have a better possibility of becoming partners with the schools and being able to act as advocates and decision-makers in the education of their children. We believe these conversations are critical for researchers, school staff, and parents to communicate in an egalitarian and informed way. Listening, rather than merely informing or talking to parents, along with conducting classroom observations with the parents, supported our effort of creating a dialogue in the academic realm, which has the potential to contribute to an inclusive education.

Acknowledgments

Some of the data in this chapter were presented at Annual Meeting of the American Educational Research Association (AERA) in April 2002. We would like to acknowledge the feedback and contributions from the three mothers who are featured in this chapter, Esperanza Ballesteros, Marisol V. López, and Jillian Velmont.

Notes

1. In this chapter we use the term *parents* to refer to the mothers or grandmothers who participated in the research component of the project. We did have fathers coming to the Math Awareness Workshops, but at the time of the study we did not have any fathers in the leadership teams.
2. Project MAPPS was funded by the National Science Foundation (NSF) under grant ESI-99-01275. The views expressed here are those of the authors and do not necessarily reflect the views of NSF.
3. Proposition 203 was a ballot initiative approved by Arizona voters in 2000, now codified as part of the Arizona Education Statutes. The measure was based on Proposition 227, a similar though somewhat less restrictive measure passed by California voters two years earlier. Both laws severely restrict bilingual education programs, replacing them with "Structured English Immersion" classes for a period "not normally intended to exceed one year" (ARS, 15-752). The law allows teachers to use a minimal amount of the child's native language for clarification, but "all children in Arizona public schools shall be taught English by being taught in English and all children shall be placed in English language classrooms" (ARS, 15-752).
4. All mothers' and teachers' names are pseudonyms.

References

Calabrese Barton, A., Drake, C., Perez, J. G., St. Louis, K., & George, M. (2004). Ecologies of parental engagement in urban education. *Educational Researcher*, *33*(4), 3–12.

Civil, M., & Andrade, R. (2003). Collaborative practice with parents: The role of the researcher as mediator. In A. Peter-Koop, V. Santos-Wagner, C. Breen, & A. Begg (Eds.), *Collaboration in teacher education: Examples from the context of mathematics education* (pp. 153–168). Boston: Kluwer.

Civil, M., & Bernier, E. (2006). Exploring images of parental participation in mathematics education: Challenges and possibilities. *Mathematical Thinking and Learning, 8*(3), 309–330.

Civil, M., Bratton, J., & Quintos, B. (2005). Parents and mathematics education in a Latino community: Redefining parental participation. *Multicultural Education Journal, 13*(2), 60–64.

Civil, M., & Quintos, B. (2006). Engaging families in children's mathematical learning: Classroom visits with Latina mothers. *New Horizons for Learning Online Journal, 12*(1), Retrieved November 29, 2008, from http://www/newhorizons.org/spneeds/ell/civil%20quintos.htm

Coleman, J. S. (1988). Social capital in the creation of human capital. *American Journal of Sociology, 94*, 95–120.

Combs, M. C., Evans, C., Fletcher, T., Parra, E., & Jiménez, A. (2005). Bilingualism for the children: Implementing a dual-language program in an English-only state. *Educational Policy, 19*(5), 701–728.

Darder, A. (1991). *Culture and power in the classroom: A critical foundation for bicultural education.* New York: Bergin & Garvey.

Delgado-Gaitan, C. (2001). *The power of community: Mobilizing for family and schooling.* Denver, CO: Rowman & Littlefield.

Delgado-Gaitan, C. (2004). *Involving Latino families in schools: Raising student achievement through home-school partnerships.* Thousand Oaks, CA: Corwin Press.

Dewey, J. (1916). *Democracy and education: An introduction to the philosophy of education.* New York: Macmillan.

FitzSimons, G. (1994). *Teaching mathematics to adults returning to study.* Geelong, Victoria, Australia: Deakin University Press.

Flecha, R. (2000). *Sharing words: Theory and practice of dialogic learning.* Lanham, MD: Rowman & Littlefield.

Henry, M. (1996). *Parent–school collaboration: Feminist organizational structures and school leadership.* Albany, NY: SUNY.

Horvat, E. M., Weininger, E. B., & Lareau, A. (2003). From social ties to social capital: Class differences in the relations between schools and parent networks. *American Educational Research Journal, 40*(2), 319–351.

Lankshear, C., Gee, P., Knobel, M., & Searle, C. (1997). *Changing literacies.* Buckingham, UK: Open University Press.

Lareau, A. (2000). *Home advantage: Social class and parental intervention in elementary education* (Rev. ed.). Lanham, MD: Rowman & Littlefield.

Lehrer, R., & Shumow, L. (1997). Aligning the construction zones of parents and teachers for mathematics reform. *Cognition and Instruction, 15*(1), 41–83.

Mapp, K. L. (2003). Having their say: Parents describe why and how they are engaged in their children's learning. *The School Community Journal, 13*(1), 35–64.

National Council of Teachers of Mathematics. (1989). *Curriculum and evaluation standards for school mathematics.* Reston, VA: Author.

National Council of Teachers of Mathematics. (2000). *Principles and standards for school mathematics.* Reston, VA: Author.

Olivos, E. M. (2006). *The power of parents: A critical perspective of bicultural parent involvement in public schools.* New York: Peter Lang.

Peressini, D. (1998). The portrayal of parents in the school mathematics reform literature: Locating the context for parental involvement. *Journal for Research in Mathematics Education, 29*(5): 555–582.

Pérez, G. C., Drake, C., & Calabrese Barton, A. (2005). The importance of presence: Immigrant parents' school engagement experiences. *American Educational Research Journal, 42*(3), 465–498.

Ramirez, A. Y. (2002). How parents are portrayed among educators. *The School Community Journal, 12*(2), 51–61.
Reay, D. (1998). Cultural reproduction: Mothers involvement in their children's primary schooling. In M. Grenfell & D. James (Eds.), *Bourdieu and education: Acts of practical theory* (pp. 55–71). Bristol, PA: Falmer.
Valencia, R., & Black, M. (2002). "Mexican Americans don't value education!"—On the basis of the myth, mythmaking, and debunking. *Journal of Latinos and Education, 1*(2), 81–103.
Valenzuela, A. (1999). *Subtractive schooling: U.S.-Mexican youth and the politics of caring.* Albany, NY: SUNY Press.
Van Manen, M. (1990). *Researching lived experience: Human science for an action sensitive pedagogy.* London, Ontario: The University of Western Ontario.
Vincent, C. (1996). *Parents and teachers: Power and participation.* Bristol, PA: Falmer Press.
Vygotsky, L. S. (1978). *Mind in society.* Cambridge, MA: Harvard University Press.

15
Culturally Responsive College Level Mathematics

MARK K. DAVIS, SHANDY HAUK, AND M. PAUL LATIOLAIS

The goal of this chapter is to describe what it might mean for college level mathematics teaching to be culturally responsive and illustrate how culturally responsive collegiate mathematics teaching and learning can look. Our focus is on effective college mathematics instruction for nonmathematics majors in service courses like calculus and liberal arts mathematics. Culturally responsive courses in the mathematics major are possible, but require a more extensive discussion about the specific nature and purpose of the mathematics major within a department before change is possible.

After providing some background, we offer common views of college mathematics teaching in the overlapping contexts of academic, workforce, and social justice concerns. Secondly, we give several short examples from the perspective of college professors about the nature of their instructional practices, including cultural responsiveness. Thirdly, we address the nature of culture and the repertoires college students and instructors build—of ways of seeing, communicating about, and engaging with these concerns. Fourthly, we provide two detailed examples of culturally responsive teaching and curricula in courses that currently exist along with some of the successes documented in these courses. We close with suggestions for how to improve the educational environment for students and instructors through the tenets of culturally responsive pedagogy. Throughout, we connect our observations with existing critical educational theories. That is, we employ common *academic mathematics cultural* practices: we start with some background information and several motivating examples, give some definitions (after already having used key terms in context), provide two extended examples, making connections along the way, and conclude with a summary of what we think these all show.

Background

For most U.S. students entering college, of all races, classes, ethnicities, and home language groups, mathematics means "computation" and mathematics beyond arithmetic is seen as having little relevance to everyday life (Hauk, 2005; Leder, Pehkonen, & Torner, 2003; Schmidt, McKnight, Cogan, Jakwerth, & Houang, 1999). In fact, mathematics "is commonly perceived as the antithesis of human activity—mechanical, detached, emotionless, value-free, morally neutral" (Mukhopadhyay & Greer, 2001). Nonetheless, like the other authors in this volume, we assert that mathematics *is* a human activity and is value-laden and culturally informed. Any human endeavor, including mathematics, that has an associated set of values (e.g., elegance), preferred ways of communicating (e.g., proof), and rules for inclusion (e.g., logical validity) is culturally in Drive, not Neutral (Davis, Hersch, & Marchisotto, 2003; Ernest, 1998).

In our view, teaching and learning in college mathematics involves managing the tensions among at least four significant factors, the demands of:

1. *Academic mathematics culture* for (re)producing mathematics in ways authentic to the traditions from which it arose;
2. *Society and the state* to produce mathematically competent workers;
3. *Global ecology and humanity* to be critical thinkers in our use of mathematics; and
4. *Multiple student communities* for mathematics teaching and learning.

These are akin to Gutstein's (2007) *classical* (he groups academic mathematics and societal demands under this one heading), *critical*, and *community* knowledge aspects of teaching mathematics. Each of the four can be seen, à la Bourdieu, as a *field*, with associated *habitus* and *relational structures* (Grenfell & James, 1998). College mathematics instructors operate at the nested intersection of these fields, where (1) is nested inside of (2), which is in turn nested in (3) while (4) may or may not overlap (1), (2), or (3). The *relational structures* at work in assuming and asserting power as an instructor in these fields depends on many factors, including where an instructor is teaching (e.g., 2-year community college or doctoral intensive research university) and what courses an instructor is teaching (e.g., major or nonmajor courses). The challenges of moving into culturally responsive college mathematics teaching for an instructor at a vocational-goals oriented community college may be relationally and structurally different from those faced by one at a community college where the primary goal is feeding students to the local university; and different again in other ways from the challenges a university mathematics professor might face. However, Bourdieu's attention to the *habitus* of people in the field—"the systems of dispositions they have acquired by internalizing a determinate type of social and economic condition" (Grenfell & James, 1998, p. 169) provides a mechanism for analysis that works across these different contexts. College mathematics instructors and students deal every day with the pulls of the intersecting fields and the sometimes dissonant aspects of habitus associated with each. Some instructors focus on one of the fields at a time: for example, looking at rich development of the classical or a sole focus on the societal in their instruction. Some have pledged allegiance to the classical, saying: "Our primary responsibility as mathematicians is not to students, but to mathematics to preserve, create, and enhance good mathematics and to protect the subject for future generations" (Palmer, 1997, p. 10).

In particular, the classical habitus has it that those things that become "non-mathematical" are excised from mathematics, including applications:

> Over the centuries, mathematics has outsourced many (usually applied) sub-domains when they developed their own ways of thinking and working (cf. Laugwitz, 1972). By considering them not to be a part of mathematics anymore, inconsistencies or conflicts could be removed in an easy way. Even today, there are disciplines of mathematics (like scientific computing or other parts of experimental mathematics) whose standards have been removed from the widely accepted mathematical standards. (Prediger, 2002, p. 8)

By contrast, pledging allegiance to (2), the societal, means the instructional goal is one of shaping students who can apply mathematics (rather than shaping conservators of mathematics). Among the societal forces at work in U.S. universities today is the push to use "business management" styles in academe. This has been felt as people from commerce become university administrators and through the less obvious but more powerful pressure exerted through the profit-based views of members of university Boards of Trustees. Additionally, state funding of public higher education means that demands felt by the state are passed on to university administration and thence on to faculty (e.g., by businesses that position themselves as customers of the state, with the products being college graduates).

Some instructors do a balancing act, taking the classic academic and societal as both important. And some, who move in the direction of culturally responsive instruction, see the classic academic and societal views as each demanding sole allegiance, but take (3), globally contextualized critical knowledge, as the driving force in making instructional decisions. That is, some instructors design college teaching for critical understanding while being responsive to the demands of the classical and societal as means to the end of critical engagement with mathematics. As Gutstein (2007) noted, "it is often the case that community knowledge is already critical, but context matters" (p. 111). One of the basic tenets of our approach to culturally responsive pedagogy is in using (4), community knowledge, as a foundation for working with college students to pose and solve problems while developing both classical and global critical knowledge.

Given that the traditions in Western education call for a knowledge of abstract concepts in mathematics and given that two out of every three new jobs in the

United States require some postsecondary education in broad and flexible critical thinking ability (Carnevale & Desrochers, 2003), how do we support the next generation of U.S. students as thinkers, workers, and global citizens? Colleges and universities must prepare culturally competent graduates who are aware of and skilled in moving among multiple social, cultural, and linguistic contexts (Middlehurst & Woodfield, 2006). Among the challenges in shaping collegiate mathematics instruction to meet quantitative literacy and cultural competence goals are the inertia of academic mathematics culture, the assimilationist underpinnings of the majority society (or as Delpit,1996, says, the *power culture*), and the very slow diversification of college mathematics faculties.

The slightly greater sociocultural diversity and difference in gender balance for college mathematics faculties from that in schools—see Tables 15.1 and 15.2 (U.S. Census Bureau, 2000; National Center for Education Statistics, 2006)—may mean that the college level instructional environment is a more fertile field for cultural responsiveness to grow in at least two ways. First, many college mathematics faculty are already interacting with colleagues who are of some "other" home culture yet who are also participants in the academic mathematics culture; that is, with colleagues who have a "dual status frame of reference" (Ogbu & Simons, 1998, p. 156). Moreover, college students may encounter, in addition to the disconnect in moving from "school" to "college," a cultural conflict when they find themselves with an instructor who is seen as "other." This otherness might come from the perception by a student that a mathematics instructor is an alien being or might come from perceived sociocultural, gender, or linguistic community differences. Moreover, this cultural disconnect happens even for the academically well-acculturated, in the mathematics graduate school experience (Herzig, 2002, 2004).

Before we move on, we position ourselves as authors, mathematicians, and college teachers. All the authors are PhDs in mathematics and each of us has taught college mathematics for more than 10 years. Within our group we have also taught elementary, middle, and high school. We have taught in North America and in Africa. We have conducted basic and applied research in mathematics

Table 15.1 Diversity of Elementary, Secondary, and Post-Secondary Faculties in the United States[a]

Category[b]	Elementary	Secondary	Post-Secondary
All others (e.g., 2 or more categories), non-Hispanic	0.5%	0.5%	1.0%
American Indian or Alaskan Native, non-Hispanic	0.5%	0.5%	0.5%
Asian, non-Hispanic	1.5%	1.5%	8.0%
Hispanic	5.5%	5.0%	4.5%
Black, non-Hispanic	9.0%	6.2%	6.0%
White, non-Hispanic	82.5%	86.0%	80.0%

a. Data are rounded to nearest tenth from 2006 projections based on U.S. Census (2000).
b. Group "race" labels are those used in the U.S. Census (2000).

Table 15.2 Gender of Elementary, Secondary Mathematics, and Post-Secondary Mathematics Faculties in the United States[a]

Category	Elementary	Secondary Mathematics	Post-Secondary Mathematics
Men	21.0%	45.1%	75.3%
Women	79.0%	54.9%	24.7%

a. Data are rounded to nearest tenth from 2006 projections based on U.S. Census (2000).

(logic, group theory, number theory, dynamical systems, climate modeling) and have done basic and applied research in mathematics education. Each of us has taken a different route in coming to our interest in culturally responsive mathematics education: one coming from the U.S. majority culture and going into teaching in very diverse and new settings; one coming from experiences rich in dealing personally with mathematical and societal racism; and one through her experiences with manifestations of sexism. Our agenda is promoting the opening of our views of instruction to include the critical perspective as we develop ourselves and as we help our students develop mathematically.

We frame the rest of our presentation by describing next the four dominant paradigms in college mathematics instruction, including their connections to classical, societal, and critical allegiances and ways these can be infused with community knowledge in culturally responsive pedagogical approaches. As promised, we will start with some examples.

The Instructor Speaks: A Collection of Short Examples

Current views of instruction fall into four broad categories (Grundy, 1987): *transmission, product, process,* and *praxis*. Below, the comments from college professors are exemplars crafted by the authors to condense actual interview responses. These come from our ongoing collegiate mathematics education research projects. It should be noted that the authors are not arguing a value-laden hierarchy to the models as we have presented them below. People come to college mathematics instruction with differing funds of knowledge, differing worldviews, and a variety of approaches to instructional change. Our contention is that learning in the context of any one of the four instructional paradigms can be made more effective by expanding instructional design to include responsiveness to community knowledge. The four models are ordered from most common to least common in collegiate mathematics instruction (according to our review of the literature and our own research).

Transmission Model

At the college level in this mathematics instructional approach, curriculum is the content of the syllabus and textbook. Students are vessels to receive this content and they are responsible for structuring it for their own future use as thinkers. Instruction is the act of speaking (transmitting) the content. Students and teachers are guided by the demands and constraints of academe (classical forces). Assessment is whatever the habitus and norms in the mathematics department suggest (most often a midterm and a final exam). The transmission model has a large and stable following at the college level and can be exemplified by the comment of Professor T: "My job is to present the information from the book to the students as clearly as possible." The traditional transmission model assumes that what is "clear" to students has already been determined by what the teacher or textbook says is important. This approach to instruction is common for lower-division nonmajor and mathematics major courses. In his student community responsive version of this curricular approach Prof. T goes on to say:

> *How* I present things depends on what does the best job of being clear to the students. When I have a lot of students from the city, I can ask them to think about financial implications for the calculus we do, but when I have a lot of kids from the farms, I change my examples so that they think about how managing water resources on a ranch can be modeled by things like difference equations. If the class is mixed, I spend a little time on each example.

Though an instructor with a transmission approach typically uses lecture as the dominant form of instruction, this is not the sole method. For example, separate computer lab sessions with very directed and structured lab activities may be added to a course. In addition to lecturing, Professor T used *Mathematica* software documents, called notebooks, where students clicked on entries to reveal computations or typed in formulas as evidence of mastery of procedures. This instructional approach was based on, as noted by Professor T, the "assumption that if a student practices a procedure enough then [conceptual] understanding will follow."

Product Model

In this instructional approach, curriculum is a set of goals about mathematical knowledge acquisition along with assessable objectives and definitions for what constitutes evidence of learning. Students are the raw material to be shaped by instruction into a certain product: the educated worker. Instruction is the calibration of presentation and assessment that results in that quality-assured end product of the college graduate as worker. Students and teacher are guided by the demands and constraints of a capital economy (societal forces). Many of the courses for mathematics majors are taught with this approach. The traditional *product* view can be illustrated by the comment of Professor I:

> The way I see it, I should present to students what they need, cover all the material, so they can solve the problems they see in the book and on the test. My goal is to prepare students for the next class…even if they say this is the last math class they're ever going to take, there is always a next class and that's what I'm getting them ready for. Some students just won't get it, usually it's the ones who shouldn't have been allowed in, to the college, in the first place, but that's the way it is.

The product view can also be seen at the college level in the assessment strategy often used in large, multisection, coordinated mathematics service courses. The same (or similar) exams are administered in all sections of the course and the tests are graded uniformly using a common rubric (or a common grader; e.g., if there are 10 instructors for 500 students in a calculus course and 10 items on the exam, Instructor X grades Item 1 on all 500 exams, Instructor Y grades Item 2 on all 500 exams, etc.). Instruction and assessment follow the assembly-line model. A community responsive product-based instructor will modify presentation and assessments based on students, like Professor B:

> For example, students need to master the idea of slope and connect it to rate of change and the derivative. So, when I teach calculus, I give students graphs of distance versus time and I make up a story that goes with it from my experiences as a hiker. Then I ask them to create their own stories about that graph and three others for homework. One or two of the stories they make up show up on a quiz later in the week: students have to work backwards, draw the graph from the story. This builds their understanding of the relationship between slope and rate of change. Because the students made up the stories, the math is connected to their lives; and because we share some stories, we get to know each other better.

In fact, the nature and use of word problems as a responsive tool in college mathematics curriculum is a fertile ground for research. As Gerofsky (2004) noted in her exploration of word problems as genre, the habitus in academic mathematics is to consider the kinds of word problems found in most college textbooks as a way to "give the student time to think" (p. 73). And, many mathematicians who teach college service courses might agree with the university professor who told Gerofsky that the contexts in word problems do not matter; that, in fact, they tend to ignore the stories—even if "horrifying" (p. 71) in content when considered carefully. This is because the purpose of word problems in mathematics is seen as stripping away the words: "a word problem is a model of a real problem and then mathematics is a model of the modeled problem" (p. 70).

Also common to the product-based model are the use of computer labs and projects. In a product-based approach, technology use may depend on how much the instructor anticipates students needing computerized mathematics skills. If the mathematics course is for engineers, computer use may be much more likely than if the course is for "pure mathematics" students. In a culturally responsive product-based approach, especially in college mathematics courses at the level of calculus and below, computer use may be more focused on worker skills like using spreadsheets or finding and distilling information from the World Wide Web rather than using computationally powerful software.

Process Model

From this perspective, curriculum is the process of developing thinking skills for "dealing with the world as it is"—each classroom full of students may learn a different collection of content, but all are being shaped for citizenship within the status quo of majority society (classical and societal forces in tension). Students are sense-making participants in the development of their own understandings. Instruction is the act of pacing and facilitating learning for the particular group of students in the room. Students and teacher are guided by the demands and constraints of the larger society. The *process* view, as it is often realized in traditional college mathematics instruction, is represented in the comments of Professor J:

> I see my responsibility as making sure students can think, can be flexible and use mathematics. They should know more than the facts, they should be able to solve problems they have never seen before. Okay, often they can't, but it's what I aim for. I cover as much as I can. It's why I have those projects the students complain about, to help them learn how to work together and think on their own.

Professor P agreed with Professor J and was working to expand on the ideas in the direction of cultural responsiveness, saying:

> Cultural responsiveness is about meeting the needs of the individual students as we, the instructors, understand that. Although it would be useful to know more about the cultural context they come from, we can be responsive to the individuals and teach them math without knowing the details of their lives. Those details come through in the project topics they pick, they show up in what the students want to work on.

That is, Professor P was open to the ideas of community responsiveness and was still working to build an understanding of sociocultural experience and of its centrality to the mathematical experience of his students (e.g., still coming to an awareness of "how the negotiation of mathematical norms in the classroom mimics and reproduces the larger social relations that exist outside of the mathematics classroom (i.e., some [students] are shut out of the process)" (Martin, 2006, p. 204). The efforts of Professor P to move from a traditional product model to a culturally responsive form of the process view are detailed below in the first of our two extended examples, about teaching applied calculus.

Praxis Model

Within the praxis instructional paradigm, curriculum is the collective practice of teacher and students engaging with and shaping the world through knowledge of mathematics and other content. Students are knowledge-generating participants who apply their experiences of the world and understandings of mathematics to analyze and influence the world around them. Instruction is the act of supporting students in critical discourse, planning, and implementation of ideas. Students and teachers explore, challenge, and redefine the demands and constraints of multiple stakeholders in local and global communities. This view is associated with the theory of *critical pedagogy* (Freire, 1970). The *praxis* view can be seen in the comments of Professor D:

> For me, *teaching* and *learning* are not "two sides of the same coin" so much as two faces of a mirrored tetrahedron. The other two faces are *person* and *community*. Well, communit*ies*, since we each belong to many communities. I teach mostly first-year students, mostly European American, and mostly from fairly stable and affluent backgrounds. They are accustomed to looking in the mirrored face I call "person" and seeing themselves. They are used to looking in the mirrored face I call "teaching" and having a Dracula-like experience where they do not see themselves, but they do see the teacher standing behind them.... My goals are for them to learn mathematics to use and define their views of the worlds they live in and to create complete reflections, with lots of background detail, and *including themselves* in each of the four faces: teaching, learning, person, and community.

Though highly consistent with culturally responsive pedagogy, Professor D's view is not especially responsive to the personal variation in experiences her students bring with them to the classroom. Professor T's transmission-based view may actually be more explicitly *responsive* to student community than Professor D's. Below, in our second detailed example, we illustrate Professor H's attempts at culturally responsive praxis-based instruction in liberal arts mathematics.

Before we move to the extended examples alluded to, we feel it is necessary to define some of the terms whose meaning the reader may have gleaned from context. The examples from instructor comments were designed to illustrate the state of college mathematics instruction and to motivate the next section where we discuss cultural repertoire, cultural dissonance, and cultural responsiveness among other things.

Culture and the Classical, Societal, Critical, and Communal

Every human living in proximity to other humans begins enculturation at birth (if not before). In the United States, even the "culture of no culture" is a culture. For example, the "culture of forgetting" among European Americans that emerged around 1930s Dust Bowl survival had values, norms, and artifacts: forgetting antecedents and moving on were valued as were careful choices about assimilation and avoidance; nuclear family structure was present; there was a norm of non-communication about a painful past; and portable tools (and portable religion) were valued over larger, more cumbersome, physical manifestations of culture (Gregory, 1989). What is quite different for many descendents of this "forgetting" culture from other ethnic-based groups in the United States is that the centrality of oral history and kinship, of family memory, may be largely absent. Instead, isolation is the basis of enculturation; perhaps originating in the nihilistic beliefs of the Christian sects who were the forebears of these White migrants. Similar analyses of other U.S. cultural groups (e.g., Grundy, 1987; Ogbu & Simons, 1998) make it clear that though the details of cultural traits may differ, including those associated with socioeconomic status, common categories describing the nature of most cultures exist.

Culture

As with any force to be reckoned with, in order to be responsive to the cultural pressures in college mathematics courses, one must first identify them. For our purposes, *culture* is a collection of learned ways of seeing and interacting with the world and a slowly evolving intergenerational template for the shaping of those learned behaviors. Key aspects of any culture are its:

1. systems of meaning (e.g., semiotics and language);
2. social organization (e.g., community, family, kinship, nation);
3. value structures (e.g., ways of determining and sustaining beliefs);
4. products (e.g., artifacts and tools).

Because mathematics is a human endeavor, it has an associated compound of culture traits. These traits include valued approaches to analyzing, judging, evaluating, interacting with, and mathematizing the world that have informed the development of mathematics as an intellectual enterprise (Hiebert, 2003; Tymoczko, 1998). These classical foundations for what is valued in mathematics and in its teaching and learning inform college mathematics textbook development and saturate the pedagogical assumptions behind the preparation of future college faculty[1] (Center for Education, 2003; Rishel, 2000).

As learners, our community knowledge—including personal life experiences, relationships, and values—may or may not coincide with the knowledge valued in the nationally dominant culture. Consequently, our engagement with learning will be mediated by the consonance (or dissonance) between personal community culture, classical mathematics culture, and large scale societal demands encountered in the classroom (Abreu, Bishop, & Presmeg, 2002; Rodriguez & Kitchen, 2005). Most implementations of the transmission, product, and process models embrace the assimilative view that all students should aspire to the majority culture. Because of this assumption, formal education in mathematics is a socializing experience that only will build smoothly on the informal education gained at home for a learner whose home culture closely resembles the power culture. For the other half of school children, whose home culture may not aspire to middle-class European/AngloAmerican male privilege, school mathematics can become an acculturative challenge requiring students, parents, and teachers to resolve conflict between personal and other cultures (Bishop, 2002; Martin, 2006; Rodriguez & Kitchen, 2005).

Cultural Conflict

Many students who make it to college mathematics courses have developed adaptive skills in moving among the cultures of different fields and negotiating the associated relational structures and aspects of habitus. Nonetheless, discord will naturally arise in any socioculturally heterogeneous group of humans. The resolution of conflict is a necessary condition for negotiating influence in a socially mediated milieu, be it a research group, a mathematics department, a classroom, or a conversation. However, since human beings are active decision makers or *agents* in their own cultures, "resolution" does not necessarily mean that one group of ideas is sacrificed to another. Such conflict can be resolved through a consensus-based balancing of cultural demands. When faced with a situation that creates cultural dissonance, people can find ways of managing themselves and their surroundings that may go beyond accepted customs and cultural prescriptions (Bates & Plog, 1980). For example, a Taiwanese immigrant graduate student teaching calculus to a diverse classroom full of U.S. undergraduates faces a different set of negotiated resolutions to linguistic and cultural conflicts than an African American PhD mathematician teaching the "same" course to a classroom of predominantly European American students. Just as cognitive dissonance and disequlibration have come to be valued as opening cognitive space for the generation of learning (Piaget, 1963), cultural dissonance can pose opportunities for the creation of new repertoires for learning classical, societal, community, and critical mathematics.

Cultural Repertoire

For one exposed to the demands of operating outside of privilege in either a well-known or foreign culture, context is likely to play a very large role in how decision making happens and in which cultural register or repertoire is relied on for interaction (Even-Zohar, 1997; Swidler, 1986). For example, the mathematical register is something mathematicians know as a privileged collection of ideas and symbols for use in communicating mathematics (Wells, 2003). All teachers have some knowledge of this tool in classical mathematics, but for most (especially grades K through 8 teachers) exposure to, familiarity with, and comfort in using this mathematical register is limited. Even more dependent on sociocultural community context are students' uses of the mathematical register. For example, mathematics classes may involve "work" for the student and her parent, "activity" for the teacher, and "problem solving" for a mathematician or mathematics education researcher (Civil, 2002). Weaving together adaptations and negotiations around cultural traits into cultural "repertoires" or "tool kits" for functioning in cultural contexts other than the first-learned is one way human beings negotiate the rapids of cross-cultural social interaction (Swidler, 1986, p. 273).

Learning and Teaching

We hold that learning is the process by which humans construct understanding as individuals and as collectives. As Paul Halmos (1994) put it: teaching "is not to tell students but to ask them, and better yet, to inspire them to ask themselves—make students solve problems, and better yet, train students, by example, encouragement, and generous reinforcement, to construct problems of their own" (p. 851). Students are often their own teachers, separately and severally. Effective teaching requires that the teacher respond to autonomous as well as communal learning needs. We presume that social and physical realities exist for each individual and for collectives (even as we do not assume we have knowledge of these realities). Such a view makes room for negotiating a social constructivist epistemology based on the two principles of radical constructivism: that knowledge is actively constructed by a person (not passively received, no matter how "passive" the person may outwardly seem) and that "the function of cognition is adaptive and serves the organization of the experiential world, not the discovery of ontological reality" (von Glasersfeld, 1989, p. 182). Note that the second condition means that the act of cognition is cultural: cognition organizes *experiences* in our physical and social realities.

Culturally Responsive Pedagogy

The phrase *culturally responsive* has acquired many interpretations over the years. For clarity, we will describe how we are using the term and illustrate its meaning in college mathematics teaching and learning. For our definition we rely most of all on Gay's (2000) representation of the idea: "Culturally responsive pedagogy simultaneously develops, along with academic achievement, social consciousness and critique, cultural affirmation, competence, and exchange; community building and personal connections; individual self-worth and abilities; and an ethic of caring" (p. 43).

Key to cultural responsiveness in curriculum and instruction are a multiculturally and community-aware definition of learning and the simultaneity of intellectual and interpersonal appropriation and feedback represented by the word *responsive*. The basic framework of culturally responsive instruction is *not* about how to get students to change their ways of seeing and interacting with mathematics to align with those of classical academic mathematics or with any other particular culture. Culturally responsive instructional approaches encourage the creation by each individual of *multiple shared repertoires*, in particular, the development of overlapping and mathematically rich cultural repertoires and the skill to identify, choose, and act within and between them.

A culturally responsive college instructor actively models actions and approaches to engaging with mathematics that are culturally aware as well as socially and ethically informed. The socioculturally heterogeneous nature of the student bodies at the universities where we have experience has shaped our views. For example, helping middle-class college students, European Americans included, to examine privilege and oppression and learn about easily realized potentials for harm (to themselves, to others, and to the world), can be a significant part of the work of culturally responsive pedagogy in college level mathematics. As was indicated in the earlier quotes from different professors, one can hold any of the four instructional views and engage in some form of culturally or community responsive pedagogy. Below, after presenting details of two different extended examples of attempts at culturally responsive college mathematics teaching, we outline six factors of culturally responsive college mathematics instruction.

Extended Example: Bringing Cultural Responsiveness to Applied Calculus

We offer details of a culturally responsive applied calculus course at a large U.S. university (17,000 students) that is part *product* and part *process*. Professor P introduced an alternative to the traditional general education calculus and statistics mathematics sequence at the university. Due to departmental constraints regarding the development of mathematics courses, these alternatives to the traditional applied calculus and introductory statistics courses had to be offered as a sequence with new titles and course numbers and offered through a unit separate from the mathematics department. Both courses, *Environmental Mathematical Modeling* and *Environmental Statistics*, were approved for use by the university as alternatives to the preexisting courses as prerequisites. The sequence was made up of two, one-quarter (10-week), classes that met four times each week, 50 minutes per session. The curriculum in Professor P's "environmental" courses emphasized communication about and student-generated projects around mathematical ideas in majority culture contexts, particularly those related to ecological models. The "traditional" courses focused on practice with procedures and computational formulas, particularly those related to business models. As a result, the few students from the environmental courses who later went to the next higher level of mathematics found themselves facing different challenges from the students who moved from the traditional courses on to the next level.

The details given below, though specific to the environmental calculus course in a particular Fall term, were representative of the course processes both before and since that term for multiple instructors. Professor P, a PhD mathematician in the mathematics department taught the course considered here with the help of a graduate assistant. The graduate assistant was present in class to work with students, took attendance (a key component of the course grade), and was responsible for reading and giving feedback on student journals.

The environmental calculus course was problem driven. There was a midterm exam (product model), but grades were also based on other activities (process model). The course grade was determined by one midterm exam, weekly working group problem-solving grades, a cooperative final project (individually reported and graded), and a collaborative project poster presentation (group presented and graded). In addition to these graded assignments, each student kept a journal reporting on engagement with mathematical ideas and course processes.[2] To obtain a particular grade, students had to demonstrate performance at a minimal level of competence on each assessment and attend class regularly (e.g., missing class more than three times would preclude an A as course grade).

Course Processes

Learning goals articulated on the syllabus involved both content and attitudinal components and reflected the instructor's weaving together the product model goals of creating workers (e.g., ability to work in research teams) and process model goals of preparing students as supporters of the status quo (e.g., "ownership" of mathematical ideas and citizenship skills in reasoning about data). The "performance goals for student progress" from the Environmental Mathematical Modeling course syllabus stipulates that students will:

1. develop a facility with and ownership of the mathematical concepts of rates of change and accumulation,
2. be able to analyze raw data to make reasonable claims using mathematical models of that data,
3. be able to communicate mathematical analyses orally and in written form to peers,
4. have increased information literacy,
5. have increased competence and confidence with respect to the use of mathematics in their lives, and
6. have increased competence and confidence working in research teams.

On the first day of class, Professor P asked the students to read the first chapter of the text and reflect on what questions they had and what was important to them. He used the e-mails they sent in response to assign initial working groups based on who the students in the room were, a process model strategy. This technique, combined with student journaling and problem contexts driven by student interests about local environmental concerns was Professor P's way of moving into culturally responsive pedagogy. The four-person student working groups Professor P created by putting together students whose responses were the closest were homogeneous by self-described ability and attitude. Students stayed in these working groups for the first half of the term. When the time came for determining working groups for the final project, three of the eight groups did not change while the other five groups rearranged their memberships.

Assessment Students completed traditional mathematics assignments, such as working on computational exercises, in class. Outside of class student work consisted of the research, analysis, and writing of results completed by the working group on topics chosen by each group. Choices were largely based on the assigned readings in the textbook and on data sets culled from online sources (e.g., the Quantitative Environmental Learning Project web data sets). Every week, each student group gave oral presentations on their weekly problems. After five weeks, the students had completed assignments covering the basic tools of differentiation and integration and took a midterm exam. The midterm exam assessed students' basic skills and ability to apply these skills to analyze raw data. A student could take the midterm up to three times, repeating problems similar to the ones that had not been answered effectively on the previous version. "Passing" was defined as the ability to correctly complete at least 90% of the exam. All students passed the midterm, with two students using all three attempts to do so.

Attendance was part of the course grade because group and whole-class discussions about mathematical concepts could only happen if students were present. A student who had three or fewer absences, passed the midterm exam, and completed the project and poster session, earned at least a C in the course. Higher grades were possible through the final project and poster. Lower grades were possible through poor attendance or not passing the midterm exam. Of the 32 students who started the course, 5 dropped during the first week and 27 finished the course; 18 students passed the course with an A, 7 earned a B, and 2 students ended the course with a C. These values for the given term were close to the averages over the life of the course: from 1999 to this writing, the distribution has been 50% A, 25% B, 10% C, and 15% drop the course.

The Final Project and Poster During the second half of the course, students designed, gathered data, analyzed data, and worked on their final project reports and group posters. First, to choose the final project, each student gave a brief oral description in class of the topic most interesting to her or him. Students then arranged themselves into interest groups. For the final project, each student analyzed a unique set of data and wrote an individual report. The working group structure was there to support the exploration of the topic and to provide a network of others also interested in the same topic to help address any mathematical challenges. Though the interest groups did not write project reports together, each interest group was responsible for creating a poster about their shared topic. During the two-hour final exam period, the class had a poster session. Each group stood next to their poster, explaining their topic and approaches to guests. Members of the faculty, graduate students, and undergraduate students in the mathematics department attended the poster session. In addition to the graded assignments, students also kept journals that were regularly reviewed by the graduate assistant.

Student Journaling

Students wrote in their journals about how the course was going. This allowed the instructor to assess and respond to the students' experiences of the various teaching and curriculum strategies. Below, we summarize the main points that arose in the student journals. The word *many* indicates at least half, *some* is between one-quarter and one-half of students, and a *few* refers to reports by one-quarter or fewer of the students.

Student Comments on Course Processes

More than 65% of students reflected at least once in journaling on how the course processes affected their learning. Early in the term, some suggested a component from the *transmission* or *product* models such as a lecture, scheduled lessons on particular topics, or articulation of specific product-based expectations, might help improve the course:

> I think that the idea of solving problems through a group is a good technique and very refreshing...however, I think that if the class could all come together and learn something current in the news or just to learn something or apply what we've learned to current events—kind of like the article projects—but *with more teacher explanation*, that could summarize all the facts. I don't know that my idea is good, but something is missing from the class. (Week 3, Student H, italics added)

Much of the frustration students reported feeling about the class seemed to be related to their discomfort with the discussion and working group-based learning environment. That is, just as a student in a transmission-based course might be concerned with the constraint of having to accept the rules of mathematics to learn the *content*, students in Environmental Mathematical Modeling found themselves having to "just go with" the nontransmission *processes* of the course: "This class seems pretty challenging and frustrating right now. I feel like we have no guidance and it gets hard sometimes. But in a way this is just a philosophy of teaching that I am unaware of so I guess I need to just go with it and accept it" (Week 8, Student K).

Student Perceptions of Group Work

The highlight of the course for many students was the group work. For some students who entered the class feeling anxiety about mathematics, working with peers in the class helped to validate and ease their concerns: "The small-group structure really helps the learning level. My other classes average 300 students!

I tend to feel really lost when I go to those classes" (Week 4, Student L). "The best part about working in groups for the complete term is the friendships that develop in the process" (Week 10, Student F).

Some students also reported that they learned from their peers when they worked so closely with other students on homework and group projects:

> Today after splitting into groups some of the math concepts finally made some sense to me. We all (at my table) were a little confused with some of the math, but once we began talking and helping each other it started to make sense. (Week 2, Student K)

> ...I must say I like the group interaction. Working in teams is always interesting but group dynamics can sometimes lead to the best of solutions or the most creative ideas. I even see that the groups who were somewhat apprehensive about doing the calculus or just the math itself are very involved in the problem solving effort. This certainly shows progress as far as the class goes. (Week 3, Student G)

The varying levels of mathematics abilities in the class provided a unique challenge for student groups. Although students generally worked in groups with students of similar abilities, often the students with calculus backgrounds provided support for students learning the concepts for the first time:

> In class today we worked in large groups on the class assignments—some students knew how to do it while others seemed overwhelmed. It was nice how the students who knew helped those who didn't. (Week 2, Student H)

> Instead of blowing off studying for it [the midterm] and daydreaming in class, I decided to try to help [other students] with their preparation. This was very satisfying to me to help them. (Week 6, Student D)

In the winter and spring terms following the fall term teaching experience described above, the instructor taught traditional calculus. It seemed that there were far more questions from students about the applicability of the material: What use was the exponential function? Why should anybody care about the Taylor series? Questions like this never came up in Environmental Mathematical Modeling, where students had a much better sense of how calculus could be used to make sense of the world. Each calculus topic was introduced as a tool to solve a particular environmental question, at which point the students used calculus to solve a problem they had identified, a problem that was their own.

Extended Example: Culturally Responsive Liberal Arts Mathematics

In this example, we offer a snapshot of Professor H's attempts to move from process- to praxis-based instruction in the context of a first-year liberal arts mathematics course at a medium sized U.S. university (11,000 students). Given the importance of community in culturally responsive curriculum and instruction, we situate Professor H's two praxis-based class sections in the context of the department and of the course—a total of 6 instructors taught 11 class sections. Each liberal arts mathematics class met for 150 minutes per week, either 50 minutes per day on Monday, Wednesday, and Friday or 75 minutes per day on Tuesday and Thursday. The two praxis-based sections taught by Professor H met on Tuesday/Thursday.

Course Design

A two-year piloting process for culturally responsive design of the course and choice of curricular materials preceded the implementation described here. At the time of our example, the textbook had been in use for two semesters by Professor H and by three of the other five instructors teaching the course. As was demanded by the administrative rules at the university, the syllabus outlined course content. Unusual to the standard format at the university, the syllabus also outlined several course processes (e.g., writing about mathematics, providing students access to at least three representations for each concept such as words, formula, graph) and instituted a "mandatory choice" of content. Five-sixths of the course content was prescribed in the syllabus through reference to topics covered in the chosen textbook while the remaining one-sixth of the course content, approximately two weeks of class, was to be negotiated on a semester-by-semester basis in each class. Each instructor chose—with or without student input, depending on the instructor's teaching style—some additional topic or topics on which to focus for the two-week "choice" part of the course.

Of the six instructors teaching in the Spring term considered here, one was culturally responsive praxis-oriented (Professor H., a PhD in mathematics), two expressed views and curricular planning that aligned with a process-based view (both with master's degrees in mathematics, one with a culturally responsive approach), and three were firmly transmission-based (one a PhD in mathematics, one with a master's degree in mathematics teaching, and one with a master's degree in mathematics; the last with a culturally responsive approach). During the semester, all instructors met with each other in a coordination seminar every week for an hour to make decisions about course material, to exchange ideas for quizzes, exams, ways of "presenting the material," and to write and fine-tune four problems that would be common to all the liberal arts mathematics final exams. Though the four final exam items were in common, the rest of each final exam was determined however the teacher saw fit, as were all other assessments in the course.

Selecting Course Content

As noted, the privilege and obligation of choosing some of the course content was left up to students or the instructor. In the given term, one of the process-based and two of the transmission-based instructors made the content choice. In the other sections of the course, the choice was made by students alone by a vote or, in Professor H's classes, as the result of an in-class discussion among students and a negotiation between student-elected representatives and the instructor. At the level of curricular materials, then, many students had at least one extended, two-week, opportunity for appropriation and feedback.

Course Processes

While in the first extended example we gave an idea of responsiveness through a broad examination of course design, in this second example we give a brief overview of course process and strive to illustrate some of the depth of responsiveness through attention to activities around a particular concept. At the level of community knowledge in Professor H's praxis-based sections, students posed and solved problems in groups during class. They also completed worksheets in class made up of problems written by students in other sections (in the same and previous terms). In- and out-of-class assessments included quizzes, exams, and presentations about brief and lengthy projects.

Problem Posing

By the third problem-posing session, in Week 5, students had begun to discuss the problems they posed with the future solver, such as a fellow student, in mind. Four-member student item-writing groups exchanged items and explicitly referred to the culturally rich context of the future problem solver in offering critique and clarification for problem statements. These problem posing activities evolved over the semester from "Pose a similar problem for a fellow student in another liberal arts mathematics class"; to "Write a similar problem in a real-world context that would be appropriate for an older student returning to college after a five-year absence due to service in the armed forces"; to "Write an item that gets at the idea of rate of inflation that would be appropriate for a middle class, European-American preservice teacher who is learning about ratio and proportion. Write a second item that she could use next year that would be accessible to her socioeconomically and ethnically diverse prealgebra students." This final problem-posing prompt occurred in the last week of the course.

Activities

Professor H's praxis-based course also included short activities to increase student awareness of the classical and societal learning and teaching cultures around them. For example, early in the semester, students read, discussed, and applied Smith and Stein's (1998) Mathematical Task Analysis Guide (TAG) and Mathematical Tasks Framework. One class time activity included a quick review of textbook problems and online homework items by students using the TAG and led to their noting that the textbook problems were largely Procedures with Connections and Doing Mathematics while online items were almost exclusively Memorization and Procedures without Connections tasks. Similarly, an introduction of the concepts covered by the words *scaffolding* and *funneling* gave students vocabulary they used throughout the term in communicating with each other and with the instructor about the nature of their own and others' learning.

Focus on Content: Consumer Price Index

The topic of Consumer Price Index (CPI) and the calculation of inflation rate as relative change in CPI[3] were covered by all 11 liberal arts mathematics sections for at least 50 minutes of class meeting time. In Professor H's praxis-based classes, the 50 minutes was made up of 20 minutes on one day and 30 on the next day of class meeting. Professor H started by asking students what inflation was and how you might measure it in the changing price of a candy bar. Within 5 minutes students generated a relative change formula and the instructor used it to introduce how CPI is derived, work two examples of translating one year's value to another, and one of finding rate of inflation (7 minutes); after this students worked in pairs on problems from the book on changing dollar-years and finding rates of inflation (7 minutes). In the next class meeting, students posed new problems (20 minutes) and critiqued posed problems (10 minutes). In all other sections, the instructors devoted one class meeting to the topic. Students in these classes took notes during a lecture and, in one process-based section, worked in groups on two problems in class. The praxis-based students completed seven problems from the text and posed two new items during the 50 minutes of time spent on the topic in class.

In Professor H's praxis-based course, the topic was spread across two class meetings to allow students to investigate—outside of class—the notion of CPI in two ways. First, by completing six on-line homework skill-building problems and secondly, by creating their own CPI after compiling price information by either: (1) visiting two supermarkets: one in a largely working-class Latino neighborhood and one in a predominantly white middle-class neighborhood or (2) comparing supermarket prices from a local English language newspaper and a local Spanish language paper—most students chose (1). Though none of the other classes did such a project, students in the nine transmission- and process-based class sections had 4 to 12 homework problems from the textbook, and four to eight online problems that were all to be completed after the one class meeting in which CPI was addressed.

A paragraph at the end of the textbook chapter on CPI introduced the idea of a Health Care CPI; however, none of the instructors brought it up in class and none assigned homework on it. Consequently, the exam item discussed below was probably a novel problem for most students. The praxis-based students' cultural responsiveness to, and awareness of, the world through mathematics can be seen, in part, in the answers they offered on the test question. One of the four common final exam items in the course was CPI-based:[4]

> The overall Consumer Price Index (CPI) in September 2002 was 185.1 and the CPI for September 2004 was 189.7. Meanwhile, the Health Care CPI for September 2002 was 308.6 and for September 2004 it was 324.0 (Source:www.bls.gov/news.release/cpi.nr0.htm).
>
> (a) What was the overall rate of inflation from September 2002 to September 2004?
>
> (b) What was the rate of inflation for Health Care from September 2002 to September 2004?
>
> (c) Compare the rate of inflation for Health Care to the overall rate of inflation. Please write using complete sentences.

Among the 270 students in the *transmission*- and *process*-based sections of the course, approximately 65% gave correct numerical answers to parts (a) and (b) and all but one of these answers was notably similar to the solution shown below:

a. 2.5%
b. 5%
c. Health care is double the rate of inflation.

In the two *praxis*-based sections of the course, 89% of the 64 students provided correct numerical answers to both (a) and (b), written using complete sentences, of the form:

a. The rate of inflation between September 2002 and September 2004 was about 2.5%.
b. The rate of inflation for Health Care between 2002 and 2004 was about 5%.

Many student answers to (c) in the two praxis-based sections of the course were quite different from the answers offered by students in the other sections. Though about 40% gave answers to (c) like the one shown above, 50% of the praxis-based students provided answers to part (c) that took a form similar to one or more of the following:

c_1. Since the health care inflation rate was double the overall rate (and assuming healthcare is part of the CPI), there must be other things that had much lower rates of inflation to balance the large increase in health care costs.

c_2. The fact that the cost of health care rose at twice the rate of inflation means that medical care will take a larger portion of a family's income than other goods and services.

c_3. Health care during those years cost more than twice what it should have, so people with lower incomes who might get a 2.5% cost of living raise would not get enough of a raise to afford the same quality of health care they could in 2001.

Students offering answers like c_1 were explicit about their assumptions regarding *how* CPI was determined. They interrogated the idea of CPI, rather than simply accepting it, and then drew mathematically logical conclusions about Health Care CPI based on those articulated assumptions.

In addition to stating the straightforward comparative information, that one was double the other, students providing answers like c_2 called upon the value of the mathematical constructs of CPI and inflation to justify assertions about the larger world. That is, they used mathematical computation and logic to support a conclusion about economic realities.

Similarly, students who gave answers like c_3 noted the comparative ratio and extended the idea, mathematically. Many talked about the relative impact of the different inflation rates on different subpopulations. In the example shown, the student focused on the life-quality inequities arising from an economic inequity in cost-of-living allotment.

The number of sections in the text read, number of homework problems posed, reviewed, and correctly completed, and depth and scope of projects completed by students was highest in the praxis-based sections and lowest in the process-based sections with the transmission-based sections in between. The scores on the common final exam items (scored independently of instructor grading, using a uniform rubric) were slightly higher in the praxis-based sections and about the same in transmission- and process-based sections.

Discussion

As in all culturally responsive *process* and *praxis* model curricula, student sense-making and communication were important components in both of the extended example courses. The proxy measurement for student sense making and communication in the process-based environmental calculus course could be found in the significance of attendance in determining course grade and the reliance on working in groups. The ability to work as a member of a team is a valuable skill for many college graduates and is responsive to the needs of one entering the middle-class working world. In environmental calculus, the course final project built student skills in examining the status quo and situating work within it, both indicators of a process view. Also, the poster brought in a communication technique valued in the mathematical culture. The culturally responsive aspects here included the focus on academic achievement as witnessed by Professor P, peers, and other faculty (in the poster session), environmental consciousness and critique, community building and personal connections, and attention to individual self-worth and abilities. Still under development for Professor P was how to operationalize the culturally responsive tenets of community knowledge, social consciousness and critique, cultural affirmation, competence, and exchange, in mathematically rich ways.

Indicators of student sense making in the praxis-based liberal arts classes included the twice monthly problem-posing sessions where students worked in small groups. In the liberal arts mathematics course, students regularly examined and mathematized cultural, socioeconomic, and political contexts and looked for alternate solutions to status quo answers—indicative of the transformative presumptions of a culturally responsive praxis approach. Still under development for Professor H was how to support students in sustaining their development as culturally responsive learners outside of and beyond their enrollment in the liberal arts mathematics class.

In the environmental calculus class, students' journal writing made clear the ways in which they were appropriating the course content and processes and was a channel for feedback to the instructor and graduate assistant of the course. Professor P's intention was to balance attention to socially important environmental issues with fostering *legitimate peripheral participation* in the mathematical community of practice of academe (Lave & Wenger, 1991). However, this intention was only partially realized. Having students choose and work with real-life data sets to answer questions and address issues in environmental science was seen as valuable and legitimate by the students. In this sense, the course was responsive. However, most members of the academic mathematics community would not be likely to say that what the students were learning was mathematics. Rather, a "pure mathematician" would identify the students' work as applied mathematics. The course content and processes did not support abstract reasoning about derivative and integral as mathematical constructs. In this sense, student participation was indeed "peripheral" to the mathematics community, but "illegitimate" to that community (Barton & Tusting, 2005), which troubled Professor P. Attempting to negotiate the tension between the demands of classical and societal knowledge may often lead to such situations. Relying on community and critical knowledge as a foundation, Professor H situated mathematics learning in service to multiple global demands of which the academy and society were two parts, also a potentially "illegitimate" form of mathematical participation in the habitus of the field of academic mathematics.

Culturally responsive curriculum and instruction offer opportunities for learning through a wide array of culturally authentic mathematical and pedagogical contexts, whether or not the contexts are from one's personal community knowledge. For example, teaching a largely European-American, middle-class, group of students through contexts that are personally relevant *and* through those that are socioculturally rich but not echoes of personal experience allows a diminishing of the perceived "otherness" of those not from White, middle-class backgrounds (Rodriguez & Kitchen, 2005). In particular, such duality of instruction can allow students the opportunity to see their own familiar culture as "other"; that is, as a culture rather than as a neutral background (Spindler, 2000).

College mathematics instructors operate at the nested intersection of several fields. College mathematics teaching lives within the larger field of academic mathematics, which itself is nested within the larger field of postsecondary education. By analyzing the habitus of agents (students, teaching colleagues, administrators), a college mathematics instructor can inform teaching decisions with pertinent community and classical knowledge. Making such analyses and using the information to change one's instruction can be dangerous to a career. Taking on culturally responsive pedagogy and attending to community and critical knowledge growth for students is a political act. However, engaging in that political act need not be a radical or abrupt move. It may start with noticing the existence of students' funds of knowledge and working to uncover and include community knowledge in framing mathematical activities. Next, one might make efforts to regularly have students become the framers of activities. A subsequent step can be inviting students to seek, with the instructor, authentic and relevant problems whose solutions may be supported by expertise in abstract and applied mathematics. Helping students to build expertise with abstract concepts while also learning how to apply them may be facilitated by being explicit with students that the instructional goal is the codevelopment of both kinds of understanding.

Learners walk into a classroom with myriad forms of habitus, including a variety of intellectual, personal, social, political, and economic resources. Most college students have learned, as they were learning mathematics, that they are expected to suppress any contribution they might be tempted to make to context. The importance of isolation and individuality having been established, students are likely to have internalized the notion that to learn mathematics they must sacrifice agency and intuition to the rules of mathematics—both as a discipline and as a classroom milieu (Boaler & Greeno, 2000). Recognizing and confronting with students this part of their habitus is one of the challenges of culturally responsive pedagogy. It is the creation of a caring environment that can facilitate change for students and for the instructor.

Responsiveness means understanding and interacting with people in context, including the variation in how that context may be created and perceived by all parties involved. Instructors' or curriculum designers' *intentions* for students' experiences of mathematics is not "context" in the sense used here. Context is mutually defined and emergent rather than wholly predetermined. It relies on the dynamics of human experience, perception, and on the interaction of the people in the room. Most of the curricular materials (from instructor-created exams to mass market textbooks) for collegiate mathematics disregard interpersonal or communal cognitive activity. With the possible exception of some reform calculus and quantitative reasoning books, college textbook development does not include addressing contextual potential—the variability in how instructors and students might want to use the books.

Conclusion

Cultural responsiveness both informs and empowers. Like the process model, a culturally responsive approach values the contributions students, colleagues, societies and policies can make to course content. At the same time, like the praxis model, culturally responsive pedagogy values the contributions that knowledge of content can make to improving society, policy, and individual lives.

Culturally responsive college mathematics curriculum and instruction foster a classroom environment where it is safe, though perhaps not especially comfortable, to engage deeply with mathematical and pedagogical ideas. In the *transmission* view, instructors can be responsive to students' by providing information through multiple modes and stating the connections among them (e.g., multiple representations: written, spoken, graphical, tabular; or multiple presentations: snapshots and animations). In the *product* view, the types of work students seek to prepare themselves for can shape the content of examples, including student-generated examples, and the forms of assessment. In the *process* view, each student can be overtly encouraged to establish personal relevance for course material while constructing a profound understanding of certain mathematical ideas. In the *praxis* view, students and instructors can explore, disagree, and come to consensus while both mastering standard representations for concepts and implementing that understanding in ways relevant to the academy, society, community, and globe.

We close with our list of five ways culturally responsive pedagogy is enacted in college mathematics, through:

- Validating the experiential capital and approaches to learning that students bring to the enterprise of learning in a college mathematics course. Validation happens when teacher and students find out about and accept each other's perceptions and then fold this awareness into resources and materials that are rich with classroom, multicultural, multiple ability, and multiple social-class connections. Explicit efforts to build bridges between socially and mathematically privileged university professors and their students can serve as a model for students' own culturally responsive interactions with others. That is, the classroom community overlaps the research mathematics community and informs a variety of cultural repertoires for students and instructor.
- Empowering students as citizens, as learners, and as teachers (for themselves and others) through implicit and explicit support and development of self-regulation and socially aware critical thinking; this overlaps the idea of teaching for social justice.

- Supporting the development of awareness among students of the knowledge, skills, and value sets—including understandings of mathematical concepts—associated with access to social, economic, and political power. In particular, codes of power, the mainstream mathematical rules and communication practices (Delpit, 1996), are explicitly discussed by students and teacher until a repertoire is established about how to translate between cultural worlds.
- Comprehensively teaching the whole learner through explicitly recognizing and valuing of the diverse ways that cultural and personal identities mediate ways of cognitive engagement as well as explicitly addressing multiple modes of learning in instructional design. In collegiate mathematics service courses this can be as simple as presentations and activities that use the multiple representations of formulas, words, tables, and graphs (common in reform calculus textbooks).
- Engaging in multidimensional assessments of learning. Such evaluations of learning in mathematics can include reflective and explanatory writing, portfolios, group-grade collaborative assignments, individual-grade cooperative assignments, projects, discussions, and peer- and self-evaluated work.

Notes

1. This may be how the Western academic mathematics culture arose from mathematics in the service of a royalty-driven society, rather than the capitalism-driven model of the state common in the U.S. today. For example, there is no ethical training in becoming a mathematician —potential ethical issues around building weapons were a non-starter when mathematics was developed in the days of monarchies rather than democracies.
2. In the term considered, the only prompt given to students was to write about the day. Subsequent analysis of student journals led to the creation and use in later terms of specific prompts in the areas of mathematical content, course process, and affect or attitude (as suggested by Dougherty, 1996).
3. For example, the rate of inflation from 1990 to 2000: $(CPI_{2000} - CPI_{1990})/CPI_{1990}$.
4. The common final exam items were written and unanimously approved by all six instructors.

References

Abreu, G. de, Bishop, A., & Presmeg, N. (Eds.). (2002). *Transitions between contexts of mathematical practices*. Dordrecht, The Netherlands: Kluwer.

Barton, D., & Tusting, K. (Eds.). (2005). *Beyond communities of practice: Language, power and social context*. Cambridge, UK: Cambridge University Press.

Bates, D. G., & Plog, F. (1988). *Cultural anthropology* (2nd ed.). New York: Knopf.

Bishop, A. J. (2002). Mathematical acculturation, cultural conflicts, and transition. In G. de Abreu, A. J. Bishop, & N. C. Presmeg (Eds.), *Transitions between contexts of mathematical practices* (pp. 191–212). Dordrecht, The Netherlands: Kluwer.

Boaler, J., & Greeno, J. G. (2000). Identity, agency, and knowing in mathematical worlds. In J. Boaler (Ed.), *Multiple perspectives on mathematics teaching and learning* (pp. 171–200). Stamford, CT: Ablex.

Carnevale, A. P., & Desrochers, D. M. (2003). Preparing students for the knowledge economy: What school counselors need to know. *Professional School Counseling, 6*, 228–236.

Center for Education. National Research Council. (2003). *Evaluating and improving undergraduate teaching in science, technology, engineering, and mathematics.* Washington, DC: National Academies Press. Retrieved November 5, 2007, from http://fermat.nap.edu/books/0309072778/html

Civil, M. (2002). Everyday mathematics, mathematicians' mathematics, and school mathematics: Can we bring them together? In M. Brenner & J. Moschkovich (Eds.), *Everyday and academic mathematics in the classroom. Monographs of the Journal for Research in Mathematics Education, 11*, 40–62. Washington, DC: National Council of Teachers of Mathematics.

Davis P. J., Hersh, R., & Marchisotto, E. A. (2003). *The mathematical experience* (Study ed.). New York: Birkhauser.

Delpit, L. (1996). *Other people's children: Cultural conflict in the classroom.* New York: New Press.

Dougherty, B. J. (1996). The write way: A look at journal writing in first-year algebra. *The Mathematics Teacher, 89*, 556–561.

Ernest, P. (1998). The culture of the mathematics classroom and the relations between personal and public knowledge: An epistemological perspective. In F. Seeger, J. Voigt, & U. Waschescio (Eds.), *The culture of the mathematics classroom* (pp. 245–268). Cambridge, UK: Cambridge University Press.

Even-Zohar, I. (1997). The making of culture repertoire and the role of transfer. *Target, 9*(2), 373–381. Retrieved April 19, 2006, from http://www.tau.ac.il/~itamarez/works/papers/papers/rep_trns.htm

Freire, P. (1970). *Pedagogy of the oppressed.* New York: Herder & Herder.

Gay, G. (2000). *Culturally responsive teaching: Research, theory, and practice.* New York: Teachers College Press.

Gerofsky, S. (2004). *A man left Albuquerque heading east: Word problems as genre in mathematics education.* New York: Peter Lang.

Gregory, J. N. (1989). *American exodus.* New York: Oxford University Press.

Grenfell, M., & James, D. (1998). *Bourdieu and education: Acts of practical theory.* London: Falmer.

Grundy, S. (1987). *Curriculum: Product or praxis?* Lewes, UK: Falmer.

Gutstein, E. (2007). Connecting *community, critical,* and *classical* knowledge in teaching mathematics for social justice. *Monograph of the Montana Mathematics Enthusiast, 1*, 109–118.

Halmos, P. (1994). What is teaching? *The American Mathematical Monthly, 101*, 848–854.

Hauk, S. (2005). Mathematical autobiography among college learners in the United States. *Adults Learning Mathematics International Journal, 1*, 36–56.

Herzig, A. (2002). Where have all the students gone? Participation of doctoral students in authentic mathematical activity as a necessary condition for persistence toward the Ph.D. *Educational Studies in Mathematics, 50*, 177–212.

Herzig, A. (2004). Becoming mathematicians: Women and students of color choosing and leaving doctoral mathematics. *Review of Educational Research, 74*, 171–214.

Hiebert, J. (2003). What research says about the NCTM Standards. In J. Kilpatrick, W. G. Martin, & D. Schifter (Eds.), *A research companion to Principles and Standards for School Mathematics* (pp. 5–23). Reston, VA: National Council of Teachers of Mathematics.

Lave, J. & Wenger, E. (1991). *Situated learning: Legitimate peripheral participation.* Cambridge, UK: Cambridge University Press.

Leder, G. C., Pehkonen, E., & Torner, G. (Eds.). (2003). *Beliefs: A hidden variable in mathematics education?* New York: Springer.

Martin, D. B. (2006). Mathematics learning and participation as racialized forms of experience: African American parents speak on the struggle for mathematics literacy. *Mathematical Thinking and Learning, 8*, 197–229.

Middlehurst, R., & Woodfield, S. (2006). *Responding to the internationalisation agenda: Implications for institutional strategy and practice.* Retrieved September 15, 2006, from http://www.heacademy.ac.uk/inclusiveteaching

Mukhopadhyay, S., & Greer, B. (2001). Modeling with purpose: Mathematics as a critical tool. In B. Atweh, H. Forgasz, & B. Nebres (Eds.), *Sociocultural research on mathematics education: An international perspective* (pp. 295–312). Mahwah, NJ: Erlbaum.

National Center for Education Statistics. (2006). *Digest of education statistics*. Retrieved February 11, 2008 from http://nces.ed.gov/programs/digest/2006menu_tables.asp

Ogbu, J. U., & Simons, H. D. (1998). Voluntary and involuntary minorities: A cultural-ecological theory of school performance with some implications for education. *Anthropology & Education Quarterly, 29*(2), 155–188.

Palmer, P. J. (1997). Teaching and learning in community. *About Campus, 2*(5), 4–13.

Piaget, J. (1963). *The origins of intelligence in children*. New York: Norton.

Prediger, S. (2002). Consensus and coherence in mathematics—How can they be explained in a culturalistic view? *Philosophy of Mathematics Education Journal, 16*. Retrieved December 23, 2004, from http://www.ex.ac.uk/~Pernest/pome16/contents.htm

Rishel, T. (2000). *Teaching first: A guide for new mathematicians*. Washington D.C.: Mathematical Association of America.

Rodriguez, A. J., & Kitchen, R. S. (2005). *Preparing mathematics and science teachers for diverse classrooms: Promising strategies for transformative pedagogy*. Mahwah, NJ: Erlbaum.

Schmidt, W. H., McKnight, C., Cogan, L. S., Jakwerth, P. M., & Hoaung, R. T. (1999). *Facing the consequences: Using TIMSS for a closer look at U.S. mathematics and science education*. Dordrecht, The Netherlands: Kluwer.

Smith, M. S., & Stein, M. K. (1998). Selecting and creating mathematical tasks: From research to practice. *Mathematics Teaching and the Middle School, 3*, 344–350.

Spindler, G. (Ed.). (2000). *Fifty years of anthropology and education 1950–2000*. Mahwah, NJ: Erlbaum.

Swidler, A. (1986). Culture in action: Symbols and strategies. *American Sociological Review, 51*, 273–286.

Tymoczko, T. (Ed.). (1998). *New directions in the philosophy of mathematics*. Princeton, NJ: Princeton University Press.

U.S. Census Bureau. (2000). *Census 2000*. Retrieved March 20, 2006 from http://factfinder.census.gov

von Glasersfeld, E. (1989) Constructivism in education. In T. Husen & N. Postlethwaite (Eds.), *International encyclopedia of education* (Supp. Vol., pp. 162–163). Oxford: Pergamon.

Wells, C. (2003). *A handbook of mathematical discourse*. West Conshohocken, PA: Infinity.

Index

Page numbers in italic refer to Figures or Tables.

B